# Interwoven Destinies

# CONTRIBUTORS

Dennis W. Archer, Dickinson, Wright, Moon, Van Dusen & Freeman

Paul C. Brophy, The Enterprise Foundation

Henry G. Cisneros, U.S. Department of Housing and Urban Development

Ernesto Cortés, Jr., Industrial Areas Foundation

Eli Ginzberg, Eisenhower Center for the Conservation of Human Resources

Nathan Glazer, Harvard University

K. Scott Hamilton, Dickinson, Wright, Moon, Van Dusen & Freeman

Walter Hook, Institute for Transportation and Development Policy

John D. Kasarda, University of North Carolina

Robert H. McNulty, Partners for Livable Places

Carol O'Cléireacáin, New York City Department of Finance

Paul E. Peterson, Harvard University

Peter D. Salins, Hunter College

Elliott D. Sclar, Columbia University

Kneeland Youngblood, University of Texas Southwestern Medical Center

**THE AMERICAN ASSEMBLY**
*Columbia University*

# Interwoven Destinies

*Cities and the Nation*

HENRY G. CISNEROS
*Editor*

*W · W · NORTON & COMPANY*
*New York   London*

Portions of Chapter 6 and Chapter 11 appeared in slightly different form in *The Public Interest.*

Copyright © 1993 by The American Assembly

Printed in the United States of America

First Edition

The text of this book is composed in Baskerville. Composition and manufacturing by the Haddon Craftsmen.

Library of Congress Cataloging-in-Publication Data
Interwoven destinies : cities and the nation / Henry G. Cisneros,
   editor.
      p.      cm.
   At head of title: The American Assembly, Columbia University.
   1. Cities and towns—United States.   2. Metropolitan areas—United
   States.   I. Cisneros, Henry.   II. American Assembly.
   HT123.I58   1993
   307.76′0973—dc20                                    93-14461

ISBN 0-393-96582-1 (Softcover)
ISBN 0-393-03571-9 (Hardcover)
W. W. Norton & Company, Inc., 500 Fifth Avenue, New York, N.Y. 10110
W. W. Norton & Company Ltd., 10 Coptic Street, London WC1A 1PU

# Contents

## LOCAL JURISDICTIONS, METROPOLITAN ECONOMIES, AND FISCAL REMEDIES

## MAKING CHANGES: COMMUNITY INITIATIVES AND NEW POLICIES FOR CITIES AND THE NATION

For my family—Mary Alice, Teresa, Mercedes, and John
Paul—and a better future for everyone.

# Preface

Cities are critical to America's economic, political, and social future. It is in our cities that the interactions must occur that will determine if the nation functions as an integrated, civil society, or if class rigidities and racial and social disorder will characterize our future.

Deeply concerned about the future of cities in our country, The American Assembly undertook a two-year project under the direction of Henry G. Cisneros, who was a trustee of The Assembly and former mayor of San Antonio, Texas. We were particularly gratified when, in January 1993, he was appointed Secretary of Housing and Urban Development, and thus one of the government officials particularly responsible for the very issues that our program was designed to address.

This volume includes the papers that were commissioned by Mr. Cisneros as background reading for a meeting that took place on April 15–18, 1993, at Arden House in Harriman, New York. Mr. Cisneros was aided in the development of these papers by an advisory committee whose names follow this preface, and he was assisted in the editing of these chapters by Professor Marc A. Weiss of Columbia University, who was deputy director of the Arden House

Assembly and is currently serving as a special assistant to the secretary of Housing and Urban Development.

The report from that Assembly meeting is also included as an appendix. It lists the authorities from across the country who adopted it as their findings and recommendations after intensive discussions over the four-day period. Mr. Cisneros was joined at Arden House as co-director by William H. Hudnut, III, former Republican member of Congress and, for sixteen years, mayor of Indianapolis, Indiana.

We gratefully acknowledge the support of the following organizations that helped to fund this undertaking:

| | |
|---|---|
| Major Funder | CITIBANK, N.A. |
| Funders | John D. and Catherine T. MacArthur Foundation<br>The Overbrook Foundation |
| Supporters | Brooklyn Union Gas Company<br>The Spencer Foundation<br>Tort & Insurance Practice Section, American Bar Association<br>M. R. Bauer Foundation<br>The Commonwealth Fund |
| Contributors | City Innovation<br>International Business Machines Corporation<br>New York Community Trust<br>Equitable Life Assurance Society of the United States<br>Merrill Lynch & Company, Inc.<br>Chase Manhattan Bank |

These organizations, as well as The American Assembly, take no position on subjects presented herein for public discussion.

It is our belief that this book continues to fulfill the mandate of

The Assembly's founder, Dwight D. Eisenhower, "to illuminate public policy" and will help citizens understand more fully what they can do to help their cities become more economically strong, pleasant, and safe.

It was also the expectation of The Assembly in initiating this project that many communities across the country would find this volume of special relevance, and would want to undertake similar programs in their areas to prepare their own policy recommendations to improve their local urban environments.

Daniel A. Sharp
President
The American Assembly

# ADVISORY COMMITTEE

## Acknowledgments

This project has been a challenge and an honor to direct. I have learned a great deal from the many experienced, wise, and caring people who have been involved during the year I spent working on the assembly and on the book. The excellent report produced by the participants of the American Assembly and the important research, analysis, and proposals contained within this volume will help reinvigorate metropolitan urban policy and create a better future for our country. To all of the authors of the chapters in this volume, to the advisory board that assisted me in choosing the chapter themes and authors, and to all of the participants in the American Assembly on "Interwoven Destinies: Cities and the Nation," I am very grateful.

As a former trustee of the American Assembly, I am pleased to have worked with this fine organization. Special thanks go to the staff, particularly Daniel Sharp and David Mortimer, and to the trustees, especially David Gergen, who served as the lead trustee for our assembly and was extremely supportive in giving thoughtful advice and participating actively in the discussions.

This book's ideas were further enriched by the assembly report and its drafters: Osborn Elliott, C. Austin Fitts, Karen Hill, Vincent

Lane, George Latimer, Kirsten Moy, Jean Nolan, Shirl Thomas, William Hudnut (my co-director), and Marc Weiss (my deputy director). I thank them for their vital work, and thank William Hudnut for the encouragement and advice he gave me throughout this long endeavor.

I am especially grateful to Marc Weiss for his support on this project. From his office at Columbia University, Marc very capably advised and assisted me with editing all of the book chapters and working with the authors.

My greatest debt is to my family: my wife, Mary Alice; my daughters, Teresa and Mercedes; and my son, John Paul. Each day they gave me love and hope, and remind me of the interwoven destinies of our lives together.

# 1

# Interwoven Destinies: Cities and the Nation

## HENRY G. CISNEROS

## The Need for National Action

All of us care about our country, about its communities, about both their promise and their peril. We are inspired by local examples of turnarounds, the national promise of Pittsburgh and Baltimore and Lowell in the East, of Indianapolis and Omaha in the heartland, of Seattle and Billings and Salt Lake City in the West. But we've also seen the peril of heightened crime, of the plague of drugs, of fear on the faces of the elderly, of neighborhoods that have lost their life force with churches closed, and ball fields empty, and

HENRY G. CISNEROS is secretary of the U.S. Department of Housing and Urban Development. He began his career in public service in 1975 with election to the San Antonio City Council, where he served until 1981, when he became the first Latino mayor of a major U.S. city. After leaving office in 1989 he became chair of Cisneros Asset Management Co., a national fixed-income asset management firm for tax-exempt institutions. Prior to his appointment to the Clinton cabinet, he served as a board member of the Rockefeller Foundation, a trustee of The American Assembly, chair of the National Civic League, and deputy chair of the Federal Reserve Bank of Dallas.

downtown stores with empty windows. We've also seen factories where weeds have overgrown the parking lots, once full of the cars of hopeful workers, in communities of all sizes in all regions, made up of people of all incomes and ages and races.

For every example of civic cooperation, such as the promise of Minneapolis or St. Paul, renowned for their civic virtue, there's another—the peril—where leaders glare across a chasm at each other, a chasm of misunderstanding, even hatred, and just refuse to work together. For every Portland, Oregon, the promise of striving to redesign its future, there's a community in peril that has surrendered to the larger forces of the global economy. For every city such as Fort Worth, the promise of sustaining attractive, graceful, and life-enhancing neighborhoods, there's a community in peril where the elderly are afraid to walk to the corner store with their Social Security checks, and where children peek out of their windows to see if the drug pushers are still at the pay phone across the street on the corner before they can go out to play.

For every city such as Tampa, meeting its promise by building homes for people, matching federal community development block grant funds in innovative ways with private capital from commercial bankers, there is the peril where the homeless look for a wind-free alcove in a department store, a sheltered stairwell, or a steam-exhaust pipe to sleep through the frozen night. And for every community of promise like Rockford, Illinois, where people have come together across traditional lines, there are communities in peril where the slow burn of anger smolders, occasionally to flare into the terrible intensity of Los Angeles in the spring of 1992.

The morning after the civil disturbances broke out in Los Angeles, I called Mayor Tom Bradley to indicate the sympathy that I knew many of us felt across the country, and also to offer my assistance. He suggested that it might be useful for me to come and help out. I arrived in Los Angeles late that afternoon, and what I smelled and felt on that occasion has enabled me to articulate a vision of urban policy with greater clarity than would have been possible before that unforgettable visit. Indeed, my experience in Los Angeles encouraged me to be willing to change my life as profoundly as accepting a cabinet position requires.

What I saw was a city in which the smoke was everywhere. It smelled of burning wire and plastic. The smoke was so thick that it obscured the lights of a helicopter circling directly overhead. Sirens screamed every few seconds, as strike teams of fire engines escorted by California highway patrol cars—literally convoys of twenty vehicles, the patrol cars to protect the firefighters—raced from one fire to the next. Men drove pickup trucks to electronics stores, bashed in the glass storefronts, and then hurriedly loaded VCRs and television sets on the trucks and sped away to the next store. There were no police anywhere in sight, because they were spread too thin across the vast city.

One man, actor Edward James Olmos, came up to me as we went in to make a plea at a television station for people to observe the curfew and keep their children at home. On the way into the TV station he said he had just come around the corner and had seen a teenager who had been shot dead. The young man was shot in the head, and he was lying arms wide, sprawled out on the city sidewalk, his eyes wide open, staring straight up. Los Angeles that Thursday night was truly the urban apocalypse in a kind of smoky orange, an assault on all of the senses, people wide-eyed, all-out panic just one more loud sound away.

This same scene could be reenacted in another American city some other night. No, you say, Los Angeles is different. It's bigger and more diverse than most cities. Perhaps it's a little tougher, too quick to take offense. What happened there can't happen in our city. Not in Miami, or Atlanta, or Cleveland. Nor in Chicago, or Detroit, or Dallas. It can't happen in Denver, or Kansas City, or Memphis, or Charleston, or Houston. Well, maybe yes, maybe no. Maybe not in the same form, or the same intensity, probably not the same exact cause of the flash point, but the white-hot intensity that became Los Angeles was the combustion of smoldering embers waiting impatiently to ignite for a long time. Like piles of dry wood with red-hot coals underneath, other American cities can also ignite. Or maybe we'll call ourselves lucky as a nation, and the embers will just continue to smolder away, quietly out of everyday sight, taking a human toll at a slower rate.

Why are so many of our communities smoldering? Perhaps it's first and foremost a matter of economics. Poverty in the United States became more widespread and severe during the 1980s, with 37 million Americans in poverty, the highest percentage of our population in over a quarter of a century, and much worse than in many other Western democracies. The real wages for the average American worker declined by almost 10 percent in the past decade, and as a result, living standards for many workers and their families have deteriorated. What has happened to our economy, to our workers, to their wages? Slower growth in national productivity touches people's lives; the loss of high-wage manufacturing jobs to overseas competition touches people's lives; the use of part-time and contract workers touches people's lives. These are not just business media abstractions. These things come home to our neighborhoods and our communities. All of these changes combine to keep incomes down for workers and families, particularly for young workers and for poor workers. And we ask, why are our cities smoldering?

Perhaps it's also a matter of race. This is not something we like to talk about. But America has yet to come to terms with race. We run from it frequently. In many of the largest cities in America, more than half the population is now a combination of African-Americans, Latinos, and Asians. A number of these cities have minority populations of more than 60 percent, including Atlanta, Baltimore, Birmingham, Chicago, Detroit, El Paso, Hartford, Los Angeles, New Orleans, Oakland, Washington, D.C., and my own city, San Antonio.

Detroit, for example, is almost 80 percent minority. It's the most segregated city in the United States. Most of Detroit's former white population has departed, some seeking the advantages of the suburbs, some fleeing a deteriorating, crime-ridden central core, and others escaping people—escaping the minority populations themselves. The result is desperation, distrust, and poverty populations left behind to fend for themselves in racial enclaves. And we ask, why are our cities smoldering?

Perhaps it's also a matter of simple rage of people who are angry beyond words. The drug-fed epidemic has resulted in a larger proportion of the United States population in jail than in any other country except South Africa. The lack of affordable housing is so severe that many of the urban poor must now spend as much as 70 percent—not 50, not 60, but 70 percent—of their incomes on shelter. And the infant mortality rate among African-Americans is worse than some Third World countries. We live in an America where every day twenty-seven children die from poverty related causes. Every day, in every part of the country, among all races, ten young people are killed by guns, thirty are wounded, and six children commit suicide. Every day 2,700 teenagers get pregnant and 1,500 teenagers drop out of school.

All of this hardship and tragic violence is not just taking place in Los Angeles—it's everywhere. In the slow burn of hundreds of communities, we're reaping a harvest of inattention, of withdrawal, of an unwillingness or incapacity to invest in all of our people. No government—certainly not the federal government alone—can address such a wide range of issues and such a broad and deep-seated series of problems confronting our country. It will take a full partnership of every level of government, of private business, of labor, civic, religious, philanthropic, and community groups, of individual citizens and families, working together to chart a new course of progress.

Central cities are the focal points of every metropolitan area, and the great majority of the American people live in these areas. Our transportation and communications systems, labor force and employment structure, environmental quality, educational and medical institutions, financial networks, governmental and judicial administration, cultural heritage, and many more aspects of our daily lives are deeply interconnected with the healthy functioning of cities.

All of us regularly interact with, depend on, and utilize cities for our livelihood and enjoyment. Even if we do not spend much time within city limits, urban vitality is essential for the entire country to generate the productivity, create the opportunity, and achieve the promise of a better future for everyone. Our nation and our cities face a common destiny. The power to shape it is in our hands.

## Metropolitan Regions, Cities and Suburbs: "All in It Together"

During the 1980s, 90 percent of the national population growth and 87 percent of the employment growth took place within central cities and metropolitan suburbs. Metropolitan areas now contain 78 percent of the total United States population and 83 percent of the household income. One-half of all Americans live in just thirty-nine metropolitan areas. Almost 80 million Americans, nearly 30 percent of the U.S. population, live in central cities (see Tables 1 and 2).

Cities are the core of metropolitan areas and play a pivotal role in the nation's economy. They provide work for millions and are the home to major private employers, the port of entry for foreign goods, capital, and workers, and the port of exit for American goods, services, and tourists. They house many of the world's premier institutions of commerce, culture, and learning.

For several reasons, the urban economic role is not adequately reflected in the national distribution of political power or in the public sector distribution of resources and responsibilities. One reason is the fixed nature of urban jurisdictions, which serve but do not

## Table 1. 30 Largest U.S. Cities by Population (thousands)

| Rank | City | Population |
|------|------|-----------|
| 1 | NEW YORK, NY | 7,323 |
| 2 | LOS ANGELES, CA | 3,485 |
| 3 | CHICAGO, IL | 2,784 |
| 4 | HOUSTON, TX | 1,631 |
| 5 | PHILADELPHIA, PA | 1,586 |
| 6 | SAN DIEGO, CA | 1,111 |
| 7 | DETROIT, MI | 1,028 |
| 8 | DALLAS, TX | 1,007 |
| 9 | PHOENIX, AZ | 983 |
| 10 | SAN ANTONIO, TX | 936 |
| 11 | SAN JOSE, CA | 782 |
| 12 | BALTIMORE, MD | 736 |
| 13 | INDIANAPOLIS, IN | 731 |
| 14 | SAN FRANCISCO, CA | 724 |
| 15 | JACKSONVILLE, FL | 635 |
| 16 | COLUMBUS, OH | 633 |
| 17 | MILWAUKEE, WI | 628 |
| 18 | MEMPHIS, TN | 610 |
| 19 | WASHINGTON, D.C. | 607 |
| 20 | BOSTON, MA | 574 |
| 21 | SEATTLE, WA | 516 |
| 22 | EL PASO, TX | 515 |
| 23 | CLEVELAND, OH | 506 |
| 24 | NEW ORLEANS, LA | 497 |
| 25 | NASHVILLE, TN | 488 |
| 26 | DENVER, CO | 468 |
| 27 | AUSTIN, TX | 466 |
| 28 | FORT WORTH, TX | 448 |
| 29 | OKLAHOMA CITY, OK | 445 |
| 30 | PORTLAND, OR | 437 |

*Source:* U.S. Bureau of the Census, *Census of Population: 1990*

fully encompass the economic production and consumption systems and the labor, housing, and transportation market areas that stretch beyond local government borders, even the boundaries of very large cities. Increasingly, new technology and the mobility of capital and labor are generating a global economy that poses greater challenges not just to central cities but to entire metropolitan regions. Another constraint is the limited constitutional standing for cities, which are highly dependent upon state governments—for legal authority to make and enforce laws, develop and manage physical infrastructure, provide services, and raise revenues through taxes and fees—and are

also dependent on the federal government for raising sufficient resources.

"All In It Together: Cities, Suburbs and Local Economic Regions," a recent study by the National League of Cities, underscores
the interwoven destinies of American cities and their surrounding
suburbs. The League found that for most U.S. metropolitan areas,
median household incomes of central cities and suburbs moved up
and down together between 1979 and 1989. When the incomes of
central city residents increased, the incomes of people living in that

**Table 2. 30 Largest U.S. Metropolitan Areas by Population (thousands)**

| Rank | Metro Area | Population | Crosses State Lines? |
|------|-----------|-----------|---------------------|
| 1 | NY–NJ–LI–CT | 18,087 | YES |
| 2 | LA–ANAHEIM | 14,532 | |
| 3 | CHICAGO–GARY | 8,066 | YES |
| 4 | SF–OAK–SJ | 6,253 | |
| 5 | PHILA–WILM–TRENT | 5,899 | YES |
| 6 | DETROIT–ANN ARBOR | 4,665 | |
| 7 | BOSTON–SALEM | 4,172 | YES |
| 8 | WASHINGTON, D.C. | 3,924 | YES |
| 9 | DALLAS–FT. WORTH | 3,885 | |
| 10 | HOUST–GALVESTON | 3,711 | |
| 11 | MIAMI–FT. LAUD | 3,193 | |
| 12 | ATLANTA | 2,834 | |
| 13 | CLEVELAND–AKRON | 2,760 | |
| 14 | SEATTLE–TACOMA | 2,559 | |
| 15 | SAN DIEGO | 2,498 | |
| 16 | MINN–ST. PAUL | 2,464 | YES |
| 17 | ST. LOUIS | 2,444 | YES |
| 18 | BALTIMORE | 2,382 | |
| 19 | PITTSBURGH | 2,243 | |
| 20 | PHOENIX | 2,122 | |
| 21 | TAMPA–ST. PETE | 2,068 | |
| 22 | DENVER–BOULDER | 1,848 | |
| 23 | CINCINNATI | 1,744 | YES |
| 24 | MILWAUKEE–RACINE | 1,607 | |
| 25 | KANSAS CITY, MO | 1,566 | YES |
| 26 | SACRAMENTO | 1,481 | |
| 27 | PORTLAND–VANC | 1,478 | YES |
| 28 | NORFOLK–VIR BEACH | 1,396 | |
| 29 | COLUMBUS, OH | 1,377 | |
| 30 | SAN ANTONIO | 1,302 | |

*Source:* U.S. Bureau of the Census, *Census of Population: 1990*

city's suburbs grew by an even higher percentage. However, when the incomes of the central city's population actually declined, so did the incomes of its suburbanites, though not by as much.

In the twenty-five metropolitan areas in which suburban incomes rose the fastest, central city incomes also increased. None of these prosperous suburban areas experienced income growth without improvement in central city incomes, nor did the cities grow without the suburbs. This suggests that urban policy debates since the 1960s may have focused too much on the city-suburban income differential and not enough on the larger unifying framework of metropolitan economic growth. Central cities and their suburbs are clearly "joined at the hip" in the structure and functioning of interrelated economic activities, stretching from the older downtown central business districts to the new "edge city" suburban office and retail centers, and from inner city manufacturing plants to suburban industrial parks.

The League of Cities report also emphasizes that each metropolitan region has its own economic growth path and cyclical patterns depending on its particular mixture of business sectors, employment base, population trends, natural resources, public investment, and other key factors. The study's authors suggest that national policy makers cannot treat all cities or metropolitan areas the same, but should assist each area to define and implement regional economic development strategies designed to promote overall growth and simultaneously to reduce city-suburban income and employment disparities. Recent research by Neal Peirce and his colleagues on "citistates," and by David Rusk on "elastic cities" and metropolitan futures, reinforces and expands upon the National League of Cities argument that federal, state, regional, and local urban policies need to start from the essential premise of "interwoven destinies."

## Economic and Social Changes: The Urban Challenge

Massive forces are converging that make this a particularly difficult time for U.S. cities. The economic functions of many major cities have been threatened both by the long-term decline of manufacturing and other important sectors of the urban economic base, and by the recent economic slowdown. Demographic changes are most visible in our central cities, with minority populations now comprising more than 50 percent of the residents of many large U.S.

cities. These changes and resulting pressures are also affecting our justice system. Federal and state governments are wrestling with their own fiscal problems, leaving city governments to battle increasingly intense human problems with the most inadequate of revenue structures. The outlook and prospects for the nation's cities are perhaps at their lowest point since the alarm about the national urban crisis in the 1960s.

Many cities have prospered in the past three decades while others have stagnated, but all are linked in a dynamic process of continual economic and social change. Urban economies have been transformed from mainly producing goods to providing services. The share of urban employment in goods production declined to only one job in five between 1970 and 1990. Larger, older cities took the biggest hits: between 1967 and 1987 Detroit lost 51 percent of its manufacturing jobs; New York City lost 58 percent; Chicago, 60 percent; and Philadelphia, 64 percent. In the last ten years the services sector accounted for 97 percent of net new employment growth in American cities.

As a consequence of this difficult urban economic transformation, during the 1980s average hourly wages fell by nearly 10 percent. At the same time, children living in poverty nationwide increased 22 percent. The wrenching social impacts of these economic changes have led to the increasing isolation of the poor and minorities in the ghettos and barrios of our inner cities. In the past thirty years, America's cities have suffered severe declines in resident incomes and tax bases due to the flight of jobs and the middle class to the suburbs. In 1960 the per capita income of cities was 105 percent of their surrounding suburbs. By 1980 per capita income of cities had fallen to 89 percent of the suburbs. A decade later, the ratio had fallen further to 84 percent, and in some cities, to less than half. Trapped by geographic boundaries that cannot expand, and disadvantaged by a labor force that is poorly prepared to compete in a global economy that places a premium on advanced education, cities on their own cannot solve the problems of the poor or of urban decay.

## Cities Are Vital to the Nation's Economic Future

Cities are vital to America's economic future. Not only are massive amounts of financial and physical capital invested in our cities, but nearly 80 percent of the American people live in metropolitan areas anchored by central cities, and more than 80 percent of the nation's jobs are located in these urban areas. Our cities are still the main centers of essential commercial activities, including international business. Not only are the nation's leading banks, communications networks, and international trading companies rooted in our cities, but so is the basic infrastructure of trade and commerce—ports, airports, roads, bridges, public transportation systems, and essential services such as public safety.

It is also in our cities that the artistic, aesthetic, educational, and scientific life of our country is spotlighted. City residents have created the symphony halls, art districts, film complexes, sports arenas, performing arts theaters, public parks, medical centers, museums, libraries, university campuses, philanthropic foundations, and historic districts in which nationally important creative and educational processes unfold. Civic interaction within cities and metropolitan areas will determine whether our nation functions as an integrated, civil society in the future, or whether class rigidities and racial and social disorder predominate. New approaches to crosscultural, crossgenerational democratic dialogue and governance must take place in America's urban neighborhoods, courthouses, and city halls.

The strength of the nation's economy, the contact points for international economics, the health of our democracy, and the vitality of our humanistic endeavors—all are dependent on whether America's cities work. It is of the greatest national importance that our cities be renewed, and it is essential that metropolitan-wide strategies of urban revitalization be in the forefront of our nation's policy priorities.

## Introduction to the Chapters

This book is divided into three sections. The first section, "Overviews: Problems and Solutions," consists of four chapters. Eli Ginzberg's introductory essay provides a broad and in-depth analysis of the most important urban trends, examining changes since the 1960s and highlighting key economic and social problems.

Elliott Sclar and Walter Hook explain the crucial economic role of central cities as efficient locations for the production of goods and services in a globally competitive economic environment. They suggest that public policies should redress the imbalance of government subsidies that for many years has heavily favored suburban sprawl, and instead create a level playing field of public support that will enhance the present and future strengths of central cities and other high-density metropolitan locations. They also outline several major urban policy initiatives in transportation, telecommunications, affordable housing, regional planning, and other key programs that can improve economic performance and productivity for cities and the nation.

John Kasarda uses newly available 1990 census data to document recent urban demographic changes, especially the increasing concentration of minorities and poverty populations in inner city neighborhoods across the United States. His detailed analysis reveals a complex and varied pattern of unemployment and economic and social problems.

Kneeland Youngblood's chapter examines—from his personal experience as a medical doctor in an urban hospital emergency room—case studies of patients related to key issues ranging from health care reform and the need for urban economic development to education reform and eliminating drug abuse. He discusses social and moral values as well as economics, and stresses the need both for new governmental actions and for more individual responsibility.

The second section, called "Local Jurisdictions, Metropolitan Economies, and Fiscal Remedies," comprises three chapters. In the first, Peter Salins provides a conceptual framework for understanding some of the economic and budgetary problems of cities. As he sees it, the main difficulty is that the real functioning of cities economically and socially takes place across the metropolitan region, and yet urban governments lack jurisdiction over much of the population and employment that they actually serve.

Carol O'Cléireacáin expands upon this theme, looking in much greater detail at city budget resources and local public sector legal and fiscal relationships with higher levels of government, particularly with state governments. She proposes several creative solutions to divide urban fiscal resources and responsibilities more equitably among governmental units.

Paul Peterson focuses on the federal government's distribution of urban oriented grants to cities and states, and how federal intergovernmental funding has changed over the past three decades. He also discusses important fiscal differences between cities in the northeastern and midwestern Rust Belt and the southern and western Sun Belt, especially in their budgetary ties to the federal government.

The third section, "Making Changes: Community Initiatives and

New Policies for Cities and the Nation," includes five chapters. Paul
Brophy describes recent successes at urban physical, economic, and
social revitalization through the emergence of entrepreneurial governments, public-private partnerships, community based nonprofit
development organizations (including his own organization, The
Enterprise Foundation), and comprehensive neighborhood improvement programs being implemented in cities such as Atlanta
and Baltimore. He advocates that the federal government should
assist and provide incentives to encourage more communities to initiate and expand neighborhood revitalization efforts.

Robert McNulty raises the important issues of quality of life and
urban amenities, arguing that maintaining cultural and recreational
opportunities, honoring historic spaces and traditions, preserving a
healthy and attractive environment, and other related policies are an
essential part of generating economic growth in urban areas. He
presents case studies of effective amenity investment and redevelopment strategies from Pittsburgh, Indianapolis, and San Antonio. He
suggests that America can learn from the European urban experience in this arena and that European urbanists can learn from
American cities the many techniques and approaches he discusses,
as well as the ones described by Paul Brophy in the preceding chapter.

Nathan Glazer explores the much-debated topic of human capital
investment in education and employment training, reviewing Germany and Japan's national experience as well as various model efforts in the United States. He stresses the need for new programs to
better serve non–college bound youth through postsecondary school
apprenticeships, community colleges, and a variety of work related
training programs to be fostered by partnerships of business, labor,
government, and educational institutions.

Dennis Archer and Scott Hamilton carefully describe the growing
difficulties and challenges of the urban judicial system. Drawing on
research by the American Bar Association and Dennis Archer's experience as a former Michigan Supreme Court justice, they offer
several thoughtful proposals for reducing the severe backlog of cases
and improving both efficiency and fairness.

Ernesto Cortés concludes the volume with a chapter on the necessity for active community organizing and mobilizing of individual
citizens and local groups to participate in urban policy decision making, particularly in low- and moderate-income and minority neighborhoods where people often have less political power due to lack of

financial resources, and fragmented organizational leadership. He firmly believes that people can be empowered individually and collectively to take actions on their own behalf, to increase their own entrepreneurial and administrative skills and self-confidence, and to make political changes that will improve the lives of disadvantaged people in our cities and nation. He cites examples from the activities of community groups that work with his organization, the Industrial Areas Foundation, in San Antonio, Fort Worth, New York, Baltimore, and other cities.

I look forward to the beginning of a new era of economic and social progress for our cities and for America. If we all work creatively and energetically together, we can put out the Los Angeles–type fires that are now smoldering in many of our urban areas, and build better communities and a brighter future for everyone.

# OVERVIEW: PROBLEMS AND SOLUTIONS

# 2

# The Changing Urban Scene: 1960–1990 and Beyond

## ELI GINZBERG

## Introduction

T he most important changes in metropolitan and urban life since
the 1960s have been:

- The steady shift of the population from the city center to the
metropolitan areas beyond the city.
- The migration of many manufacturing and service sector jobs to
the outlying areas.
- The substantial growth within cities of employment in advanced
business services, particularly in finance, insurance, and real estate.

ELI GINZBERG is the director of the Eisenhower Center for the Conservation of Human Resources; director of the Revson Fellows Program for
the Future of the City of New York; Hepburn Professor Emeritus of Economics and special lecturer, Graduate School of Business and School of
Public Health, Columbia University. He was the chair of the National
Commission for Employment Policy and its antecedent bodies from 1962–
1981, and is the author of more than 100 books on human resources and
health policy. He acknowledges the assistance of Anna Dutka of the Eisenhower Center staff in the preparation of this chapter.

- The increasing concentration of minority and immigrant populations in the inner city, replacing many working and upper-income whites who relocated to the suburbs.
- The substantial difficulties of most large city public education systems in serving the increasingly large number of minority students, many of whom drop out without high school diplomas, thereby becoming handicapped in the search for jobs.
- The growing social disorder of many low-income inner city neighborhoods that are characterized in part by crime, drugs, homelessness, poverty, and despair.
- The relatively small financial contribution of the federal government in the late 1980s to the nation's largest cities.
- The much higher per capita governmental outlays by the largest cities compared to the smaller cities. Most of the differential reflects additional expenditures in the large cities for education, health and hospitals, and public welfare.
- Increased funding for large cities by state governments, filling some of the gaps left by the federal government's cutbacks.

In sum, the last three decades have seen a decline in population and jobs in many of the nation's largest cities simultaneous with an increased demand for public services, particularly for special education, health care, and welfare.

The nation's cities enjoyed a substantial rate of population growth during the past three decades, but most of the growth was concentrated in cities with populations below 250,000. According to the *Statistical Abstract* (1992), the nation had 130 cities of over 100,000 population in 1960 and 194 in 1990. The largest growth occurred in cities with populations of between 100,000 and 250,000, which increased in number from 79 to 131. Cities with populations ranging between 10,000 and 25,000, and 50,000 to 100,000, also increased considerably. Only the smallest cities, those under 10,000, had substantially no growth. The total urban population increased by 32 percent over the three decades, from 115.9 to 152.2 million.

The nation's seven largest cities, those with populations of 1 million or more, increased their total population by 6.4 percent from 18.8 to 20 million, considerably below the 16 percent rate of increase for all cities. The next largest category, cities of between 500,000 and 1 million, had a total population decrease of 3 million. On the other hand, the next two categories of cities, those between 250,000 and 500,000, as well as those between 100,000 and 250,000, enjoyed substantially higher rates of growth, 35 percent and 37 percent respectively.

The three categories of cities between 10,000 and 100,000 had an increase in total population of 12 million at a time when the population of all the nation's cities increased by 21 million. As Table 1 indicates, some of the nation's best known cities suffered double-digit percentage losses in population in the single decade between 1980 and 1990. Except for Chattanooga, Newark, and New Orleans, these were all major midwestern manufacturing centers that were seriously afflicted in the 1980s when technological obsolescence and the overvalued U.S. dollar undermined their markets both at home and abroad.

## Metropolitanization

The "city story" has been increasingly overshadowed by the "metropolitan story," which now dominates the U.S. landscape. In 1990 the twenty-one largest metropolitan areas (each with over 2 million population) accounted for about 100 million population, or four out of every ten Americans. The New York–New Jersey–Connecticut consolidated metropolitan statistical area (CMSA) accounted for 18 million, and the Los Angeles–Anaheim–Riverside CMSA for 14.5 million. Phoenix, Arizona, in twentieth position among the nation's metropolitan centers, came in with just over 2.1 million.

The next eighteen metropolitan areas, each with between 1 and 2 million residents, adds another 28 million to the previous 101 million. This means that slightly more than one out of every two Ameri-

### Table 1. Percent of Population Loss, 1980–1990

| City | |
|------|------|
| Chattanooga, TN | 10.1 |
| Cleveland, OH | 11.9 |
| Detroit, MI | 14.6 |
| Flint, MI | 11.8 |
| Gary, IN | 23.2 |
| Newark, NJ | 16.4 |
| New Orleans, LA | 10.9 |
| Pittsburgh, PA | 12.8 |
| St. Louis, MO | 12.4 |
| Warren, MI | 10.1 |

cans is a resident of one of the nation's forty largest metropolitan areas, each of which boasts at least 1 million population.

In 1960 the federal government had designated 212 areas as "metropolitan" with a combined population of 113 million out of a national urban total of 179 million. Sixty-three percent of the urban population lived in these metropolitan areas. Three decades later, nearly four out of every five city, suburban, and town dwellers were living in these vast metropoles. In 1990 (with some change in the definition of a metropolitan area), there were 284 such areas with a population total of 193 million, or 78 percent of the 249 million national total. During the last third of a century the United States has become more, not less, urbanized, or at least more metropolitanized.

The core of urban life has shifted dramatically from the city center to the metropolitan area, with a growing proportion of the population living and working in the suburbs and in the outlying metropolitan areas. However, this shift from city center to the outlying metropolitan areas should not be exaggerated. In 1960 the three largest groups of cities—starting with those over 250,000 population—accounted for 34 percent of the nation's total population. In short, one out of every three Americans was a resident of a large central city. Thirty years later, in 1990, the proportion of large-city residents had declined by five percentage points, to 29 percent of the nation's total population. Thus nearly one-third of the American people remind us every day of the continuing importance of large cities in the nation's pattern of life and work.

## The Dynamics of Urban Change: 1960–1990

Several major influences have shaped the urban transformations of the last three decades, including demographic shifts and changes in the labor market, housing patterns, and government policies. The three dominant trends have been:

- *Urbanization patterns: increasing metropolitan growth.*
  The U.S. is an increasingly urbanized society—nearly four out of every five persons lived within a metropolitan area in 1990.
- *Regional shifts: people move to the Sun Belt.*
  Most of the nation's larger cities, particularly in the Northeast and Midwest, lost population over the decades 1970 to 1990. During

the same time period, many of the larger cities in the South and West gained population.

- *Ethnic population changes: emergence of big city "minority majorities."* Minorities have become the majority in many of the nation's most populous urban centers.

In 1960 the national birth rate stood at twenty-four births per 1,000 people, reflecting the end stages of the baby boom generation that had started in 1946 and ended in 1964, some eighteen years later. By the mid-1970s the birth rate had declined from twenty-four to less than fifteen, or by just under 40 percent, a decline as spectacular as the dramatic increase that began in 1946. By 1990 the birth rate had once again advanced but very slightly—from a low of around 14.7 in the mid-1970s to 16.7 in 1990.

During these three decades the United States became both a healthier and increasingly older society. The death rate declined from 9.6 per thousand in 1960 to 8.7 in 1990, with a substantial drop in the infant mortality rate from twenty-nine to under ten per thousand. At the same time, the number and proportion of persons sixty-five years and older increased about 100 percent over the three decades, from 16.7 million to 32 million. The most striking increases occurred in persons seventy-five years and over. In 1960 there were 5.6 million in this age group, a figure that rose to over 13 million in 1990 with more than half (7.2 million) in the eighty years and older category.

The last third of a century also saw a significant shift in the regional distribution of the U.S. population from north to south and east to west. The Northeast and the Midwest each suffered a relatively large decline from 25 and 29 percent of the nation's total population to 20.4 and 24 percent respectively; while the South and the West had increases from 30.7 to 34.4 percent and 15.6 to 21.2 percent respectively. These were the years when "Frost Belt" and "Sun Belt" entered the national vocabulary, with the fastest regional population and economic growth in the metropolitan Sun Belt.

In 1965 the United States undertook the first substantial liberalization of its immigration policy since the early 1920s. As a consequence, the increase in the number of immigrants more than doubled, from 2.5 million in the 1950–1960 period to 5.8 million between 1980 and 1990. These recorded increases do not include the sizable number of illegal immigrants who enter without authorization or who stay beyond their allotted time. Most importantly, the sources of immigration shifted away from Europe to the predominant number of immigrants consisting of persons whose parents and forebears came from Latin America or Asia.

Owing to the large numbers of immigrants and their children, the American population has become much more diverse. Subtracting from the total population the 30 million African-Americans, the almost 7 million Asian-Americans and Pacific Islanders, and 1.7 million Native Americans and Alaskan Natives leaves 209 million Caucasians, 84 percent of the total population of 249 million. But this 209 million includes 22 million Latinos. If Latino-Americans are also counted as a "minority" group, then nearly one out of four Americans—24 percent—belongs to a racial or ethnic minority. When the age and relative fertility trends of African-Americans and Latinos are taken into account, it is predictable that minorities will account for a growing proportion of the total U.S. population in the decades ahead.

The focus on African-Americans, Latinos, and other minorities is that much more relevant because of their heavy concentration in the nation's largest metropolitan areas. Of the twenty most populated metropolitan areas, the minority population is equal or greater than its national proportion in all but the following: Philadelphia/Wilmington/Trenton, Boston/Lawrence/Salem, Seattle/Tacoma, Minneapolis/St. Paul, and Pittsburgh/Beaver Valley.

Even more relevant is the high proportion of minorities living in the nation's largest cities, those with over 1 million inhabitants in 1990:

- Chicago (2.8 million) is 39 percent African-American, 19.6 percent Latino, 4 percent other; *62.4* percent total minority.
- Dallas (1 million) is 29.5 percent African-American, 20.9 percent Latino, 2.7 percent other; *53.1* percent total minority.
- Detroit (1 million) is 75.7 percent African-American, 2.8 percent Latino, 1.2 percent other; *79.7* percent total minority.
- Houston (1.6 million) is 28.1 percent African-American, 27.6 percent Latino, 4.4 percent other; *60.1* percent total minority.
- Los Angeles (3.5 million) is 14 percent African-American, 39.9 percent Latino, 10.3 percent other; *54.2* percent total minority.
- New York (7.3 million) is 28.7 percent African-American, 24.4 percent Latino, 8.1 percent other; *51.2* percent total minority.
- Philadelphia (1.6 million) is 39.9 percent African-American, 5.6 percent Latino, 2.9 percent other; *48.4* percent total minority.

• San Diego (1.1 million) is 9.4 percent African-American, 20.7 percent Latino, 12.3 percent other; *42.5* percent total minority.

Many cities with a population between 500,000 and 1 million also have large minority concentrations, though somewhat less than in the nation's largest urban centers (see Table 2).

Of the nation's eight largest cities with 1 million or more population in 1990, only two—Philadelphia and San Diego—were less than half minority. Among cities with at least 500,000 or more inhabitants, only Indianapolis, Jacksonville, Phoenix, and Seattle had minority populations less than one-third of the total; Boston had a 42 percent minority population; and in each of the remaining eight cities, the minority population accounted for more than half of the total.

## The Dynamics of Urban Decision Making

Since the 1960s, three urban trends have predominated:

• The growth of outlying metropolitan areas largely at the expense of the inner cities.
• The large numbers of people who continue to reside in the inner city.

### Table 2. Minority Concentrations

|  | Population in Thousands | Total Minority |
|---|---|---|
| Baltimore | 730 | 61.7 |
| Boston | 574 | 42.0 |
| Cleveland | 506 | 52.5 |
| El Paso | 515 | 74.0 |
| Indianapolis | 731 | 24.8 |
| Jacksonville | 635 | 30.0 |
| Memphis | 610 | 55.5 |
| Milwaukee | 628 | 38.2 |
| Phoenix | 983 | 28.5 |
| San Antonio | 936 | 83.2 |
| San Francisco | 724 | 53.8 |
| San Jose | 782 | 51.5 |
| Seattle | 516 | 25.9 |
| Washington, D.C. | 607 | 73.5 |

• The increasing proportion of large-city population accounted for
by minorities.

## Suburbanization

Most Americans look forward to owning their own homes, and
have been willing to work hard to pay off their mortgage loans. To
become homeowners, they have also been willing to commute long
distances to work. Since the end of World War II, when the Federal
Housing Administration (FHA) and Veterans Administration (VA)
made low down-payment home and mortgage loans widely available, an increasing number of middle class and working class families
have been able to exchange their urban rental housing for a suburban home.

Home ownership has been a major factor in attracting urban
families to the suburbs. Almost as strong a factor has been the concerns of many urbanites with deteriorating inner city living conditions resulting from the influx of new groups, the declining quality of
local schools, and rising crime rates.

Much of the concern stems from a fear of racial and ethnic change
in urban neighborhoods. Many white Americans have been unwill-
ing to live near African-Americans who during the past several
decades have relocated to the large cities in the North and West
seeking a new and better life.

The African-American urban in-migration spurred substantial
white out-migration to the suburbs. More recently, there has also
been significant suburban migration of middle class African-Americans and other minorities. This underscores that suburbanization
has not been motivated simply by a "push factor." Still, there can be
no doubt that crime and racism made a major contribution to speeding the exodus of many white urban residents to the suburbs.

This metropolitan population shift resulted initially in related job
shifts, as the rapidly increasing suburban population required access
to a growing number of services, many of which had to be provided
locally. But substantial job shifts out of the inner city reflected even
more long-term decisions by employers to relocate, both in the manufacturing and business service sectors.

When the time came for employers to consider new investments
in their urban manufacturing plants, an increasing number recognized that they would be better off making investments in less
crowded settings where their operations would be free of the many

negative factors of the city environment, from traffic congestion to environmental regulations. The development of the interstate highway system increased the advantage of truck transportation over rail. Highways and trucking accelerated the relocation of factories from the city center to the suburbs.

Employers believed that such relocations out of the city would also give them access to an improved labor supply. In many instances they were able to draw on the underemployed population that lived on the periphery just beyond the metropolitan area.

The out-migration of urban manufacturing plants began well before the 1960s. But the trend intensified during the 1970s and 1980s, with many employers now favoring the suburbs over inner city locations. The national and regional headquarters of a growing number of U.S. firms, as well as the North American headquarters of many foreign firms, have increasingly shifted to a suburban location. Their rationale for moving includes lower business costs, a more attractive labor force, and access to adequate space so that large firms can consolidate the administrative divisions of their headquarters in a single location. Such consolidations have been reinforced by a desire of senior executives for shorter commuting times for themselves and escape from the negatives of working in the city, as well as their belief that if the entire corporate staff were based in a single complex, their productivity would increase. No one of these factors alone could have resulted in the reconfiguration of the urban-suburban business location patterns, but together they speeded corporate relocations away from the city center.

The third major force reconfiguring the urban-suburban scene was government—federal, state, and local. Massive investments in the interstate highway system played a key role, as did the substantial federal income tax benefits for suburban homeowners who deduct both the interest payments on their home mortgages and the cost of their property taxes.

In addition to federal subsidies, many states have invested heavily in establishing and maintaining an improved road system, although an increasing number have of late fallen behind in their maintenance and expansion efforts. The prominent position of suburban representatives in state legislatures has assured that suburban communities generally receive favorable treatment in the distribution of state funds for such purposes.

In the 1960s and 1970s the federal government began to play an important role in the financing of selected functions of large city governments, contributing at the peak year in 1980 close to 26 percent of the total annual expenditures of cities via grants for urban renewal and housing, education, training and employment, and a great many other programs from health care to environmental improvements. But the repeated successes after 1968 of the Republican party in winning presidential elections led to the curtailment of such programs once Ronald Reagan came into office in 1981. But party differences aside, the population shift away from the inner city to the suburban areas was the main reason for the increasingly difficult economic and fiscal circumstances that most large municipal governments encountered once federal funding was drastically cut back in the 1980s.

These urban fiscal difficulties were compounded by the federal revision of the immigration statutes in 1965 and again in 1986 that placed additional burdens on cities that were the magnets for the rapidly expanding inflows of immigrant and refugee populations, many of whom required special income assistance and social services. Although the federal government made some targeted appropriations for immigrants and refugees with special needs, it generally has not covered the costs of immigrant absorption in large urban centers.

Finally, there is the pervasive city drug problem. The last decades have seen a marked expansion in the drug culture, with the nation's largest cities experiencing explosive growth in the sale and use of addictive drugs. This urban drug scourge has contributed to weakening many inner city neighborhoods and has deprived many young people of the preparation necessary to engage in productive lives. While the federal government has increased the outlays required to interdict the importing of illegal drugs from abroad, its success has been minimal. This failure has led to rising local government expenditures for police, jails, and hospital care, as well as abandoned babies, rising unemployment, housing deterioration, homelessness, and many more undesirable consequences of the drug culture.

The mayors of the nation's leading cities have sought to make clear to successive presidents, Congress, and the voters that they are facing great difficulty in meeting the economic and social challenges in their communities. At present, urban officials confront too many people with large unmet needs for services and support, and too few tax dollars to address these problems. While the easy answer is that local governments should levy additional taxes, municipal tax increases are often neither feasible nor practical. Local governments

are the creatures of the states to which they belong, and their right to
levy additional taxes is frequently subject to the prior approval of
their state legislatures. Even when such approval is forthcoming, a
tax raising strategy is often ineffective or counterproductive. Most
urban employers have a continuing option of choosing to remain in
the city or move out. Large-city tax rates are already considerably
above the national average for all local tax burdens. Further tax
increases could result in additional job losses and a shrinking city tax
base in the future.

## The Last Third of a Century:
## A Trial Balance Sheet

In the last third of this century there have been several major
population changes: (1) the growing concentration of the American
population in metropolitan areas; (2) the more rapid growth of suburbs and outlying areas in contrast to the city proper; (3) the even
more rapid growth of the smaller metropolitan areas, those with
fewer than 250,000 population; (4) the increasing dominance of minority groups in both the nation's leading metropolitan areas and in
the nation's leading cities; and (5) the disproportionately rapid
growth in the number of elderly in the population, particularly those
over seventy-five years old.

The substantial movements of the population to the suburban and
outlying parts of metropolitan areas have resulted in the relocation
of a large number of jobs, especially service sector jobs most closely
linked to residential location patterns, such as retailing, health care,
education, and public safety. At the same time, manufacturing jobs
as well as administrative and business services have grown rapidly in
the suburbs, reflecting the preference of many large and small corporations to move their operations out of the central city.

Despite considerable out-migration of jobs, many people who
moved to the suburban areas to live still continue to commute to
central cities for work. Moreover, as the U.S. economy has come to
depend increasingly on college educated "knowledge workers,"
these suburban commuters fill a number of the better-paying positions in the central city business services sector, particularly in the
finance, insurance, and real estate sectors.

A major consequence of this employment trend has been a growing disadvantage for the less educated minority population that accounts for such a high proportion of urban residents but whose

members have limited access to both preferred urban jobs and the expanding jobs in outlying areas. The lower-skilled urban population has been particularly vulnerable because of the out-migration of such a high percentage of manufacturing jobs that in earlier decades offered entry-level employment opportunities. The problematic performance of most urban public school systems has only added to the difficulties facing minority youth, many of whom drop out of high school and thereby further jeopardize their chances to find a regular job. Because of the declining availability of low-skill jobs in the inner city, the poorly educated face greater hurdles today in finding a job and securing a regular source of income than they have in prior decades.

The well-being of the nation's large cities requires a fast-growing regional, national, and international economy, but since the onset of the recession of 1989–92, the larger economic environment has been negative and unsupportive. The unprecedented volume of recently built commercial space standing vacant is all that one need notice to underscore the problems that most metropolitan areas currently confront. There is little prospect that the surplus urban and suburban office space will be soon absorbed. The 1992 riots in Los Angeles should serve as a potent reminder that cities with large numbers of unemployed and underemployed young persons and adults face social disintegration that can lead to widespread destruction of lives and property.

The American people must address a long list of unsolved problems awaiting attention and improvement, including putting their federal finances in order; attending to their deteriorating infrastructure; improving the conditions in which so many of the nation's children and youth are being reared; finding more effective responses to crime, drugs, AIDS, homelessness, and other growing pathologies; and above all creating a national understanding for and support of the federal government's central obligation to help solve our nation's urgent economic and social challenges. The future well-being not only of the nation's cities, but of the nation itself, depends on broad federal initiatives.

## Looking Ahead

What does the future hold in store for the nation's largest cities, the sixty-three with a total of at least 250,000 population in 1990? The slow rate of growth of the U.S. economy since the early 1970s may be replaced by more rapid growth in the near future. However, the odds are currently against this scenario. In the face of a very large increase in the federal debt from about $1 to $4 trillion since the early 1980s and with the annual federal deficit in the $300 billion range, the prospect of any early return to a more generous revenue-sharing policy between the federal government and the nation's cities looks problematic.

Will state governments increase the amount of dollars that they are able and willing to share with their respective large cities? In the absence of a significant increase in the annual rate of national economic growth, which appears unlikely in the near term, the probability of substantially more state aid for cities is quite low. In fact, there are signs that a disturbing fiscal trend may be underway, in Massachusetts, New York, California, and in many other states. State legislatures, facing acute budgetary problems, have reduced rather than increased their grants to large cities.

What about the revenue-raising potential of large cities to raise more taxes locally? As noted earlier, cities are in competition with their outlying areas as well as with other cities both in the United States and abroad. The well-managed city will think twice before adding to the tax burden of businesses or households that are already paying above-average amounts of taxes. In short, increasing the revenues available to the nation's large cities from their own tax base does not appear to be a realistic short-term strategy. Under the best of circumstances there might be specific functions for which additional federal dollars would be forthcoming, such as funds for absorbing new immigrants, or subsidies to help equalize the uneven spending between inner city and suburban school systems. But such enhancements, if available at all, are likely to be modest.

The United States has the lowest average total tax burden of any nation in the world, equaled only by Japan—around 30 percent of the gross national product (GNP). Ever since President Reagan persuaded the Congress in 1981 to cut the federal income tax rate on both persons and corporations, the doctrine that the American people cannot afford to pay more taxes has gained widespread credence, a doctrine reinforced by the American distaste for big government. While it will be difficult to wean the American people from its strongly held view that higher taxes lead only to more government waste, the possibility for a change in the public's attitude and behavior is always present. In the mid-1990s the governmental fiscal environment may take a more friendly turn in favor of what are known as "investment expenditures" involving education, infrastructure, the environment, technology, and research. Such a shift has already been indicated by President Clinton.

Still, the outlook for financial relief of our large cities is not propitious. Without increased federal and state assistance, will the cities be able to contribute to their own survival and revival? While it is true that there has been a steady shift of population from the inner city to the suburbs and the outer areas, the fact remains that in 1990 the 200 largest cities, each with more than 100,000 people, have a total population of almost 72 million, or about 30 percent of the population of the United States. These cities remain in many respects the economic hubs for their respective metropolitan areas that are home for over 185 million people—or about three out of every four Americans. Only a nation set on self-destruction would turn its back on its major urban and metropolitan centers, which remain the apex of such a large part of the country's physical and human capital—as well as the decision-making complex that determines the shape and direction of the American economy and culture.

Some of our leading cities in the East, Midwest, South, and West have been singled out as preferred locations by immigrants who have come to the United States to seek their fortune and secure their future. Admittedly, many of these immigrants need a helping hand to assist them in surmounting the multiple challenges that they face, including finding a job and a home, and learning a new language. We know from the experience of the last two centuries that our cities have profited from the inflows of hard-working immigrants who have helped to revitalize neighborhoods, start new businesses, provide scientific and technical talent to our research based industries, and have made important contributions to the prosperity and growth of urban areas.

Many other immigrants have added to the problems facing urban areas, contributing to crime and drugs and expanding the welfare rolls. But these negatives are closely tied to the continuing shortfall in jobs that has characterized most inner cities during the past three decades, even in the face of a substantial increase in the nation's total employment. Sustained full employment would result in a substantially lower demand by the poor—native-born and immigrant alike—for governmentally financed social welfare services.

Even more than a full-employment economy is needed for the future well-being of our cities and the nation. We must also pay close attention to the following additional challenges:

- A broadened understanding is necessary by all Americans of the growing economic and social risks confronting the nation. We need a sense of common purpose between suburbanites and the inner city population. The United States cannot survive, much less prosper, if it permits its cities to languish and die.
- There is urgent need to build new political structures that are metropolitan-wide so that the two interdependent populations, city centered and metropolitan based, can cooperate on a host of common projects from regional transportation to regional medical centers.
- There is need for an ongoing public debate as to the future costs and benefits of the continuing flight from our nation's cities. The United States may well be reaching the point where the costs of dispersal are much greater than the social returns.

The genius of the United States since its inception has been its ability to design and redesign federal, state, and local governmental policies so that they support and strengthen decision making in the public and private sectors, thereby maintaining a strong base for economic and social progress.

In a nation that spans over 3 million square miles and boasts a diverse population of nearly 260 million, tensions between city and suburb, between regions, between national and international policy, are inevitable. But a commitment of the entire population to "E Pluribus Unum" (From Many, One) has provided the glue that guided the nation's vision in the past, as it must continue to do in the future.

# 3

# The Importance of Cities to the National Economy

## ELLIOTT D. SCLAR
## AND WALTER HOOK

### Urban Policy as Spatial Economic Policy

Since 1980 federal policy has looked at cities as places where many poor people live, rather than as efficient sites of production for the leading industries of the twenty-first century. The deteri-

---

ELLIOTT D. SCLAR is professor of urban planning in the Graduate School of Architecture, Planning and Preservation at Columbia University, where he has chaired the Urban Planning Program. An economist who specializes in economic development planning, Dr. Sclar recently co-authored a monograph for the U.S. Conference of Mayors entitled *Does America Need Cities?* He has acted as a consultant to city governments and community groups as well as labor unions, and currently serves on Mayor Dinkins's New York City Economists Roundtable. The author of numerous books and articles on urban economic development and infrastructure planning, Dr. Sclar is currently undertaking a study for the Twentieth Century Fund on the economics of public service privatization.

WALTER HOOK is the executive director of the Institute for Transportation and Development Policy. He is a doctoral candidate in Columbia University's Urban Planning Program, where he teaches urban economic development and research methods. He worked with Elliott Sclar, Joseph Persky, and Wim Weiwol on *Does America Need Cities?*

oration of American cities has been treated as a social problem as intractable as the problem of poverty itself. But the deterioration of urban America, while a reflection of continuing poverty and inequity, is also partly the result of public policies that have undermined the viability of urban areas as places of production. These policies are not only inequitable, but they also pose a threat to the economic competitiveness of the nation.

The problems of the American urban poor must be addressed as part of a broader national policy effort to strengthen the economic viability of urban centers and the productivity of the urban labor force that lives there. It may be impossible for the United States to remain a prosperous middle class society in the next century unless the country begins to appreciate the vital economic importance of central cities and designs new policies to encourage public and private reinvestment in one of our most important economic assets.

Historically, cities have been the most efficient locations for commercial and industrial activity. There is growing evidence that the information-intensive nature of many of the new jobs being created is actually increasing rather than decreasing the importance of central locations to minimizing telecommunications and transportation costs. In recent years, some businesses have chosen to relocate to office parks or freestanding corporate headquarters in suburban and exurban locations accessible by interstate highways. This has not happened because these locations are inherently more efficient, but because the costs of these locations have been underwritten by public subsidies. As a result, the efficiency savings of central city locations are lost because the inadequacy of urban services and difficult social problems have made the urban business environment increasingly unpleasant and unsafe.

## Links between City and Suburb

Although we think of the United States as an amalgam of fifty sovereign states, the economic reality is different. Much of the economic strength of the United States rests in its metropolitan regions. In 1990, 75 percent of the U.S. population lived in metropolitan areas, and over 83 percent of the nation's income was derived from these same areas. Over half of the entire U.S. population lives in just thirty-nine metropolitan areas.

While employment in urban areas as a percentage of total metropolitan area employment has continued to decrease since World War II, there are signs that this downward trend is abating. Although the long-term trend in metropolitan New York shows the city's share of employment falling from 56 percent to 41 percent between 1960 and 1990, from 1980 to 1990 it fell only 1 percent, from 42 percent to 41 percent. Total employment in the Manhattan central business district actually increased during the 1980s by 10.7 percent.

Central city jobs also constitute the higher paying jobs in most metropolitan areas. While central city jobs constitute 32.2 percent of total jobs nationally, they garner 37.7 percent of nationwide earnings. Wages of central city jobs are on average 20 percent higher than suburban jobs, and this earnings gap has been widening in many metropolitan areas, though many of these jobs are held by suburban residents.

People living in suburban areas continue to have a considerable stake in the economic vitality of cities. A large share of central city earnings, and in some cases an absolute majority of these earnings, goes to families living in suburban areas. A recent survey by Arthur Goldberg of people living in the suburban areas of the nation's 100 largest cities found that half of suburban families had at least one family member working in the city.[1] In Baltimore 59.2 percent of total earnings from city jobs went to suburban residents. In Washington D.C. 70.5 percent of total urban earnings went to suburban residents, while in Denver, Philadelphia, St. Louis, San Francisco, and New Orleans the figures are over 45 percent. Furthermore, 67 percent of suburban residents depend on the city for major medical care, and 43 percent have family members attending or planning to attend a city based institution of higher learning, while 46 percent believe their property values would be adversely affected by economic decline in nearby cities. Thus national prosperity depends on metropolitan prosperity, which in turn depends on the economic health of central cities.

## Central Location and Producer Services

The improvement in employment growth in many central business districts has been driven primarily by the growing importance of information-intensive producer services in the national economy. Services constitute an increasing share of employment and gross national product (GNP), accounting for 71 percent of employment and 68 percent of GNP as of 1985. Not all of these services are growing at the same rate, however. As Saskia Sassen has pointed out in *The Global City,* while the share of retail services has been flat, producer services have grown dramatically.[2] Producer services include such office based activities as legal services, advertising, finance, insurance, real estate, data processing, and telecommunications services, as well as occupations such as security and custodial services and messenger and package delivery services.

As Manuel Castells showed in *The Informational City,* of the new jobs created in the United States between 1980 and 1985, only 33,-200 were in manufacturing, while 3,477,800 were in services, most of them information processing producer services.[3] While job growth between 1980 and 1985 grew by 8 percent nationally, jobs in producer services grew by 20 percent. Currently, employment in manufacturing has declined to around 14 percent of the total work force, while employment in information based producer service industries has increased to 13.9 percent. Percentages of GNP have followed similar patterns.

Producer services firms have been concentrating in central urban locations, bidding up rents and in some cases driving corporate headquarters and "back-office" activities out to suburban areas. The top twenty-four central counties accounted for 39 percent of all employment in information-intensive industries, while these counties only constituted 27 percent of total U.S. employment. The pay for such jobs located in downtown Boston was 3.55 times higher than jobs under similar categories in suburban areas, and 2.37 times higher in downtown New York than in suburban areas.

## The Economic Advantages of Central Locations

### Why Producer Service Firms Choose Central Locations

Despite some evidence of revived corporate interest in central locations, particularly in producer services, many jobs continue to relocate from urban to suburban areas. The question is not whether this trend is in fact continuing; it is. But what is causing this decentralized employment trend and is it strengthening or weakening the competitiveness of the U.S. economy?

The growth in job relocation from central cities to suburbs has been encouraged by outmoded public policies. These policies were developed before the globalization of the economy made competitiveness a serious concern. This decentralization pattern now poses a problem for U.S. economic vitality.

Historically, cities develop and grow because it is more efficient to produce and market goods in central locations where the transportation and telecommunications costs for both producers and consumers can be minimized. Transportation costs are minimized because inputs into production are close by, and outputs are near to final consumers. Furthermore, because urban areas represent a single contiguous market, larger-scale production becomes possible, with increased returns from economies of scale and efficiency gains from increasing product specialization, known as agglomeration economies. Telecommunications costs and the cost of information are also minimized. Locations near concentrated markets provide producers with critical up-to-date information about changes in market prices, supply, and demand. Despite advances in telecommunications technology, these information flows are still very important. In fact, with the growing importance of information based industries and just-in-time production, differences in transportation and telecommunications costs may be increasing in importance.

Unlike the large mass industrial production that dominated the U.S. economy prior to the 1970s, which was very land-intensive, the information based economy has different spatial dynamics. An information based economy depends upon the quality and efficiency of information systems and information analysis.

The best analysis is conducted in environments in which a diverse range of experts have easy face-to-face contact with one another. Further, the cutting edge of research and development seems to increasingly be coming from networks of small independent firms rather than large isolated firms. This, combined with the intensive use of telecommunications infrastructure, seems to be favoring both central city locations and centralized clusters of dense suburban development, or "edge cities."

Many of the functions performed by producer service firms, such as legal or data processing services, for example, were previously performed by in-house departments within major corporations. By contracting out these activities to specialist companies known as producer service firms, economies of scale that were impossible before recent advances in computer technology can be realized in office functions. These specialized firms, in turn, are highly information-intensive. Every time a corporation contracts out its payroll processing work, its demand for telecommunications services increases. The contractor must be able to send a large amount of information to the corporate client. As the competitive producer services firm has many business clients in order to realize the necessary economies of scale, it is natural for the firm to locate in a central location in order to reduce its telecommunications and transportation costs.

With worldwide trade in producer services growing rapidly, central locations are becoming critical for facilitating international transactions. Firms like Merrill Lynch or Morgan Stanley rely on constant flows of data from around the world that then have to be retransmitted to clients through local networks. This transmission can only occur at minimum cost in a place where the telecommunications infrastructure is sufficient to support such volume. It is only with great difficulty and at high expense that noncentral locations can have sufficient telecommunications infrastructure and a sufficient local network to be economically competitive for this type of activity.

Central locations also make possible a high level of specialization of producer services. A firm might need the assistance of a lawyer specializing in Indonesian product liability law. The larger the urban area, the more likely that it can sustain such a highly specialized practice. Meanwhile, it is to the lawyer's advantage to be located as centrally as possible to minimize marketing, telecommunications, and travel costs and to make the business accessible to the maximum number of current and potential clients.

## Why Exurban Growth Continues

If central locations are much more efficient, why would the current trend still be toward firm relocation to suburban and exurban areas? A principal reason is that the increased costs resulting from firm relocation are not borne directly by the private firm, but rather by its employees and the public taxpayers. As a result, important efficiency gains from central locations are lost.

Given the strategic importance of central urban locations in minimizing production costs, particularly for producer services firms, it should be a matter of economic policy concern that no other advanced industrial nation has decentralized employment and allowed cities to deteriorate to the same degree as the United States. If central location were no longer economically efficient, we would see similar employment suburbanization among our international competitors, but they have not done it to the same extent.

The current policy approach to urban America evolved in the three decades following World War II at a time when the U.S. economy was globally preeminent. With wide differences between the productivity of labor in the United States and other countries, and with European and Japanese spending power weakened by the war, U.S. policy was more concerned with maintaining consumer demand for U.S. products than with minimizing the costs of production. Thus U.S. public policy was used more to stimulate consumption and less to maximize productive efficiency. As a result, many public investments led to changes in the spatial distribution of economic activity that have imposed significant additional costs on the economy. Since that time, as the European and Japanese economies rebuilt their industrial infrastructure, the competitive position of the U.S. economy has deteriorated, and these past inefficiencies in the built environment are beginning to take their toll.

While the process of suburbanization is complex, several key public policies encouraged urban deconcentration beyond what would likely have happened in a purely market-driven urbanization process. The Federal Housing Administration (FHA) insured home mortgages and Veterans Administration (VA) government guaranteed loans for home buyers strongly encouraged suburbanization. Before the 1960s civil rights movement, the underwriting criteria for FHA and VA loans effectively restricted their use to single-family suburban homes in racially segregated neighborhoods. This suburban bias remained until the 1970s. Because home builders wanted their product to be eligible for the FHA and VA programs, most new construction was located in the suburbs.

Furthermore, the mechanization of southern agriculture in the 1950s and 1960s resulted in a large migration of southern rural African-Americans into northern cities. African-Americans clustered in urban areas both because the costs of living were lower and because they were kept out of suburban areas by private restrictive covenants and exclusionary public zoning. Those African-Americans who could afford to buy a home were often unable to secure mortgage loans from financial institutions, and had to borrow funds for home purchase with "land-installment contracts," dealing through speculators who often charged the equivalent of 20 percent interest rates.

The concentration of African-Americans and lower-income groups in central cities and the lack of financing for inner city home ownership meant that many urbanites remained renters. As renters they were ineligible for the other major U.S. government benefits for private home ownership: the federal income tax deductibility of mortgage interest payments and state and local property taxes. Together, FHA-VA and income tax deductions created strong financial incentives for anyone who could buy a home and relocate to a suburban area. Once this urban decentralization process got underway, banks and other lenders encouraged it by withdrawing private financing from moderate income central city neighborhoods through mortgage "redlining."

As a result, a private dollar invested in a new suburban single-family house went much further than a comparable dollar spent in the urban rental housing market. In light of these generous housing subsidies, much of the newly prosperous middle class moved to the suburbs after World War II.

Government transportation policies have also encouraged suburbanization. Until the late 1960s and early 1970s, most forms of public transportation serving urban areas, such as buses, subways, and commuter railroads, were either supplied by private companies at a profit, or by public authorities expected to at least "break even" on revenues and expenses. In a typical example, New York's subway system was expected to pay for all of its capital investments and operating costs out of user charges, while fares were kept low by government regulation. The New York City Transit Authority lost money, quality of service declined, and financing for routine maintenance, let alone capital improvements or line expansion, was unavailable. Deteriorating service alienated riders. Public subsidies to the subway system were not made available until 1968 when the state government ended the fire-wall between highway tolls and subway financing. Federal subsidies using gasoline tax revenues finally were provided in the 1970s.

U.S. urban commuter rail lines were caught in the same trap as the city subways. Regulations made them unable to raise fares in order to cover necessary capital and operating expenses. The poor quality of their service made them unable to compete with the private automobile, which was highly subsidized because taxpayers financed most of the costs of building and maintaining streets and highways. Had the federal and state governments not intervened in the mid-1960s, urban commuter rail lines would have gone bankrupt and been closed, and the rights-of-way sold off.

Meanwhile, as suburban commuters became increasingly dependent on the private automobile, subsidies to roads and highways have increased. By 1955 total subsidies to road based modes had already risen to $1.34 billion annually. They are currently around $24.27 billion annually, representing 30 percent of the total cost of road provision.

Most people who can afford to buy a suburban home and commute by automobile are heavily subsidized and encouraged to do so. These public policies have contributed to dividing the residents of cities and suburbs along income and racial lines. Lower-income and minority residents have become concentrated in urban centers while higher-income people have relocated to suburban areas.

The nature of regulation in telecommunications pricing also helped to underwrite the costs of suburbanization. The prices for basic telephone service were fixed at a flat rate negotiated between AT&T and the Federal Communications Commission. This rate was determined by allowing AT&T to make a fixed percent of profit above the total cost of providing service to all users. The flat-rating system meant that differences in the cost of providing service to different areas were not reflected in the prices of these services. Since most of the cost of providing telephone service is in providing and maintaining the wire network, and it is much cheaper to provide a single line to a high-density city building than to provide lines to sprawling suburban locations, city users were effectively subsidizing suburban and rural users.

As a result of these and many other public policies, business firms as well as individuals based their commercial, industrial, and residential location decisions partly on price signals that were somewhat distorted by government subsidies and incentives. These suburban oriented subsidies helped to counteract some of the economic efficiency advantages of central city locations.

## The Costs of Continued Urban Dispersal

By encouraging the dispersal of economic activity, past U.S. public policies have imposed significant costs on the inputs of U.S. firms. Private firms, however, have not adjusted their location patterns to avoid these costs because they do not face them directly. Rather, these costs affect firms only indirectly in the form of higher taxes and labor costs.

In Holland, for example, high urban density and a network of safe and efficient bicycle and pedestrian paths make it possible for an employee's commuting needs to be met at minimal cost. A one-time purchase of a $200 bicycle can take care of all of a person's commuting costs for five years. A Dutch worker therefore only needs to be paid around $40 a year to cover commuting costs. The public costs of maintaining bicycle and pedestrian infrastructure are also minimal, thus reducing taxes.

In the United States, however, low density suburbanization has undermined the viability of lower-cost modes of transportation such as public transportation, bicycling, and walking. As a result, 86 percent of the population is dependent on automobiles for commuting, and each employee must be paid more than $2,500 per year for the purchase and maintenance of an automobile. Furthermore, taxes have to be collected to pay the estimated $2,400 per passenger car of public subsidy to make the roads and highways viable for automobile transportation. These costs are all indirectly reflected in the prices of goods produced in the United States. In increasingly competitive global markets, such costly inefficiencies harm the competitiveness of U.S. products.

America's dependence on automobiles is also exacerbating its international trade deficit. In 1989 Japan produced 9,052,000 passenger cars while consuming only 4,404,000 cars. In the same year the United States produced 6,823,000 passenger cars, while consuming 9,853,000 cars. If each one of these imported cars cost $10,000, then $30 billion of our total annual trade deficit, or roughly 15 percent, can be directly attributed to our deficit in automobiles. Oil imports add another 30 percent, meaning U.S. dependence on automobile commuting accounts for 45 percent of the trade deficit. While many scholars have asked why the United States has lost its competitive edge in the production of cars, fewer have asked why we consume so many compared to other nations.

The inefficiencies in the U.S. transportation system are clearly linked to the decentralized pattern of urbanization. The amount of money the United States spends for transportation, telecommunications, and related infrastructure is high relative to other countries. The United States spends between 15 and 18 percent of GNP on transportation, while Japan spends only 9 percent of its GNP on transportation. American families spend from between 15.2 percent and 22.5 percent of their annual income on transportation related expenses, whereas Japanese families spend only 9.4 percent of their income on transportation.

The growing traffic congestion associated with the U.S. metropolitan development patterns also imposes severe costs on the economy. According to a recent study by G. Bruce Douglas, every time a firm relocates from a central city to a suburban location the number of automobile trips made by the firm's employees during the day increases by twelve times.[4] Thus a large part of the growth in vehicle miles traveled by U.S. citizens—and the consequent increase in traffic congestion—is being driven by the relocation of firms from urban to suburban areas.

Traffic congestion has worsened considerably in the United States in the last ten years. According to Anthony Downs's study, *Stuck in Traffic,* since 1975 the percentage of miles people have to travel in congested conditions during rush hour has increased from 42 percent to 63 percent, with levels expected to further increase dramatically in the next ten years.[5] At the current level of growth in automobile traffic, many metropolitan regions will find their average travel speeds cut in half within the decade. The current costs of this congestion nationally are estimated to be $168 billion a year.

Traffic congestion increases the costs of shipping goods and the costs of commuting, and takes away from time that could be spent more productively or enjoyably. Yet the cost of building more highways to ease increasing traffic congestion is prohibitive. In 1987 the Federal Highway Administration estimated that our current U.S. annual expenditures on highways of $14.6 billion would have to be increased by 35 percent just to bring the existing physical infrastructure back up to the 1983 level of congestion and quality.[6] In order to maintain average user costs (which include the costs of congestion) at current levels of $400 billion per year, current expenditures would have to be increased by 113 percent. A much more cost-effective way of resolving U.S. automobile traffic congestion problems is to encourage reurbanization and higher density living and working patterns. This would reduce the need for travel and make mass transit options more viable.

The highly dispersed U.S. pattern of metropolitan development is also contributing to environmental degradation. Currently 29 percent of energy consumption—and 25 percent of toxic emissions that cause global warming—come from the transportation sector. While more fuel efficient vehicles and alternative fuels may offer some hope, the current explosion of vehicle miles traveled is undermining the progress on air and water pollution that these innovations could make.

The U.S. automobile-dependent suburban development patterns

are highly wasteful of land. Because of cars, most metropolitan areas have to dedicate over half of their available land to road infrastructure, compared to less than 25 percent in Japanese cities. If mainland China were to have as many automobile commuters per capita, it would need to pave 40 percent of its arable farmland in order to provide sufficient road infrastructure.

These inefficiencies caused by decentralization manifest themselves in the higher costs of other forms of infrastructure as well, such as telecommunications, electricity, water, sewerage, and drainage. Supporting the same level of economic activity in suburban and rural areas requires that transportation, water, sewer, and power lines be extended and maintained over far longer distances. The 1974 study by the Department of Housing and Urban Development (HUD), *The Costs of Sprawl*,[7] indicated that the cost of providing housing in low-density unplanned suburban areas was 60 percent higher than providing the same number of units in planned, high-density urban areas. More than half of these costs are paid for by the taxpayers.

## Why Urban Deconcentration Has Led to Declining Public Investment in Infrastructure and Human Capital

The continued process of urban deconcentration may be hurting the U.S. economy in other ways as well. Continuing suburbanization of employment and residences has undermined the tax base of urban areas. Urban governments have thus been increasingly unable to invest in infrastructure and in the education and training of the labor force, both of which are critical to making cities competitive sites of production. Declining public investment could partially explain the long-term slowdown in U.S. labor productivity and economic growth.

Many U.S. economists have become alarmed at U.S. economic growth trends relative to other advanced industrial countries. The higher the productivity of U.S. labor, the more U.S. employees can be paid while maintaining the competitiveness of U.S. products in international markets. After World War II, the United States enjoyed a substantial productivity advantage in comparison with other developed countries. However, since 1960 productivity in the United States has only grown at an annualized rate of 1.21 percent, while productivity levels in Japan have grown at an annual rate of

5.71 percent, in Italy at 3.78 percent, and in Germany at 2.87 percent. Between 1979 and 1988 annual productivity in the United States grew by only 1.09 percent, while in Japan it grew by 2.93 percent, in England by 1.79 percent, and in Germany by 1.12 percent. These recent differences, though considerably smaller than the initial gap, are still sufficiently high to warrant concern.

According to recent studies by David Aschauer and Alicia Munnell, there is a significant correlation between the level of public investment and the level of productivity growth.[8] With current tax revenues at only 30 percent of GNP, the United States is the second lowest-taxed nation among Organization for Economic Cooperation and Development (OECD) countries after Turkey. Japan, with tax revenues accounting for only 30.2 percent of gross domestic product (GDP) is also not heavily taxed. The key difference, however, is that Japan, despite its very low tax levels, spends a tremendous amount of its money on public investment. Japan is projected to increase its level of public investment from 6 percent of GDP to 10 percent of GDP from 1991 to 1996, while in the United States public investment constitutes less than 1 percent of GDP. There is thus significant evidence that the slowdown in economic growth since the late 1970s can be partly attributed to the relatively low level of U.S. public investment.

The urban crisis in the United States is both part of the explanation for why public investment has fallen, and also a reflection of this falling public investment. Even before World War II, with U.S. policies encouraging decentralization, city governments found themselves in fiscal distress, making it difficult to finance their needed infrastructure improvements and the education and training of their residents. With federal policy underwriting many of the costs of urban dispersal, city governments were not able to raise their taxes significantly without the threat of driving away more residents and businesses. The beginnings of deindustrialization in the 1970s exacerbated these problems, driving many cities into severe fiscal crisis.

The beginning of the urban fiscal crisis coincides with the slowdown in economic growth in the United States and the decline of the aggregate productivity of the U.S. workforce. Until the end of the 1970s, the federal government attempted to compensate for the declining tax base of central cities resulting from middle and upper class residential and corporate flight to suburban areas by increasing loans and grants to cities. After 1980, however, cities increasingly had to rely on property taxation for revenue. Federal aid as a percentage of city budgets was reduced by 64 percent from an average of 17.7 percent in 1980 to an average of 6.4 percent in 1990. In 1991, 60.9 percent of our nation's cities had fiscal difficulties, and 26.5 percent were in serious fiscal distress.

To make matters worse, cities also were locked into destructive competition with their own suburbs as well as other cities to attract corporate investors. With urban tax bases increasingly dependent on property taxation, metropolitan regional competition virtually assured that whatever federal money was received through urban development action grants (UDAG) and community development block grants (CDBG) was spent encouraging immobile real estate development that promised to yield new property tax revenues. Investments in the education of the more mobile urban workforce was easily overlooked. Similarly, the long-term gains from improvements in the quality of urban infrastructure and urban services were too far in the future for badly strapped cities. As a result, federal aid to cities in the late 1970s did not lead to significant increases in urban productivity.

Consider Baltimore. Between 1970 and 1985 Baltimore City lost 45 percent of its manufacturing jobs. This dealt a devastating blow to the city's tax base. Knowing that the welfare of its citizens depended on the city's ability to deliver public services such as education and transportation, Baltimore tried to revive its property tax base. The city embarked on public development projects using federal grant funds to construct the well-known redevelopment of their inner harbor in the hopes of setting off a construction boom. Indeed, the supply of downtown office space exploded. By 1985 roughly $50 million of public investment had attracted $540 million of private investment, with another $700 million in private investment in various planning stages.

Despite all of this furious construction activity and the praise the city won for its reconstruction efforts, including the award-winning Harbor Place festival market, Baltimore entered the 1990s poorly equipped to compete with other locations for the jobs of the future. The city's focus on downtown real estate had increased the supply of office space but it had led to a serious underinvestment in the critical factors of production: labor and infrastructure.

By 1990 this redevelopment strategy began to draw critics even among the business community. The Greater Baltimore Committee, long the voice of the established downtown sector, pointed out that while Baltimore's Harbor Place complex may have created some jobs and expanded the tax base in the short run, in the long run it had failed to address the key problems with Baltimore as a place of production in the 1990s. Of the twenty largest U.S. cities, Baltimore had the lowest percentage of adults over twenty-five years old with a high school degree and the third lowest number with a college degree.

The committee's report concluded that if Baltimore hoped to compete for investment dollars against other cities and against its own surrounding suburban areas, it would have to improve the education and productivity of its citizens and improve urban services. The new, service-driven economy of the 1990s requires a computer literate workforce. The city of Baltimore still had classrooms without schoolbooks, let alone computers.

With homelessness on the rise, particularly among children, and the overcrowding of housing, obvious from the 35,000 people on the Baltimore Housing Authority's waiting list, the ability of children to get an education has declined. Forty-three percent of school age homeless children do not attend school. The vast increase in the incidence of homelessness among children is likely to have profound effects on the labor force of tomorrow.

The point is not to blame city mayors for bad policies. Almost every city around the country was forced by deindustrialization to attract businesses and expand its tax base by adopting similar domestic development strategies. The point is that the federal government, by systematically pulling back from its support for cities in the 1980s, forced them to rely increasingly on their own resources. Trying to bolster the local tax base, city governments dedicated the bulk of public development dollars to real estate ventures, and hoped that the new business activity located in the city would make up for the tax concessions they granted to attract the new investment.

Meanwhile, those public investments that are the most critical to the productivity growth of the U.S. economy, and hence the competitiveness of U.S. products in international markets, have shrunk considerably. Urban infrastructure is in disrepair after years of deferred maintenance. U.S. investment in education through the high school level is the lowest among the seven most industrialized nations, with the United States spending only 4.1 percent of GNP, compared to 4.6 percent of GNP in West Germany and 4.7 percent in Japan. Furthermore, the extremely localized nature of public education means that many poor communities are underfunded. At the same time, these schools are being asked to deal with problems such as drug abuse, homeless students, and the reemergence of public health concerns ranging from measles to AIDS.

## Urban Policy as a
## Form of Industrial Policy

U.S. Secretary of Labor Robert Reich in *The Work of Nations* points out that national economic vitality depends less on the nationality of a firm's ownership and more on where actual production is located.[9] This in turn means that the competitiveness of the U.S. economy hinges directly on the relative strengths and weaknesses of the United States as a site of production. Thus the reason a firm chooses to locate in the United States rather than someplace else will be a reflection of the business environment in the United States. That, in turn, is critically affected by public policy.

The United States maintains a commanding lead in many high-technology areas, as it has in the past. The problem is not that the new ideas are not coming from the United States, but that the resulting products are not being manufactured here. The transistor was invented at Bell Laboratories, yet Japanese firms dominate the worldwide consumer electronics industry. Anyone can buy or license a patent. An innovative new product may be invented by a high-technology research firm in California, but there is little benefit to the American people if the product is manufactured overseas.

In recent decades important changes have occurred in the nature of production that have made old economic categories such as "manufacturing" and "services" obsolete. What has emerged is a type of integrated activity that combines these categories in new and different ways. The Japanese call it "just-in-time production," Reich has labeled it "flexible production," and a team of MIT researchers has dubbed it "lean production."

By closely linking what a factory produces to what it buys from its suppliers, and to up-to-the-minute changes in what customers are demanding, just-in-time (JIT) gives firms important comparative advantages. First, because smaller batches are produced, firms are able to respond more quickly to rapid changes in consumer demand. This reduces the risk of overproducing outmoded goods. Second, less of the firm's capital is tied up in stockpiled inputs or unsold inventory. The system also requires employees to understand the production process, which then allows them to constantly monitor quality control. This process also allows manufacturers to make frequent minor technological innovations in the production process and to closely customize a product to a specific customer's needs. Thus design, marketing, and manufacturing have been collapsed into overlapping steps in a seamless circular process of product output and evolution.

While a great deal of attention has focused on the changes necessary to internal firm management to make just-in-time production possible in the United States, scant attention has been given to the changes in infrastructure and public policy required. While there is a growing consensus around the competitive advantages of just-in-time production inside the firm, Toyota found that factors outside the production process were just as important. Toyota found that the distribution and sales functions were generating 20 percent to 30 percent of a car's cost to the customer—an amount that exceeded Toyota's cost to manufacture the car. Furthermore, while it took two days to manufacture the car, it took from fifteen to twenty-six days to close the sale, transmit the order to the factory, get the order scheduled, and deliver the car to the customer. While some of these costs are unavoidable, some reflect the constraints of the transportation and telecommunications infrastructure. These costs will be brought down only by public policies that encourage increasing efficiencies in the transportation and telecommunications systems.

Several factors may give U.S. cities important advantages as sites for future just-in-time production facilities. First, the new producers do not require as much land to store raw materials and finished goods. Second, the close communication between customers, manufacturers, and suppliers of intermediate goods greatly increases the importance of the efficiency and reliability of the transportation and telecommunications networks, and the information processing skills of a firm's workers. As has been demonstrated, central locations hold the potential for significant cost savings in these areas when not distorted by misguided public policy. Third, as a close relationship between the manufacturer and the suppliers becomes increasingly important, the agglomeration economies possible in urban areas through increased product and service specialization become more important. Finally, competitive advantage through technological innovation makes locational proximity to research and development institutions invaluable.

We must begin to think of urban policy as a potent form of economic and industrial policy. Urban policy that directs private investment to efficient sites of production by investing in infrastructure and human capital is critical to making just-in-time viable in the United States. It is noteworthy that in Japan, where just-in-time production evolved, manufacturing is largely an urban phenomenon.

## Urban Areas and the Culture Industry

Abandoning our nation's cities is also abandoning our nation's history. If this were not a serious problem in and of itself, abandoning our history is also abandoning a growing international market—tourism. Many nations earn a significant percentage of their GNP and foreign exchange from tourist dollars. But tourists do not flock to U.S. cities the way they flock to Paris and Rome largely because we have made them so unpleasant.

Cities are also home to most of our major research and cultural institutions. Many major universities are becoming incubators for small research and development firms. Increasingly, these firms are the engines of economic growth. Recently, a major biotechnology firm announced it was establishing a principal manufacturing facility on unused industrial land in Boston. Critical to this choice, according to the firm's president, was the quality of local research and development facilities. As many of our major universities are in urban locations, the ability of these firms to develop into the businesses of the twenty-first century will depend on the viability of the urban business environment. In a world increasingly dominated by ideas and culture, industries like entertainment and art, the social diversity of our cities is an important economic asset. The costs of allowing these institutions to stagnate would represent an enormous lost opportunity in terms of the nation's economic well-being.

## Reinventing Urban Policy

Cities are critical sites of production in the future information based global economy. The fortunes of the national economy will rise or fall based on the viability of our nation's cities. That the United States has allowed its cities to deteriorate is not only a social problem from the perspective of equity and social harmony. It is also an economic liability we could be living with for decades unless we take action to change course and begin a new urban economic policy.

If the United States is to restore its cities to their economically strategic role, first it will be necessary to reorient the strategy behind national economic policy. For much of the last two decades the implicit assumption behind America's response to a changing global economy emphasized lowering the costs of existing operations rather than encouraging a more efficient restructuring. That assumption manifests itself in the policy emphasis at all levels of government on lowering business taxes and in pursuing budget cutbacks and social policies that are most harmful to low- and moderate-income families. The policy rationale was that American methods of doing business were fine, and the only problem was that they cost too much.

As we survey the economic damage of the 1970s and 1980s, it is clear that the tax-cutting approach to boost profits did not work in restoring economic competitiveness. Instead, the drop in public revenues has led to a loss of critical public investments in both the infrastructure and workforce, making our economic activities more costly and less efficient. In addition, the upward redistribution of income implied by such policies has not led to a new burst of productive private investment. Instead, it has caused domestic consumer demand to stall, which has further postponed economic revitalization. Because of the historic distribution of economic activity between cities, suburbs, and rural areas, the brunt of the cost of this policy has been borne by the central cities and older suburbs.

It is now time for the United States to reorient its approach to international competition. Instead of treating the symptoms of the problem, America must focus on the cause: low productivity. Public policy can contribute to enhanced private sector productivity by pursuing policies that lower the costs of doing business by making the spatial infrastructure more efficient for a restructured world economy, and by lowering the upward pressure on wages by cutting prices and the cost of living through more efficient and affordable education, health care, housing, transportation, day care, and other services.

In the remainder of this chapter we will review the policy changes needed to simultaneously enhance U.S. economic performance and revitalize American cities.

## Increase Federal Support for Cities

The "new federalism" of the Reagan-Bush years led to drastic cutbacks in federal funding to urban areas, and to increasing flexibility of state and local decisions on the spending of federal grant funds. The result of these two policies was a serious underinvestment in urban infrastructure and human capital.

This form of federalism occurred at the same time that the economy was being deindustrialized. Deindustrialization, according to William Julius Wilson, left large segments of the inner city population facing long-term unemployment or the replacement of $350 a week industrial jobs with $150 a week service sector jobs.[10] The net result was the reduction of incomes for inner city residents that undermined the tax base. This in turn led to the fiscal crisis in the late 1970s. To prevent businesses from fleeing in the wake of deteriorating public services, city governments used tax concessions on an unprecedented scale.

In a growing national economy, such tax competition would not be all bad. It could help to better distribute economic activity and encourage the public sector to be more efficient. Over time, however, as urban areas found they had to provide tax incentives, tax competition merely exacerbated the problem it was intended to address: the decrease in the city tax base.

Urban policies that maximized the value of real estate but did little to increase the income of city residents made the tax base increasingly dependent on property taxation. Fiscally insecure urban governments used the flexible federal funding that was available for festival marketplaces and downtown revitalization schemes aimed at encouraging increased real estate development, rather than for education, infrastructure, or neighborhood development. These policies, however, left cities vulnerable to fluctuations in real estate values. According to Michael Pagano, with the collapse of the real estate market in the late 1980s, 60.9 percent of city governments are facing fiscal difficulties, and 26.5 percent are in serious fiscal distress.[11] Cutbacks in federal support for cities combined with their declining local tax base have caused cities to underinvest in the two major factors of production that they influence, public capital (the modernization of transport, telecommunications, water, sewer, and power infrastructure) and human capital (the health, safety, education, housing, and retraining of the workforce). Thus the most neglected areas were those where public action most directly affected private sector productivity.

A new urban policy must begin by increasing federal fiscal responsibility for urban areas, thereby allowing cities to lower the tax burden on the residential population and business communities. The economically relevant regions of the twenty-first century rarely conform to the political boundaries that evolved in the nineteenth century. In most major metropolitan areas nearly half of the income from city jobs is earned by noncity residents. A justification therefore exists for redistributing these economic benefits back into cities through federal taxation in order to cover the higher costs of maintaining urban infrastructure.

Unlike buildings and infrastructure, urban residents are not bound to central city locations. The U.S. labor market is increasingly mobile, which means that the beneficiaries of a city's educational investments are national in scope. Thus there is a strong rationale for increased national investments into human capital, such as education and health care.

Finally, the case for increased federal support can be based on the size of the federal tax base relative to that of states and localities. The only level of government that can successfully sustain the new initiatives of a revived national urban policy is the federal government.

Further, federal income and corporate taxes are far less regressive than local taxation. As the polarization of incomes has weakened the purchasing power of the middle class and put a damper on domestic demand, more progressive tax policy would help stimulate economic growth.

Some form of federal revenue sharing aimed at increasing productivity should be studied as a method to effect this financing. It is critical that states, regions, and localities be given the necessary autonomy to respond creatively to unique local circumstances. Revenue sharing can provide that autonomy. However, cities cannot be allowed to spend all federal dollars on tourist attractions and private real estate development while neglecting investments in human capital and public infrastructure. Only a significant injection of federal aid can help to stem the self-defeating, beggar-thy-neighbor fiscal policies where localities attempt to steal each other's tax base while trying to drive away undesired social groups and land uses. It must be made clear that ultimately no locality is an island (even if it is on an island).

## Encourage the Recentering of New Development

A key to encouraging long-term economic growth is to make new public investments that increase spatial efficiency. This in turn means public interventions to encourage higher-density development by revitalizing our center cities and older, larger suburbs. For that to happen, the structure of public subsidies that has in the past encouraged lower-density development must be reversed, and public investment targeted to modes of transportation and telecommunications that must encourage higher-density metropolitan development patterns in cities and suburbs.

## Transportation

The goal of U.S. transportation policy should be the maximization of mobility, convenience, and fairness, and the minimization of costs and environmental damage. Minimizing the costs of inputs and the costs of living does not necessarily mean building more highways in the hope of reducing traffic congestion. Rather, it means removing the need to build an extra lane on a suburban highway by making public transit as viable an option as the private car.

Studies indicate that the relocation of firms from urban to exurban areas is a principal cause of the rapid increase in vehicle miles traveled. More commuting leads to greater traffic congestion and the need for expanded suburban road infrastructure. Extra infrastructure costs can be avoided if firms are not compelled to relocate out of urban areas. One recent estimate indicated that if families were able to commute to work and to shop by public transportation, the need for a second car would be removed. These families would save up to $3,000 annually by "junking the clunker." Making this option viable for the vast majority of Americans will require a fundamental rethinking of our transportation and land use policies. We can borrow several ideas already practiced by other countries.

First, subsidies to transportation modes that encourage sprawling land development must be phased out. Thirty percent of the cost of the nation's road infrastructure is currently subsidized by tax revenues. The first step, from the point of view of economic efficiency, is to increase user charges to cover these costs. User charges for the private automobile would therefore have to increase over time by the amount of the subsidy. The easiest way to do this would be to increase gasoline taxation to the point where it entirely covered the costs of maintaining and servicing the motorized road traffic network.

From an economic point of view, road taxation offers the best way to discourage the overuse of the scarce resource known as road infrastructure. Such taxation would discourage new construction in exurban areas by making these locations more expensive to commuters. In addition, congestion pricing, which increases road taxes during peak times, could also be implemented. Congestion pricing, by encouraging commuters to travel during off-peak hours, could help relieve traffic congestion, increase road speeds, and decrease pollution. The other advantage from an equity perspective is that road taxation, unlike the gasoline tax, could be made progressive by keeping tolls low in lower-income urban and rural areas.

Second, we should increase subsidies to transport modes that encourage efficient transportation and land use patterns and are less polluting. Tax credits currently available to employers who provide parking to their employees should gradually be removed, while tax credits to firms that provide transit allowances should be increased and tax credits for providing bicycle facilities such as secure bicycle parking and showers with locker rooms for changing clothes should be provided.

Increasing the subsidies for commuter railroads, buses, and subways is also critical to encouraging their use. Lowering fare costs and increasing the quality of service over time could actually lower the average operating costs of mass transit by increasing ridership.

Finally, nonmotorized modes of transportation such as bicycling and walking, which have the lowest costs and are nonpolluting, must be supported. Cities should be encouraged to undertake bicycle and pedestrian network planning, to give subsidies to parking garages that provide bicycle parking facilities and to buildings that provide parking and showers. Cities should also be encouraged to build a network of bicycle and pedestrian ways that are safely segregated from automobile traffic. These lanes could also be used by people commuting with roller blades, an increasing phenomenon in large cities like Los Angeles and New York. Local commuter rail and transit authorities should provide bicycle parking facilities, and make provisions for commuters to bring their bicycles onto trains.

The new Intermodal Surface Transportation Efficiency Act (ISTEA) offers some hope that federal transportation dollars will be used to encourage more efficient modes of transportation. This legislation ties federal funding to the existence of regional plans that must be in compliance with the Clean Air Act Amendments of 1990 (CAAA). The increasing flexibility with which states can use federal transportation funds under ISTEA is also grounds for hope. However, the playing field between transportation modes must be leveled. Federal funding should encourage higher-density land use patterns around public transit modes. Otherwise, federal dollars will continue to be used on automobile based modes and the costs of automobile dependence will continue to harm both the national economy and metropolitan efficiency.

## Telecommunications

With the increasing role of telecommunications in the global economy, and the growing importance of information based industries and information-intensive production methods, public policies that help minimize telecommunications costs for society should be encouraged. A recent study by the Commerce Department indicated that the private U.S. system of telecommunications has not spent as much on modernization as other industrialized nations. According to the study, U.S. investment in telecommunications system modernization fell by an average of 8.1 percent a year between 1980 and 1989, the lowest among the Group of Seven leading industrialized nations, whereas West Germany increased their annual investment by 5.1 percent a year during the same period.[12] There is thus considerable concern that if the United States is to remain competitive, our telecommunications system must be modernized more rapidly. The ways in which the system is modernized, and telecommunications costs thus reduced, will have important ramifications for the spatial location of future economic activity, and therefore the efficiency of future production.

Public sector investment in the United States could hasten the development of a fiber-optic cable network at both the long distance and local level, such as the Clinton administration's proposed nationwide telecommunications "highway." Both developments could help to bring down telecommunications costs, thus improving national economic competitiveness in the coming decades. However, the rates charged should reflect the actual costs of supplying the network to a particular location. Otherwise, as with the interstate highway system, the U.S. government will be subsidizing further inefficiencies in telecommunications, transportation, and land use systems. There are two basic issues involved in reducing telecommunications costs and system modernization. First, the question is how to upgrade the long distance services to fiber-optic cable. The second question is how to upgrade the local network to fiber-optic cable. The issues are different because long distance service is provided in a quasi-competitive market, while the local network is much closer to a "natural monopoly," where federal regulation has protected the local monopolies of the Bell system.

For long distance service, debate has focused on whether the planned "electronic highways" should be built by the federal government at taxpayers' expense, or by the private sector, encouraged by federal tax benefits. Those advocating public construction believe that given the competition in the long distance service, no single firm will be able to raise its prices sufficiently to finance the construction of a fiber-optic superhighway, nor will any be willing or able to risk borrowing sufficient funds to construct the network. Vice President Gore and others have thus suggested that the federal government finance the construction of the system, then turn over its management to a private firm and publicly regulate its use. This would have the advantage of speeding up the construction of a fiber-optic network, reducing telecommunications costs, and facilitating public access information services for government and perhaps also for non-profit organizations.

Given the performance of U.S. long distance telecommunications firms in the last decade relative to other nations, an increased federal role is justified. However, if the federal government decides to embark on a massive public telecommunications infrastructure project similar to the construction of the interstate highway system, it will need to be very careful about how it structures the rates. If the rate structure does not reflect the actual costs of installing the service to a particular location, then further suburban sprawl and its associated inefficiencies will be encouraged. Wiring "edge cities" with fiber-optic cable would be far more expensive than simply wiring together the central business districts of urban areas. If these additional costs of suburban expansion are not reflected in the rate structure, as they are not in the current private telecommunications system, then the costly inefficiencies of metropolitan sprawl will once again be underwritten by the taxpayers.

Upgrading the local telecommunications network presents slightly different issues. There is little discussion of direct public financing to upgrade the local networks to fiber-optic cable. Rather, the issue is whether or not regulators will allow rate increases on basic services to finance the private construction and ownership of local fiber-optic networks by the "Baby Bells." The danger of this approach is that allowing increases in the rates for basic services could put the cost of telephone service out of reach of low-income families, or force them to pay for expensive infrastructure to support services that they are unlikely to need or use. According to Alfred Kahn, upgrading local

911 service in New York City, which connects the caller to the nearest patrol car, is costing an extra $0.35 a month on local service.[13] A fiber-optic cable directly linked to every home would increase the cost of basic service significantly more. Losing access to telephone service would further worsen the social isolation of low-income groups, which William Julius Wilson argues in *The Truly Disadvantaged* is the key cause of long-term concentrations of continuous urban poverty.[14] It would also hurt the small business community that has been responsible for most of the job growth in the last decade. Regulators must insure that the costs of building new local telecommunications infrastructure be paid for by the business community and higher-income users who are the most likely beneficiaries, rather than by basic service users. One way to avoid this problem would be direct public support for upgrading, to be financed by progressive income taxation.

While cities already have considerable advantages in telecommunications infrastructure, an increased public role could also be used to further centralize economic activity. One approach, used in several states including New York, is subsidizing the construction of public-private partnership teleports. The New York Teleport is a joint venture between New York City, the Port Authority of New York and New Jersey, Merrill Lynch, Western Union, and Cox Communications. It serves two functions: (1) by providing facilities that connect two different long distance carriers, it allows users to bypass the local network, thus reducing telecommunications costs; and (2) it is also a real estate development of "smart buildings" on Staten Island in New York City. The site allows local residents to save money on telecommunications by bypassing the local network. By offering lower telecommunications costs and low rents, while connected to Manhattan and New Jersey by fiber-optic cable, the teleport has been able to keep some back-office functions within New York City.

## Increase Public Investments in the Productivity of the Urban Workforce

Although much of the policy discussed in this chapter relates to investments in physical infrastructure, the key to increased productivity lies in improving the ability of our workforce to produce efficiently. The best way to reduce upward pressure on wages is to reduce the costs of living.

## Housing and Homelessness

Homelessness and high housing costs must be dealt with if our urban areas are to revive as locations for production. The large number of homeless people on city streets is the reason given by many businesses for not locating in urban areas. The presence of the homeless on the mass transit system discourages many people from using public transportation. If every American had a job that paid sufficient wages to cover the costs of decent and safe housing, the federal government would not have to get so directly involved in the housing market. Short of a program for full employment, the housing problem has to be dealt with directly.

If U.S. policy seeks to reduce the costs faced by businesses in order to promote economic growth, then the costs of living faced by employees must be brought down by reducing the costs of housing. This can only be done if the federal government increases funding for programs that expand the supply of affordable housing, both for renters and owners. Since many people living in urban areas are renters, increased housing certificates and vouchers are necessary. Such certificates and vouchers, however, tend to bid up rents on available low-rent housing unless they are accompanied by policies that expand the supply of rental units for low-income tenants. Increasing the supply of low-cost rental housing not only helps the direct beneficiaries of the housing, but also the entire renting population who may see their rents lowered. If rents are lower, there will be less upward pressure on wages because existing wages would increase in purchasing power. The wages of city workers could become more competitive with workers in other places that now have lower living costs. Their increased disposable income could also help stimulate economic growth.

Different strategies are needed for different market segments. For the poor that will mean the direct subsidy of housing. The supply of low-cost housing can be expanded in a flexible manner, channeling federal dollars to community organizations that in the past decade have become quite skilled at rehabilitating and building low-income housing.

For the working class and middle class, it means making renting and home ownership more affordable by encouraging an expansion of the supply of housing and facilitating the necessary financing. A revitalized Federal Housing Administration mortgage insurance program should actively target home ownership in urban areas.

The federal tax incentives such as the low-income housing tax credit and state and local mortgage revenue bonds, plus funds leveraged by the Community Reinvestment Act, have helped expand the supply of financing available for affordable housing. But almost everyone working in the housing field now agrees that the level of private commitment will never be sufficient to remove the gap between the need for subsidized housing and the current level of available units without a significant increase in federal commitment.

## Health Care Reform

One of the key factors undermining the productivity of the urban workforce and increasing the level of crime in urban areas is the lack of a universal health care system.

The United States has one of the most ineffective and inefficient health care systems in the developed world. A study by Woolhandler and Himmelstein estimated that 25 percent of health care costs covers administering the complicated multiparty insurance system.[15] The United States now spends about 12 percent of gross domestic product on health care compared to less than 10 percent in other advanced industrial nations. Yet two-thirds of the American people are either uninsured or underinsured. A significant proportion of those lacking some form of insurance live in urban areas.

Access to insurance is provided by the nation's employers. In 1993, however, the nation's biggest industrial company, General Motors (GM), recorded the largest loss in the history of corporate America—$23 billion—the equivalent of $3,000 for every vehicle sold in 1992. GM's loss is practically equal to the $22.2 billion it spent to fund the health care benefits of its retirees. It is simply impossible for GM and other major businesses to compete internationally when firms in other countries do not pay nearly as much for the health care insurance coverage of their employees and retirees.

Lack of universal health care has a devastating effect, particularly on lower-income urban families. The homeless, for example, arrive at health facilities with similar medical conditions as other low-income persons, but their lack of housing aggravates their problems. Bed-rest is a near impossibility, and medication is difficult to administer on a regular basis. Another example is substance abuse and drug addiction. Recent policy has focused on enforcement. Drug treatment, which is also critical to fighting the problem, is not adequate to meet the burgeoning demand. While the impact can be seen on the streets in terms of increased crime, it can also be seen in the health care system in terms of increased numbers of AIDS cases among intravenous drug users.

Unless the United States initiates national health care reform, it is estimated that by the year 2000 close to 20 percent of GDP will be spent on health care. Providing universal coverage without tackling the massive inefficiencies created by the administration of private health insurance will merely shift the costs without reducing them. If health care is not made universal, both in terms of access and financing, the most visible effects will continue to be seen in urban areas. The haunting image of people with various illnesses too poor to find adequate health care living on city streets will continue.

## Education

Education is central to the problems of the urban United States, and to the productivity of American workers. The main reason middle class families leave urban areas is the lack of quality public education. Education in our cities has suffered as a result of the fiscal crisis. As most public schools are funded primarily through local property taxation, there is a close correlation between school quality and the wealth of the residents in the school district. This has historically condemned people in low-income areas to lower-quality education. While the per pupil expenditures in our education system lag behind the levels of many other developed nations, the spending differences are not sufficient to explain the problems in the U.S. education system. As Robert Reich has pointed out in *The Work of Nations,* not only are there tremendous inter- and intraregional differences in per pupil expenditures in the United States, but the lack of a public health care system, the lack of affordable day care, and the growing problems of homelessness mean that many of our children are bringing a host of social problems into the schools that the education system is not equipped to address.[16] Resolving the problems of our nation's schools is linked to resolving the problems of homelessness and health care. Increased state and federal support for local schools will help to redress regional imbalances. Another possible reform is school choice within the public school system, where children in poor communities would be allowed to go to better funded schools in other neighborhoods or districts. Such a program may have certain advantages, but it also may help perpetuate the divisions in the quality of education between students of different incomes and qualifications.

## Day Care

Critical to making it feasible for women and men with young children to participate in the workforce is the availability of affordable day care. Day care services are not easy to find and are often quite expensive. Key to increasing productivity and reducing the costs of living is reducing the costs and time commitments of child care. Currently the Clinton administration is talking of ending welfare dependency in favor of assisting welfare recipients to find jobs. Yet the primary program of public assistance is Aid to Families with Dependent Children. This program was created in recognition of the importance of the role of mothering. If "welfare" is to be replaced, publicly supported day care will need to be a key component.

## Reinventing Regional Planning

The competition to attract investment from private firms between cities and suburbs within metropolitan areas and between states in multistate metropolitan regions is ultimately undermining the ability of state and local governments to make the sorts of public investments required to increase the productivity of the U.S. economy. This competition has nothing to do with the comparative advantage of any particular community, and everything to do with interjurisdictional tax competition. Instead of administrative competition, the driving force behind the spatial location of firms must once again become the relative comparative advantage of a region. Only this will ensure an economically optimal spatial distribution of economic activity.

In place of destructive competition between cities, suburbs, and rural areas for private investment, the United States must establish a coordinated regional approach to economic development. The goal is to make sure that regional infrastructure is provided in the most efficient and timely manner. Decisions to grant private land development rights must be made at the regional level in order to tie them to planned infrastructure improvements and environmental concerns. Only a planned metropolitan development effort is capable of avoiding interjurisdictional tax competition, thereby strengthening the hand of local governments to collect tax revenues for critical public investments. A regional approach will maximize the efficiency of this public investment, thereby lowering the costs of living and the costs of doing business.

Leadership for regional planning efforts must come from Washington. The federal government has the economic resources and political power to help foster the necessary cooperative planning effort. That is especially the case when regions have an important interstate component such as the tristate region around New York City or the bistate region north of Boston, where interstate competition has been particularly destructive. It is also important when the relevant private sector firms have an international orientation. The CAAA and the ISTEA legislation provide a strong basis for such an effort. Housing programs should also be developed and managed in the context of regional planning.

While the federal government must provide the leadership, regional planning will only be successful if it is fully embraced within the metropolitan areas. To some extent local support will depend upon making the case for the benefits of such an approach, and to some extent it will depend upon giving the local actors a free hand in making decisions.

Because it is unlikely that the administrative boundaries will change, or that local authorities will give up their jurisdiction to some supraregional planning body, federal and state incentives must be used to encourage regionalism. For example, many land use policies have generally been locally controlled while most transportation policies have been controlled at the state and federal level. As a result land use and transportation have not been well coordinated. It makes little sense for the federal government to fund a fixed rail transit system if the community that it serves does not adjust its zoning to permit the higher-density land use that transit can generate. Federal or state level financial assistance should be used as incentives to encourage local land use plans to conform with regional plans. This is especially true where metropolitan regions cross state lines.

## Conclusions: Toward a Progrowth Urban Policy

The following recommendations are first steps to begin shifting spatial development patterns so they become more efficient in the national economy and more supportive of the urban based society needed for the United States to remain a world leader in the next century.

(1) The playing field between city and suburb must be leveled. The implicit subsidies for continued deconcentration must either be equalized with subsidies to central cities, or eliminated entirely. Unless the true costs of sprawl are borne by those who engage in the deconcentration process, it will continue on its inefficient path.

(2) The physical infrastructure (i.e., water, sewerage, power, transportation, communications, and housing) and the service levels in education, public safety, and transit in central cities must be restored. It is not enough to level the playing field. It is also necessary to make up for past disinvestment. Unless the urban public realm works well, it will be difficult to effectively create the level playing field and to entice an expanded middle class back into the central cities. Without an expanded middle class, the problems of social and spatial urban polarization will intensify.

(3) The disincentives of local governments to invest in "human capital"—the health, education, and welfare of their residents in a highly mobile labor market—must be recognized. The American people, and the physical infrastructure and natural resources on U.S. soil, are the only truly national assets. It is these assets that we must nurture to promote economic growth and job creation. Consequently both federal leadership and federal financial support will be necessary to induce the necessary public and private investments.

(4) The industrial land and abandoned neighborhoods of central cities and older suburbs should be primary targets for revitalization. The vast expanses of under- or unutilized land that lie within ten miles of central cities must be given high priority as efficient locations for production in the new era of transportation and telecommunications-intensive just-in-time manufacturing. Similarly, urban residential neighborhoods with their excellent stock of older buildings must be thought of once more as locations for housing all classes of citizens. Many of these communities are located near already developed public transportation, and can be very cost-effective sites for the revitalization of America's economic base.

## Notes

[1] Goldberg (1990).
[2] Sassen (1991).
[3] Castells (1989).

4 Douglas (1990).
5 Downs (1992).
6 *Trends and Forecasts of Highway Passenger Travel* (1987).
7 Department of Housing and Urban Development (1974).
8 Aschauer (1989) and Munnell (1990).
9 Reich (1991).
10 Wilson (1987).
11 Pagano (1991).
12 Quoted in Edmund Andrews, "U.S. Warns of Phone Industry Lag," *New York Times,* October 23, 1991, p. D1.
13 Kahn (1991).
14 Wilson (1987).
15 Woolhandler and Himmelstein (1991). See also Woolhandler and Himmelstein (1986).
16 Reich (1991).

# 4

## Cities as Places Where People Live and Work: Urban Change and Neighborhood Distress

JOHN D. KASARDA

The targeted attacks of rioters in Los Angeles on Korean businesses reveal that racial conflict in urban America is no longer a black and white issue. Rather, it is a street-level collision of hopes and opportunities in the face of dramatically changing inner city demographic and economic contexts. Let's briefly look at these changing contexts.

For one, the nation's poverty population, once predominantly

JOHN D. KASARDA is a Kenan Professor of Business Administration and director of the Kenan Institute of Private Enterprise at the University of North Carolina at Chapel Hill. Dr. Kasarda has published more than fifty scholarly articles and eight books on urban development, demographics, and employment issues. He serves on the editorial boards of a variety of major professional journals. He has also served as a consultant on national urban policy to the Carter, Reagan, and Bush administrations and has testified numerous times before U.S. congressional committees on urban and employment issues. Dr. Kasarda has been the recipient of many grants and awards from such organizations as the National Science Foundation, the National Academy of Sciences, the U.S. Department of State, and the Agency for International Development and is a fellow of the Urban Land Institute.

rural, has increasingly urbanized. In 1959 only 27 percent of our poor resided in metropolitan central cities. By 1991 central cities housed 43 percent of the U.S. poverty population. During the same period, the proportion of poor African-Americans living in the central cities rose from 38 percent to 80 percent.[1] In 1991 the central cities housed 60 percent of the nation's poor living in census tracts with high concentrations of poverty, up from just one-third in 1972.[2]

This growth and concentration of poverty populations in our major cities occurred at a rapid pace despite targeted infusions of public assistance, affirmative action programs, and civil rights legislation (programs traditionally supported by liberals) and persisted during periods of national and urban economic recovery (the solution espoused by many conservatives). One reason why neither set of prescriptions worked, I propose, is that both were overwhelmed by fundamental changes in the structure of inner city economies, particularly affecting the employment prospects of disadvantaged African-American residents whose families simultaneously fragmented and internal social and economic support networks dissolved.

As a place where people work, it must be recognized that the American city is much different today than it was in the 1960s when our assumptions about poverty were formed. Advances in transportation, communication, and industrial technologies, interacting with the changing structure of the national and global economy, have transformed our major cities from centers of material goods production to centers of information exchange, finance, and administration. Manufacturing dispersed to the suburbs, exurbs, nonmetropolitan areas, and abroad. Warehousing facilities relocated to more regionally accessible beltways, expressways, and interstate highways. Retail establishments, following the suburbanizing middle class clientele, shifted to outlying shopping centers and malls.

In this process, many traditional goods-processing industries that once constituted the economic backbone of cities, and provided entry-level employment for lesser-skilled African-Americans, vanished. These industries were replaced, at least in part, by knowledge-intensive white-collar service industries that typically required education beyond high school and therefore precluded most poorly educated inner city minorities from obtaining employment. For example, by 1990 New York City and Boston each had more employees in white-collar service industries—where executives, managers, professionals, and clerical workers dominate—than in their manufacturing, construction, retail, and wholesale industries combined.

This is a dramatic metamorphosis since the 1950s, when employment in these goods-processing industries outnumbered information-processing employment by a three-to-one margin.[3]

Hit hardest was the central city manufacturing sector. Between 1967 and 1987 Detroit lost 51 percent of its manufacturing jobs; New York City, 58 percent; Chicago, 60 percent; and Philadelphia, 64 percent.[4] Even Sun Belt cities such as Atlanta and Los Angeles experienced manufacturing job losses during this period.

Blue-collar employment decline was exacerbated by the urban exodus of working class and middle-income residents and the neighborhood business establishments that once served them. This exodus further drained low-skill service jobs such as domestic workers, gas station attendants, and local delivery personnel.

Declines in urban blue-collar jobs disproportionately affected African-Americans, since as late as the 1968–70 period over 70 percent of all African-Americans working in metropolitan areas held blue-collar jobs. Among all metropolitan workers less than half were in blue-collar occupations at that time.[5] Moreover, of urban African-Americans classified as blue collar in the late 1960s, more than half were employed in goods-producing industries (primarily manufacturing and construction).

With the ready availability of urban blue-collar jobs, requiring little more than a strong back and a willingness to work, four-fifths of central city adult African-American males with less than twelve years of schooling were actually working between 1968 and 1970. This is in contrast to under 50 percent of comparably educated urban African-Americans working between 1990 and 1992 (computed from Current Population Survey machine-readable files, designated years).

During the 1980s a number of large cities experienced considerable overall job growth, led by employment gains in white-collar services. Yet manufacturing employment in these cities continued to decline. New York City, for instance, gained 333,209 jobs from 1980 to 1990—a nearly 10 percent overall city increase—but lost 162,739 jobs in its manufacturing sector—a 32 percent drop. Likewise, Boston added 40,715 jobs in the net during the 1980s while losing 21,365 manufacturing jobs—a 38 percent decline in this sector.[6]

While millions of blue-collar jobs were disappearing from our cities—the very jobs that in the past attracted and socially upgraded waves of disadvantaged persons—minority residents who lack the education for employment in the new information-processing industries were increasing. This includes the large cohorts of baby boom sons and daughters of African-American urban migrants of the 1950s and 1960s who reached labor force age during the 1970s and 1980s.

Following the Immigration Act of 1965, African-American inner city population growth was demographically supplemented by waves of Latino and Asian immigrants, while white flight to the suburbs continued apace. As a result, by 1990 racial-ethnic minorities composed the demographic majority in most of our largest cities—57 percent in New York, 62 percent in Chicago, 63 percent in Los Angeles, 70 percent in Atlanta, 79 percent in Detroit, and 88 percent in Miami.

The largest increments of immigrants to the inner cities during the 1970s and 1980s were Latinos. This group has the poorest educational distribution of any large minority population, with 43 percent of Latino immigrants age twenty-five to fifty-four having eight years of schooling or less in 1989.[7] In addition, during the 1980s, while many of the better educated Asian immigrants were settling directly in the suburbs, those with more limited education continued to be attracted to the central cities.

The conflicting residential and employment base changes described above placed the demographics and economies of our cities on a collision course, with the poorly educated impacted the most. While overall educational attainment of urban minorities improved during the 1970s and 1980s, these gains were not sufficient to keep pace with even faster rises in the education required to work in the new urban information based economy. It did an African-American high school dropout in the South Bronx little good to learn that the old footwear factory that closed near his home was replaced by a gleaming new Manhattan office tower, just a short bus ride away.

A significant portion of lesser-educated Asian and Latino immigrants adapted to urban structural transformation, English language limitations, and outright discrimination through self employment, strong kinship support networks, and ethnic economic solidarity. Family owned Asian and Latino businesses sprung up throughout the inner city, many in the most distressed parts such as the South Bronx in New York, Liberty City in Miami, and South Central Los Angeles. African-American small business formation did not nearly keep pace. Indeed, between 1977 and 1982, while the number of Asian-American owned firms with paid employees expanded by 160 percent, the number of African-American owned firms with employees actually declined by 3 percent. With small business formation becoming the key to inner city job growth in the new urban economy, African-Americans slipped further behind Asians and Latinos in joblessness in most cities.[8]

Moreover, slow improvements in city minority residents' overall education level meant that the least educated African-Americans fell further behind in the hiring queue of remaining traditional urban industries. As a result, jobless rates among poorly educated urban African-Americans skyrocketed.

Table 1 documents the outcome. It presents data on jobless rates of central city African-American and white males, by education completed, in cities for which comparable trend data could be obtained from the late 1960s to the early 1990s. Most striking are the increases in jobless rates of African-American males with less than a high school degree, rising from 18.8 percent during the 1968–70 period in northeastern cities to 57.1 percent during 1990–92 and from 23.5 percent in the midwestern cities in the 1968–70 period to 63.3 percent in the 1990–92 period. African-American males with a high school degree also fared poorly, with their jobless rate in northeastern cities rising from 10.8 percent in the late 1960s to 31.1 percent in the early 1990s, and in midwestern cities from 9.8 percent to 40.5 percent.

The limits of a poor education in our economically transforming cities, regardless of race, are highlighted by the substantial increases in jobless rates of lesser-educated white males in the same set of cities. By the 1990–92 period, more than one-third of white out-of-school males who had less than twelve years of schooling completed were not working. The sharp drops in jobless rates as one moves to each higher level of education for both African-Americans and whites during the 1990–92 period give further testimony to the critical importance of education for work in the new urban economy.

While many white lesser-educated workers were able to follow deconcentrating blue-collar jobs and relocate to working class suburbs, suburbanization of the lesser-educated African-Americans was limited by housing discrimination and their low incomes. Spatially confined to inner cities of blue-collar employment decline, many African-Americans began to rely on two surrogate economies to stay economically afloat: (1) the underground economy, composed of drug trade, prostitution, theft, and other illicit activities, and (2) the welfare economy, based on a variety of cash and in-kind public assistance transfers.

The inner city confluence of blue-collar job decline with rising illicit activities, high rates of welfare dependency, and middle class

**Table 1. Percentage Not at Work of Out-of-School Central City African-American and White Male Residents Age 16–64 by Region and Education: 1968–70 to 1990–92**

| Education | 1990–92 | 1980–82 | 1968–70 |
|---|---|---|---|
| NORTHEAST | | | |
| **African-American** | | | |
| Less than High School | 57.1 | 44.4 | 18.8 |
| High School Graduate | 31.1 | 27.2 | 10.8 |
| Some College | 19.9 | 17.2 | 11.2 |
| College Graduate | 7.3 | 4.3 | 8.6 |
| **White** | | | |
| Less than High School | 36.7 | 33.6 | 15.1 |
| High School Graduate | 23.9 | 17.1 | 6.6 |
| Some College | 14.4 | 10.7 | 7.4 |
| College Graduate | 11.9 | 6.0 | 5.6 |
| MIDWEST | | | |
| **African-American** | | | |
| Less than High School | 63.3 | 51.6 | 23.5 |
| High School Graduate | 40.5 | 29.6 | 9.8 |
| Some College | 29.8 | 15.0 | 6.9 |
| College Graduate | 11.5 | 10.0 | N.A. |
| **White** | | | |
| Less than High School | 34.4 | 29.1 | 11.5 |
| High School Graduate | 18.3 | 15.8 | 5.1 |
| Some College | 11.5 | 15.7 | 3.8 |
| College Graduate | 5.2 | 6.2 | 2.6 |

*Note:* Northeast cities are: Boston, Newark, New York, Philadelphia, Pittsburgh. Midwest cities are: Chicago, Cleveland, Detroit, Milwaukee, St. Louis.
*Sources:* Bureau of the Census, *Current Population Survey: March File:* 1968, 1969, 1970, 1980, 1981, 1982, 1990, 1991, and 1992.

black flight resulted in a powerful spatial interaction. Associated with this interaction were a plethora of concentrated social problems further aggravating the predicament of people and neighborhoods in distress, such as high degrees of poverty, family dissolution, out-of-wedlock births, school dropout, and joblessness. Negative stereotyping and distancing by outsiders (frequently with racial connotations) resulted in further spatial and social isolation of these distressed neighborhoods, magnifying their predicament.

In the remainder of this chapter I will detail the rise of concentrated poverty areas and socially distressed neighborhoods in the nation's 100 largest central cities. Fundamental questions necessary for the development of national urban policies will be answered. Did the growth of concentrated poverty areas and deterioration of social conditions, so well documented in our cities for the 1970 to 1980 period, continue between 1980 and 1990? Did the geographic locus of urban neighborhood distress, which was disproportionately found in old, large cities in the Northeast and Midwest in 1980, diffuse to younger, smaller cities and to major cities in the South and West by 1990? What happened to the racial/ethnic composition of the poorest urban neighborhoods during the 1980s? What role if any did the burst of immigration to cities between 1980 and 1990 play in the composition of distressed urban neighborhoods? Did our major cities become more or less residentially segregated during the 1980s?

## Measuring Urban Neighborhood Distress

Defining an urban neighborhood for analytical purposes is no easy task. The closest measurable unit to an urban neighborhood is the census tract that the Bureau of the Census defines as "a relatively homogeneous area with respect to population characteristics, economic status, and living conditions with an average population of 4,000."

Research based on 1970 and 1980 census tract data shows that over 80 percent of the nation's concentrated poverty areas and socially distressed tracts are found in the nation's 100 largest central cities.[9] It also shows that census tracts in these cities accounted for the vast majority of the growth of concentrated poverty and underclass neighborhoods between 1970 and 1980.[10] The 100 largest central cities as of 1980 will therefore serve as the urban units for cross-sectional and longitudinal analysis. As shown in the tables at the end of this chapter, these cities provide an excellent representation across region, city size, and city age categories.

Economic and social characteristics of the approximately 13,000 census tracts in the 100 cities in 1970, 1980, and 1990 were derived to obtain various indicators of urban neighborhood distress. The most common focus on census tract poverty rates and poverty population concentration within and across tracts of individual cities or metropolitan areas. Thus *poverty tracts* are typically considered to be those with at least 20 percent of their residents falling below the poverty level while *extreme poverty tracts* are those where at least 40 percent of the residents are in poverty.[11] Both indicators will be used herein to assess growth, concentration, and compositional shifts of poverty areas in the 100 cities over time.

Neighborhood distress is also often thought to reflect detrimental social conditions. For example, Erol Ricketts and Isabel Sawhill classify urban underclass tracts as those with disproportionately high rates of joblessness, female-headed families, teenage school dropout, and welfare recipiency.[12] Likewise, Mark Alan Hughes labels tracts with concurrently high levels of adult male joblessness, mother-only families, and welfare recipiency as "deprivation neighborhoods."[13]

This study combines census tract measures of poverty, underclass, and deprivation neighborhoods to create two baseline indicators that will herein be noted as *distressed neighborhoods* and *severely distressed neighborhoods*. Distressed neighborhoods are census tracts that simultaneously exhibit disproportionately high levels of poverty, joblessness, female-headed families, and welfare recipiency. Severely distressed neighborhoods are those tracts that have all the characteristics of distressed tracts, plus exceptionally high rates of teenage school dropout. (The rationale for this differentiation will be noted shortly.)

In terms of precise measurement, severely distressed tracts are those tracts that simultaneously fall at least one standard deviation above the 1980 national tract mean on the following five measures:

- *Poverty:*
  proportion of the resident population below the poverty line.
- *Joblessness:*
  proportion of out-of-school males age sixteen and older who worked less than twenty-six weeks a year.
- *Female-headed families:*
  proportion of families with children under age eighteen that are headed by a woman (spouse absent).
- *Welfare recipiency:*
  proportion of families receiving public assistance income.
- *Teenage school dropout:*
  proportion of persons age sixteen to nineteen not enrolled in school and not high school graduates.

Readers familiar with the literature on the urban underclass will recognize that the definition of severely distressed tracts combines high rates of poverty with the full set of Ricketts-Sawhill underclass tract measures. The 1980 national tract standard deviation cutoffs were used to classify distressed and severely distressed tracts in 1970, 1980, and 1990 and to benchmark and compare intercensal (1970 to 1980 and 1980 to 1990) changes during the past twenty years in each of the 100 cities.[14]

Teenage school dropout is singled out as a differentiating measure of severely distressed tracts for two reasons. First, completing high school, as shown above, is critically important for work in our economically transforming urban centers. Second, by 1990 a much larger proportion of the nation's youth (age sixteen to nineteen) were either in school or received their high school degree than was the case in 1980. Thus a city census tract that in 1990 was one standard deviation above the 1980 national tract teenage school dropout rate would be especially disadvantaged.

## Growth and Change in Poverty Tracts and Distressed Neighborhoods

Table 2 presents an overview of the number and proportion of tracts meeting the above described criteria for poverty or neighborhood distress status at the three time points. The sharp rise in the number and percent of poverty and extreme poverty tracts during the 1980s can be clearly observed. By 1990 approximately two in five urban tracts had at least 20 percent of their population in poverty, and nearly one in seven urban tracts had at least 40 percent of their population in poverty. The net addition of extreme poverty tracts in the 100 cities between 1980 and 1990 (624) was actually greater than that between 1970 and 1980 (579).

Both the number of distressed and severely distressed tracts increased between 1980 and 1990. Yet such growth was modest for distressed tracts and marginal for severely distressed tracts, particu-

**Table 2. Number of Census Tracts, by Poverty and Distress Status, 100 Largest Central Cities, 1970–1990**

| Census Tracts | 1970 | 1980 | 1990 |
|---|---|---|---|
| Total Number of Tracts | 12,584 | 13,777 | 14,214 |
| (% of City Total) | 100.0 | 100.0 | 100.0 |
| Poverty Tracts | 3,430 | 4,713 | 5,596 |
| (% of City Total) | 27.3 | 34.2 | 39.4 |
| Extreme Poverty Tracts | 751 | 1,330 | 1,954 |
| (% of City Total) | 6.0 | 9.7 | 13.7 |
| Distressed Tracts | 296 | 1,513 | 1,850 |
| (% of City Total) | 2.4 | 11.0 | 13.0 |
| Severely Distressed Tracts | 166 | 562 | 566 |
| (% of City Total) | 1.3 | 4.1 | 4.0 |

*Sources: 1990 Census of Population,* Summary Tape File 3A; *1980 Census of Population,* Summary Tape File 3A; *1970 Census of Population,* Fourth Count machine-readable file.

larly compared to the huge increases in the latter between 1970 and
1980. Indeed, there was a marginal decline in the percent of tracts in
the 100 cities that were classified as severely distressed in 1990 compared to 1980 (4.0 vs. 4.1 percent).

A fundamental conclusion to be drawn from Table 2 is that while
poverty neighborhoods became a more prominent feature of urban
space in 1990, internal social disadvantages that constitute neighborhood distress did not deteriorate substantially out of line with 1980
national tract averages. Later, changes in these tract social characteristics will be documented.

## Regional Patterns

One of the primary findings on the growth of poverty and underclass areas was that this growth was concentrated in large cities in the
Northeast and Midwest, with much less growth in the South and
West. For example, four northern cities alone (New York, Chicago,
Philadelphia, and Detroit) accounted for two-thirds of the increase
in poor people living in extreme poverty tracts between 1970 and
1980.[15]

Table 3 shows the number of poverty, extreme poverty, distressed,
and severely distressed census tracts in the central cities, by region,
for 1970, 1980, and 1990. It also shows the proportion of city tracts
falling in each distress category. The number and proportion of
tracts in all poverty and distress neighborhood categories increased
in the midwestern cities. By 1990 nearly one out of every two central
city tracts in the Midwest had at least 20 percent of its population
below poverty, and nearly one out of five tracts had at least 40
percent of its residents below poverty. Indeed, the number of extreme poverty tracts in midwestern cities nearly doubled between
1980 and 1990. The number of distressed neighborhoods increased
by almost as much, with one in five central city tracts in the Midwest
meeting neighborhood distress criteria in 1990 compared to only one
of forty in 1970. In absolute terms, distressed tracts in Midwest cities
increased from 91 in 1970 to 722 in 1990. Severely distressed tracts
increased from 53 in 1970 to 209 in 1990, with all but twenty-six of
this increase in severely distressed tracts occurring between 1970 and
1980.

A listing of individual cities (to be shown later) revealed that Detroit led the Midwest in growth in poverty and distressed tracts. In
1970 only 29 percent of Detroit's tracts were classified as poverty

tracts (i.e., 20 percent or more of its residents below poverty). Detroit's poverty tracts rose to 48 percent of the city's total in 1980 and to *75 percent* of the city's total in 1990. The number of extreme poverty tracts in Detroit rose from 4 in 1970 to 45 in 1980 and to 133 in 1990, representing an increase from under 4 percent of the city tracts in 1970 to 37 percent in 1990. Detroit's severely distressed tracts climbed from 4 in 1970 to 39 in 1980 and to 53 in 1990, or from 1.4 percent of the city's total in 1970 to 9.6 percent in 1980 and 15.3 percent in 1990.

The pattern in the Northeast, where a number of the region's large cities exhibited economic recovery during much of the 1980s, was considerably more favorable than that of the Midwest. The number of poverty tracts in northeastern cities actually declined slightly, while the aggregate number of extreme poverty tracts increased by only one between 1980 and 1990. This compares to a growth of 506 poverty tracts and 332 extreme poverty tracts in northeastern cities between 1970 and 1980. Both distressed and severely distressed census tracts declined substantially in the Northeast during the 1980s, in contradistinction to dramatic growth in these distressed neighborhoods during the 1970s.

Leading the turnaround in the Northeast was New York City with declines in all categories of poverty and distressed tracts between 1980 and 1990. For example, while extreme poverty tracts in New York City rose from 73 in 1970 to 311 in 1980, they dropped to 276 (or 13 percent of the city total) in 1990. Likewise, severely distressed tracts, which expanded from 22 in 1970 to 126 in 1980, dropped to 81 (3.6 percent of the city's total tracts) in 1990.

Southern cities experienced modest increases in their poverty, extreme poverty, and distressed tracts during the 1980s and marginal increases in the number of their severely distressed tracts. No one city stood out in the South as a major contributor to increases in poverty or distressed tracts during the 1980s. Note, as well, that while some growth did occur in the number of extreme poverty and severely distressed tracts, that their percentages of the city tract totals in these categories are much lower in the South than in the Northeast and Midwest.

Even lower percentages of poverty and distressed tracts are found in larger cities in the West. In 1990 only 5.8 percent of central city tracts in the West met extreme poverty criteria, and 1.3 percent severely distressed criteria. Note, as well, that both the percentage of distressed and severely distressed tracts in western cities declined between 1980 and 1990, with an absolute drop in the number of severely distressed tracts, while the percentage of poverty tracts and extreme poverty tracts increased slightly. Thus while the number of poor neighborhoods expanded, the number with serious social disadvantages (e.g., mother-only households) did not.

Conditions in Los Angeles, which has received so much attention since the 1992 riot, did get somewhat worse, however. L.A.'s extreme

**Table 3. Number and Proportion of Census Tracts, by Poverty and Distress Status, By Region, 1970–1990**

| Central Cities | 1970 | 1980 | 1990 |
|---|---|---|---|
| **Midwest** | | | |
| Total Number of Tracts | 3,377 | 3,465 | 3,424 |
| (% of City Total) | 100.0 | 100.0 | 100.0 |
| Poverty Tracts | 915 | 1,314 | 1,633 |
| (% of City Total) | 27.1 | 37.9 | 47.7 |
| Extreme Poverty Tracts | 168 | 374 | 678 |
| (% of City Total) | 5.0 | 10.8 | 19.8 |
| Distressed Tracts | 91 | 485 | 722 |
| (% of City Total) | 2.6 | 14.0 | 20.1 |
| Severely Distressed Tracts | 53 | 183 | 209 |
| (% of City Total) | 1.6 | 5.3 | 6.1 |
| **Northeast** | | | |
| Total Number of Tracts | 3,365 | 3,426 | 3,409 |
| (% of City Total) | 100.0 | 100.0 | 100.0 |
| Poverty Tracts | 828 | 1,334 | 1,311 |
| (% of City Total) | 24.6 | 38.9 | 38.5 |
| Extreme Poverty Tracts | 133 | 465 | 466 |
| (% of City Total) | 4.0 | 13.6 | 13.7 |
| Distressed Tracts | 66 | 547 | 496 |
| (% of City Total) | 1.9 | 16.0 | 14.1 |
| Severely Distressed Tracts | 44 | 190 | 155 |
| (% of City Total) | 1.3 | 5.5 | 4.5 |
| **South** | | | |
| Total Number of Tracts | 3,257 | 3,970 | 4,284 |
| (% of City Total) | 100.0 | 100.0 | 100.0 |
| Poverty Tracts | 1,139 | 1,378 | 1,782 |
| (% of City Total) | 35.0 | 34.7 | 41.6 |
| Extreme Poverty Tracts | 362 | 391 | 629 |
| (% of City Total) | 11.1 | 9.8 | 14.7 |
| Distressed Tracts | 89 | 372 | 517 |
| (% of City Total) | 2.2 | 9.4 | 11.3 |
| Severely Distressed Tracts | 50 | 145 | 162 |
| (% of City Total) | 1.5 | 3.7 | 3.8 |

| Central Cities | 1970 | 1980 | 1990 |
|---|---|---|---|
| **West** | | | |
| Total Number of Tracts | 2,585 | 2,916 | 3,097 |
| (% of City Total) | 100.0 | 100.0 | 100.0 |
| Poverty Tracts | 548 | 687 | 870 |
| (% of City Total) | 21.2 | 23.6 | 28.1 |
| Extreme Poverty Tracts | 88 | 100 | 181 |
| (% of City Total) | 3.4 | 3.4 | 5.8 |
| Distressed Tracts | 50 | 109 | 115 |
| (% of City Total) | 1.9 | 3.7 | 3.7 |
| Severely Distressed Tracts | 19 | 44 | 40 |
| (% of City Total) | 0.7 | 1.5 | 1.3 |

Sources: *1990 Census of Population*, Summary Tape File 3A; *1980 Census of Population*, Summary Tape File 3A; *1970 Census of Population*, Fourth Count machine-readable file.

poverty tracts, which expanded from twenty-five in 1970 to only thirty in 1980, increased to forty-five (6.6 percent of the city's total tracts) in 1990. Likewise, the number of severely distressed tracts in L.A. rose from ten in 1970 to thirteen in 1980 and seventeen (2.6 percent of the city tract total) in 1990. It needs to be pointed out, however, that even in 1990 these are relatively small numbers and percentages, well under those found in major urban centers of the Northeast and Midwest.

## Population Characteristics

The above information describes the growth or decline in the *number* of poverty and socially distressed tracts during the past two decades. What happened to the size and racial/ethnic composition of those residing in these tracts during each of the past two decades? Table 4A answers this question in terms of extreme poverty tracts, while Table 4B addresses it in terms of distressed tracts. Recall that an extreme poverty tract is 40 percent or more of the census tract population below poverty at the time of the census (1970, 1980, or 1990). Distressed tracts pertain to census tracts in 1970, 1980, and 1990 that are *simultaneously* one standard deviation above the 1980 national tract mean in proportions of poverty population, joblessness, mother-only families, and welfare recipiency.

The percentages shown below the absolute numbers in each upper half of the two panels are the percent of each racial/ethnic group in the cities residing in either extreme poverty or distressed

**Table 4A. Population Size and Composition of Extreme Poverty Tracts, 100
Largest Central Cities, 1970–1990**

| Population | 1970 | 1980 | 1990 |
|---|---|---|---|
| Total Population in Extreme Poverty Tracts | 2,690,970 | 3,833,288 | 5,495,852 |
| (% of City Total) | 5.2 | 7.9 | 10.7 |
| Non-Latino White | 501,129 | 559,772 | 850,078 |
| (% of all NL Whites) | 1.4 | 2.0 | 3.2 |
| Non-Latino African-American | 1,743,828 | 2,469,776 | 3,147,239 |
| (% of all NL African-Americans) | 15.7 | 19.9 | 24.2 |
| Latino | 408,072 | 740,156 | 1,306,977 |
| (% of all Latinos) | 9.8 | 12.3 | 15.4 |
| **Racial Composition of Extreme Poverty Tracts** | | | |
| Non-Latino White | 18.6 | 14.6 | 15.5 |
| Non-Latino African-American | 64.8 | 64.4 | 57.3 |
| Latino | 15.2 | 19.3 | 23.8 |

**Table 4B. Population in Distressed Tracts, 100 Largest Central Cities,
1970–1990**

| Population | 1970 | 1980 | 1990 |
|---|---|---|---|
| Total Population in Distressed Tracts | 1,022,479 | 4,893,371 | 5,704,094 |
| (% of City Total) | 1.7 | 10.0 | 11.1 |
| Non-Latino White | 150,992 | 492,769 | 591,411 |
| (% of all NL Whites) | 0.4 | 1.7 | 2.2 |
| Non-Latino African-American | 783,390 | 3,542,614 | 3,861,023 |
| (% of all NL African-Americans) | 6.6 | 28.6 | 29.7 |
| Latino | 72,215 | 793,964 | 1,117,299 |
| (% of all Latinos) | 1.6 | 13.2 | 13.2 |
| **Racial Composition of Distressed Tracts** | | | |
| White | 14.8 | 10.1 | 10.4 |
| African-American | 76.6 | 72.4 | 67.7 |
| Latino | 7.1 | 16.2 | 19.6 |

*Sources: 1990 Census of Population,* Summary Tape File 3A; *1980 Census of Population,* Summary Tape File 3A; *1970 Census of Population,* Fourth Count machine-readable file.

tracts. For example, in 1990 there were 24.2 percent of non-Latino African-Americans residing in extreme poverty tracts while 29.7 percent of non-Latino African-Americans in the 100 cities resided in distressed tracts, as defined above. This percent measures the degree of concentration of the racial/ethnic group in either extreme poverty tracts or distressed tracts at each point in time.

The percentages in the bottom portion of each panel refer to the racial/ethnic composition of the tracts themselves. Thus African-Americans made up 57.3 percent of the population in extreme poverty tracts in 1990, while Latinos made up 23.8 percent and non-Latino whites 15.5 percent. The small residual that would make the percentages sum to 100 are non-Latinos of "other" races (mostly Asians and Pacific Islanders).

Reflecting growth in the number and proportion of city tracts that were classified as extreme poverty or distressed (see Table 2), Table 4A reveals that both the number of city residents and proportion of city residents living in such tracts increased during the 1980s. The upper portion of Table 4A shows that both the number and concentration of all racial/ethnic groups in extreme poverty tracts rose fairly steadily throughout the 1970s and 1980s. This was not the case for distressed tracts. As shown in the top portion of Table 4B, growth and concentration of the overall city population and of each racial/ethnic group residing in distressed tracts was substantially greater in the 1970s than in the 1980s. This is especially the case for African-Americans and Latinos, where virtually no increase in their concentration in distressed tracts occurred.

In terms of racial/ethnic mix of the tracts themselves, the bottom half of each panel shows that non-Latino whites marginally increased their proportions between 1980 and 1990 in both extreme poverty and distressed tracts. African-Americans declined in their proportions, due largely to substantial increases in the absolute number of Latinos in extreme poverty and distressed tracts. Nonetheless, observe that in 1990, non-Latino African-Americans still accounted for more than two-thirds of persons residing in distressed tracts in the 100 cities.

## Poverty Populations

Let us now focus on the poorest segment of our urban citizens, those in poverty, describing their growth and spatial concentrations within our cities during the decade 1980 to 1990 and comparing these most recent trends with trends during the 1970s.

Table 5 displays the total poverty population, by race, for the 100 cities and the degree to which it is concentrated in poverty tracts and distressed neighborhoods. For example, the third row shows that of the 7,542,479 city residents in poverty in 1970, 1,240,855 (or 16.5

percent) resided in extreme poverty tracts of the 100 cities. Poverty population in extreme poverty tracts expanded to 1,828,576 in 1980 and to 2,650,142 in 1990. By the latter date, 28.2 percent of the poverty population resided in extreme poverty tracts. Similarly, the percent of poverty population concentrated in distressed tracts rose from 6.6 percent in 1970 to 27.0 percent in 1980 and to 28.1 percent in 1990. While the absolute number of poor persons residing in severely distressed tracts increased between 1980 and 1990 (from 772,452 to 810,678), their concentration in these tracts declined slightly. Table 5 again highlights the fact that while poverty neighborhoods experienced consistent growth in the number of poor residents and their concentration between 1970 and 1990, the vast majority of the growth and concentration of poor persons in distressed and severely distressed neighborhoods took place during the 1970s.

Table 6 looks at African-American and Latino poverty population concentration over time. The top panel reveals that the concentration of poor African-Americans in extreme poverty tracts increased considerably between 1980 and 1990, from 33.8 percent to 41.6 percent. Thus by 1990 more than two out of five poor African-Americans residing in the 100 central cities were located in extreme poverty tracts. At the same time, more than one out of two poor African-Americans resided in distressed tracts. The concentration of poor African-Americans in severely distressed tracts also increased slightly from 13.1 percent of the cities' total African-American poverty population in 1980 to 13.7 percent in 1990.

**Table 5. Size and Concentration of Poverty Population, by Census Tract Poverty and Distress Status, 100 Largest Central Cities, 1970–1990**

| Poverty Population | 1970 | 1980 | 1990 |
|---|---|---|---|
| **Total Poverty Population** | | | |
| All 100 Cities | 7,542,479 | 8,113,277 | 9,392,953 |
| (% of City Total Population) | 14.5 | 16.7 | 18.3 |
| In Poverty Tracts | 4,156,543 | 5,178,509 | 6,466,097 |
| (% of Total) | 55.1 | 63.8 | 68.8 |
| In Extreme Poverty Tracts | 1,240,855 | 1,828,576 | 2,650,142 |
| (% of Total) | 16.5 | 22.5 | 28.2 |
| In Distressed Tracts | 496,430 | 2,187,867 | 2,640,454 |
| (% of Total) | 6.6 | 27.0 | 28.1 |
| In Severely Distressed Tracts | 322,906 | 772,452 | 810,678 |
| (% of Total) | 4.3 | 9.5 | 8.6 |

*Sources: 1990 Census of Population,* Summary Tape File 3A; *1980 Census of Population,* Summary Tape File 3A; *1970 Census of Population,* Fourth Count machine-readable file.

**Table 6. African-American and Latino Poverty Population Size and Concentration by Census Tract Poverty and Distress Status, 100 Largest Central Cities, 1970–1990**

| Poverty Population | 1970 | 1980 | 1990 |
|---|---|---|---|
| **African-American Poverty Population** | | | |
| All 100 Cities | 3,182,881 | 3,428,593 | 4,002,094 |
| (% of City African-American Total) | 27.7 | 27.2 | 29.9 |
| In Poverty Tracts | 2,567,429 | 2,827,386 | 3,328,625 |
| (% of Total) | 80.7 | 82.5 | 83.2 |
| In Extreme Poverty Tracts | 895,920 | 1,157,537 | 1,664,872 |
| (% of Total) | 28.1 | 33.8 | 41.6 |
| In Distressed Tracts | 408,450 | 1,507,520 | 1,894,868 |
| (% of Total) | 12.8 | 44.0 | 47.3 |
| In Severely Distressed Tracts | 262,904 | 450,568 | 547,273 |
| (% of Total) | 8.3 | 13.1 | 13.7 |
| **Latino Poverty Population** | | | |
| All 100 Cities | 966,413 | 1,575,569 | 2,394,890 |
| (% of City Latino Total) | 100.0 | 100.0 | 100.0 |
| In Poverty Tracts | 664,735 | 1,162,367 | 1,842,990 |
| (% of Total) | 68.8 | 73.8 | 77.0 |
| In Extreme Poverty Tracts | 196,202 | 378,832 | 650,747 |
| (% of Total) | 20.3 | 24.0 | 27.2 |
| In Distressed Tracts | 35,189 | 394,226 | 547,854 |
| (% of Total) | 3.6 | 25.0 | 22.9 |
| In Severely Distressed Tracts | 28,183 | 190,640 | 177,083 |
| (% of Total) | 2.9 | 12.1 | 7.4 |

*Note:* the race/ethnicity category is for whites, African-Americans, and Latinos.
*Sources: 1990 Census of Population,* Summary Tape File 3A; *1980 Census of Population,* Summary Tape File 3A; *1970 Census of Population,* Fourth Count machine-readable file.

The bottom panel of Table 6 reveals that the number of poor Latino residents in the 100 cities climbed from 966,413 in 1970 to 1,575,569 in 1980 and to 2,394,890 in 1990. This growth was matched with an increased concentration of poor Latinos in poverty tracts and extreme poverty tracts. The number and percent of poor Latinos concentrated in severely distressed tracts, which climbed dramatically in the 1970s, actually declined during the 1980s. Thus by 1990 only 7.4 percent of poor Latinos compared to 13.7 percent of poor African-Americans were concentrated in severely distressed tracts. Poor Latinos also showed considerably less concentration than poor African-Americans in extreme poverty tracts and distressed tracts.

What about regional differences in the growth and concentration of urban poverty populations? These differences are described in

Table 7, which shows that the greatest increases in poverty population concentration took place in midwestern cities. Concentration of
poor persons in extreme poverty tracts in these cities rose from 12.8
percent in 1970 to 36.2 percent in 1990. Absolute numbers of poor in
extreme poverty tracts in midwestern cities climbed from 222,722 in
1970 to 439,550 in 1980 to 789,778 in 1990, a nearly fourfold increase
over the twenty-year period.

The Midwest is the only region where the concentration of poor
in severely distressed inner city tracts actually increased between
1980 and 1990. By the latter date, 13.2 percent of the poverty pop-

**Table 7. Poverty Population Size and Concentration by Census Tract
Distress Status and Region, 1970–1990**

| Poverty Population | 1970 | 1980 | 1990 |
| --- | --- | --- | --- |
| **Midwest** | | | |
| Total | 1,736,284 | 1,881,635 | 2,179,774 |
| (% of City Total) | 13.2 | 16.8 | 20.3 |
| In Extreme Poverty Tracts | 222,722 | 439,550 | 789,778 |
| (% of Poverty Population) | 12.8 | 23.4 | 36.2 |
| In Severely Distressed Tracts | 98,872 | 211,961 | 271,174 |
| (% of Poverty Population) | 5.7 | 11.3 | 12.4 |
| **Northeast** | | | |
| Total | 1,957,449 | 2,280,389 | 2,245,702 |
| (% of City Total) | 14.9 | 19.8 | 19.4 |
| In Extreme Poverty Tracts | 226,686 | 699,224 | 693,260 |
| (% of Poverty Population) | 11.6 | 30.7 | 30.9 |
| In Severely Distressed Tracts | 82,325 | 284,443 | 230,249 |
| (% of Poverty Population) | 4.2 | 12.5 | 10.3 |
| **South** | | | |
| Total | 2,520,793 | 2,463,537 | 2,925,198 |
| (% of City Total) | 16.9 | 16.8 | 18.9 |
| In Extreme Poverty Tracts | 683,783 | 583,945 | 886,341 |
| (% of Poverty Population) | 27.1 | 23.7 | 30.3 |
| In Severely Distressed Tracts | 113,096 | 214,403 | 228,990 |
| (% of Poverty Population) | 4.5 | 8.7 | 7.8 |
| **West** | | | |
| Total | 1,327,953 | 1,487,716 | 2,042,279 |
| (% of City Total) | 12.2 | 13.2 | 15.2 |
| In Extreme Poverty Tracts | 107,664 | 105,857 | 280,763 |
| (% of Poverty Population) | 8.1 | 7.1 | 13.7 |
| In Severely Distressed Tracts | 28,613 | 61,645 | 80,265 |
| (% of Poverty Popluation) | 2.2 | 4.1 | 3.9 |

*Sources: 1990 Census of Population,* Summary Tape File 3A; *1980 Census of Population,* Summary
Tape File 3A; *1970 Census of Population,* Fourth Count machine-readable file.

ulation of Midwest central cities resided in severely distressed tracts.

Larger northeastern cities actually experienced a decline in over-all poverty population during the 1980s, in contrast to a considerable increase during the 1970s. The number of poor persons in extreme poverty tracts and severely distressed tracts also declined between 1980 and 1990, with virtually no increase in concentration in extreme poverty tracts and substantial declines in poverty population concentration in severely distressed tracts in northeastern cities.

Southern cities, which exhibited an absolute decline in poverty population during the 1970s and a decrease in the size and concentration of their poverty populations in extreme poverty tracts, reversed this trend in the 1980s. Between 1980 and 1990, the number of poor residing in extreme poverty tracts in southern cities rose from 583,945 to 886,341 while their concentration of poor in these tracts rose from 23.7 percent to 30.3 percent. A quite different pattern may be observed for the growth and concentration of poor in severely distressed tracts during the past two decades in southern cities. After expanding considerably during the 1970s, poverty population residing in severely distressed tracts slowed in the 1980s, while poverty population concentration in these tracts declined from 8.7 percent to 7.8 percent. This occurred despite a slight increase in the number of severely distressed tracts in southern cities (see Table 3).

Western cities followed the trends in southern cities with declines in the number and concentration of poor residing in extreme poverty tracts during the 1970s and sharp rises in the 1980s. This increase reflects the 80 percent growth in the number of extreme poverty tracts in western cities between 1980 and 1990 (Table 3).

The size and concentration of poverty population in severely distressed tracts in western cities rose during the 1970s by a considerable amount. Absolute increases moderated during the 1980s, and the amount of poverty population concentration in severely distressed tracts declined slightly between 1980 and 1990, again reflecting the decline in severely distressed tracts. It is important to point out that in 1990 poverty population concentration in extreme poverty tracts and severely distressed tracts was considerably less in the West than other regions of the nation.

## Social Characteristics

We have been working with the assumption that distressed and severely distressed urban neighborhoods imply more than high proportions of poor people. These neighborhoods are also posited to exhibit social disadvantages such as high rates of school dropout, out-of-wedlock births, persistent joblessness, welfare dependency, and racial/ethnic segregation that reinforce poverty and limit upward mobility. In this section, we look at basic trends in these urban social and spatial indicators. Our focus will be on female-headed families with children, poorly educated adult residents, teenage school dropouts, unemployment, welfare recipiency, and residential segregation.

Table 8 reveals how family fragmentation has disproportionately afflicted the African-American residents of large cities. In 1970, 35 percent of African-American families with children under age eighteen were female-headed. By 1980 this had risen to 48 percent and by 1990 to 55 percent. The 1990 African-American female-headed household rate was twice that of Latinos and three times that of whites in the 100 largest cities. Note, as well, that the proportion of white and Latino female-headed households with children stayed essentially constant between 1980 and 1990 when cities are considered in the whole.

Looking at trends within their extreme poverty areas, one again observes continuous increases in African-American female-headed households with children during the past two decades, whereas the proportion of white and Latino female-headed households showed no increase between 1980 and 1990. In fact, Latinos showed a proportional decline in this social indicator. By 1990 nearly 75 percent of African-American households with children who resided in extreme poverty tracts were female-headed compared to 40 percent of white households and 46 percent of Latino households in these poverty neighborhoods.

Education completed has been consistently documented to be among the strongest correlates of workforce attachment and social mobility in our economically transforming cities.[16] Those without a high school degree have become especially disadvantaged.[17] The top panel of Table 9 reflects steadily reduced proportions of all urban racial/ethnic groups who have not completed high school. Yet as late as 1990, 36.2 percent of the urban African-American population age twenty-five and over and 54 percent of urban Latinos had not completed high school. The 21.9 percent of white urban adults who had not completed high school reflects the fact that the census tract data used for this table did not permit separation of Latino whites from the total white population.

Despite steady declines in the number and proportion of adult

**Table 8. Female-Headed Households with Children Under Age 18 in 100 Largest Central Cities and Their Extreme Poverty Areas, by Race/Ethnicity 1970–1990**

| Total City Area<br>**Female-Headed with Children** | 1970 | 1980 | 1990 |
|---|---|---|---|
| Total Population | 1,158,408 | 1,662,480 | 1,781,540 |
| (% of Households with Children) | 17.2 | 27.8 | 30.1 |
| White Population | 593,857 | 608,172 | 602,256 |
| (% of White Households with Children) | 11.9 | 18.1 | 18.8 |
| African-American Population | 544,346 | 818,030 | 943,796 |
| (% of African-American Households with Children) | 34.5 | 48.1 | 54.7 |
| Latino Population | 118,557 | 246,717 | 330,088 |
| (% of Latino Households with Children) | 18.0 | 26.8 | 27.9 |

| Extreme Poverty Areas<br>**Female-Headed with Children** | 1970 | 1980 | 1990 |
|---|---|---|---|
| Total Population | 151,437 | 317,630 | 420,372 |
| (% of Households with Children) | 45.4 | 61.1 | 61.6 |
| White Population | 27,017 | 31,116 | 48,563 |
| (% of White Households with Children) | 30.7 | 40.8 | 40.4 |
| African-American Population | 122,830 | 222,603 | 312,755 |
| (% of African-American Households with Children) | 51.1 | 67.6 | 73.0 |
| Latino Population | 19,400 | 59,299 | 85,607 |
| (% of Latino Households with Children) | 31.2 | 48.8 | 45.7 |

*Note:* The race/ethnicity category is for whites, African-Americans, and Latinos. Latinos here may be white or black and are therefore included in these racial categories.
*Sources: 1990 Census of Population,* Summary Tape File 3A; *1980 Census of Population,* Summary Tape File 3A; *1970 Census of Population,* Fourth Count machine-readable file.

white and African-American city residents with less than twelve years of education completed, the bottom panel of Table 9 shows increases in all racial/ethnic groups residing in extreme poverty tracts in this low-education category, implying greater concentration of the least educated in these neighborhoods. Moreover, as late as 1990, 53 percent of all adult residents of extreme poverty tracts had not completed high school, while half of the adult white and African-American residents had not completed high school. Nearly 70 percent of adult Latinos residing in extreme poverty tracts had not completed high school.

The above data refer to education completed by adults. What about the youth, so important to the future of cities? Table 10 looks at the critical factor of school dropout trends among persons age

**Table 9. Population 25 and Over with Less Than High School Education in 100 Largest Central Cities and Their Extreme Poverty Areas, by Race/Ethnicity 1970–1990**

|  | Total City Area | | |
| **Less than High School Education** | 1970 | 1980 | 1990 |
| --- | --- | --- | --- |
| Total Population | 14,155,232 | 10,227,130 | 9,095,288 |
| (% 25 and Over) | 48.9 | 35.4 | 27.9 |
| White Population | 10,463,277 | 5,956,316 | 4,601,844 |
| (% 25 and Over) | 45.7 | 30.6 | 21.9 |
| African-American Population | 3,445,272 | 2,776,739 | 2,774,040 |
| (% 25 and Over) | 63.5 | 45.3 | 36.2 |
| Latino Population | 1,189,636 | 1,661,918 | 2,385,305 |
| (% 25 and Over) | 66.4 | 58.8 | 54.0 |

|  | Extreme Poverty Areas | | |
| **Less than High School Education** | 1970 | 1980 | 1990 |
| --- | --- | --- | --- |
| Total Population | 901,357 | 1,149,148 | 1,518,452 |
| (% 25 and Over) | 76.7 | 62.8 | 52.7 |
| White Population | 291,311 | 246,398 | 363,455 |
| (% 25 and Over) | 75.1 | 61.0 | 49.4 |
| African-American Population | 599,996 | 672,578 | 869,579 |
| (% 25 and Over) | 77.7 | 61.4 | 50.8 |
| Latino Population | 139,136 | 243,469 | 447,168 |
| (% 25 and Over) | 86.9 | 76.0 | 69.8 |

*Note:* The race/ethnicity category is for whites, African-Americans, and Latinos. Latinos here may be white or black and are therefore included in these racial categories.
*Sources: 1990 Census of Population,* Summary Tape File 3A; *1980 Census of Population,* Summary Tape File 3A; *1970 Census of Population,* Fourth Count machine-readable file.

sixteen to nineteen for our cities and within their poverty and distressed census tracts. The bottom half of the panel shows the consequences of school dropout in the cities and subareas on prospects of working.

While nationwide figures reveal steady reductions in the school dropout rate of young persons between 1970 and 1990, the top panel of Table 10 offers little encouragement that urban youth dropout conditions have improved much during the same period. For the cities as a whole, youth dropout rates declined from 16.8 percent in 1970 to 14.6 percent in 1990. While slow declines in youth dropout characterized all subareas between 1980 and 1990, extreme poverty tracts, distressed tracts, and severely distressed tracts experienced only marginal declines during the 1980s.

**Table 10. Percentage of Persons Age 16–19 Who Are High School Dropouts, by Distress Status, 100 Largest Central Cities**

| | Panel A | | |
| | 1970 | 1980 | 1990 |
|---|---|---|---|
| City Total | 16.8 | 16.3 | 14.6 |
| In Poverty Tracts | 24.6 | 21.4 | 18.9 |
| In Extreme Poverty Tracts | 24.2 | 21.9 | 19.4 |
| In Distressed Tracts | 26.7 | 23.1 | 21.4 |
| In Severely Distressed Tracts | 36.0 | 36.2 | 35.5 |

**Percentage Not Working Among Young High School Dropouts, by Distress Status, 100 Largest Central Cities**

| | Panel B | | |
| | 1970 | 1980 | 1990 |
|---|---|---|---|
| City Total | 56.8 | 63.6 | 65.0 |
| In Poverty Tracts | 61.9 | 72.0 | 70.4 |
| In Extreme Poverty Tracts | 64.4 | 80.7 | 79.2 |
| In Distressed Tracts | 71.3 | 81.0 | 81.0 |
| In Severely Distressed Tracts | 71.7 | 80.0 | 81.7 |

Sources: *1990 Census of Population,* Summary Tape File 3A; *1980 Census of Population,* Summary Tape File 3A; *1970 Census of Population,* Fourth Count machine-readable file.

Apropos joblessness, the bottom panel of Table 10 shows that 65 percent of city residents age sixteen to nineteen who were not in school and had not completed high school were not working in 1990. Joblessness among younger school dropouts residing in the cities' poverty areas was 70 percent, 79 percent in extreme poverty tracts, 81 percent in distressed tracts, and 82 percent in severely distressed tracts.

Public assistance recipiency, which rose sharply during the 1970s, leveled off during the 1980s. Table 11 reveals that, while the absolute number of households receiving public assistance in the 100 central cities rose marginally between 1980 and 1990, the proportion actually declined marginally. These proportional declines characterize all but the severely distressed poverty subareas of the cities. It is worthwhile to point out that even in extreme poverty tracts, two-thirds of the households do not receive public assistance, while 62 percent do not receive public assistance in the cities' severely distressed neighborhoods.

The negative consequences of residential segregation and isola-

**Table 11. Households Receiving Public Assistance, in the 100 Largest Central Cities, 1970–1990**

|  | 1970 | 1980 | 1990 |
|---|---|---|---|
| **Total Public Assistance Households** | | | |
| All 100 Cities | 971,870 | 2,107,190 | 2,149,132 |
| (% of City Households) | 7.5 | 11.4 | 11.0 |
| In Poverty Tracts | 545,549 | 1,321,582 | 1,432,575 |
| (% of Households in These Tracts) | 18.8 | 23.2 | 21.5 |
| In Extreme Poverty Tracts | 151,890 | 467,105 | 597,090 |
| (% of Households in These Tracts) | 28.1 | 36.4 | 32.8 |
| In Distressed Tracts | 75,024 | 609,104 | 665,596 |
| (% of Households in These Tracts) | 36.2 | 36.4 | 34.6 |
| In Severely Distressed Tracts | 49,065 | 211,267 | 205,896 |
| (% of Households in These Tracts) | 36.7 | 36.7 | 37.6 |

*Note:* In 1970, the unit is families.
*Sources: 1990 Census of Population,* Summary Tape File 3A; *1980 Census of Population,* Summary Tape File 3A; *1970 Census of Population,* Fourth Count machine-readable file.

tion for a range of inner city problems have been well documented in the scholarly literature during the past two decades.[18] These problems include inferior public schools, networking constraints affecting job prospects, negative stereotyping by outsiders, and many others.

We computed the index of dissimilarity, which is the most conventional measure of segregation, to examine trends in African-American–white segregation in the 100 central cities between 1970 and 1990. The index of dissimilarity measures the amount of residential segregation between two racial groups by contrasting their proportional makeup of individual census tracts in the city with their proportions in the entire city population.[19] The index of dissimilarity may be interpreted as the percentage of persons who would have to move among census tracts to achieve African-American–white tract compositions equivalent to the overall African-American–white city composition.

Table 12 presents the means of the segregation indexes for the 100 cities and for cities classified by region, city size, and city age. Results reveal that residential segregation in the central cities increased during the 1970s and that this increase characterized central cities in most regions and all size categories. The only declines between 1970 and 1980 in mean level of segregation were found in the West and for young cities, that is, those cities that achieved metropolitan status (50,000 or more population) in 1950 or later.

Table 12. Mean Measures of Segregation (Index of Dissimilarity)

|                              | 1970 | 1980 | 1990 |
|------------------------------|------|------|------|
| **All Cities**               | 63.6 | 66.8 | 60.3 |
| **Region**                   |      |      |      |
| Northeast (12)               | 63.3 | 71.3 | 66.0 |
| Midwest (23)                 | 63.4 | 70.0 | 66.0 |
| South (40)                   | 65.9 | 71.4 | 64.1 |
| West (25)                    | 60.1 | 53.8 | 46.1 |
| **Size**                     |      |      |      |
| Less Than 250,000 (45)       | 62.1 | 62.7 | 56.0 |
| 250,000–499,999 (33)         | 63.6 | 68.2 | 61.2 |
| 500,000–999,999 (16)         | 66.5 | 70.7 | 64.9 |
| 1 Million & Over (6)         | 66.2 | 79.5 | 75.1 |
| **Age[1]**                   |      |      |      |
| Pre-1990 (45)                | 65.4 | 71.3 | 66.6 |
| 1900–1940 (40)               | 62.9 | 66.3 | 58.5 |
| 1950 & Later (15)            | 59.6 | 54.3 | 45.9 |

[1]City age is defined as the year at which the city achieved 50,000 population size, which is the basis for metropolitan central city status.
*Note:* The number of cities in each category is shown in parenthesis.
*Sources: 1990 Census of Population,* Summary Tape File 3A; *1980 Census of Population,* Summary Tape File 3A; *1970 Census of Population,* Fourth Count machine-readable file.

Mean levels of African-American–white segregation declined between 1980 and 1990 for the 100 central cities as a whole and for all regional, city size, and city age categories. Comparing 1970 with 1990, mean levels of segregation rose in the Northeast and Midwest and declined in the South and West. Mean levels of segregation were considerably higher in 1990 than 1970 for cities with more than 1 million residents, but lower among smaller city size categories. Our oldest central cities (those reaching 50,000 population before 1900) also had slightly higher segregation in 1990 than 1970. Thus in 1990 segregation was highest in larger, older cities in the Northeast and Midwest. With two-thirds of the residents in older cities and Frost Belt cities required to shift residence to achieve a racially balanced residential pattern and three-quarters of the residents of our largest cities having to move to achieve neighborhood racial balance, African-American–white residential segregation remains a prominent feature of our city landscape.

Before briefly describing trends for individual cities it is useful to provide a comparative summary of demographic, social, and economic indicators juxtaposing these conditions in extreme poverty and severely distressed tracts with nonpoverty tracts and the city as a whole. Table 13 does this. For the most part, the data presented speak for themselves. Suffice it to highlight a number of points.

• While the number of city tracts steadily went up between 1970 and 1990, the number of nonpoverty tracts (less than 20 percent residents below poverty) went steadily down. In 1970 four out of five city residents lived in nonpoverty tracts; by 1990 more than one-third of the population in the 100 cities resided in poverty tracts.
• Two of three households with children living in severely distressed tracts were female-headed in 1990, compared to less than one in five households with children in nonpoverty tracts.

**Table 13. Population Characteristics by Tract Distress Status, 100 Largest Central Cities, 1970–1990**

| Characteristic by Year | City Total | Non-Poverty[1] | Extreme Poverty | Severely Distressed |
|---|---|---|---|---|
| Number of Tracts, 1970 | 12584 | 9154 | 751 | 166 |
| Number of Tracts, 1980 | 13777 | 9064 | 1330 | 562 |
| Number of Tracts, 1990 | 14214 | 8618 | 1954 | 566 |
| Percentage of Population, 1970 | 100.0 | 74.5 | 5.2 | 1.2 |
| Percentage of Population, 1980 | 100.0 | 67.2 | 7.9 | 3.4 |
| Percentage of Population, 1990 | 100.0 | 62.7 | 10.7 | 3.2 |
| % Female-headed HH with Children, 1970 | 17.2 | 12.0 | 45.4 | 55.5 |
| % Female-headed HH with Children, 1980 | 27.8 | 18.8 | 61.1 | 59.8 |
| % Female-headed HH with Children, 1990 | 30.1 | 19.8 | 61.6 | 65.4 |
| % Persons with less than HS Education, 1970 | 48.9 | 43.3 | 76.7 | 78.6 |
| % Persons with less than HS Education, 1980 | 35.4 | 28.1 | 62.8 | 63.9 |
| % Persons with less than HS Education, 1990 | 27.9 | 19.8 | 52.7 | 54.6 |
| % Males with no Work in Previous Year, 1970 | 18.1 | 15.6 | 30.9 | 38.9 |
| % Males with no Work in Previous Year, 1980 | 23.8 | 19.5 | 42.8 | 44.2 |
| % Males with no Work in Previous Year, 1990 | 23.8 | 19.3 | 40.4 | 44.6 |
| % HS Dropouts not Working, 1970 | 56.8 | 52.9 | 64.4 | 71.7 |
| % HS Dropouts not Working, 1980 | 63.6 | 54.9 | 80.7 | 80.0 |
| % HS Dropouts not Working, 1990 | 65.0 | 57.0 | 79.2 | 81.7 |

| Characteristic by Year | City Total | Non-Poverty[1] | Extreme Poverty | Severely Distressed |
|---|---|---|---|---|
| % Youths that are HS Dropouts, 1970 | 16.8 | 13.4 | 24.2 | 36.0 |
| % Youths that are HS Dropouts, 1980 | 16.3 | 13.1 | 21.9 | 36.2 |
| % Youths that are HS Dropouts, 1990 | 14.6 | 10.9 | 19.4 | 35.5 |
| Total Employed per 100 not Working, 1970 | 127.1 | 139.1 | 72.5 | 60.4 |
| Total Employed per 100 not Working, 1980 | 131.5 | 158.5 | 57.8 | 58.9 |
| Total Employed per 100 not Working, 1990 | 145.6 | 182.3 | 65.5 | 58.1 |
| % Population Foreign-Born, 1970 | 8.1 | 8.8 | 3.3 | 2.6 |
| % Population Foreign-Born, 1980 | 11.4 | 10.9 | 7.4 | 8.2 |
| % Population Foreign-Born, 1990 | 14.9 | 13.6 | 11.8 | 9.0 |
| % African-American Households without a Vehicle, 1970 | 47.0 | 32.2 | 64.2 | 73.0 |
| % African-American Households without a Vehicle, 1980 | 40.2 | 22.3 | 64.7 | 62.2 |
| % African-American Households without a Vehicle, 1990 | 39.5 | 23.9 | 59.0 | 62.9 |

[1]Nonpoverty tracts are defined as those with fewer than 20 percent of their residents below the poverty level at each census year.

*Sources: 1990 Census of Population,* Summary Tape File 3A; *1980 Census of Population,* Summary Tape File 3A; *1970 Census of Population,* Fourth Count machine-readable file.

- The high school completion rates of nonpoverty tract residents improved markedly between 1970 and 1990 with more than four of five adult residents of these tracts having a high school degree compared to fewer than half the residents of extreme poverty and severely distressed tracts.
- More than 40 percent of out-of-school males age sixteen to sixty-four in extreme poverty tracts and severely distressed tracts had not worked at all in 1989, compared to less than one in five comparable males in the nonpoverty tracts.
- Four of five younger males in extreme poverty tracts who had dropped out of school were not working in 1990. Even in nonpoverty areas of the city, if you are a school dropout, you probably are not working.
- Only 11 percent of younger people in nonpoverty tracts drop out of high school compared to 36 percent in severely distressed tracts.
- Whereas the number of persons employed per 100 not working went up considerably within nonpoverty tracts between 1970 and 1990, it went down in extreme poverty tracts and severely distressed neighborhoods. In 1990 the ratio of employed to those not

working was three times greater in nonpoverty tracts than in either extreme poverty tracts or severely distressed tracts.

• The percentage of the population that is foreign-born steadily
went up in the cities between 1970 and 1990 but increased the
fastest in extreme poverty and severely distressed tracts. By 1990,
11.8 percent of extreme poverty tracts were composed of foreign-
born compared to 3.3 percent in 1970, while in 1990, 9 percent of
the severely distressed tracts were composed of foreign-born compared to 2.6 percent in 1970.

• Approximately 60 percent of the African-American households in
extreme poverty tracts and severely distressed neighborhoods do
not own a private vehicle compared to 24 percent in nonpoverty
areas.

## Individual City Patterns

The aggregate trends described above blur some important differences and crosscurrents among individual cities. For example,
while New York City led the nation by a wide margin in growth of
concentrated poverty between 1970 and 1980, its concentrated poverty population declined considerably between 1980 and 1990. Still,
by 1990 the city maintained a wide lead in the absolute numbers of
poverty tracts and distressed neighborhoods. On the other hand,
Chicago, which experienced the second largest gain in extreme poverty and severely distressed neighborhoods between 1970 and 1980,
was again the second largest gainer between 1980 and 1990.

Detroit, which also was among the nation's leaders between 1970
and 1980 in growth of concentrated poverty and severely distressed
neighborhoods, fared the worst of all cities in the 1980s as its downward spiral accelerated. Between 1980 and 1990 Detroit *added* the
most extreme poverty tracts (88), severely distressed tracts (14), population in extreme poverty tracts (261,323), population in severely distressed tracts (41,953), poverty population in extreme poverty tracts
(127,411), and poverty population in severely distressed tracts (28,-
816). Coming in second behind Detroit in growth of extreme poverty
and socially distressed population was Los Angeles, a city that
showed limited growth in such neighborhoods during the 1970s.

Because it is not feasible to discuss the multitude of individual city
patterns of growth of concentrated poverty and socially distressed
neighborhoods, this chapter adds Tables 14 to 21 ranking the cities
on a variety of concentrated poverty and distressed neighborhood

indicators. It begins with a complete ranking in 1990 of all 100 cities on the number of tracts and population residing in these tracts for each of the four concentrated poverty and neighborhood distress categories. It then provides listings of the top ten cities regarding change between 1970 to 1980 and 1980 to 1990 within the four major poverty and distressed neighborhood categories of number of tracts, population, and poverty population. The tables also list the ten largest cities in 1990 in terms of non-Latino African-American population and Latino population in concentrated poverty and distressed neighborhoods.

The final table is a complete ranking of the 100 largest cities in terms of degree of African-American–white segregation in 1970, 1980, and 1990. This table reveals that Cleveland was the most segregated city in the country in 1990 and that 88 percent of the city's neighborhood (tract) residents would have to move for the tracts to exhibit the same black-white composition as the city as a whole. The high degree of segregation that exists in America's cities is further testified to by the fact that for seventy-eight of the largest 100 cities more than half of their neighborhood residents would have to move to achieve neighborhood racial balance equivalent to the city racial composition.

## Concluding Remarks

This chapter provides a snapshot of economic change and neighborhood distress in our major cities. As places of work, cities have transformed from centers of goods processing to centers of information processing. With this transformation has come a considerable increase in the amount of education required for urban employment. As a result, those at the bottom end of the schooling-completed ladder have found themselves increasingly displaced from employment opportunities.

Cities continued to expand as the place of residence of African-Americans, other minorities, and immigrants, many of whom lack the education to participate in new urban growth industries. While some immigrant groups, such as Asians and certain Latinos, have adapted by creating small businesses, African-Americans have tended to be less successful in entrepreneurial pursuits. Increasingly confined to areas of blue-collar job decline, inner city African-American joblessness and poverty have grown substantially during the past twenty years and with this associated social problems. Analysis has shown that poverty concentration and neighborhood distress continued to worsen in our major cities as a whole between 1980 and 1990, with the greatest deterioration occurring in large cities in the Midwest, especially Detroit and Chicago.

Cities like Los Angeles, whose neighborhoods showed limited concentrations of poverty population in the 1970s, slipped in the 1980s. Conversely, New York City's neighborhoods, which deteriorated markedly in the 1970s, reversed their downward spiral in the 1980s. Why these different patterns emerged is not clear. Does it simply represent a regression toward the mean among our largest cities, or did something really different take place in Los Angeles than in New York City during the 1980s? The other chapters in this book shed light on this and many other important questions raised by the inner city data presented herein.

## Notes

[1] Bureau of the Census (1982 and 1992).
[2] Reischauer (1987) and Bureau of the Census (1992).
[3] Kasarda (1985).
[4] Bureau of the Census (1969 and 1991).
[5] Bureau of the Census (1968–1992), machine-readable data file, various years.
[6] Bureau of Economic Analysis, *Regional Economic Information System, 1992,* cd-rom data files.
[7] Meisenheimer (1992), pp. 3–19.
[8] Kasarda (1989), pp. 26–47.
[9] Jargowsky and Bane (1991) and Mincy, Sawhill, and Wolf (1990), pp. 450–453.
[10] Kasarda et al. (1992).
[11] Bureau of the Census (1992) and Jargowsky and Bane (1991).
[12] Ricketts and Sawhill (1988), pp. 316–325.
[13] Hughes (1989), pp. 187–207.
[14] The 1980 national tract standard deviation cut points (the mean plus one standard deviation) are (a) female-headed families with children: cutoff = 0.368; (b) male joblessness: cutoff = 0.454; (c) teenage school dropout: cutoff = 0.272; (d) welfare recipiency: cutoff = 0.176; and (e) poverty: cutoff = 0.332.
[15] Jargowsky and Bane (1991).
[16] Moss and Tilly (1991).
[17] Bluestone, Stevenson, and Tilly (1991) and Kasarda (1990), pp. 234–264.
[18] Jencks (1988), pp. 23–32; Jencks and Peterson (1991); Massey and Eggers (1990), pp. 1153–1188; Wilson (1987).
[19] Duncan, Cuzzort, and Duncan (1961) and Massey and Eggers (1990).

**Table 14. Cities Ranked on Number of Tracts by Poverty and Distress Status, 1990**

| City | Extreme Poverty Tracts No. | Rank | Poverty Tracts No. | Rank | Distressed Tracts No. | Rank | Severely Distressed Tracts No. | Rank |
|---|---|---|---|---|---|---|---|---|
| New York | 276 | 1 | 732 | 1 | 295 | 1 | 81 | 1 |
| Chicago | 179 | 2 | 417 | 2 | 197 | 2 | 64 | 2 |
| Detroit | 133 | 3 | 244 | 4 | 165 | 3 | 53 | 3 |
| Cleveland | 68 | 4 | 159 | 6 | 83 | 4 | 24 | 6 |
| Milwaukee | 60 | 5 | 109 | 9 | 56 | 7 | 15 | 8 |
| New Orleans | 59 | 6 | 121 | 8 | 56 | 6 | 15 | 9 |
| Philadelphia | 53 | 7 | 152 | 7 | 57 | 5 | 24 | 5 |
| Houston | 51 | 8 | 191 | 5 | 37 | 11 | 7 | 18 |
| Los Angeles | 45 | 9 | 257 | 3 | 39 | 10 | 17 | 7 |
| Memphis | 44 | 10 | 76 | 15 | 42 | 9 | 12 | 11 |
| Baltimore | 35 | 11 | 97 | 11 | 43 | 8 | 25 | 4 |
| Atlanta | 35 | 12 | 73 | 16 | 35 | 12 | 9 | 13 |
| San Antonio | 35 | 13 | 98 | 10 | 23 | 18 | 6 | 21 |
| Pittsburgh | 34 | 14 | 80 | 13 | 29 | 15 | 7 | 20 |
| Dallas | 33 | 15 | 97 | 12 | 21 | 20 | 7 | 17 |
| Cincinnati | 30 | 16 | 66 | 19 | 26 | 16 | 8 | 16 |
| Miami | 26 | 17 | 59 | 24 | 13 | 37 | 5 | 31 |
| Columbus, OH | 23 | 18 | 60 | 23 | 22 | 19 | 10 | 12 |
| Minneapolis | 23 | 19 | 55 | 26 | 18 | 23 | 5 | 27 |
| Newark | 21 | 20 | 63 | 21 | 31 | 13 | 14 | 10 |
| St. Louis | 20 | 21 | 70 | 17 | 30 | 14 | 9 | 14 |
| Dayton | 20 | 22 | 35 | 46 | 16 | 25 | 4 | 35 |
| Buffalo | 20 | 23 | 53 | 29 | 26 | 17 | 5 | 30 |
| Oklahoma City | 19 | 24 | 63 | 22 | 13 | 36 | 9 | 15 |
| Rochester | 19 | 25 | 52 | 32 | 18 | 21 | 6 | 22 |
| Phoenix | 18 | 26 | 56 | 25 | 6 | 56 | 5 | 26 |
| Kansas City | 18 | 27 | 69 | 18 | 14 | 32 | 4 | 36 |
| Mobile | 18 | 28 | 39 | 40 | 12 | 39 | 2 | 48 |
| Akron | 18 | 29 | 35 | 47 | 17 | 24 | 2 | 50 |
| El Paso | 17 | 30 | 53 | 30 | 7 | 53 | 0 | 100 |
| Toledo | 16 | 31 | 48 | 35 | 18 | 22 | 4 | 33 |
| Shreveport | 15 | 32 | 30 | 57 | 16 | 27 | 4 | 32 |
| Baton Rouge | 15 | 33 | 36 | 45 | 14 | 33 | 3 | 42 |
| Fresno | 15 | 34 | 34 | 49 | 5 | 65 | 2 | 51 |
| Birmingham | 14 | 35 | 40 | 38 | 15 | 28 | 1 | 56 |
| Boston | 14 | 36 | 77 | 14 | 13 | 35 | 2 | 49 |
| Tampa | 14 | 37 | 36 | 42 | 12 | 40 | 7 | 19 |
| Syracuse | 14 | 38 | 26 | 63 | 11 | 41 | 6 | 24 |
| Fort Worth | 14 | 39 | 55 | 27 | 9 | 48 | 3 | 46 |
| Flint | 14 | 40 | 30 | 56 | 15 | 29 | 3 | 43 |

| City | Extreme Poverty Tracts | | Poverty Tracts | | Distressed Tracts | | Severely Distressed Tracts | |
|---|---|---|---|---|---|---|---|---|
| | No. | Rank | No. | Rank | No. | Rank | No. | Rank |
| Norfolk | 13 | 41 | 22 | 71 | 12 | 38 | 3 | 41 |
| Jackson | 13 | 42 | 32 | 53 | 16 | 26 | 6 | 25 |
| Tulsa | 13 | 43 | 40 | 39 | 3 | 76 | 0 | 100 |
| Jacksonville | 12 | 44 | 29 | 58 | 9 | 43 | 3 | 39 |
| Nashville-Davidson | 11 | 45 | 36 | 43 | 9 | 45 | 5 | 28 |
| Columbus, GA | 11 | 46 | 20 | 74 | 8 | 49 | 5 | 29 |
| Portland | 11 | 47 | 36 | 44 | 5 | 66 | 1 | 63 |
| Louisville | 10 | 48 | 48 | 34 | 14 | 31 | 3 | 37 |
| Washington, D.C. | 10 | 49 | 65 | 20 | 14 | 30 | 4 | 34 |
| Denver | 10 | 50 | 42 | 37 | 9 | 44 | 3 | 38 |
| Montgomery | 10 | 51 | 19 | 76 | 9 | 47 | 3 | 45 |
| Indianapolis | 10 | 52 | 54 | 28 | 9 | 46 | 0 | 100 |
| San Diego | 10 | 53 | 44 | 36 | 5 | 67 | 3 | 47 |
| Tucson | 10 | 54 | 35 | 48 | 1 | 88 | 0 | 100 |
| Knoxville | 9 | 55 | 28 | 59 | 6 | 57 | 3 | 44 |
| Charlotte | 9 | 56 | 24 | 67 | 3 | 74 | 1 | 59 |
| St. Paul | 9 | 57 | 34 | 51 | 6 | 59 | 0 | 100 |
| Austin | 8 | 58 | 51 | 33 | 5 | 68 | 1 | 67 |
| Omaha | 8 | 59 | 31 | 55 | 5 | 63 | 0 | 100 |
| Richmond | 8 | 60 | 31 | 54 | 7 | 51 | 3 | 40 |
| Corpus Christi | 8 | 61 | 22 | 72 | 6 | 62 | 1 | 68 |
| Sacramento | 8 | 62 | 36 | 41 | 8 | 50 | 1 | 64 |
| Lubbock | 8 | 63 | 27 | 62 | 4 | 71 | 1 | 75 |
| Chattanooga | 7 | 64 | 23 | 70 | 6 | 55 | 1 | 60 |
| Springfield, MA | 7 | 65 | 16 | 82 | 7 | 52 | 6 | 23 |
| Seattle | 7 | 66 | 28 | 60 | 3 | 72 | 0 | 100 |
| Amarillo | 7 | 67 | 26 | 64 | 1 | 89 | 0 | 100 |
| Oakland | 6 | 68 | 52 | 31 | 9 | 42 | 1 | 65 |
| Gary | 6 | 69 | 34 | 50 | 14 | 34 | 2 | 52 |
| Spokane | 6 | 70 | 24 | 68 | 6 | 58 | 1 | 69 |
| Stockton | 6 | 71 | 28 | 61 | 4 | 70 | 2 | 53 |
| Wichita | 6 | 72 | 17 | 79 | 6 | 60 | 0 | 100 |
| Long Beach | 5 | 73 | 19 | 77 | 4 | 69 | 1 | 62 |
| Honolulu | 5 | 74 | 10 | 92 | 1 | 87 | 0 | 100 |
| Tacoma | 5 | 75 | 16 | 83 | 6 | 61 | 2 | 55 |
| Raleigh | 5 | 76 | 13 | 86 | 2 | 79 | 1 | 66 |
| St. Petersburg | 4 | 77 | 15 | 84 | 3 | 73 | 1 | 58 |
| San Francisco | 4 | 78 | 33 | 52 | 2 | 77 | 0 | 100 |
| Madison | 4 | 79 | 12 | 91 | 0 | 100 | 0 | 100 |
| Grand Rapids | 4 | 80 | 20 | 75 | 3 | 75 | 1 | 71 |
| Providence | 4 | 81 | 23 | 69 | 5 | 64 | 1 | 57 |
| Fort Wayne | 4 | 82 | 13 | 89 | 1 | 84 | 1 | 70 |

| City | Extreme Poverty Tracts | | Poverty Tracts | | Distressed Tracts | | Severely Distressed Tracts | |
|---|---|---|---|---|---|---|---|---|
| | No. | Rank | No. | Rank | No. | Rank | No. | Rank |
| Salt Lake City | 3 | 83 | 21 | 73 | 0 | 100 | 0 | 100 |
| Lexington-Fayette | 3 | 84 | 13 | 87 | 2 | 80 | 1 | 61 |
| Albuquerque | 3 | 85 | 25 | 65 | 0 | 100 | 0 | 100 |
| Des Moines | 3 | 86 | 12 | 90 | 1 | 85 | 0 | 100 |
| Fort Lauderdale | 2 | 87 | 9 | 94 | 2 | 82 | 0 | 100 |
| Little Rock | 2 | 88 | 16 | 81 | 7 | 54 | 1 | 74 |
| Lincoln | 2 | 89 | 9 | 93 | 0 | 100 | 0 | 100 |
| Jersey City | 2 | 90 | 24 | 66 | 2 | 78 | 1 | 72 |
| Colorado Springs | 2 | 91 | 17 | 80 | 0 | 100 | 0 | 100 |
| Worcester | 2 | 92 | 13 | 88 | 2 | 81 | 2 | 54 |
| Greensboro | 2 | 93 | 8 | 95 | 1 | 86 | 0 | 100 |
| Las Vegas | 1 | 94 | 8 | 96 | 2 | 83 | 1 | 73 |
| Anaheim | 1 | 95 | 6 | 97 | 0 | 100 | 0 | 100 |
| San Jose | 0 | 100 | 15 | 85 | 0 | 100 | 0 | 100 |
| Anchorage | 0 | 100 | 4 | 99 | 0 | 100 | 0 | 100 |
| Riverside | 0 | 100 | 5 | 98 | 0 | 100 | 0 | 100 |
| Santa Ana | 0 | 100 | 19 | 78 | 0 | 100 | 0 | 100 |
| Virginia Beach | 0 | 100 | 1 | 100 | 0 | 100 | 0 | 100 |

*Sources: 1990 Census of Population,* Summary Tape File 3A.

**Table 15. Cities Ranked on Population Size by Poverty and Distress Status, 1990**

| City | Extreme Poverty Tracts No. | Rank | Poverty Tracts No. | Rank | Distressed Tracts No. | Rank | Severely Distressed Tracts No. | Rank |
|---|---|---|---|---|---|---|---|---|
| New York | 952484 | 1 | 2733603 | 1 | 1168932 | 1 | 262061 | 1 |
| Chicago | 381866 | 2 | 1179229 | 3 | 472790 | 3 | 159532 | 2 |
| Detroit | 375548 | 3 | 768091 | 4 | 485659 | 2 | 157575 | 3 |
| Los Angeles | 230338 | 4 | 1415445 | 2 | 205936 | 5 | 92061 | 5 |
| Philadelphia | 191515 | 5 | 657484 | 6 | 248521 | 4 | 103593 | 4 |
| Houston | 156223 | 6 | 766715 | 5 | 108627 | 11 | 19422 | 18 |
| San Antonio | 152420 | 7 | 452666 | 7 | 106817 | 13 | 24222 | 14 |
| New Orleans | 151624 | 8 | 316500 | 11 | 142376 | 7 | 42263 | 8 |
| Milwaukee | 140831 | 9 | 273471 | 14 | 136445 | 9 | 35329 | 10 |
| Memphis | 126866 | 10 | 274893 | 13 | 133352 | 10 | 38434 | 9 |
| Baltimore | 104212 | 11 | 330847 | 9 | 138251 | 8 | 76798 | 6 |
| Cleveland | 100422 | 12 | 326120 | 10 | 157083 | 6 | 45766 | 7 |
| Atlanta | 91944 | 13 | 234219 | 18 | 91770 | 15 | 17642 | 20 |
| Miami | 90644 | 14 | 257437 | 15 | 58505 | 19 | 22750 | 15 |
| El Paso | 82197 | 15 | 309440 | 12 | 31553 | 39 | 0 | 100 |
| Fresno | 81765 | 16 | 182606 | 24 | 25592 | 49 | 15087 | 24 |
| Dallas | 80383 | 17 | 348738 | 8 | 53194 | 23 | 10197 | 38 |
| Columbus, OH | 74889 | 18 | 192214 | 22 | 67363 | 17 | 26256 | 13 |
| Cincinnati | 68376 | 19 | 172359 | 27 | 65736 | 18 | 14430 | 26 |
| Buffalo | 61277 | 20 | 187002 | 23 | 107413 | 12 | 14727 | 25 |
| Minneapolis | 61054 | 21 | 139946 | 36 | 42760 | 29 | 11284 | 32 |
| St. Louis | 60842 | 22 | 249338 | 17 | 100868 | 14 | 30834 | 12 |
| Baton Rouge | 59040 | 23 | 131264 | 42 | 53190 | 24 | 6546 | 50 |
| Pittsburgh | 56985 | 24 | 140795 | 35 | 53307 | 22 | 12608 | 28 |
| Phoenix | 56036 | 25 | 228239 | 19 | 17894 | 58 | 15519 | 23 |
| Dayton | 49496 | 26 | 106380 | 50 | 44611 | 27 | 11755 | 30 |
| Shreveport | 49447 | 27 | 103445 | 53 | 53513 | 20 | 6361 | 51 |
| Newark | 49189 | 28 | 167186 | 29 | 78232 | 16 | 32898 | 11 |
| Flint | 46076 | 29 | 104860 | 52 | 53488 | 21 | 10837 | 35 |
| Birmingham | 45505 | 30 | 149759 | 32 | 51576 | 25 | 4154 | 59 |
| Tucson | 38965 | 31 | 171172 | 28 | 1238 | 88 | 0 | 100 |
| San Diego | 38739 | 32 | 219000 | 20 | 30820 | 42 | 13983 | 27 |
| Syracuse | 38150 | 33 | 70651 | 70 | 36893 | 32 | 16532 | 21 |
| Norfolk | 36749 | 34 | 61029 | 76 | 33303 | 36 | 8831 | 41 |
| Toledo | 36041 | 35 | 139416 | 37 | 42624 | 30 | 8594 | 43 |
| Rochester | 33232 | 36 | 108515 | 49 | 32237 | 38 | 11028 | 34 |
| Nashville-Davidson | 32834 | 37 | 109127 | 47 | 31112 | 41 | 15969 | 22 |
| Akron | 32566 | 38 | 84995 | 61 | 32298 | 37 | 2984 | 62 |
| Mobile | 32219 | 39 | 81938 | 63 | 27933 | 46 | 1118 | 75 |
| Montgomery | 32002 | 40 | 72593 | 69 | 29083 | 45 | 8104 | 47 |

| City | Extreme Poverty Tracts | | Poverty Tracts | | Distressed Tracts | | Severely Distressed Tracts | |
|---|---|---|---|---|---|---|---|---|
| | No. | Rank | No. | Rank | No. | Rank | No. | Rank |
| Jackson | 31748 | 41 | 108604 | 48 | 45373 | 26 | 11599 | 31 |
| Louisville | 31646 | 42 | 122425 | 43 | 41224 | 31 | 8593 | 44 |
| Tampa | 31426 | 43 | 100667 | 54 | 31527 | 40 | 18491 | 19 |
| Fort Worth | 31202 | 44 | 164855 | 31 | 23894 | 51 | 7711 | 48 |
| Springfield, MA | 30281 | 45 | 65716 | 74 | 26053 | 48 | 20950 | 17 |
| Boston | 28738 | 46 | 252109 | 16 | 34640 | 33 | 2946 | 63 |
| Tulsa | 27808 | 47 | 96831 | 56 | 5982 | 82 | 0 | 100 |
| Madison | 27744 | 48 | 59954 | 77 | 0 | 100 | 0 | 100 |
| Oklahoma City | 27623 | 49 | 133973 | 41 | 29867 | 43 | 21514 | 16 |
| Jacksonville | 27005 | 50 | 115229 | 45 | 33639 | 35 | 9665 | 39 |
| Austin | 26998 | 51 | 172544 | 26 | 16956 | 62 | 2762 | 65 |
| Corpus Christi | 26222 | 52 | 95989 | 57 | 20987 | 55 | 1925 | 72 |
| Knoxville | 25355 | 53 | 69671 | 72 | 14699 | 66 | 6880 | 49 |
| Columbus, GA | 25113 | 54 | 49009 | 84 | 17166 | 60 | 11858 | 29 |
| Charlotte | 24756 | 55 | 62968 | 75 | 7805 | 77 | 2884 | 64 |
| Kansas City | 24049 | 56 | 136349 | 39 | 23805 | 52 | 8769 | 42 |
| Stockton | 23492 | 57 | 114266 | 46 | 22265 | 54 | 10773 | 36 |
| Indianapolis | 23297 | 58 | 166060 | 30 | 24516 | 50 | 0 | 100 |
| Denver | 22796 | 59 | 146972 | 33 | 23271 | 53 | 8214 | 46 |
| Seattle | 22283 | 60 | 105055 | 51 | 11816 | 70 | 0 | 100 |
| Richmond | 22257 | 61 | 83885 | 62 | 19397 | 56 | 10468 | 37 |
| Washington, D.C. | 20609 | 62 | 202759 | 21 | 44006 | 28 | 11159 | 33 |
| Lubbock | 19428 | 63 | 78189 | 66 | 9568 | 72 | 1247 | 73 |
| Oakland | 18626 | 64 | 181000 | 25 | 29459 | 44 | 9192 | 40 |
| Sacramento | 18466 | 65 | 121571 | 44 | 33662 | 34 | 5324 | 52 |
| St. Paul | 17834 | 66 | 90210 | 60 | 11751 | 71 | 0 | 100 |
| Long Beach | 17480 | 67 | 138503 | 38 | 16972 | 61 | 2086 | 71 |
| Omaha | 16825 | 68 | 74798 | 68 | 8506 | 74 | 0 | 100 |
| Portland | 15764 | 69 | 91346 | 59 | 12499 | 68 | 2603 | 67 |
| Wichita | 15104 | 70 | 46501 | 86 | 15178 | 65 | 0 | 100 |
| Raleigh | 14612 | 71 | 41021 | 90 | 7345 | 78 | 3616 | 60 |
| Chattanooga | 13963 | 72 | 54154 | 81 | 16699 | 64 | 5306 | 53 |
| Tacoma | 12688 | 73 | 42913 | 88 | 17286 | 59 | 4829 | 55 |
| San Francisco | 12127 | 74 | 143905 | 34 | 11932 | 69 | 0 | 100 |
| Lexington-Fayette | 10836 | 75 | 52529 | 82 | 7188 | 79 | 3281 | 61 |
| St. Petersburg | 10274 | 76 | 46750 | 85 | 8838 | 73 | 2395 | 70 |
| Gary | 9569 | 77 | 100151 | 55 | 26312 | 47 | 4565 | 57 |
| Greensboro | 9552 | 78 | 27563 | 96 | 4439 | 84 | 0 | 100 |
| Providence | 9406 | 79 | 81341 | 64 | 16815 | 63 | 2586 | 68 |
| Fort Lauderdale | 8731 | 80 | 44763 | 87 | 6526 | 81 | 0 | 100 |
| Jersey City | 8445 | 81 | 79778 | 65 | 8445 | 75 | 4658 | 56 |
| Amarillo | 8093 | 82 | 54872 | 80 | 368 | 89 | 0 | 100 |

| City | Extreme Poverty Tracts | | Poverty Tracts | | Distressed Tracts | | Severely Distressed Tracts | |
|---|---|---|---|---|---|---|---|---|
| | No. | Rank | No. | Rank | No. | Rank | No. | Rank |
| Des Moines | 7943 | 83 | 38794 | 92 | 3787 | 85 | 0 | 100 |
| Worcester | 7674 | 84 | 58981 | 78 | 8396 | 76 | 8396 | 45 |
| Grand Rapids | 7042 | 85 | 67854 | 73 | 5296 | 83 | 2435 | 69 |
| Honolulu | 6911 | 86 | 21197 | 98 | 2390 | 87 | 0 | 100 |
| Spokane | 6674 | 87 | 69989 | 71 | 14132 | 67 | 4998 | 54 |
| Albuquerque | 6478 | 88 | 91601 | 58 | 0 | 100 | 0 | 100 |
| Fort Wayne | 5080 | 89 | 25263 | 97 | 2612 | 86 | 2612 | 66 |
| Little Rock | 4960 | 90 | 42730 | 89 | 19312 | 57 | 1244 | 74 |
| Las Vegas | 4193 | 91 | 36675 | 93 | 6598 | 80 | 4193 | 58 |
| Lincoln | 3442 | 92 | 27983 | 95 | 0 | 100 | 0 | 100 |
| Colorado Springs | 1640 | 93 | 50240 | 83 | 0 | 100 | 0 | 100 |
| Salt Lake City | 1512 | 94 | 58315 | 79 | 0 | 100 | 0 | 100 |
| Anaheim | 1041 | 95 | 30530 | 94 | 0 | 100 | 0 | 100 |
| San Jose | 0 | 100 | 76962 | 67 | 0 | 100 | 0 | 100 |
| Anchorage | 0 | 100 | 14033 | 99 | 0 | 100 | 0 | 100 |
| Riverside | 0 | 100 | 39389 | 91 | 0 | 100 | 0 | 100 |
| Santa Ana | 0 | 100 | 134517 | 40 | 0 | 100 | 0 | 100 |
| Virginia Beach | 0 | 100 | 6322 | 100 | 0 | 100 | 0 | 100 |

*Sources: 1990 Census of Population,* Summary Tape File 3A.

**Table 16. Panel A: Cities Ranked on Growth of Tracts by Poverty and Distress Status, 1970–1980**

| City | Extreme Poverty Tracts | | Poverty Tracts | | Distressed Tracts | | Severely Distressed Tracts | |
|------|------|------|------|------|------|------|------|------|
| | No. | Rank | No. | Rank | No. | Rank | No. | Rank |
| New York | 238 | 1 | 334 | 1 | 333 | 1 | 104 | 1 |
| Chicago | 85 | 2 | 149 | 2 | 143 | 2 | 39 | 2 |
| Newark | 28 | 3 | 17 | 18 | 39 | 5 | 19 | 4 |
| Philadelphia | 28 | 4 | 45 | 5 | 51 | 4 | 11 | 8 |
| Cleveland | 22 | 5 | 46 | 4 | 34 | 7 | 3 | 26 |
| Detroit | 22 | 6 | 33 | 7 | 80 | 3 | 35 | 3 |
| Atlanta | 16 | 7 | 24 | 9 | 26 | 9 | 11 | 7 |
| Columbus, OH | 15 | 8 | 23 | 10 | 16 | 14 | 14 | 6 |
| Baltimore | 12 | 9 | 34 | 6 | 35 | 6 | 15 | 5 |
| Buffalo | 11 | 10 | 19 | 14 | 12 | 17 | 1 | 54 |

**Panel B: Cities Ranked on Growth of Tracts by Poverty and Distress Status, 1980–1990**

| City | Extreme Poverty Tracts | | Poverty Tracts | | Distressed Tracts | | Severely Distressed Tracts | |
|------|------|------|------|------|------|------|------|------|
| | No. | Rank | No. | Rank | No. | Rank | No. | Rank |
| Detroit | 88 | 1 | 65 | 2 | 77 | 1 | 14 | 1 |
| Chicago | 47 | 2 | 37 | 4 | 28 | 5 | 10 | 2 |
| Milwaukee | 42 | 3 | 35 | 5 | 29 | 3 | 6 | 8 |
| Houston | 38 | 4 | 114 | 1 | 29 | 4 | 5 | 9 |
| New Orleans | 30 | 5 | 21 | 14 | 28 | 6 | 7 | 5 |
| Cleveland | 26 | 6 | 43 | 3 | 34 | 2 | 10 | 3 |
| Miami | 18 | 7 | 24 | 9 | 8 | 18 | 2 | 16 |
| Pittsburgh | 16 | 8 | 17 | 18 | 9 | 14 | 7 | 7 |
| San Antonio | 16 | 9 | 22 | 12 | 14 | 7 | − 1 | 69 |
| Dallas | 15 | 10 | 31 | 6 | 9 | 11 | 1 | 21 |

*Sources: 1990 Census of Population,* Summary Tape File 3A; 1980 Census of Population, Summary Tape File 3A; 1970 Census of Population, Fourth Count machine-readable file.

**Table 17. Panel A: Cities Ranked on Growth of Population by Poverty and Distress Status, 1970–1980**

| City | Extreme Poverty Tracts | | Poverty Tracts | | Distressed Tracts | | Severely Distressed Tracts | |
|---|---|---|---|---|---|---|---|---|
| | No. | Rank | No. | Rank | No. | Rank | No. | Rank |
| New York | 697693 | 1 | 662034 | 1 | 1179582 | 1 | 312116 | 1 |
| Chicago | 211626 | 2 | 360449 | 3 | 422200 | 2 | 90027 | 3 |
| Philadelphia | 114089 | 3 | 225650 | 4 | 245690 | 3 | 24663 | 10 |
| Newark | 72326 | 4 | 27127 | 25 | 117897 | 5 | 54881 | 4 |
| Detroit | 58974 | 5 | 144089 | 5 | 228119 | 4 | 94709 | 2 |
| Columbus, OH | 33719 | 6 | 33956 | 17 | 46964 | 15 | 39320 | 5 |
| Atlanta | 32158 | 7 | 74717 | 8 | 73993 | 9 | 29508 | 7 |
| Buffalo | 27298 | 8 | 47193 | 12 | 37839 | 17 | − 4969 | 94 |
| Baltimore | 25409 | 9 | 90172 | 7 | 116008 | 6 | 33563 | 6 |
| Dayton | 23935 | 10 | 26982 | 27 | 27143 | 25 | 7192 | 33 |

**Panel B: Cities Ranked on Growth of Population by Poverty and Distress Status, 1980–1990**

| City | Extreme Poverty Tracts | | Poverty Tracts | | Distressed Tracts | | Severely Distressed Tracts | |
|---|---|---|---|---|---|---|---|---|
| | No. | Rank | No. | Rank | No. | Rank | No. | Rank |
| Detroit | 261323 | 1 | 185775 | 3 | 227912 | 1 | 41953 | 1 |
| Los Angeles | 134432 | 2 | 422782 | 2 | 38792 | 9 | 30030 | 2 |
| Houston | 111309 | 3 | 458016 | 1 | 77403 | 3 | 12050 | 11 |
| Milwaukee | 109927 | 4 | 106239 | 7 | 82130 | 2 | 16824 | 8 |
| Fresno | 73809 | 5 | 111705 | 6 | 14597 | 25 | 11546 | 12 |
| San Antonio | 72595 | 6 | 90835 | 9 | 63945 | 4 | − 7207 | 86 |
| New Orleans | 57896 | 7 | − 1079 | 81 | 44306 | 7 | 19809 | 5 |
| Miami | 55669 | 8 | 60231 | 17 | 38572 | 10 | 9395 | 16 |
| El Paso | 51915 | 9 | 77446 | 11 | 20668 | 16 | − 7262 | 87 |
| Flint | 42581 | 10 | 45768 | 25 | 43615 | 8 | 5254 | 20 |

*Sources: 1990 Census of Population,* Summary Tape File 3A; 1980 Census of Population, Summary Tape File 3A; 1970 Census of Population, Fourth Count machine-readable file.

## Table 18. Panel A: Cities Ranked on Growth of Poverty Population by Poverty and Distress Status, 1970–1980

| City | Extreme Poverty Tracts | | Poverty Tracts | | Distressed Tracts | | Severely Distressed Tracts | |
|------|------|------|------|------|------|------|------|------|
| | No. | Rank | No. | Rank | No. | Rank | No. | Rank |
| New York | 342267 | 1 | 331951 | 1 | 527662 | 1 | 148758 | 1 |
| Chicago | 119766 | 2 | 162787 | 2 | 199929 | 2 | 43764 | 2 |
| Philadelphia | 57723 | 3 | 88462 | 4 | 107874 | 3 | 15782 | 6 |
| Newark | 37006 | 4 | 28421 | 7 | 54375 | 5 | 25657 | 4 |
| Detroit | 27673 | 5 | 62415 | 5 | 89118 | 4 | 36636 | 3 |
| Columbus, OH | 17278 | 6 | 16653 | 14 | 18261 | 15 | 16276 | 5 |
| Atlanta | 15794 | 7 | 27990 | 8 | 36434 | 8 | 15111 | 8 |
| Baltimore | 15180 | 8 | 32359 | 6 | 50628 | 6 | 15295 | 7 |
| Buffalo | 13265 | 9 | 18637 | 13 | 17185 | 17 | − 1212 | 93 |
| Dayton | 10870 | 10 | 10011 | 21 | 11991 | 24 | 3578 | 31 |

## Panel B: Cities Ranked on Growth of Poverty Population by Poverty and Distress Status, 1980–1990

| City | Extreme Poverty Tracts | | Poverty Tracts | | Distressed Tracts | | Severely Distressed Tracts | |
|------|------|------|------|------|------|------|------|------|
| | No. | Rank | No. | Rank | No. | Rank | No. | Rank |
| Detroit | 127411 | 1 | 108222 | 3 | 116789 | 1 | 28816 | 1 |
| Los Angeles | 59501 | 2 | 149668 | 2 | 16676 | 10 | 14512 | 2 |
| Milwaukee | 57305 | 3 | 55240 | 4 | 46430 | 2 | 11990 | 6 |
| Houston | 52554 | 4 | 151748 | 1 | 36293 | 3 | 5737 | 12 |
| San Antonio | 36012 | 5 | 39354 | 7 | 31187 | 4 | − 1725 | 81 |
| Fresno | 33123 | 6 | 46145 | 5 | 5210 | 34 | 4328 | 15 |
| New Orleans | 28547 | 7 | 12181 | 36 | 22478 | 6 | 12435 | 5 |
| Miami | 26205 | 8 | 29620 | 11 | 15220 | 11 | 2408 | 19 |
| El Paso | 25899 | 9 | 36956 | 9 | 13222 | 14 | − 4382 | 93 |
| Dallas | 20945 | 10 | 45443 | 6 | 7006 | 27 | − 4976 | 94 |

*Sources: 1990 Census of Population,* Summary Tape File 3A; 1980 Census of Population, Summary Tape File 3A; 1970 Census of Population, Fourth Count machine-readable file.

**Table 19. Panel A: Cities Ranked on Poverty Population by Poverty and Distress Status, 1980**

| City | Extreme Poverty Tracts | | Poverty Tracts | | Distressed Tracts | | Severely Distressed Tracts | |
|---|---|---|---|---|---|---|---|---|
| | No. | Rank | No. | Rank | No. | Rank | No. | Rank |
| New York | 476161 | 1 | 984917 | 1 | 562592 | 1 | 183029 | 1 |
| Chicago | 194094 | 2 | 429751 | 2 | 248994 | 2 | 77562 | 2 |
| Philadelphia | 104660 | 3 | 248802 | 4 | 143072 | 3 | 43946 | 4 |
| Baltimore | 60912 | 4 | 140295 | 6 | 78838 | 5 | 34259 | 5 |
| New Orleans | 55378 | 5 | 119789 | 7 | 56187 | 9 | 12084 | 14 |
| Newark | 52003 | 6 | 94988 | 10 | 60412 | 8 | 28668 | 6 |
| Detroit | 51709 | 7 | 188286 | 5 | 102511 | 4 | 46989 | 3 |
| Memphis | 48318 | 8 | 106662 | 9 | 68982 | 6 | 6280 | 28 |
| Atlanta | 46709 | 9 | 93151 | 12 | 47553 | 10 | 22413 | 8 |
| Los Angeles | 41444 | 10 | 290093 | 3 | 67455 | 7 | 24227 | 7 |

**Panel B: Cities Ranked on Poverty Population by Poverty and Distress Status, 1990**

| City | Extreme Poverty Tracts | | Poverty Tracts | | Distressed Tracts | | Severely Distressed Tracts | |
|---|---|---|---|---|---|---|---|---|
| | No. | Rank | No. | Rank | No. | Rank | No. | Rank |
| New York | 454908 | 1 | 959390 | 1 | 520323 | 1 | 117977 | 1 |
| Chicago | 205733 | 2 | 430748 | 3 | 236681 | 2 | 88005 | 2 |
| Detroit | 179120 | 3 | 296508 | 4 | 219300 | 3 | 75805 | 3 |
| Los Angeles | 100945 | 4 | 439761 | 2 | 84131 | 5 | 38739 | 5 |
| Philadelphia | 93303 | 5 | 223605 | 6 | 113894 | 4 | 54183 | 4 |
| New Orleans | 83925 | 6 | 131970 | 8 | 78665 | 6 | 24519 | 7 |
| San Antonio | 72909 | 7 | 158771 | 7 | 51668 | 11 | 14299 | 12 |
| Houston | 72757 | 8 | 241964 | 5 | 50383 | 12 | 9168 | 19 |
| Milwaukee | 70282 | 9 | 106548 | 13 | 67881 | 8 | 20059 | 9 |
| Memphis | 63745 | 10 | 104417 | 14 | 66137 | 9 | 19555 | 10 |

*Sources: 1990 Census of Population,* Summary Tape File 3A.

**Table 20. Panel A: Cities Ranked on Non-Latino African-American Population by Poverty and Distress Status, 1990**

| City | Extreme Poverty Tracts | | Poverty Tracts | | Distressed Tracts | | Severely Distressed Tracts | |
|---|---|---|---|---|---|---|---|---|
| | No. | Rank | No. | Rank | No. | Rank | No. | Rank |
| New York | 409271 | 1 | 1074190 | 1 | 546179 | 1 | 123886 | 2 |
| Chicago | 315406 | 2 | 714147 | 2 | 415490 | 2 | 134074 | 1 |
| Detroit | 308606 | 3 | 610920 | 3 | 401263 | 3 | 112134 | 3 |
| New Orleans | 131857 | 4 | 244942 | 8 | 130993 | 5 | 38978 | 7 |
| Memphis | 117833 | 5 | 229605 | 9 | 127732 | 6 | 35917 | 8 |
| Philadelphia | 114727 | 6 | 415976 | 4 | 180143 | 4 | 63807 | 4 |
| Baltimore | 93080 | 7 | 255538 | 7 | 122242 | 8 | 63686 | 5 |
| Milwaukee | 91529 | 8 | 142595 | 15 | 99537 | 9 | 24315 | 12 |
| Houston | 91257 | 9 | 308385 | 5 | 91724 | 11 | 14856 | 14 |
| Atlanta | 81186 | 10 | 203696 | 10 | 88388 | 13 | 16496 | 13 |

**Panel B: Cities Ranked on Latino Population by Poverty and Distress Status, 1990**

| City | Extreme Poverty Tracts | | Poverty Tracts | | Distressed Tracts | | Severely Distressed Tracts | |
|---|---|---|---|---|---|---|---|---|
| | No. | Rank | No. | Rank | No. | Rank | No. | Rank |
| New York | 459099 | 1 | 1113035 | 1 | 544656 | 1 | 122075 | 1 |
| Los Angeles | 133027 | 2 | 842746 | 2 | 97830 | 2 | 42333 | 2 |
| San Antonio | 128952 | 3 | 352276 | 3 | 84792 | 3 | 21815 | 4 |
| El Paso | 74933 | 4 | 260453 | 6 | 30900 | 6 | 0 | 100 |
| Houston | 54573 | 5 | 288207 | 4 | 13902 | 12 | 4130 | 16 |
| Philadelphia | 44391 | 6 | 64410 | 16 | 42633 | 4 | 29942 | 3 |
| Chicago | 42851 | 7 | 285413 | 5 | 36335 | 5 | 19768 | 5 |
| Phoenix | 35986 | 8 | 105115 | 10 | 9012 | 19 | 8161 | 10 |
| Fresno | 33171 | 9 | 71696 | 13 | 11437 | 15 | 8778 | 9 |
| Miami | 31920 | 10 | 145904 | 7 | 26188 | 7 | 15326 | 6 |

*Sources: 1990 Census of Population,* Summary Tape File 3A.

**Table 21. Cities Ranked by Degree of African-American–White Segregation (Index of Dissimilarity) in 1970–1990**

| Rank | City | 1990 Score | 1990 Rank | 1980 Score | 1980 Rank | 1970 Score | 1970 Rank |
|------|------|-----------|-----------|-----------|-----------|-----------|-----------|
| 1 | Cleveland | 87.6 | 1 | 88.1 | 2 | 65.1 | 55 |
| 2 | Chicago | 85.9 | 2 | 89.9 | 1 | 66.3 | 43 |
| 3 | Philadelphia | 82.4 | 3 | 83.2 | 5 | 64.3 | 58 |
| 4 | Atlanta | 81.4 | 4 | 79.7 | 11 | 78.4 | 2 |
| 5 | Dayton | 79.3 | 5 | 81.5 | 9 | 69.0 | 24 |
| 6 | Jackson | 79.1 | 6 | 79.2 | 13 | 64.8 | 57 |
| 7 | St. Louis | 78.2 | 7 | 83.7 | 4 | 65.2 | 54 |
| 8 | Miami | 77.8 | 8 | 81.5 | 8 | 80.5 | 1 |
| 9 | St. Petersburg | 77.2 | 9 | 84.7 | 3 | 64.0 | 60 |
| 10 | Washington, D.C. | 76.7 | 10 | 76.0 | 28 | 71.3 | 13 |
| 11 | New York | 76.3 | 11 | 77.2 | 23 | 60.8 | 71 |
| 12 | Baltimore | 76.1 | 12 | 78.9 | 14 | 73.2 | 9 |
| 13 | Flint | 75.7 | 13 | 77.6 | 20 | 69.7 | 18 |
| 14 | Newark | 75.4 | 14 | 76.9 | 25 | 68.7 | 28 |
| 15 | Louisville | 75.2 | 15 | 82.8 | 6 | 69.1 | 22 |
| 16 | Pittsburgh | 74.8 | 16 | 77.7 | 19 | 68.9 | 26 |
| 17 | Fort Lauderdale | 74.3 | 17 | 78.8 | 16 | 77.8 | 4 |
| 18 | Boston | 74.0 | 18 | 77.9 | 17 | 72.0 | 11 |
| 19 | Los Angeles | 74.0 | 19 | 82.0 | 7 | 76.3 | 5 |
| 20 | Milwaukee | 73.7 | 20 | 76.6 | 26 | 66.9 | 40 |
| 21 | Omaha | 73.2 | 21 | 77.4 | 22 | 70.4 | 16 |
| 22 | Baton Rouge | 72.6 | 22 | 74.7 | 36 | 65.7 | 48 |
| 23 | Buffalo | 72.1 | 23 | 76.5 | 27 | 69.6 | 19 |
| 24 | Memphis | 71.2 | 24 | 75.9 | 29 | 73.2 | 8 |
| 25 | Shreveport | 70.7 | 25 | 75.7 | 32 | 67.3 | 37 |
| 26 | Kansas City | 70.6 | 26 | 80.3 | 10 | 64.2 | 59 |
| 27 | Toledo | 69.7 | 27 | 75.8 | 31 | 59.8 | 74 |
| 28 | Mobile | 69.3 | 28 | 77.5 | 21 | 61.0 | 70 |
| 29 | Indianapolis | 68.2 | 29 | 74.4 | 37 | 65.8 | 47 |
| 30 | Montgomery | 67.8 | 30 | 71.7 | 44 | 62.2 | 65 |
| 31 | Houston | 67.0 | 31 | 77.0 | 24 | 69.2 | 20 |
| 32 | Birmingham | 67.0 | 32 | 74.9 | 35 | 65.0 | 56 |
| 33 | Knoxville | 66.9 | 33 | 69.8 | 50 | 69.1 | 21 |
| 34 | Cincinnati | 66.6 | 34 | 72.7 | 41 | 63.3 | 62 |
| 35 | Fort Wayne | 66.5 | 35 | 71.4 | 48 | 65.6 | 50 |
| 36 | Tulsa | 65.8 | 36 | 79.6 | 12 | 59.2 | 77 |
| 37 | Denver | 65.8 | 37 | 71.4 | 46 | 70.2 | 17 |
| 38 | Seattle | 65.7 | 38 | 71.6 | 45 | 69.0 | 25 |
| 39 | Detroit | 65.1 | 39 | 67.7 | 56 | 60.0 | 73 |
| 40 | Dallas | 65.0 | 40 | 78.8 | 15 | 71.8 | 12 |
| 41 | Tampa | 64.6 | 41 | 75.1 | 34 | 67.2 | 38 |
| 42 | Nashville-Davidson | 64.5 | 42 | 71.4 | 47 | 74.3 | 6 |

| Rank | City | 1990 | | 1980 | | 1970 | |
| | | Score | Rank | Score | Rank | Score | Rank |
| --- | --- | --- | --- | --- | --- | --- | --- |
| 43 | Portland | 64.3 | 43 | 68.6 | 54 | 67.5 | 36 |
| 44 | Columbus, OH | 64.1 | 44 | 69.3 | 51 | 65.5 | 53 |
| 45 | Fort Worth | 63.6 | 45 | 77.9 | 18 | 66.9 | 39 |
| 46 | Charlotte | 63.1 | 46 | 72.9 | 40 | 73.4 | 7 |
| 47 | Grand Rapids | 63.1 | 47 | 68.6 | 55 | 68.8 | 27 |
| 48 | Syracuse | 62.9 | 48 | 66.2 | 61 | 56.3 | 85 |
| 49 | Akron | 62.9 | 49 | 69.1 | 53 | 59.8 | 75 |
| 50 | Amarillo | 62.8 | 50 | 75.9 | 30 | 57.5 | 81 |
| 51 | Wichita | 62.7 | 51 | 73.9 | 38 | 62.4 | 64 |
| 52 | Columbus, GA | 62.5 | 52 | 61.0 | 78 | 58.0 | 80 |
| 53 | New Orleans | 62.2 | 53 | 64.4 | 67 | 61.1 | 68 |
| 54 | Richmond | 61.9 | 54 | 69.2 | 52 | 71.1 | 15 |
| 55 | Chattanooga | 61.7 | 55 | 64.9 | 66 | 68.4 | 29 |
| 56 | Oklahoma City | 60.7 | 56 | 75.3 | 33 | 57.2 | 83 |
| 57 | Greensboro | 60.6 | 57 | 70.9 | 49 | 66.1 | 44 |
| 58 | Des Moines | 60.4 | 58 | 65.5 | 63 | 65.9 | 45 |
| 59 | Jersey City | 60.3 | 59 | 66.7 | 59 | 62.9 | 63 |
| 60 | Lubbock | 60.1 | 60 | 73.1 | 39 | 53.2 | 88 |
| 61 | Jacksonville | 60.0 | 61 | 72.1 | 42 | 71.2 | 14 |
| 62 | Little Rock | 59.4 | 62 | 67.2 | 58 | 67.6 | 35 |
| 63 | San Diego | 58.9 | 63 | 63.2 | 71 | 66.8 | 41 |
| 64 | Providence | 58.7 | 64 | 63.0 | 72 | 54.2 | 87 |
| 65 | Rochester | 58.0 | 65 | 62.7 | 73 | 65.6 | 51 |
| 66 | San Francisco | 57.5 | 66 | 62.0 | 77 | 66.5 | 42 |
| 67 | Gary | 57.3 | 67 | 64.0 | 69 | 68.1 | 32 |
| 68 | Norfolk | 57.2 | 68 | 71.9 | 43 | 63.4 | 61 |
| 69 | Minneapolis | 57.1 | 69 | 62.1 | 76 | 59.0 | 79 |
| 70 | Lexington-Fayette | 56.4 | 70 | 66.6 | 60 | 68.1 | 31 |
| 71 | Austin | 55.7 | 71 | 64.1 | 68 | 69.1 | 23 |
| 72 | Springfield, MA | 55.3 | 72 | 63.7 | 70 | 65.7 | 49 |
| 73 | Raleigh | 55.1 | 73 | 65.4 | 64 | 67.7 | 34 |
| 74 | San Antonio | 54.2 | 74 | 65.4 | 65 | 68.0 | 33 |
| 75 | Oakland | 54.1 | 75 | 56.7 | 81 | 61.3 | 67 |
| 76 | Phoenix | 51.5 | 76 | 62.5 | 74 | 60.5 | 72 |
| 76 | Phoenix | 51.5 | 76 | 62.5 | 74 | 60.5 | 72 |
| 77 | St. Paul | 51.1 | 77 | 67.5 | 57 | 65.6 | 52 |
| 78 | Long Beach | 50.6 | 78 | 60.3 | 80 | 68.2 | 30 |
| 79 | Las Vegas | 48.7 | 79 | 65.5 | 62 | 78.3 | 3 |
| 80 | Fresno | 47.8 | 80 | 62.3 | 75 | 72.6 | 10 |
| 81 | Corpus Christi | 46.9 | 81 | 60.7 | 79 | 61.1 | 69 |
| 82 | Honolulu | 46.5 | 82 | 48.6 | 85 | 39.5 | 98 |
| 83 | Colorado Springs | 44.2 | 83 | 44.1 | 91 | 55.3 | 86 |
| 84 | Lincoln | 43.4 | 84 | 47.6 | 87 | 47.7 | 92 |
| 85 | Sacramento | 43.2 | 85 | 52.9 | 83 | 59.1 | 78 |

| Rank | City | 1990 Score | 1990 Rank | 1980 Score | 1980 Rank | 1970 Score | 1970 Rank |
|------|------|------------|-----------|------------|-----------|------------|-----------|
| 86 | Salt Lake City | 42.7 | 86 | 45.1 | 89 | 42.9 | 96 |
| 87 | Worcester | 41.4 | 87 | 48.7 | 84 | 51.9 | 89 |
| 88 | El Paso | 41.1 | 88 | 37.9 | 95 | 44.6 | 95 |
| 89 | Stockton | 38.6 | 89 | 56.7 | 82 | 65.8 | 46 |
| 90 | Spokane | 38.5 | 90 | 37.8 | 97 | 48.0 | 90 |
| 91 | San Jose | 37.0 | 91 | 45.3 | 88 | 45.7 | 94 |
| 92 | Tacoma | 37.0 | 92 | 44.2 | 90 | 56.9 | 84 |
| 93 | Madison | 35.7 | 93 | 34.3 | 99 | 41.4 | 97 |
| 94 | Anchorage | 35.1 | 94 | 37.9 | 96 | na | 100 |
| 95 | Albuquerque | 34.1 | 95 | 40.4 | 93 | 47.9 | 91 |
| 96 | Tucson | 33.2 | 96 | 48.4 | 86 | 59.5 | 76 |
| 97 | Riverside | 30.5 | 97 | 39.2 | 94 | 62.1 | 66 |
| 98 | Santa Ana | 29.8 | 98 | 41.1 | 92 | 57.3 | 82 |
| 99 | Virginia Beach | 29.4 | 99 | 33.3 | 100 | 36.2 | 99 |
| 100 | Anaheim | 22.8 | 100 | 36.1 | 98 | 46.1 | 93 |

*Sources: 1990 Census of Population,* Summary Tape File 3A; *1980 Census of Population,* Summary Tape File 3A; *1970 Census of Population,* Fourth Count machine-readable file.

# 5

## Stopping the Hemorrhaging: Human Problems at a Crisis Point

### KNEELAND YOUNGBLOOD

It must be remembered that there is nothing more difficult to plan, more doubtful of success, nor more dangerous to manage than the creation of a new system. For the initiator has the enmity of all who would profit by the preservation of the old institution and merely lukewarm defenders in those who would gain by the new ones.—Machiavelli

As a physician specialist in emergency medicine, my view of urban problems in America is a very personal one. In my ten years of clinical practice, the emergency department has served as a microscope through which to examine and treat various illnesses and injuries affecting a cross-section of the American public. The emergency department also has served as a great laboratory to evaluate

KNEELAND YOUNGBLOOD is a practicing emergency medicine physician at HCA Medical Center-Plano and a clinical instructor at Parkland Memorial Hospital, the University of Texas Southwestern Medical Center in Dallas. Dr. Youngblood is a trustee of the Democratic National Committee, was appointed by Texas Governor Ann Richards in 1991 to the Task Force on Revenue, and serves as a member of the Health Professions Review Committee advising the President's Health Policy Task Force headed by Hillary Rodham Clinton.

larger issues affecting the cities and the nation and the extensive challenges that confront our country. While the degree and volume of problems are larger in urban settings, the extent of various maladies affecting American society is pervasive. Each setting, be it urban, suburban, or rural, has its own unique challenges. While often these problems are characterized as "health care" or "urban" issues, in fact, they are broader social, economic, and educational issues that confront our entire society. Thus solutions will have to occur not just from the health care or urban perspective, but from broader national economic and social policies.

This chapter will cite examples of patients I have cared for personally. The purpose in reciting these cases is to put a human face on the statistics we often see and hear in the news. While the incidents I describe have all taken place in a hospital setting, they represent much more than medical or clinical problems. This chapter will document with each case the failure of specific national policy issues such as economic development, substance abuse, education, health care delivery, and human values. There will be a policy discussion of each of the subjects and some recommendations, followed by three cases that reflect positively on American society and its efforts.

## The Need for Health Care
## Reform and Universal Coverage

Health of mind and body is so fundamental to the good life that, if we believe men have any rights at all as human beings, they have an absolute right to such a measure of good health as society, and society alone is able to give them.—Aristotle

A prominent physician in the community, he was a friend and colleague. He had the time bomb of cystic fibrosis ticking away at his life and his life's accomplishments. He lived a remarkable life by any measure. He was forty-three, still living and functioning productively as a physician, caring for others much less ill, when he knew it was time. He didn't think it would happen this way. He always expected to go out alone, quickly and in a blaze of glory. Yet he found happiness later in his life with a woman and her two sons, and married her. He provided well for his new family but now he knew this would end soon. His only healthwise hope was a lung transplant. To obtain it required that he quit his job, move to North Carolina (where the best cystic fibrosis care was being given) and wait with beeper for "the call." Lung transplants are an experimental treatment, therefore not covered by medical insurance. Furthermore, this was a pre-existing illness and wouldn't be insured anyway. Consequently, the procedure would require $200,000 cash up front. How about disability insurance? He had some, but this was a pre-existing illness, so not much could be obtained. Any chance to cash in on life insurance? Hardly, but he managed to secure a small amount through a policy loophole.

Thus he waits, a product and victim of the system. As knowledgeable about the illness that confronts him as any of his doctors, nurses, and health professionals, he is a victim of the system that will cause him to mortgage his and his family's financial future, possibly forever.

Failure to provide universal health care for our citizens, experimental or not, has meant that patients must choose between economic health and physical and mental health. Rising from $41.6 billion in 1965 to $808.5 billion in 1992, national health care spending has increased from 5.9 percent of gross national product (GNP) in 1965 to 13.4 percent in 1992. Moreover, by the year 2000 health care expenditures in the United States could increase to as much as $1.6 trillion, or 16 percent of GNP, according to the Department of Health and Human Services.

Despite spending more on health care than on all of education, defense, prisons, farm subsidies, food stamps, and foreign aid, approximately 35 million Americans still lack basic health insurance coverage. While these 35 million Americans lack health coverage, they do receive health care. The problem is that they can be and very likely will be financially devastated because they do not have health insurance. In addition, because they may not be able to afford health services, the cost for the rest of the American public goes up as hospitals, physicians, and other entities try to recoup the cost of this uncompensated care.

Multiple health care reform initiatives have been advocated by various groups and institutions including President Clinton, members of Congress, and various private sector groups. Critical to the success of any initiative will be the inclusion of all significant parties, hospitals, physicians, federal and state government representatives, nurses, dentists, auxiliary health care personnel, and patient advocate groups. A milestone has been reached among these groups already in that each recognizes that current trends cannot continue without bankrupting our country, economically and spiritually.

There is general consensus on three issues. First, the United States should have universal health care for all of its citizens. Second, there needs to be better access to health care. Third, the cost of health care needs to be made more affordable. The problem occurs in deciding how best to accomplish these three objectives.

Regardless of the plan adopted, there are some fundamental elements that should be included in it. These elements should include retaining the private nature of the U.S. health care system. Anyone who has been at a Veterans Administration hospital, controlled by the federal government, will understand why the federal government should not run the health care system. It is bureaucratized and inefficient, and does not deliver the best, most cost-effective care. The system should have universal coverage, some degree of consumer choice, insurance and tax reform, tremendous consumer and patient education about the health care system with realistic expectations, and finally, malpractice reform. The United States needs meaningful reform of the health care system, while at the same time retaining its unique and positive American character. The American public must come to understand that health care reform will affect everyone's life. The attitude that Americans support health care reform except when they are ill and then everything must be done on their behalf, regardless of cost, must change. Health care reform will require personal sacrifices on everyone's part, but the nation as a whole will be better off.

## The Challenge of Economic Development

The society which scorns excellence in plumbing because plumbing is a humble activity and tolerates shabbiness in philosophy because it is an exalted activity will neither have good plumbing nor good philosophy. Neither its pipes nor its theories will hold water.—John Gardner

As I explained to Mr. Johnson that his wife could be having early signs of a heart attack and needed hospitalization, he was immediately stricken with fear. He lost all color in his face and then slowly regained his composure. First he wanted to know if she already had suffered a heart attack. No, I explained, but we needed to hospitalize her to try to prevent that from occurring. He looked at her and then at me and said no, she's not going to be hospitalized. Initially I thought, what a cruel, unloving man. Yet as I looked at the two of them gaze into each other's eyes, I knew there was love, pure and simple. I was confused and angry as to how he could jeopardize his wife's health and well-being. With tears in his eyes, he spoke to me and explained how he and his wife had been married forty-seven years, that he loved her more than he loved himself, but they could not afford for her to be hospitalized. They had no health insurance, and everything they had worked for together would be wiped out.

He had worked at a large construction firm for many years and had received health insurance through his employer, but with the downturn in the Texas economy after the oil boom years, he had been laid off. Though he continued to work as an independent contractor, he did not qualify for nor did he want any government assistance (i.e., Medicaid), yet he did not earn enough money to pay for private health insurance. He stated that he simply could not afford for his wife to be hospitalized. After considerable convincing by me, he eventually agreed for her to be hospitalized, but for one day, and one day only.

While this case study further reinforces the need for universal health care, it more fundamentally illustrates the need for greater economic development. Economic development at its most basic level is a decent job. Every job should mean at least the ability to provide for one's self and one's family the basic needs of sustenance: food, shelter, and clothing. The government's role is not to guarantee a living to each individual, but to help generate opportunities to make a good living for all those who choose to do so. As a nation, we have failed in this regard. Too many of our citizens have unsuccessfully sought to better themselves and have been denied because of lack of opportunity. It should be the role of the federal government directly, or indirectly through the private sector, to emphasize not only full employment as one of its fundamental missions, but jobs that allow everyone to provide well for one's self and one's family.

The U.S. government has thus far failed to provide adequate job training and retraining to mitigate the adverse effects of a dynamic and global economy. Job losses to the Pacific Rim or Mexico have left laid off workers in certain business sectors with no alternative skills and therefore no ability to care for themselves and their family. The proposed North American Free Trade Agreement (NAFTA), with its tremendous opportunities to make the United States and the North American continent more globally competitive, will be a miserable failure in the United States if our business and government leaders do not adequately address and prepare the U.S. workforce with greater job training and retraining to mitigate the negative impacts of the agreement.

The current state of research and development further illustrates an essential component of economic development and America's responsibilities in this area. Research and development on a public and private level have been essential to define new technologies, be they in defense, biotechnology, telecommunications, information technology, or other new products and processes. As a consequence of new technologies, industries have blossomed employing both highly paid professionals and technicians and low-skilled wage earners.

While America used to lead the world in research and development, that is no longer the case. According to Lester Thurow:

Today American non-defense R&D [research and development] spending is lower than it was twenty years ago, while the Germans and Japanese have upped the intensity of their effort. Total R&D spending (defense plus non-defense) matches that of Germany and Japan, but non-defense spending has been flat at 1.8% of the GNP, for most of a decade, while German and Japanese spending is rising and now stands at 2.6 and 2.8% of the GNP respectively. Looking at total R&D spending as a fraction of the GNP, America holds the fifth position, Japan the third, Germany the fourth. First place is held by Sweden. If military spending is subtracted and only civilian spending is included, America slips to tenth in R&D spending. If all government spending is subtracted and only civilian spending remains, America was almost at the bottom, ranking twentieth out of twenty-three industrial countries. Unless one believes that Americans are smarter than Germany or the Japanese, today's spending levels will eventually lead to a secondary position for American science and engineering and lower rates of growth in productivity.[1]

Thus failure to reinvest in America through research and development both in the public and private sector has contributed to our declining economic prospects. This poor economic outlook is especially harmful to urban America because the cities have been America's manufacturing headquarters—the places where new industries were born and blossomed.

Finally, the financial future of the United States will depend largely on the success or failure of its nonwhite population. By the year 2000, nonwhites will make up the majority of the U.S. workforce. Failure to recognize, invest in, and promote this group has led and will continue to lead to further economic decline. This workforce is in a sad state of affairs. The New York City unemployment rate for African-Americans was 14.3 percent in August 1992, compared with an overall rate of 7.6 percent. The rate for whites was 6.6 percent. The rate for African-American teenagers during the summertime was 36.9 percent compared with 16.9 percent for white

STOPPING THE HEMORRHAGING

teenagers. According to the the *New York Times*,[2] a study by the Sentencing Project, a Washington based group that promotes sentencing reforms and alternatives, reported that nationwide on any given day almost one in four African-American men between the ages of twenty and twenty-nine is either in prison or jail or on parole or probation. The figure for white non-Latino men of the same age was one in sixteen, or 6.2 percent. The rate for Latino men was 10.4 percent, or one in ten.

The most visible impact of economic development failure is seen in the ghettos of our nation's major metropolitan areas. The deterioration of our urban centers has been multifactorial. Forced integration such as school busing was an important impetus to white flight from central cities to the suburbs. In pursuit of this migrating suburban labor and consumer market, many companies also left the cities, cutting business volume, trimming jobs, and decreasing the urban tax base. This cumulative effect resulted in declining urban schools, job opportunities, and city services, making cities less attractive for business to reverse the economic decline. Further, big cities tended to create legislation that was perceived as antibusiness while the suburbs got federal and state incentives that made them more attractive areas to relocate.

The point is that to the extent nonwhites fail, white America will succeed less. Our destinies are inextricably linked. Consequently, we must have an ongoing honest dialogue of constructive criticism to better one another. Each of our communities has its respective strengths and weaknesses. We must begin by acknowledging and not exploiting these differences, and then pursue the sometimes painful task of redirecting our communities' attitudes and actions. This honest and continuing dialogue can improve national economic development policy as federal government leaders better understand how and why America's diversity is a strength rather than a weakness, and can frame new policies accordingly.

## Social Values and the
## Battle against Drug Abuse

Success is to be measured not so much by the position that one has reached in life as by the obstacles which one has overcome while trying to succeed.—Booker T. Washington

As I spoke to the nineteen-year-old mother of three, my years in the emergency department made the patient a quick study even before speaking to her. She was 5'5", medium build, African-American, with a disheveled appearance, in need of a hairdo, or at least her hair combed. She probably was on welfare, unemployed, and single. She was looking for free medical advice on her lower abdominal pain. My first assumption was probably another pregnancy. A quick and knowing glance from the nurse revealed that she shared my cynical view of the situation.

As I took the medical history, I found that indeed my patient was a mother of three, on welfare, and unemployed. But to my surprise, she was also in school trying to complete her GED. I had to ask, perhaps in a judgmental tone, why she had quit school. She responded that she was unable to care for her kids, husband, and household while going to school. She could not afford to have someone else care for them either. I could not help but wonder where her husband was now and why she married at such a young age. I asked her about it. "We have separated," she told me, "and I got married at such a young age because my mother gave me to him." Excuse me? Excuse me? Her mother, whom she didn't like to talk about, had and still has a chronic, severe drug habit, and when she was twelve, her mother gave her to the man who became her husband in a drug deal.

One day she was out on the playground, jumping rope with her friends like everybody else, and then one night she awoke and a man was in her bed. She had never been with a man before and didn't know him. But he was eighteen and had bargained for her in exchange for giving her mother drugs. She left with him the next morning and became his property. They gradually got to know each other and eventually he quit dealing drugs. They got married and subsequently had three kids. He was good to her, but now they were separated. She wasn't sure if they would get back together again, but she was determined to try to make it on her own. She not only had her three kids, but two of her younger brothers, whom her mother had abandoned, lived with her, and she was trying to care for them also. Fortunately, her medical problem was not serious. Later, as the nurse and I reflected on our initial attitude and presumptions about this woman, which had proved to be incorrect, we were both embarrassed and sad. It was difficult to comprehend that someone so young could have had such a terrible experience. We were humbled by this person who had a very different life experience from our own. One could not but admire this woman for her efforts to improve her life circumstances—circumstances with which we would not have fared nearly as well.

Drug abuse has had a devastating impact on the values of our nation. There is no greater love than the love between a mother and her child. Yet drugs have helped destroy this natural and seemingly unshakable bond.

Drug abuse represents a cancer that is seriously harming American society. While it may have begun in urban America, it has now invaded America's suburbs as well as its rural areas. Largely ignored initially because it affected the "other America"—urban African-Americans and Latinos—the drug issue now has permeated all levels of American society. The flourishing drug trade has found its home in the United States for many reasons, but singularly, I believe the most important factor responsible for this scourge is the decline of moral values. While politics has exploited the word "values," there is still a legitimate place for discussion and new initiatives in this arena. Essentially, a failure of the sense of shared community responsibility is at the heart of the debate about values.

Crime is the most obvious manifestation of the loss of values and the declining sense of shared community responsibility. Between 1958 and 1973 the prison population of the United States remained almost constant at approximately 200,000. However, from 1974 to 1979 the prison population expanded to 300,000. In 1982 it reached 400,000, and by 1990 the population had exploded to 755,425. Multiple factors are responsible for this dramatic increase, including the imposition of longer sentences and the decrease in parole releases, but ultimately the major reason for this rapid rise in the prison population is the increase in crime itself. Further, while the percentage increase in crime from 1960 to 1980 was a staggering 296 percent, the increase in *violent* crime during the same period was a colossal 367 percent.

Nevertheless, passing more laws, imposing stiffer sentences, and revoking bail will not solve our country's problems of community security and responsibility. These measures in varying degrees are important for a well-ordered society and the restoration of confidence in America's criminal justice system. Further, crime prevention and strict punishment must be maintained and strengthened. Yet anticrime initiatives do not address the underlying condition that results in drug problems. For example, upfront spending commensurate with the urgent need for prenatal care for teenage and poor mothers will produce healthier infants who can then start with the necessary tools to compete effectively in their school classrooms. Similarly, programs to reduce school dropout rates produce enormous savings in lowered welfare and law enforcement costs. The

Austin Project in Austin, Texas, embodies the concept of early intervention for youth opportunities. It is a multidisciplinary approach to solving the urban problems facing the city using both public and private sector leadership to agree on specific challenges the city faces and on methods to accomplish the goals. According to a *New York Times* interview, project director Walt Rostow relates that the fundamental goal of the project is "to see how you create an operational unit out of a community."[3] The hope is by getting the different public and private sector agencies to focus on a particular project, there will be a reduction in duplication and costs. Most importantly, according to the *Times,* it is his belief that "a common purpose greatly multiplies ingenuity and commitment."

America has long held the correct principle of separating church and state. Nevertheless, I believe the nation's leaders should embody and morally anchor the country in terms of helping people understand right from wrong, truth from falsehood, the importance and necessity of hard work with head or hand versus laziness, discipline versus immediate gratification, merit versus who you know, and inclusion versus exclusion. While the federal government cannot and should not dictate morality, it should lead by example and set the tone for what its citizens should be about and the consequences of one's actions, good or bad. Our nation has failed in this regard, and as a consequence many young people especially lack a moral compass to decide right from wrong.

Drugs are simply a manifestation of this underlying moral cancer. As a step toward reestablishing a sense of shared community responsibility, I think it is important to incorporate in the daily education of our children the issue of ethics. While there have been changes in American family structures that have made moral education more difficult to transmit, truth and justice should remain essential fabrics of understanding among all of our citizenry. Certainly one should learn these issues in the context of one's family circumstances, but I feel the nation has a vested interest in making sure that all of its young citizens are exposed early and throughout their public or private schooling. Inclusion of ethics topics in educational curricula will hopefully reinforce philosophies already established. However, ethics instruction may also be an opportunity to expose those less fortunate to expectations. For example, everyone should be taught that regardless of their fortunate or unfortunate circumstances in life, society will hold them accountable for their actions.

## The Fundamental Importance
## of a Good Education

The only method of education is experiment, and its only criterion is freedom.—Tolstoy

As the twenty-nine-year-old woman rushed her fourteen-year-old daughter into the emergency department, you could see the look of frustration and exasperation on her face. The girl had been complaining all night about her back hurting and wouldn't let anyone else sleep as a consequence of her discomfort. Unkempt in appearance, mother and daughter both looked rather aged beyond their years. The mother had quit high school after getting pregnant in the tenth grade. She didn't bother to get married; it was not even an option for her. The fourteen-year-old girl was her first child, and while she had three others including a six-month-old, the mother was like a child herself in many ways.

Inarticulate and unable to express themselves well, both mother and daughter were silent in their effort to communicate the problem. It just hurts. It just hurts. What does it hurt like? It hurts like a pain. Where does it hurt? It hurts in my back. In your lower back or your upper back? Just all over. The overweight, pimply faced redhead was increasingly more difficult to talk to as her pain became more intense. Without understanding exactly what I was treating, I began a general evaluation and screening of the patient. Evaluation of her back did not reveal any particular pathology. Examination of her abdomen, however, showed intense, frequent contractions. In attempting to question the patient about her menstrual history, she was unsure what that all meant. As she screamed in pain, I looked below and was shocked to see a head emerging. A delivery tray was made available, and the delivery of a 7 lb. 8 oz. redheaded boy was swift and without incident. In all of the excitement, the girl and her mother only knew she was in pain. They had no idea that she was pregnant and about to deliver. The mother noted she was getting a bit overweight, but never thought about the possibility of her being pregnant. Moreover, the girl was so ignorant of her own bodily functions, she never understood the changes she was going through during the course of her pregnancy. Now I was facing a twenty-nine-year-old grandmother, a fourteen-year-old mother, and a newborn child who stands little chance of getting out of this perpetual cycle of ignorance and poverty.

This case underscores the importance of education. Education is that precious asset that gives people hope because we can see greater possibilities than our immediate situation. Education allows us to be able to communicate to others a new and different vision of the world. It allows us to change ourselves and the world around us. Without it we are limited in our scope of thinking and are much more likely to miss new lights of opportunity and hope. The United States has failed, in this regard, to provide each child and young adult the fundamental education necessary to succeed in the larger, real world. We cannot force someone to learn. However, we can make education a national priority and challenge children and young people to learn. It is the lack of education that creates the cycles of poverty and welfare that permeate much of America's inner city neighborhoods. The welfare mentality of an expected and perpetual handout has bred a cycle of dependency and nonexpectation that has crippled millions of Americans. We must educate our youth and provide adequate training and jobs as well as child care to prevent this cycle of dependency.

The cities and the nation must develop strategic alliances to complement and achieve educational excellence not only in college bound students, but non–college bound and secondary school students. According to Lester Thurow:

The United States is unique among industrial countries in that it does not have an organized post-secondary education system for the non–college bound. Relative to their respective sizes, for every dollar in taxpayer money invested in education for the non–college bound, $55 is spent subsidizing those going to college—a ratio that is neither fair nor efficient. Other national governments invest heavily in the post-secondary skills of the non–college bound. Britain, France and Spain spend more than twice as much as the United States; Germany more than three times as much; and Sweden almost six times as much.[4]

These educational programs should not only be alternative opportunities for poor and minority students but should be comprehensive in scope. The programs should encourage all non–college bound students to participate and to seriously and actively acquire skills and training, enabling them to compete for well-paying and relatively secure positions in U.S. industries. It is important that this non-college track be perceived as a successful alternative, not a poor second choice for these students. If it is perceived as a successful alternative, it can invigorate the U.S. workforce with confident, trained personnel who do not require as much on-the-job training, because they will be prepared to do the job immediately.

My purpose in reciting these specific clinical cases is first to document the decline of American values and the sense of shared community responsibility. A second purpose is to introduce some of the people who have been negatively affected by the lack of sufficient economic development in the United States. Finally, a third purpose is to underscore the importance and impact of poor education, as well as the necessity for health care reform. Can the federal government play a role in helping with these issues? I firmly believe that it can and must. While some people may be able to succeed on their own, I believe a majority will need assistance in some form or fashion. Nevertheless, it is important to recognize that people make the difference. Ultimately, it takes personal initiative, desire, and drive to succeed. We must give each citizen the understanding that with their individual tools, desire, and hard work, they have the opportunity to succeed in our society.

I began this chapter with personal examples of the emerging character of human crisis that confronts cities today. As emergency department physicians, we examine patients with a variety of illnesses and injuries. However, we also see a larger America, which allows us to evaluate the maladies that affect the country as a whole. Although we medically treat the patients, a greater therapy is required to heal the nation.

## A Helping Hand and a Commitment to Change

In this we have one great consolation: that the more difficult the conflict, the more glorious the triumph.—Thomas Paine

The twenty-two-year-old muscle-bound young man was anxious to get out of the emergency department. He had been brought in by his girlfriend, at her insistence, and did not want to be there. She had brought him in because he had been complaining about chest pain over the past few days but refused to seek any medical attention for his condition. She was concerned about him, because in addition to his chest pain, he had become increasingly hostile. Upon assessing the patient, I noted his blood pressure and heart rate were quite elevated. He was anxious and somewhat combative but was cooperative enough to eventually complete the medical history and examination. Significant in the patient's evaluation was a history of steroid abuse. He had been taking anabolic steroids off and on for the past few years, beginning in high school in an attempt to do better as a varsity athlete. He continued to abuse anabolic steroids intermittently over the course of the past few years, and now it was beginning to affect his physical and mental health.

The young man's skin was slightly jaundiced from the impact of the steroids on his liver. Laboratory studies further revealed in addition to his liver insufficiency, he also had begun to have kidney failure. The patient was beginning to have multisystem failure because of his steroid abuse, but unfortunately, he was in no mood to hear of his condition. His girlfriend and I begged and pleaded for him to recognize his condition and permit hospitalization to try to reverse his illness. He was verbally abusive and at times taunting in defiance of his condition.

Eventually, however, he agreed to be hospitalized for at least one night. One night turned into two days, which turned into a week, which turned into who knows how many days, as I lost track of his case. A year later, however, on two occasions I received messages that someone had been trying to reach me through the emergency department and finally, on the third day, he found me. Less muscular than before, he generally appeared to be in good health. He was very, very gracious and thankful for my convincing him to come into the hospital. He had turned around his physical health as well as his life. He had accepted God, and given up his substance abuse. He had come to say thank you and asked for my forgiveness for initially acting so hostile toward me. Of course, I forgave him for his actions and explained that they were not unexpected given his condition. I was only grateful that he was fully rehabilitated.

This patient wanted and needed help, even though at the time he did not recognize it. Because of the efforts of others, he was made aware of his severe condition, but also was given the tools and assistance with hospitalization to physically and mentally recover his health. Many people in poverty also want and need help, though they don't always recognize it. It sometimes takes society to forcefully intervene with policies and initiatives that challenge people to recognize their deficiencies. Concurrently, we must provide structure and assistance that allow people to turn their lives around and be responsible citizens.

Often, people in poor circumstances don't know the answers, and don't know that they don't know the answers. Further, they may not even know the right questions to ask. We as a nation must effectively provide the tools through social service mechanisms that assist, cajole, educate, challenge, and give sufficient incentives for people to be the best they can be. Just as the hospital is a refuge to care for illness, so should the social service network be a refuge to assist people with their needs. Further, it should return them to the larger society healthier because of the experience, and more motivated to be contributing members of society. This case of steroid abuse and full recovery represents hope, hope that with society's help, medical and otherwise, individuals will be able to make the right choices about their own personal condition and be given a second chance to turn their lives around.

## Hope, Spirit, and Technology

Concern for man himself and his fate must always form the chief interest of all technical endeavor; never forget this in the midst of your diagrams and equations.—Albert Einstein

As the thirty-five-year-old woman came into the emergency department, she looked very well. She was three weeks postpartum, having delivered a healthy 6 lb. 8 oz. little girl without any attendant complications. However, over the past couple of days, she felt a little short of breath and not up to her usual level of stamina. She had some vague chest discomfort, but no true pain.

She was immediately hooked up to the cardiac monitor, which revealed no evidence of any abnormality. My colleague initially assessed the patient and ordered the appropriate studies to further evaluate her condition. While these tests were pending, the patient requested to go to the restroom. After checking her vital signs, the nurse detached the patient from the monitor. The patient walked a few feet and then suddenly collapsed on the floor. She was immediately taken into the major cardiac resuscitation room. The emergency department staff and my clinical colleague converged on the patient with lightning speed, initiating rapid cardiac resuscitation. Despite their efforts, the patient remained without pulse, blood pressure, or spontaneous breathing. The look of apprehension across the emergency department staff was profound. As the possible causes of this catastrophic event raced through my colleague's mind, he was joined by the on-call cardiologist who also tried in vain to resuscitate the patient.

After forty-five minutes, a last-resort medication called TPA was given in an effort to dissolve what might be a blood clot to the patient's lungs causing her condition. It was new and at $3,000 a dose, it was a medication that could not be given without thought. It was given, however, and within seconds the patient's cardiac function returned. She was subsequently transferred to the cardiac care unit in critical condition. Despite bleeding from every orifice because of the strong medication, over the course of the next few weeks the patient made gradual, yet remarkable improvements. Eventually, she was transferred from the intensive care unit and ultimately discharged home. The discharge was made all the more miraculous because she essentially had a full and complete recovery. She was able to hold her child in her arms again, and walk out of the hospital with her husband. While it took a few weeks to totally regain her strength, given the ordeal she had been through, she had a miraculous recovery.

Nowhere in the world would this woman have lived except in the United States. Because of the advanced technology and medicine present in the United States, we are able, unlike other parts of the world, to give first-rate and new cutting edge technology that often makes the difference between life and death. Granted, it was an expensive medication that turned her condition around, and an even more expensive hospitalization. However, she lived. As a consequence she is a productive citizen, raising a family and contributing to our society. The cost was well worth the investment.

The United States continues to lead the world in medical technology and pharmaceuticals. We should continue this effort. Granted, we must better understand, prioritize, and allocate those resources, but we should not decrease our efforts to provide the best technology and medication available.

## A Case for Welfare Reform

The important thing is this: To be able to sacrifice at any moment what we are for what we could become.—Charles DuBois

She was a frequent flyer in the emergency department. She and her children had been seen so many times for so many different ailments that we all knew her and the kids as if they worked there. Time and time again I quizzed her about her condition and the condition of her children. She was on welfare, not working, and not looking for work. They had no doctor, so they used the emergency department as their family practice office. This got to be old. The staff was tired of caring for her and her children for routine medical care.

On occasion, she would be involved in a fight with her boyfriend or other friends, but she continued to go back to the same environment with the same attitude of nonachievement and failure. We talked again and again on her numerous visits about the condition of her life and how she could change it. The lectures appeared to fall on deaf ears for she seemed never to want to improve herself or her family's situation.

One day, however, I did notice that she hadn't visited the emergency department in some time. Then, several months later, she came into the emergency department, but she came in bringing a friend who needed help. She was dressed in a fast food uniform and was elated to tell me that she had gotten a job and had found a relative to take care of her kids. We were both happy about her progress. She came in several months later and told me that she had become a nurse's aid and was working at one of the local nursing homes. She also related that she now had medical insurance, had found herself a private physician, and that she and her family were doing much better. She stated that she just got tired of being a loser and being around losers. She was much happier than I had ever seen her before, and it was nice to see that she appreciated how different her life could and should be when one takes control of one's circumstances and is not simply a victim of one's circumstances.

While there will be ups and downs associated with this particular person and her family, she has at least begun to understand how to direct her life as opposed to having it directed by others. Her former sense of victimization permeates the underclass in our society. The calls for welfare reform advocated by the Clinton administration are a concrete vehicle to change the perception of hopelessness and victimization. The proposal that welfare or Aid to Families with Dependent Children (AFDC) eligibility be limited to two years for healthy individuals should be instituted. Commensurate with that, the federal government must stress job placement, and subsidize work if necessary so that individuals are financially better off working than they are on welfare. The program should also be complemented by access to affordable child care and health care in order that these parents can work and work effectively.

## Conclusion: Personal Responsibility
## and National Urban Policy

If there is no struggle, there is no progress. . . . Power concedes nothing
without demand. It never did and it never will. Find out just what any
people will quietly submit to and you have found out the exact measure of
injustice and wrong which will be imposed upon them, and these will
continue till they are resisted with either words or blows, or both. The limits
of tyrants are prescribed by the endurance of those whom they oppress.—
Frederick Douglass

Whether through economic development, education, health care
reform, welfare policy reform, or values, we must provide people
with the necessary tools and a level playing field to compete. Ultimately, we must recognize that national achievement of our goals is
predicated on personal initiative and responsibility. Those who
choose the path of personal initiative and responsibility should be
promoted and rewarded. However, for those who choose not to act
responsibly, we should not supplement and thereby encourage their
dependency. Now characterized as "tough love," my grandfather
once refused to give my father $100 to help our family avoid being
evicted from our home. My grandfather told his son: "If I give you
$100 now, you will be back in two months for $100 more." He
believed that if $100 was the only difference between my father's
success or failure, then he didn't deserve to succeed. My grandfather
stated that he (my grandfather) was a failure if he hadn't instilled
enough confidence in his son given his (my father's) education and
experience. He never gave my father the $100, but my father met the
challenge, and succeeded and we weren't evicted. Consequently, my
father encouraged all of his children to be responsible for ourselves
just as his parents had done.

The challenges we face as a nation begin with changing individual
habits. Just as government represents individual citizens, so too do
national policies reflect on urban America. Their destinies are intertwined. The decline of America's cities is an indictment of past federal policies, and their resurrection will occur only with national
leadership and citizen demands for such action. We must all work
together to achieve these important goals. Restoration of America's
preeminence in education, economic development, social values,
health care reform, and welfare reform, among others, will enable
cities to improve the human conditions that confront them today in

such challenges as homelessness, drug abuse, health problems, poverty among children, and crime. These very real human problems are at a crisis point, and we must stop the hemorrhaging.

## Notes

[1] Thurow (1992), p. 157.
[2] *New York Times,* September 13, 1992, p. 15.
[3] *New York Times,* January 31, 1993, p. 97.
[4] Thurow (1992), p. 275.

# LOCAL JURISDICTIONS, METROPOLITAN ECONOMIES, AND FISCAL REMEDIES

# 6

## Metropolitan Areas: Cities, Suburbs, and the Ties that Bind

### PETER D. SALINS

### Introduction

**M**any Americans believe that cities, as we have known them, are now an optional feature of the U.S. economic landscape. In the conventional view, late twentieth century urban life has been irreversibly altered by the technology of instant communication—of graphic as well as visual and aural messages, by the available infrastructure of high-speed travel by car and plane, and by the apparently successful decentralization of manufacturing, office, and mass retailing functions. Some argue that we no longer need the kind of

---

PETER D. SALINS is professor of urban planning at Hunter College and chair of its Department of Urban Affairs and Planning. He is also a senior fellow of the Manhattan Institute and a member of the editorial board of the Institute's quarterly publication *The City Journal.* He was formerly co-editor of the *Journal of the American Planning Association.* Among his other professional activities, he is director of the Citizens Housing and Planning Council of New York and a trustee of the Lavanburg Foundation. Dr. Salins's most recent book is *Scarcity by Design: The Legacy of New York City's Housing Policies,* written with Gerard Mildner.

geographically concentrated, dense, economic conurbation of factories, offices, and stores, surrounded by the homes of their workers, that we have come to think of as the archetypal city. At the same time the apparent problems of U.S. cities—their residential populations increasingly characterized by growing cohorts of the nation's poor, unemployed, criminal, drug-dependent, old, and sick—has made their perceived economic obsolescence something for many Americans to cheer rather than lament. In this posturban America most people can find not only their homes, but their livelihoods in the suburbs. The United States has become, according to this view, the world's first suburban nation. This is why the pleas of the mayors of the larger cities for a federal government rescue, a national "agenda for our cities," have not been acted upon. Only the occasional big-city social explosion, like that in Los Angeles in the spring of 1992, can briefly mobilize a small increment of attention, and an even smaller increment of economic assistance, while confirming in the public mind the difficult conditions in such places.

The trouble, however, with the death notices being written for the American city is that like Mark Twain's many years ago, they are exaggerated. They mistake the changing function and role of older cities for obsolescence, they fail to account for the complex patterns of contemporary urbanization, and they do not recognize how many of America's urban problems are caused more by the governmental structure of its urban regions than by any intrinsic failings of its cities.

The contemporary American city may not look very much like it did forty years ago, and may look even less like the traditional cities of Europe that have profoundly shaped the popular view of what constitutes a true city. Nevertheless, the city as an economic entity, the city as a more or less concentrated collection of businesses, homes, and institutions, interconnected by a dense and costly infrastructure of transportation, utilities, and telecommunications, is alive, well, and a permanent, indeed growing, feature of American life. All of the arguments and debates about the viability of cities really revolve around the proper definition of what constitutes a city, and where we draw its boundaries.

The fundamental confusion lies in only classifying as "cities" those municipal corporations chartered as such by their respective states. American cities can only be understood in connection with their suburbs, and the distinction between city and suburb is a false one. No U.S. city, so-called, is a freestanding entity. Every one, even New York, the nation's largest, is locked in a symbiotic relationship with

its surrounding suburban communities in an economically and socially integrated urban entity referred to by demographers and
economists, and officially sanctified by the U.S. Census Bureau, as a
*metropolitan area.*

Metropolitan areas constitute the true cities of the United States.
The places that most people think of as the nation's important cities,
municipalities such as Los Angeles, San Antonio, Baltimore, or Boston, for example, are only the *central cities* of their much larger, but
organically unified metropolitan complexes. Such other places referred to as cities, like Yonkers and Oakland, are just oversized suburbs, satellites in the metropolitan constellations of New York City
and San Francisco, respectively. In other words, all the places that
we have chosen to think of as cities, the places that are formally
incorporated as cities under the charters of their states, even places
that have hundreds of thousands or, perhaps, millions of residents,
are mere pieces of the urbanized regions where more than 80 percent of all Americans live.

At the same time, the places we think of as suburbs are not independent competitors of the cities. These eclectic groupings of urban
communities are natural extensions of the central cities, just as dependent on, and integrated into, the overall metropolitan fabric.
They may not acknowledge it, but the citizens of Winnetka and
Cicero are every bit as much Chicagoans as the residents of Chicago's near northside or the stockyards. Likewise, the people of Anaheim, Inglewood, and Beverly Hills are all members of the same city:
metropolitan Los Angeles.

The aptly designated *central* city at the heart of the typical American metropolitan complex, the place that lends its name to the entire
region, usually only accounts for a fraction of its population and jobs.
Sun Belt cities like Houston and Phoenix and the country's municipal giants, New York, Chicago, and Los Angeles, contain nearly half
their metropolitan regions' activities. At the other extreme, cities like
San Francisco and Boston barely make up a sixth of theirs. Surrounding the single municipal and service jurisdiction of every central city lies a vast array of other jurisdictions, large and small, simple
and complex, that collectively comprise "the suburbs": counties, cities, townships, villages, and school districts, as well as a variety of
specialized districts for such services as police, fire protection, water,
sewerage, education, health care, transportation, and countless others. Robert C. Wood described this phenomenon in 1961 in a book
about metropolitan New York's many local jurisdictions titled *1400*

*Governments.* Today the New York region contains many thousands of governments.

The boundaries that circumscribe and separate the nation's cities and suburbs have been drawn and maintained, for the most part, through a combination of historical accident and political calculation. But regardless of the circumstances under which it has evolved, the fact that a matrix of jurisdictions is superimposed on the organic unity of an American metropolitan area has profound and troublesome practical consequences. The jurisdictional fragmentation of our metropolitan areas, and the typical pattern of that fragmentation, have seriously distorted residential and employment markets and bedeviled decades of government attempts to implement effective "urban" policies.

Generations of political scientists and public administrators have agonized over the confusion and inefficiency engendered by the jurisdictional chaos of the suburban rings, and numerous limited reforms have been implemented to rationalize the government of some metropolitan regions. But the real problem is not the chaos of the contemporary metropolitan system; far more problematical are its underlying order and rationale. For all sectors of American society—city dwellers and suburbanites, politicians and planners, liberals and conservatives—have failed to comprehend the organic unity of metropolitan regions, and have come to accept the city-suburban distinction as real, even definitive. Thus "urban" problems are seen exclusively as problems of "the cities" (meaning, for the most part, *central* cities), and an "urban policy" is seen as something that will be mainly beneficial to "the cities." In a nation where more than half the urban population lives in "the suburbs" this perception is fatal to an informed discussion of urban problems and a sensible urban policy. Unless America's suburbanites understand that they are every bit as much passengers on the country's leaky urban boats as the people of "the cities" they will not endorse the financial or institutional measures that will improve urban life for all metropolitan residents.

In this chapter it is my intention to sketch, in greater detail, the actual nature of metropolitan economic and social dynamics, how they are affected and distorted by jurisdictional fragmentation, the problems that arise or are exacerbated by these jurisdictional patterns, and the implications for a rational and effective national urban policy.

## Natural Patterns

The organizing principle of metropolitan regions today is the same one that has caused cities to arise and flourish since prehistoric times, namely, the economic efficiency of having a great many interdependent activities, especially those whose participants must meet every day, located near enough to each other to minimize the time and money costs of their interaction. For workplaces and their workers, stores and their shoppers, businesses and their suppliers or customers to get together on a regular and reliable basis, they must be reasonably close together, or plugged into effective transport and telecommunications networks. As transport and telecommunications technology improves, the cost per unit of distance of regular interaction declines. This permits businesses and households to either reduce their travel and communication costs, or alternatively, to move farther apart.

The process of moving farther apart is called decentralization, and while U.S. metropolitan areas have been decentralizing for 100 years, there are built-in limitations to the extent of this process. Even with modern technology, transport costs remain high, both in money and time. While telecommunications is relatively cheap and getting cheaper, costs do increase with distance. But more to the point, there are limits to the ability to substitute telecommunications for travel. Most employers still want their workers to show up in person; most people still prefer to shop in person, especially in an age when shopping is as much about entertainment as the acquisition of needed goods; and most key business deals still need to be consummated in person.

Therefore, the continuing decentralization of metropolitan activities does not mean that the age-old benefits of urban concentration have disappeared, nor that the downtowns of central cities are necessarily obsolete. Above all, decentralization does not mean that households or businesses can locate anywhere at will, without regard to distance or the costs of travel. Decentralization means merely that the benefits of improved transport and telecommunications technology have mainly been taken in increased space rather than reduced costs. Rather than save money, many businesses and households have chosen, over time, to spread out, but as they do, their relative location and juxtaposition within the metropolitan area are maintained. As a result of decentralization the average metropolitan density declines, even as total regional activity increases (measured in growth of population and employment), by the addition of newly urbanized land at the perimeter of the region. Paradoxically, the decentralization process will actually increase local densities in most of the formerly urbanized portions of the region, as many suburban areas become more developed and congested. The notable exception is the metropolitan core, meaning the central areas of the central city, where the decentralization process will result in an absolute decrease in jobs and residents, and a corresponding reduction in density. Again, paradoxically, in the core of the metropolitan core, the central city's central business district (CBD), activity density may rise because the CBD hosts the growing metropolitan region's expanding command and control operations, and increasingly, the region's more sophisticated leisure attractions.

In addition to decentralization, the other critical process shaping the metropolitan area is specialization. Both household and business profiles differ markedly in different sections of any urban region. The specialization and differentiation of activities become more pronounced the closer one gets to the center of the region. The reason for this is that the closer one gets to the center, the greater are the benefits of higher accessibility and reduced travel costs. The price of centrally located land is generally higher because competing activities bid against each other to secure the most advantageous sites. But only certain kinds of businesses and households need or value central locations enough to pay the high monetary costs these sites command.

Specialization begins with the highly skewed spatial distribution of a metropolitan region's jobs. Even after a century of decentralization, two-thirds of a typical region's businesses and other employment sites will be found near its center. Even where jobs are located outside the central city, the majority will be found in clusters or strips that follow a natural pattern established by a transportation system with the central city as its hub. Within the metropolitan region's specialized economic zones there is further fine-grained specialization by industry. Each region's CBD will host a unique and specialized array of office functions, retail, service, and entertainment establishments, medical and educational institutions, and the seats of its local and regional governments. Not far away, in grimy—but still functional—industrial zones, one can find many of the region's warehouses and truck depots, power plants, and freight yards, and the remnants of high-density, inner city manufacturing. The region's remaining jobs will be scattered among a widely dispersed array of metropolitan subcenters, in dense clusters of shopping, office, institutional, or manufacturing complexes, or stretched out along arterial ribbons of commercial activity.

The existence of regional subcenters is nothing new, and the way they are spatially distributed, in a nested hierarchy, follows principles of urban economics described by land economists and geographers more than sixty years ago. What has changed is that as most U.S. metropolitan areas spread out far beyond the central city limits, more of these employment subcenters are in the suburbs, sometimes referred to as "edge cities." However, the intensity of employment, even in this highly decentralized universe, declines rapidly with distance from the regional core, a fact neatly confirmed by the pattern of lights seen from the air as one flies over any U.S metropolitan area at night.

The homes of the metropolitan region's households are as spatially specialized as its businesses. The residential heart of the larger metropolitan central cities is dominated by three kinds of dwellings and populations: (1) architecturally distinctive, expensive housing occupied by the younger and older members of the region's wealthy elite; (2) sophisticated but less luxurious housing for many of the area's not-so-affluent but well-educated young professionals; and (3) large concentrations of deteriorated housing, public developments, and private slums, settled by some of the region's poorest minority households.

The wealthy elite once dominated the housing of the core, and the elite neighborhoods of major cities like New York's Upper East Side, Philadelphia's Rittenhouse Square, or San Francisco's Nob Hill are still legendary sites of America's upper class in the popular and media imagination. Much of the elite long ago deserted the core, but a sizable proportion of its younger and older members continue to live there for the same reasons as their lifestyle cousins, the "yuppies." The elite and the "yuppies" are attracted to the core because it is the only part of the metropolitan area offering the stimulus and diversions of the traditional city. But only a handful of larger metropolitan areas like New York, Chicago, San Francisco, Boston, Philadelphia, and Washington have truly cosmopolitan cores. As part of the redevelopment of their downtowns, a growing number of medium-sized cities like Milwaukee and Baltimore have created pockets of "luxury" housing aimed at this market. In general, however, the smaller the metropolitan area, the more limited the number of homes occupied by elite and young professional households in the city center.

That leaves the poor, by far the most robust segment of the market for inner city housing. The vast majority of the poorest inner city households are recent migrants to urban America or the children of migrants. Migrants to every urban area first settle in the core because that is where the region's cheapest housing can be found, and that is where they have the easiest access to the region's largest concentration of jobs, especially jobs with limited skill demands. U.S. cities experienced two great waves of migration since World War II. In the first wave, in the 1950s and 1960s, African-Americans came to the cities looking for work, fleeing the collapsing rural economy of the South. In the second wave, in the 1970s and 1980s, immigrants from Latin America, the Caribbean, and Asia came after immigration rules were liberalized in 1968. How can the poor afford to live in the center if it is also home to many of the region's elite, and land there is supposed to be more expensive? In the non-elite areas of the metropolitan core the residential *structures* will be cheaper because they are the region's oldest and most deteriorated, and also because they have the region's densest occupancy. In other words, in the city's innermost neighborhoods many potentially expensive sites are occupied by large numbers of inexpensive dwellings. The boundary within the core between areas occupied by the elite and "yuppies" and those settled by the poor is often very unstable. Obviously, many deteriorated former homes of the affluent fall to the poor. But also, in a reversal of this process, many homes of the poor are reclaimed by the affluent in cities where the ranks of young professionals have swelled, and the architectural charm lurking behind deteriorated facades has been discovered. This urban reentry of the affluent is sometimes called gentrification.

Beyond the core, residences are arrayed in circumferential zones declining in density from the edge of the CBD to the perimeter of the metropolitan region; elevator apartment buildings blending into developments of row houses and garden apartments, older homes on small lots giving way to tracts of newer houses on sites as large as an acre or more. At any given distance from the center, each zone is more or less homogeneous with respect to density and dwelling type. By the time one is five miles from almost any metropolitan downtown other than New York City's, one will be in neighborhoods comprised mainly of one- and two-family homes, on small to medium-sized lots, with a scattering of apartment houses on the major roads. At ten miles, even in New York, you will be surrounded by detached houses on larger lots, some in charming communities of traditional architecture, others in post–World War II subdivisions, with garden apartment and townhouse complexes in the suburban centers and near highways and major arterial streets.

However similar the dwellings of these concentric zones may be on the outside, they are extremely heterogeneous with respect to the socioeconomic and ethnic profile of their occupants. The socioeconomic variation is typically anchored by an axis of high-status housing that runs from the elite neighborhoods of the CBD to the region's outermost communities, interrupted at various points by natural features, nonresidential activities, and pockets of low-income minority settlements. As one travels from Beacon Hill in central Boston to suburban Weston, or from the White House to Potomac, Maryland, one will move through an attractive chain of mostly upper-income communities. A similar journey through the lower- and middle-income residential metropolitan corridors will reveal much more differentiation in housing conditions as one moves from shabby central neighborhoods, to tidy communities of modest homes in the inner suburbs, to modern homes on large properties in the outer suburbs nearly indistinguishable from their higher-income counterparts.

Somewhere, one-third to halfway across this metropolitan ocean of housing, is drawn the arbitrary line that separates the central city from the suburbs. The line may be arbitrary but it is not unimportant. As will be spelled out in greater detail, the presence of myriad governmental jurisdictions outside the central city significantly distorts the tidy land economics model of metropolitan neighborhoods differentiated only by smooth density and status gradients. Some of these jurisdictional effects are accidental, but many are the result of conscious suburban land use policies that aim to restrict development to lower-than-market densities, and impose greater-than-market levels of housing type and demographic homogeneity. Because even the central city has long adopted such policies in its high-income neighborhoods, along the elite axis the central city–suburban boundary is hardly perceptible. Suburban–central city land use policies have been most divergent along the nonelite corridors so that journeys through them will often reveal abrupt changes in housing conditions and ethnic profiles at the central city–suburban frontier.

In reviewing the natural and not-so-natural dynamics of America's metropolitan areas, the key point to remember is that central cities will always be the functional heart of U.S. metropolitan areas. They have one unique asset not possessed by any suburb or "edge city": their centrality. Decentralization notwithstanding, some metropolitan functions *must* take place in or near the center of metropolitan regions. No matter how rapid and sweeping the advances in transport and telecommunications technology yet to come, they will not eliminate the friction of distance. Central locations will always yield important transport based efficiencies, and there will always be a large number and variety of businesses and institutions that can benefit from them. As a result, a major share of the nonresidential enterprises already in the central cities will stay there, and some new ones will continue to move in.

For the same reason there will always be households that prefer or can benefit from inner metropolitan locations for their homes. As indicated, not only the poor prefer to live in the central residential precincts of the metropolitan area. Some proportion of affluent young singles and married couples will always value convenience, urban stimulation, and denser quality housing over the space and tranquility of the suburbs. Even many of the middle-aged homeowners in most metropolitan areas still value the central city's less dense outer neighborhoods for their easy access to downtown, their greater variety of local shopping, and often, their distinctive architecture.

Nevertheless, the ongoing process of decentralization will continue to reduce the total number of businesses and households in most central cities, making them less populous and less dense. These are perfectly natural developments and are not, by themselves, to be considered harbingers of central city decline. It is only because decentralization occurs in metropolitan areas characterized by governmental fragmentation and suburban indifference that it appears as such a significant urban problem.

## Central Cities and the Urban Crisis

The universally lamented urban crisis of U.S. cities really boils down to two very different dilemmas. One is the fact that all U.S. metropolitan areas have large numbers of very poor, usually disproportionately minority, households, households suffering not just from poverty, but with many attendant social problems. The other is that the natural locational forces of U.S. metropolitan areas, in combination with the effects of their jurisdictional fragmentation, conspire to keep most of these households in the central city. This degree and extent of poverty is perceived as a crisis primarily because the central cities remain, in fact, the functional hearts of all metropolitan areas. Thus because many of the social problems of the metropolitan poor are concentrated in every urban region's core, they are highly visible to the leaders and visitors of metropolitan America, and they are disruptive of the central city's image, enjoyment, and perhaps even its economic life.

The external face of these problems is revealed in a visit to any U.S. metropolitan area. For example, just outside the redeveloped central city downtown, with its new office towers, "festival markets," new museum and library additions, reclaimed waterfronts, and gentrified townhouse blocks, one finds a sea of urban squalor. Here are dozens to hundreds of blocks of deteriorated and abandoned residential structures amidst filthy and ill-maintained streets, parks, schools, and public housing developments. Behind the wretched physical facade of the area lie the troubling statistics of unemployment, family breakdown, substance abuse, crime, and welfare dependency.

The problems of urban poverty do not have municipal or metropolitan causes or cures. They are mostly caused by national economic and social factors that only national policies can correct. But the concentration of these problems in the neighborhoods of the central cities and some unlucky suburban municipalities, and the strain on these overstressed municipalities to fund and manage appropriate municipal responses, is primarily a product of America's *metropolitan* policies. National, state, and local policies for metropolitan areas affect the way these problems are spatially distributed, they allow most suburban communities to strategically keep them outside their own gates, and they make these problems mainly the burden and responsibility of the places where they are situated.

Under present arrangements, municipalities—cities and suburbs—must finance and manage not only the usual array of broad based local services—education, infrastructure, and public safety—but where necessary, offer critical health, housing, income assistance, and social services to their poor. The latter services are not only costly, difficult to administer, and often ineffective, but the resources they consume also make it harder for cities to provide high-quality educational and other services for the rest of the population. Because most cities, and even some suburbs, cannot limit or determine their population mix, a mix created by the metropolitan-wide spatial distribution of economic and residential activities among governmental jurisdictions, the particular profile of businesses and households that reside within their boundaries will determine whether or not the city or suburb is a desirable place to live.

The most obvious and urgent impact of having large concentrations of the poor is on the affected municipalities' *quality of life*. The term, while vague and difficult to precisely define, measures three things: the attractiveness, functional adequacy, and cleanliness of the physical environment (streets, sewers, parks, housing, and so on); the quality of local education and other ordinary municipal services; and the level of civil order (the extent of crime, graffitti, drugs, homelessness, or other real and perceived threats).

It is in the realm of quality of life that the central cities are at the greatest disadvantage relative to their suburbs. The need to provide an expensive array of social, health, and housing services for the poor keeps cities from lavishing more money and attention on education, parks, and roads. Education, to take the most critical example, consumes about half of most suburban budgets, but rarely more than a third of most central cities'. Perhaps even more importantly from the point of view of other urban residents, the social problems of the poor contribute to the cities' physical blight and civil disorder. A key symbolic measure of disorder affecting popular perceptions is crime, and the differences in crime rates between central cities and their metropolitan areas is dramatic. From Boston to Seattle, from Milwaukee to New Orleans, central city crime rates are more than twice the metropolitan average.

Because the quality of life disparities between cities and suburbs have become so great, and so widely perceived, metropolitan jurisdictional fragmentation, by creating suburban fiscal and quality-of-life sanctuaries, has profoundly distorted the natural locational choices of metropolitan households and businesses. While the economic benefits of centrality, as indicated earlier, keep many businesses and households in the central cities no matter what, a large complement of other metropolitan activities moves to the suburbs without suffering serious inconvenience or economic loss. Under these circumstances the spatial distribution of metropolitan activities no longer remains entirely "natural"—that is, determined purely by the iron logic of urban economics. Since a locality's mix of activities can spell the difference between its governmental success or failure, and the difference between affording its citizens a luxurious or squalid level of quality-of-life services, self-interest motivates each jurisdiction to bend market forces to recruit as advantageous a mix of higher-income households and businesses as they can. If localities vary not only in their populations and other intrinsic characteristics, but in the quality of their services and the taxes they levy to pay for them, then households and businesses will choose to live in the more "successful" communities. Unfortunately for the central cities and low-income suburbs, this is not a game all municipalities can successfully play.

In the real metropolitan world in which jurisdictions are pitted against each other for social, fiscal, and economic survival, the most important, and most sensitive, variable distorting locational choices, and affecting local conditions, is *race*. Race is not only highly correlated with the central city poverty that middle-income households and businesses try to escape, it is its most visible symbol. That age-old habits of class and race bias should result in class and racial segregation within the metropolitan region is not surprising, even in the absence of governmental fragmentation. But jurisdictional fragmentation has made segregation economically and socially functional for metropolitan businesses and residents. Firms and families intent on reducing contact with African-Americans and other minorities, by not merely distancing themselves from concentrations of minority settlement within cities, but actually moving to jurisdictions where they are diminished or absent, secure several distinct advantages. For starters, by moving from the large and heterogeneous central city or from an inner metropolitan satellite city to a small suburb, they are often subject to lower taxes by not having to share the costs of servicing the costly infrastructure of older business districts or the social needs of poor minority residents. Even if taxes are not lower, they make themselves eligible for local services like education and parks that are better funded because local revenues aren't used to pay for other urban functions, and are patronized primarily by middle- to upper-income whites.

Finally, perhaps most important to those who segregate themselves by local jurisdiction as well as geography, they can exercise land use regulatory powers. In most states, "home rule" has devolved zoning and subdivision regulations to incorporated municipal governments, giving suburban jurisdictions, even very small ones, the power to regulate the kinds of housing and business they will permit within their borders. This means that once middle- and high-income households manage to isolate themselves in the sanctuary of a suburb, they have the power to resist and thwart the metropolitan-wide economic and social forces that would normally make even outer communities more economically and residentially diverse.

As a result of these strategems, all U.S. metropolitan areas are intensely segregated by race. Large or small, northern or southern, with sizable minority populations or not, most of every metropolitan area's minorities, and even more of its minority poor, are concentrated in the central cities. Here is a comparison of central city and suburban minority percentages for a sample of larger metropolitan areas (central city percentage/suburban percentage): Atlanta: 69/22; Cleveland: 51/10; Detroit: 78/7; New York City: 48/18; Philadelphia: 46/13; Sacramento: 40/15; Washington, D.C.: 70/18.

The magnitude of these jurisdictional distortions is very much related to the central city's share of the metropolitan pie. The greater the central city relative to its metropolitan region, and the more it resembles the rest of the region economically and demographically, the better off it will be. That is the only reason why the sprawling cities of the Sun Belt appear to be much healthier and more vital than the apparently decaying cities of the Rust Belt. Having annexed many of their suburbs in recent decades, the municipal boundaries of Sun Belt cities encompass a much larger range of metropolitan households and businesses. There is actually far more crime and poverty in the center of metropolitan Phoenix or Dallas than there is in the center of metropolitan Cleveland or Pittsburgh, for example, but the *cities* of Phoenix or Dallas seem far less troubled, and have far fewer budgetary problems, than the *cities* of Cleveland or Pittsburgh. An exception is San Francisco, a city so small relative to its region that it comprises hardly more than the metropolitan area's "downtown." As such, it benefits from the cosmopolitan activities and high tax revenues that characterize large metropolitan cores while its limited territory doesn't extend far enough out to capture most of the poverty and costly service needs of typically larger central cities. Much of what would normally be San Francisco's poverty can be found across the bay instead, in the "satellite" city of Oakland.

## The Role of Federal and State Governments

The decentralization of metropolitan regions was made possible by advances in transport and telecommunications technology, but federal and state policies going back to the 1950s have been instrumental in accelerating and expanding the process. Federal highway construction programs have paid for the network of expressways that brought the far-flung outer reaches of suburbia within plausible commuting range of metropolitan job sites, permitting the urbanization of a metropolitan frontier far from the edge of the central city. Federal income tax rules and federal home mortgage programs brought home ownership within financial reach of millions of middle-income city residents, creating a market for new housing subdivisions at the metropolitan frontier. Federal water and sewer construction subsidies underwrote the infrastructure of newly created, or newly populated, suburban jurisdictions, and federal grants paid for the preparation of their land use and infrastructure plans. Not insignificantly, federal corporate tax rules have made it more profitable for manufacturing firms to build new plants in the suburbs than to rebuild their old ones in the central city.

As the federal government was laying the economic foundation for the sprawling, suburbanized metropolitan region, state governments devised the fiscal and jurisdictional arrangements that made sprawling metropolitanization functionally possible. Most states created metropolitan-wide, and in cases interstate, agencies to organize critical regional transportation, infrastructure, and environmental functions. All states developed programs of assistance to local governments, especially for schools, which made it possible for even the smallest jurisdictions, with little in the way of taxable commercial property, to offer a full-blown set of municipal services. Of course, as stated earlier, state laws and constitutions grant service and regulatory powers to localities in the first place.

These federal and state arrangements do not explicitly discriminate against central cities. Central city travelers use the federally financed highways; central city homeowners deduct their property tax and mortgage payments from their income taxes; and central city businesses depreciate their new and rebuilt facilities. Likewise, state aid for education and other local services is as essential in balancing the budgets of central cities as it is for those of the suburbs. The discriminatory impact of these policies lies, rather, in their subsidization of locational dynamics and governmental structures that increasingly handicaps central cities vis-à-vis their suburban neighbors. By these policies the federal government subsidizes decentralization and sprawl, and more importantly, the states subsidize the jurisdictional fragmentation that facilitates rigid patterns of segregation by class and race.

The obvious unfairness of central cities having to absorb, disproportionately, what are metropolitan-wide problems and fiscal burdens has not escaped notice. As metropolitan areas grew in population and territory in the decades after World War II and central cities appeared to be increasingly disadvantaged, a rationale was elaborated for a system of intergovernmental aid designed explicitly to address the issue.

At the federal level three formats of assistance were devised. The costly welfare and health programs for which the metropolitan poor are eligible were expanded, with their costs shared equally by the federal government and the states, but with responsibility for their management and clientele assumed by municipalities. Categorical assistance programs were instituted that addressed a wide variety of central city needs (housing, infrastructure, job training, law enforcement, compensatory education, and so on), but whose limited funds were awarded competitively, requiring applicant cities to prepare elaborate plans and justifications (and exercise some political muscle) if they hoped to receive any assistance. Among the most visible fruits of the categorical repertoire are the dramatically redeveloped cores of U.S. metropolitan areas, which have transformed the appearance, if not the economic base, of most large central city downtowns. In the early 1970s, reflecting a Nixon era notion of federal-city relations called "fiscal federalism," Congress finally launched unrestricted "revenue-sharing" and "block grant" programs that, by tying levels of aid to population and indicators of distress, more directly engaged the fiscal needs of central and satellite cities. The most generous and functionally nonspecific of these programs, "general revenue sharing," was relatively short-lived, however, being terminated in 1986. What remain are programs of functionally targeted, but relatively unrestricted, local assistance for community development, social services, and education.

Aside from picking up the nonfederal share of public assistance and health grants, most states provide substantial assistance to local communities for education, and many supplement local funding for social and health services, roads, and criminal justice. Most state programs of assistance to localities are supposed to be correlated with local need, and aim to compensate for variations in local government tax bases. Programs of federal and state intergovernmental aid were explicitly designed to offset much of the fiscal burden of the central cities and the more hard-pressed suburbs. Less explicitly, these programs, by making the fragmented distribution of resources within metropolitan regions more tolerable, have helped to facilitate the white middle class suburbanization of metropolitan regions and to maintain the concentration of low-income minorities in the central cities and the older suburban satellite cities. Thus a kind of Faustian metropolitan bargain exists between the leaders of the older cities and the residents of the expanding suburbs: the cities agree to serve increasingly as the poorhouses of the metropolitan community, as long as the suburbanites—with Washington and the state capitals acting as brokers and intermediaries—underwrite the extra costs this role imposes.

## Recasting the Destinies of Cities and Suburbs

It becomes more apparent with time that this Faustian metropolitan bargain is not viable in the long run. For one thing, the growing stringency of federal and state budgets has caused both federal and state governmental levels to renege significantly on their part of the bargain. As a result of recurrent cuts in federal and state aid, most central and satellite cities are having great difficulty balancing their budgets without Draconian reductions in local services or excessive levels of taxation. In rebellion, some cities like Bridgeport, Connecticut, have even threatened to file for bankruptcy.

But there is a more profound problem with this metropolitan compact. The cities cannot continue to play a growing and dominant role as their metropolitan regions' poorhouses if they are to survive as healthy urban communities, no matter how much intergovernmental aid they receive as compensation. If central and satellite suburban cities are populated disproportionately by poor, often minority, households, plus an aging cohort of middle-income families leavened only by a small cadre of "yuppies" near their downtowns, then the strains on their educational, social, and other municipal services, the diminution of their quality of life, and their crime, homelessness, and other problems may persuade too many of the cities' remaining successful businesses and middle-income families to decamp for more agreeable metropolitan communities in the suburbs. Even a continued resurgence of the cities' downtown cores will only partially offset the damage wrought by such a negative downward spiral. Bear in mind also that only the largest and most cosmopolitan of U.S. metropolitan areas can sustain vibrant central city cores.

Thus national and state "urban" policies should move away from the traditional concern with reimbursing disadvantaged municipalities (the "cities," for the most part) and move toward the promotion of a healthier and more economically natural integration and distribution of metropolitan regional resources and responsibilities. What does this mean in terms of specific policy objectives and concepts?

What is *not* being proposed is any form of metropolitan-wide government. A scheme of metropolitan governance is not politically viable in most regions of the United States, nor is it especially desirable. The concept would obviously be opposed most bitterly by the suburban municipalities and their legislators. But it might not be enthusiastically embraced by central city politicians and their constituencies either, because of the resulting loss of central city autonomy in situations where cities would be outnumbered by their suburban partners with respect to service needs, priorities, and the allocation of revenues. But metropolitan government also does not make much sense logistically any more. Most metropolitan areas are simply too extensive and populous to submit to any form of centralized regional decision making or management. In fact, the larger central cities, which comprise half or less of their metropolitan areas, are increasingly ungovernable from city hall. The Sun Belt cities still engage in a form of metropolitan government, as the central cities expand into the suburbs by annexation. This has been tolerated by suburbanites as the price for obtaining access to regional infrastructure systems to serve their rapidly growing populations. But even in the Sun Belt, metropolitan government may not play well in the long run.

Rather than promoting metropolitan government, federal, state, and local policies should focus on creating a level metropolitan playing field. No longer should the well-being and service capabilities of metropolitan localities, central city or suburban, be hostage to their economic, social, or demographic profiles, nor should they be harmed by the beggar-thy-neighbor scramble of their sister municipalities for regional economic advantage. The kinds of policies and concepts that might help to achieve this level playing field include the following.

(1) *Break the nexus between services to disadvantaged households and residence in a particular jurisdiction.* Programs of income and health assistance, as well as poverty and child related social services, should be funded and managed at the national or state level, their benefits available to eligible households without regard to place of residence. Making public assistance, social service, or health benefits portable, at least within states, and administering and funding them entirely at a higher-than-municipal level of government would do two things. It

would lift from local jurisdictions with the largest disadvantaged populations, especially the cities, their most onerous service and fiscal burdens. More importantly, it would permit the disadvantaged and dependent households of the cities to settle anywhere they wished within metropolitan areas. Most of these households might well prefer to stay where they are in the central or older satellite cities, but many might find cheaper homes, better jobs, or more responsive municipal services in the suburbs.

(2) *Prevent localities from using their land use and other regulatory powers to shape their population and economic base, or to secure competitive advantages over other metropolitan communities.* States should make sure that the regulations of all metropolitan localities make room for the balanced and rational growth of their regions. Municipalities have a legitimate objective in deploying regulations to protect, as the Constitution stipulates, the health and welfare of their residents. But many suburban communities go much further. When such communities reserve most of their residential districts for large houses on two-acre lots, when they ban multifamily housing or commercial activity, when they set impossible environmental standards, or prevent any new development, they go too far. At best they are motivated by a wish to secure a very beneficial quality of life at the expense of their metropolitan neighbors, or less justifiably by a wish to recruit a favorable local demographic and economic mix, and to discriminate on the basis of race and income. Either way, they are using public powers to achieve a largely private benefit. States, holding the actual constitutional powers of local land use regulation, should restrict their uses to legitimate health and welfare issues.

(3) *Assure some level of equity in local revenues.* Programs of state and federal fiscal assistance to localities should be aimed primarily at smoothing out variations in aggregate municipal revenues. As it stands, the specialization of business and household locations driven by metropolitan-wide economic and other factors creates enormous disparities in local tax bases. These disparities have been recognized, and partially compensated for, by programs of formula based functionally specific state and federal aid. It would be preferable to replace this assistance with unrestricted grants, allowing municipalities to set their own service priorities and standards.

(4) *Encourage central cities to decentralize the management and delivery of basic services.* One of the most important advantages possessed by the suburbs relative to the central cities is the manageable and responsive scale of their municipal service delivery. But this is one advan-

tage that the cities can secure for themselves by devolving to their neighborhoods the provision, and perhaps funding, of many of their locally based services such as schools, police, sanitation, and others. Many cities have wards or other submunicipal administrative districts, but they rarely have much authority, and almost never their own funds. Cities should be encouraged and assisted to design and implement plans that effect meaningful decentralization, giving their neighborhoods roughly the powers of a typical suburb.

In combination, these policy ideas, if implemented even in part, would go a long way toward mitigating some of the thorniest aspects of U.S. "urban" problems. They would address the most visible and distressing social phenomenon of the cities: poor households trapped in crumbling central city ghettos, and the attendant and extreme level of intrametropolitan racial and class segregation. They would address the fiscal distress of metropolitan cities and tax-poor suburbs. And they would help to restore a more natural, and more efficient, distribution of homes and businesses across the metropolitan landscape, as people and businesses would choose sites for their intrinsic benefits, rather than their municipal jurisdiction, and would receive the same amount and quality of governmental services, wherever they choose to settle.

# 7

## Cities' Role in the Metropolitan Economy and the Federal Structure

### CAROL O'CLÉIREACÁIN

This chapter argues that cities are the forgotten players in the American federal structure. At the core of U.S. metropolitan areas, cities play a pivotal role in the nation's private economy, but that role is not reflected in the distribution either of political power or of the fiscal resources and responsibilities of the public economy. Various ad hoc measures over the years to reform political institutions have resulted in blurred lines of accountability without elimi-

CAROL O'CLÉIREACÁIN is finance commissioner of New York City. Appointed by Mayor David N. Dinkins in January 1990, she is the second woman—and first professional economist—to hold this post. Ms. O'-Cléireacáin came to New York City at the height of the fiscal crisis in 1976, beginning thirteen years as chief economist at District Council 37, AFSCME, the city's largest union, whose pension funds rescued the city. She has taught at a number of universities and served as chief economic advisor to Rev. Jesse L. Jackson during his 1988 campaign for president and later advised the Dukakis campaign. She is on the editorial board of *Dissent*. The author wants to thank Michael Hyman for his diligent work checking the facts and Bill Thomas for his ongoing help on the issues of fiscal federalism in New York.

nating the fiscal stress and inequities faced by cities. States have proved unable to generate adequate city fiscal health. The time has come to create a permanent fiscal relationship from the federal government to cities that reflects the economic role that cities serve in the national economy.

This chapter proceeds to describe briefly the growing discontinuity between city political and legal boundaries and the functioning of the real economy. The second section critiques the fiscal inadequacy imposed on cities by America's federal-state-local divisions of authority, including Ronald Reagan's "new federalism." The third section discusses a number of possible changes in the state and federal fiscal relationship with cities. The conclusion adds the author's proposals for a more public role for mayors to secure their fiscal relationship with the national government.

## The City Political and Economic Mismatch

The Constitution created a federal system of government where responsibilities not expressly designated to the central government belong to the states, as guaranteed in the Tenth Amendment. Cities were, and continue to be, invisible in the document.

The states devolved, through home rule arrangements, responsibilities to more than 80,000 local governments—counties, cities, school districts, and so on. The division of responsibilities and the delineations of services to be provided by these local governments vary widely from state to state and even within states. In short, there is no standard definition of what constitutes a city as a public jurisdiction.

For example, in California alone, San Francisco is a coterminous county and city, with both sets of responsibilities, while Los Angeles and San Diego have overlying city and county boundaries. Chicago and Detroit are each part of larger counties; New York City is comprised of five counties. Each of these states—California, Illinois, Michigan, and New York—specifies different city and county service responsibilities, taxing authority, and budgetary arrangements.

As legal creatures of their states, cities are subject to state authority in virtually all aspects of city governance—boundaries, political structures, taxation, and the provision of services, especially education and criminal justice. City powers to tax are dependent upon delegation of state authority. About half of the states allow cities to levy some form of sales tax; only a dozen states allow city income taxes. The only significant tax considered to belong to local government is the property tax; even that is levied under state constitutional limitations and statutory controls, and is often subject to state or local referenda.

As greater flows of goods, services, people, and money have tied together the U.S. economy, fiscal arrangements among levels of governments have become both more complicated and less sensible. Originally, cities were to provide basic services to their resident population. Today, all cities provide police and fire protection and refuse collection, while many also provide education, health, welfare, and other services. The older and larger cities spend proportionately more on services to assist their growing low-income and immigrant populations. In 1989 the ten largest cities welcomed more than half of America's immigrants.

Cities house more than their share of America's poverty—43 percent. They generally experience higher rates of unemployment, crime, drug abuse, and AIDS. For example, nationally, the central city poverty rate is 18.6 percent, compared to 12.5 percent in the typical metropolitan area. The ten largest cities now account for half of the country's AIDS cases.

The real economy of U.S. central cities stretches far beyond their political boundaries as every day millions of people travel from suburban areas or beyond to work, study, and do business. In a recent survey of Americans living outside the country's largest cities, half of the households had at least one member working in the city; two-thirds depended on the city for major medical care; and four out of ten had members either attending or planning to attend a city based institution of higher education.[1] According to the National League of Cities, suburban household income and central city household income rise and fall together, and do not appear to be independent of one another.

The urban economy everywhere crosses county lines (ten, on average); in the Northeast and parts of the Midwest, crosses state lines; and in the Northwest and Southwest even crosses national borders. Further, urban economies now stretch beyond the United States. City taxpayers are increasingly foreign businesses. In New York City, for example, annual foreign investment averaged almost 4 percent of gross city product from 1985–89, resulting in foreign ownership of business worth $60 billion, while more than 7 percent of private sector employees work in foreign owned establishments, and foreign banks provide 60 percent of city bank tax revenues. The extension of the border patrol's roadblocks well into U.S. territory north along the San Diego Freeway suggests that the Southern California economy stretches from Mexico through San Diego and beyond Long Beach–Los Angeles. One immigration expert has documented a three-day response time from Guatemalan villages to changes in the low-skill job market in Houston.[2]

It is the constitutional role of state government to ensure that public services are provided, that such service provision is fair and efficient, and that crossborder inequities do not occur. Sometimes state government is uninterested in such issues; sometimes it is ill-equipped; at best, it is slow to act. Many state legislatures are dominated by a long-standing tension between city and noncity legislators, especially in states where there is one large city, such as New York, Illinois, Georgia, Massachusetts, and Michigan. Reflecting its major share of state population, New York City only musters 40 percent of the representation in the state legislature, not enough to carry the day on its behalf, but far greater than other big cities such as Chicago or Detroit.

Suburban legislators generally reflect the higher incomes of their voters, many of whom left the city in search of a lower tax burden and a different mix of public services and neighbors. Suburban voters and their elected representatives do not often see their interests aligned with the central cities. In most states with more than one urban center, such as Texas, Pennsylvania, and Ohio, the concerns of the city-only elected officials still do not dominate the state legislature. California, where counties with major urban centers comprise a majority of the population, offers the best potential for a state with, if not a city focus, at least a metropolitan one. Yet even there, suburban districts frequently do not support city interests.

## Fiscal Federalism: The Flow of Grants, Revenues, and Mandates

The porousness of city borders and the concentration of poverty, unemployment, homelessness, and a number of serious social problems make it almost impossible for cities to have control over their own budgets. On one side of the ledger, they cannot easily control their revenues. Vigorous competition by business for low-cost locations constrains tax levels, while tax bases and tax rates are largely determined by state legislation or state referenda. In New York, for example, the state controls all city taxes, even charging a fee to administer the income and sales taxes, and setting rules for the property tax. In California, Massachusetts, and Florida, statewide property tax limitations passed by referenda severely constrain localities from funding education and other essential services. In Colorado, since the 1992 election, local tax increases must be approved by a referendum at a general election before they can take effect.

On the other side of the ledger, an increasing number of spending and service provision decisions, in education, criminal justice, water resources, health, and welfare, are predetermined by legislated and judicial mandates from state and national government. Again, in the case of New York City, the state provides some funding for elementary and secondary education through a formula set each year. But much of city spending on education, criminal justice, health care, and welfare services must meet state standards and is subject to fiscal penalties and sanctions if the standards are violated.

## Who Does What?

Since the Employment Act of 1946, the national government has taken responsibility for keeping the economy at high levels of employment and growth with reasonable price stability, using tools of monetary controls and fiscal policy. In addition, the national government has largely played the role of redistributor of income and wealth, modifying the market determined distribution in line with the goals of social equity, especially in providing assistance to the poor. As Edwin Cannan noted in 1896:

Measures adopted to produce greater equality are . . . exceedingly unsuitable for local authorities. The smaller the locality the more capricious and ineffectual are likely to be any efforts it may make to carry out such a policy. It seems clearly desirable that all such measures should be applied to the largest possible area. . . .[3]

While the national government provides some public goods, like national defense, that are not easily divisible for individual consumption, the bulk of publicly provided goods and services is provided through state and local governments. Generally, states limit their direct services to higher education, highways, criminal justice (courts and prisons), and aid to the poor. Local governments provide elementary and secondary education, police and fire protection, sanitation and waste disposal, streets, water, public health, and a range of cultural and recreational institutions and facilities.

Economic theory posits that individuals and businesses locate based on the package of public services and taxes offered by different localities. Yet with a highly mobile population, "purely local" is a shrinking concept. It is not easy to find services that ultimately do not have "spillover" effects onto nonresidents. For example, New York City's police provision is driven, at least in part, by a national proliferation of handguns, since more than 90 percent of the guns recovered in city crimes are purchased outside of the city. The "efficient" solution to public service provision is to determine the exact reach of the service and provide it through a government whose boundaries coincide with that reach. However, that would generate a system of government with a huge number of overlapping rather than coterminous service districts, which is not easily coped with by politics in theory or in practice.

## Federal Grants and Revenue Sharing

There have been a number of innovations that sought, until the Reagan-Bush years, to better balance the fiscal flows with the actual economic and political responsibilities. The federal government has, in this century, greatly expanded its role in the intergovernmental system. All three branches of the federal government have cooperated in this expanded role, including the courts, which, through rulings on the reach of the Tenth Amendment and the interstate commerce clause, increasingly have told states to protect their rights through the exertion of political power in Congress.[4]

A key to the expanding federal role was the introduction of a federal income tax that provided a basic mechanism to redistribute income from rich to poor. Both the tax's progressivity and the responsiveness of the revenues to economic growth demonstrated, through time, that the federal government had a powerful tool not only to repair some of the inequalities of the private economy but also to redistribute revenues within the public sector, from the highest level of government to the lowest.

Another key federal innovation was the introduction of intergovernmental grants. Given the responsive federal income tax and constitutionally designated political boundaries, economists set about channeling growing federal revenues to where the service problems are, through a system of grants. Different types of grants pursue different goals. Matching or categorical grants encourage state and local spending on activities with positive spillovers. Unconditional, "lump-sum," or "block" grants equalize fiscal capacity and, ultimately, public service provision. General revenue-sharing grants, based on population and income, establish a more efficient and more equitable tax system by substituting, to some degree, a more progressive federal tax system for more regressive state and local taxes.

As Figure 1 demonstrates, prior to 1981 federal grants directed to cities were an important component of fiscal federalism in the 1960s and 1970s. President Reagan's "new federalism," however, rewrote fiscal federalism dramatically and attempted to make all levels of government smaller.

First, Reagan did not accept that redistribution belonged at the national level, stating in 1982 that "financial assistance to the poor is a legitimate responsibility of states and localities." Second, he crippled the main engine for progressivity and elasticity of revenues, the federal income tax, by lowering, flattening, and indexing the rates. Third, his "new federalism" involved a complete "turnback" to the states and localities of a number of federal programs, without any accompanying revenue to fund them. Finally, he consolidated a number of categorical grants into block grants, which eliminated the incentive for states and localities to spend in these areas because state or local matching efforts were not required by the federal government.

According to the U.S. Conference of Mayors, federal aid to state and local governments fell by $34 billion in real terms during the 1980s. Local governments were hit harder than states. Of the seventy-seven categorical grant programs consolidated into block grants in 1981, forty-seven had been directly for local governments.[5] Real per capita federal aid to localities fell by 55 percent during the 1980s as compared to a 15 percent decline to states.[6]

## The State Role

States play a different and more complex role vis-à-vis cities in the economics of the federal structure. Grants are only one of the several mechanisms by which states influence city fiscal health. States directly establish the fiscal rules and institutions under which cities operate and determine the services that cities must provide.

As Helen Ladd and John Yinger demonstrate in *America's Ailing Cities,* even before the new federalism of the 1980s, states did not give

**Figure 1. Direct Federal aid to Cities 1965–1990
As a Percentage of Own-Source Revenue**

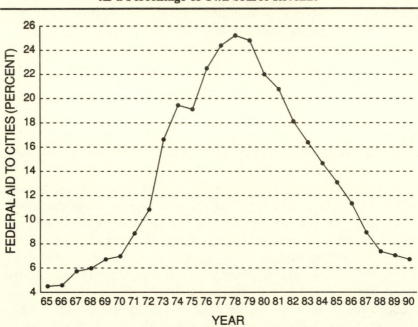

*Source:* U.S. Bureau of the Census, City Government Finances, various years

city governments policy tools powerful enough to ensure adequate
city fiscal health. Large cities and those with poor residents have
been in particular need "of outside resources to achieve the same
quality of services at the same tax burden as the average city. . . .
*Between 1972 and 1982,* state assistance . . . offset approximately one-
half of the decline in city fiscal health caused by economic and social
trends."[7]

Unfortunately, the "new federalism" of the 1980s further weakened the ability of states to help cities. Taxpayer revolts limited the
option of raising state (or local) taxes. Cutbacks in federal aid to
states and rolling recessions made states effectively poorer and less
flexible. Medicaid, the federal health care program for the poor,
whose costs are outside of state control, took an increasing share of
state resources. And largely due to tax constraints, many states developed "structural deficits, where the revenue from their existing tax
systems falls persistently below current services spending."[8]

With states forced to balance their budgets, something had to
give. So in the 1980s they cut back significantly on their help to cities.
Whether they would have cut back more if there had not also been

massive federal cutbacks in urban aid is an unanswered question. Helen Ladd suggests "that state actions probably did not offset the impact on cities of the recent cuts in federal aid to cities" and that states do not view their own federal aid as additional revenue to pass on to localities.[9]

Unfortunately for cities, states also have been unwilling to allow cities greater taxing authority or to relieve them of some service obligations.[10] For example, since the beginning of the Reagan administration, no additional cities have been given the ability to tax nonresidents. Worse, in several significant ways, states have robbed cities of some major revenues. New York, for example, has levied state taxes on uniquely city tax bases, such as hotel rooms costing more than $100 a night and real property gains exceeding $1 million, thus eliminating these options for raising city revenues. California Governor Peter Wilson's 1993 budget proposal would shift $2.6 billion of city, county, and district property tax revenue to the state budget.

In addition, there have been very few substantial state takeovers of city responsibilities. According to the National Association of State Budget Officers (NASBO), state takeover or assumption of local services between 1982–87 concentrated primarily on courts and jails. In most states assumptions of local services accounted for less than 5 percent of total aid in 1989.

## The Mandates

Mandates represent a range of different demands that higher levels of government impose on lower ones. The Advisory Commission on Intergovernmental Relations (ACIR) defines a mandate as "any constitutional, statutory or administrative action that limits or places requirements on local governments."[11] In some sense, all city spending is mandated, since cities operate under state delegated home rule authority; so "mandates," per se, cannot be categorized as bad.

The items most often cited by cities as *burdensome* mandates are educational requirements, landfill cleanup, sewer treatment plant facilities, federal road requirements, welfare and medicaid costs, health care/retiree costs, pension increases, and FICA.[12]

This list highlights the special location of cities in the mandate game: they get hit from all sides. Mandates come from all *three* branches of *two* higher levels of government! Legislative mandates may, potentially, bring funding with them. Major federal programs, however, often allocate funds only to states and leave the determination of the local share to the state legislature. Executive mandates are meant to generate uniformity. They almost always come in the form of procedures, guidelines, and paperwork, with the resulting disallowances, sanctions, and penalties. They generate considerable compliance costs. Judicial mandates cannot include funding. In some instances the courts have demonstrated sensitivity to the costs their decisions will impose, particularly in the area of retroactive pension liabilities. But ultimately, courts can neither generate revenues nor prioritize spending demands.

The key question for mandates is whether a higher level of government should help pay for part or all of the cost. There is clearly no easy answer. In part, it depends on whether the mandate is something that the city should be doing anyway. In part it depends on whether the level of activity is excessive. The three levels of government may not agree on the answer in each particular case, but they certainly should all be asking the questions.[13] That does not appear to be the case at present.

Unfortunately, there is no measure of the total of unfunded mandates that cities face from both state and federal government. Chicago estimates that mandated spending annually amounts to approximately $160 million. New York City easily spends $5 billion on mandates, about one-quarter of its "own funds" budget. Since cities carry different responsibilities and, therefore, very different budgets, comparisons and aggregation are meaningless.

## Redesigning Federalism to Meet Cities' Needs

For cities, there were both strengths and weaknesses to pre-Reagan fiscal federalism. The strengths lay in the clear reliance on the federal government, with its progressive and elastic income tax, as the engine of redistribution; some direct provision of federal aid to cities, without passing through the states; and a recognition of the role of categorical matching grants to induce certain types of spending.

However, the system was far from ideal. What Paul Peterson refers to in his chapter as "marble-cake" federalism represented a patchwork that had developed over time but had never been pruned or prioritized. There was no clear division of responsibility and, therefore, no clear accountability to the public. This "marble cake" was also a "layer cake," with cities at the bottom. If the two top layers leaned, the lower layer crumbled. If the two top layers soaked up the resources, the lower layer went dry.

Further, cities had no permanent standing of their own. The responsibilities they bore and the resources to pay for them varied dramatically from state to state. A city's ability to receive a net gain from the state pass-through component of federal aid differed from place to place and from year to year. Worse, there was no serious long-term policy aimed at changing the growing economic disparities between cities and their suburbs.

Even if the pre-Reagan federalism were the ideal, it would not be easy to go back to it. Neither the actors, the needs, nor the economics are the same. Mandates went unnoticed in the beginning; they are on everyone's lips now. State governments were isolated, weak, and unprofessional in the beginning; they are organized and professional bureaucracies now. Homelessness and AIDS were unknown then; they are concentrated in cities now. Suburbanization and regional economic segregation were a problem then; they are more firmly entrenched problems now. The burden of the federal deficit used to be an academic discussion; it is a very real constraint now.

### Making Change at the State Level

The state role in fiscal federalism is the elimination or leveling of economic disparities within the urban region. Examples of improving that role abound.[14] The options presented here focus on changing the governmental structure and enhancing revenues. This chapter does not address other government policies on housing, employment, and education that have a considerable effect on segregation and the distribution of economic gains in a region, nor does it discuss the special issue of the relationship of education finance and property taxes.[15] What follows is not an exhaustive list.

*Increase Assistance.* The most direct way for states to help cities in poor fiscal condition is through equalizing grants. These grants should be allocated according to measurable factors, such as a high percentage of low-income people or disproportionately high budget needs. Refining these measurements and attempting to include factors to account for high, uncontrollable public service costs would improve the targeting further. When seeking to improve the quality of particular services, states should use categorical matching grants. To lower city tax burdens, lump-sum state grants are the most efficient.[16] This is easier said than done. The politics of state assistance to localities has degenerated into a frenzy of "hold harmless" provisions that make significant city budget changes a different challenge.

**Tax Relief.** States have a number of ways to offer cities fiscal relief through the tax system. One, of course, is to increase directly city taxes. Better yet, states should devolve to large cities the authority to determine broadly based tax rates and define selected business and excise tax bases. This would place city tax responsibility with city elected officials and remove from rural and suburban state legislators the burden and political blame for annual city tax increases.

Another option is to increase the range and flexibility of taxes that cities can levy, including income and business taxes. A fourth is to extend the reach of city taxes to the wider economy by, for example, allowing cities to levy taxes that are easily exported. While there are a number of taxes whose incidence would fit this description, including a portion of the commercial-industrial real estate tax, the best examples are the nonresident (commuter) earnings/income tax and a city payroll tax. Of the eighteen city nonresident income or earnings taxes, six are not fully exportable; and of the ten least fiscally healthy cities, New Orleans, Chicago, Buffalo, and Los Angeles do not have an earnings tax, and Baltimore has one that is restricted to residents.[17]

New York City, one of the six cities with a restricted nonresident earnings tax, tried during the recession of the early 1990s to get the state legislature to remove certain restrictions and expand the tax base. Even with a proposal that shares the resulting city revenues with surrounding New York suburbs, the state legislature will not vote this tax. State legislators from suburban New York feel the antitax mood so strongly that they do not want to vote for any tax increase on their constituents, even when it will be rebated and the only net liability remaining would be on New Jersey and Connecticut residents. The politics appear as a loser to suburban legislators: the counties (and their executives) would get the "glory" of windfall revenues to either reduce property taxes or improve county services, while state legislators would get the "black mark" of voting a tax increase.

**Consolidation and Annexation.** Major governmental reorganization, through consolidation of units of government or annexation, eliminates fiscal disparities by creating a political unit that can take advantage of economies of scale in both the provision of services and the benefits received. Consolidation is most commonly used for school districts. Examples of general government consolidations include: Miami and Dade County (Florida); Indianapolis and Marion County (Indiana); and Nashville and Davidson County (Tennessee). Unfortunately, issues of political accountability and local control rarely allow local governmental consolidation on a very large scale, although there have been recently some city-county consolidations of note: Jacksonville–Duvall County (Florida); Lexington–Fayette County (Kentucky); Columbus–Muskogee County (Georgia). Annexation has been pursued aggressively in Albuquerque, New Mexico, and Huntsville, Alabama, and is most common for newer, growing cities.

Jurisdictional consolidation and city annexation of surrounding areas can be encouraged actively through state policies that require a minimum size for service provision, reward or punish based on size, provide incentives by defraying the costs of feasibility studies or holding harmless taxpayers during transition periods, or require consolidation when cities and their overlying counties automatically reach a certain size.

**Takeovers by Higher Levels of Government.** During the New York City fiscal crisis of the mid-1970s, the state permanently shifted the funding and administration of the senior colleges of the City University of New York and the city court system to the state government. Other states have done similarly with the courts during the past decade. In several states, counties have taken over central city responsibilities for zoos, parks, art museums, and other cultural and athletic facilities. Usually this has only been done during severe city fiscal stress and when there are evident spillover effects to suburban residents, as in the case of Detroit.

Despite the previous takeover, New York City remains a unique case. The state continues to impose fiscal burdens on the city that are required in very few other states. These are for major redistributive programs. New York City annually spends about $1.6 billion for its share of Medicaid, a cost it would not have to bear if it were in any of thirty-seven other states. New York is one of only thirteen states that require localities to pay a share of Medicaid costs, and the 50 percent local share it requires is far higher than in all but one of these states. Annually, New York City spends about $730 million for welfare, again due to state requirements. New York is one of only nine states that require localities to pay a share of welfare costs; the 50 percent share requirement is the highest of any state. At the same time, the state collects only ninety-four cents for every dollar of local taxes—the lowest ratio of any state in America (except New Hampshire). Governor Mario Cuomo has proposed a phased takeover of the local share of Medicaid, only with an accompanying assumption by the state of certain local taxing authority for the funding. The legislature has so far shown little interest. While the city strongly supports a takeover, the timing, tax component, and resulting distribution of burdens in the governor's proposal present a number of problems.[18]

***Service Sharing and Regional Authorities.*** In general, cities have not been particularly successful in getting the surrounding area to help in the provision of city services. Education would seem to be an obvious service that could benefit from the economies of crossjurisdictional sharing. However, with the exception of controversial school desegregation in Missouri, including Kansas City and St. Louis, which is spreading the burden of educating many central city students to the richer suburbs, most school district revenue sharing has not happened. Emotional and political issues of local control and racial integration make this very controversial. In fields less emotionally charged than schooling, and with clear private sector benefits, regional authorities have been very successful. The New York City area has the New York–New Jersey Port Authority, one of the oldest multistate examples, which covers the harbors, airports, bridges, and tunnels. New York City also has a regional transportation authority as do Chicago; Washington, D.C.; Portland, Oregon; and San Francisco. The Chicago and Boston areas have both formed Metropolitan Sanitary Districts.

***Tax Base Sharing.*** Metropolitan sharing of the tax base offers fiscal relief without the loss of political control inherent in consolidation, takeovers, and annexation. It requires a recognition by the city and surrounding suburbs that they are all part of a metropolitan economy and that new economic development is a metropolitan resource to be shared by all. The largest and most famous example of this approach is that of the Minneapolis–St. Paul Twin Cities area in Minnesota, where the growth of the commercial-industrial property tax base within the metropolitan region is redistributed to all municipalities by formula, based on population and existing market value. According to the Research Department of the Minnesota House of Representatives, since the law went into effect in 1975, the disparity in commercial-industrial tax base among the communities has been reduced to four to one; without the program the ratio would be twenty-two to one.[19]

## Making Changes at the National Level

Changing the role and responsibilities of the federal government, and thus redesigning federalism, has finally become a topic of serious conversation. The legacy of the Reagan-Bush years and the worsening plight of cities, and the poor within them, have brought into public focus the need to overhaul the federal system.

*Restoring Federal Aid to Cities.* Restoring federal aid to cities requires raising greater federal income tax revenues and controlling the growing federal budget deficit, thus generating excess federal revenue as "revenue sharing." Revenue sharing must be distributed to cities directly. The essential element in any new federal aid to cities is to target it directly to those cities hardest hit by national economic and social forces beyond their own, or their states', control. It is possible to design efficient grants to cities and to take into account the role of overlying counties and their responsibilities.[20]

*Encouraging State Aid and Support to Cities.* Empirical evidence does not support the notion that federal aid to states is an effective way for the federal government to assist cities. Further, since state policy makers seem to view their grants to cities as twice as powerful, dollar-for-dollar, than allowing cities to raise taxes, if federal grants were increased to reward states for giving high levels of city aid, states would likely cut back more on their tax-raising support to cities, leaving cities worse off in the long run.[21]

A different approach would be the creation of incentives for states to allow cities to levy income taxes, covering residents and nonresidents, or to have states take over welfare spending. It is not easy to know how best to structure such incentives, especially since the federal income tax deduction for state and city taxes does not seem to have been enough to induce the widespread use of such city income taxes. Penalties on states with large cities that do not allow income taxes are another option. An even stronger version would be a direct federal prohibition on states requiring a local share of welfare spending.

*The European Approach.* It is hard, and probably dangerous, to generalize from international experience. However, the European

Community (EC), with a much smaller budget than the United States and very different constitutional and economic structures, is struggling, too, with fiscal federalism. It has created a permanent mechanism to redistribute resources to achieve greater equity. The primary mechanism is three long-standing structural funds: the European Regional Development Fund, the European Social Fund, and the Guidance Section of the European Agricultural Guidance and Guarantee Fund, which have been significantly redesigned as the EC has expanded and adopted the goal of economic integration. In addition, the European Investment Bank provides capital specifically for infrastructure, for enterprises in less developed areas, and for modernization.

As part of the 1992 program to remove remaining trade barriers among members, the resources of these three structural funds are now targeted to regions with severe problems of poverty, unemployment, and underdevelopment. Although the funds are quite separate, they are directed at the common goal of cohesion among EC members by: promoting economic development in regions where per capita gross domestic product (GDP) is at least 25 percent below the community average; converting of industrial areas in decline; combating long-term and teenage unemployment; and generating rural development. In general, these funds flow directly from Brussels to regional projects, particularly cities; however, three member states (Greece, Ireland, and Portugal) form their own complete development regions. Brussels has denied funds to member states when they have violated rules of "additionality" by substituting EC funds for national funds.

***The Rivlin Approach.*** The most complete attempt at redesigning the federal role is contained in Alice M. Rivlin's *Reviving the American Dream: The Economy, the States and the Federal Government.*[22] Unfortunately, it does not directly address cities, their needs, place, or role.

Rivlin seeks to separate out lines of authority and revenues between the national government and the states. The federal government would provide for the national defense, international affairs, various interstate activities, and Social Security, and move to control the growth of health care costs and ensure coverage for everyone. The federal budget would gradually move from deficit to surplus through the state takeover of funding for most domestic programs. Rivlin argues that most domestic programs are better suited to state and local governments because policies in education, social services, and housing require adaptation to local conditions to be effective. The new *state* responsibilities would be financed through increased revenues coming from a new system of *common shared taxes*.

There is strong appeal to portions of the Rivlin proposal. The federal takeover of health coverage and health cost containment, including Medicaid, would remove the fastest rising unfunded mandates from states and restore the national government to its supreme role in income distribution programs. Common shared taxes offer states, for the first time, real ability to increase and broaden their tax bases rather than narrowing them in the beggar-thy-neighbor game of location competition. This would leap well beyond the fledgling attempts by states to form compacts to act collectively in taxation. It would also require a significant change in the relationship between the Internal Revenue Service (IRS) and states. Presently, the IRS makes many administrative decisions, such as allowing limited liability corporations, which cost states billions of dollars of revenues. Yet the IRS does not consult with states or estimate the potential impacts of these decisions.

Although Rivlin presents her proposals as a logical sorting out of functions, she ignores the tremendous problems in the state-local government relationship. The issue of education, with numerous state court decisions finding inequities in local financing and school aid formulas, should generate a national debate over which level of government is most responsible and responsive. There is a strong case that can be made for the financing of elementary and secondary education at the state, not the local, level.

Most importantly, the absence of cities, their problems, and their needs is a glaring omission in Rivlin's work. Cities are relegated to complete dependence on states for the equalization of fiscal resources. Rivlin *assumes* that states will be more disposed and do a better job of aiding cities than they do at present; it is hard to see why. For example, one can argue that common shared taxes might make states even more reluctant to allow cities expanded taxing authority as they jealously guard their remaining revenue sources.

## Conclusion

American fiscal federalism does not work for cities. The system needs to be fixed, but a return to the pre-Reagan days is neither possible nor would it be sufficient to insure the fiscal viability of America's cities. Then, what?

The need for serious change at the state level is compelling. However, the fact that there are not more and better examples to help the country's largest and most fiscally distressed cities than the options discussed above suggests that such reforms are very difficult to achieve. The largest single obstacle to improved state fiscal federalism is the lack of city political muscle in state legislatures.

The importance of the city to the suburban, regional, and national economies and the concentration of much of America's poverty, unemployment, social pathologies, AIDS, and immigrants in cities make the case for a stronger role for the national government in narrowing the fiscal disparities of America's cities. Unfortunately, there is not, as yet, a master solution. Alice Rivlin's approach is incomplete because it relies on state governments to "do the right thing" for cities and ignores the problem of cities being unable to shape the decision making of their state governments.

In theory, the ideal solution would be constitutional reform to create states that far better coincide with the real economy. It is hard to imagine, however, that the American political system is ready to reopen the Constitution, even in a limited way. Short of constitutional standing, cities should be seeking every possible means to carve out a permanent, separate role for themselves in relation to the national government.

Cities should push the federal government for a system of urban and regional assistance along the lines of the European Community's structural funds. There is a compelling argument for a direct link from the national government to city governments, so fund assistance should flow directly from the national to the city government, with the city playing the role of the regional center, disbursing the aid further for the regional component. There should be a permanent structural assistance program as well as a countercyclical program designed and ready to kick in automatically for labor markets experiencing high unemployment, low labor force participation, and large training needs, including absorption of immigrants.

For such a program to work properly, the data on which federal funds are disbursed must be accurate. That will require significant improvements in the census to capture the undocumented, homeless, and noninstitutionalized mentally ill. Further, economic and special reports will have to be generated specifically for cities, since labor market data are generally reported by county, making accurate aid and policy decisions difficult.

Cities whose labor markets will be affected by the North American Free Trade Agreement (NAFTA), at least the nation's largest and those along the Mexican and Canadian border, should propose to the federal government that the supplemental agreement on labor issues establish new crossborder regional authorities to levy taxes and share revenues to handle the burdens of the crossborder flows.[23] This will also help to establish cities as the centers in negotiations over issues that affect their labor markets.

Cities and their mayors must enunciate a coherent statement of federalism, delineating national, state, and city responsibilities. Mayors have too often in the past seemed unwilling to accept that certain state and federal mandates are essential. Accepting that, mayors should focus on creating incentives for states to sort out their program responsibilities with their cities and to improve city fiscal institutions. While we have a multilayered system of government, there is, ultimately, only one layer of taxpayer.

- The mayors should seek a special federal task force to design a mechanism for federal encouragement of more responsive and progressive city taxes. The long-standing deductibility of state and local taxes is clearly not a great enough incentive. The mayors must direct an effort to reform city tax structures and suggest a mechanism for federal encouragement.
- The mayors should design a federal aid formula to states that would reward states for giving institutional support to cities. Notwithstanding the substitution problems, federal mandatory pass-through of aid to cities is certainly a place to start.
- The mayors should propose federal awards to states for new and creative support that relieves city stress.

Finally, cities have to move beyond their political limitations. Severely hampered by their lack of constitutional standing and lack of political power in state capitals, cities have to create a third way. Mayors can carve out a wider and more statesman-like role by working for the benefit of their metropolitan area in the national and international economy. In the end, America's economy depends on America's cities. The challenge is to turn that central economic role into a matching political and fiscal one. Experience indicates that mayors must raise their issues and needs to the national and international level. Pushing to create regional structures and gaining jobs and investment for the metropolitan region can help bring people together around a common interest.

# Notes

[1] Persky, Sclar, and Wiewel (1991).
[2] Economic Policy Council of the UNA-USA (1993).
[3] Cannan (1896).
[4] *Garcia v. San Antonio Metropolitan Transit Authority,* 469 US 528 (1985), at 556.
[5] Ladd (1991), p. 479.
[6] Gold (1993).
[7] Ladd and Yinger (1989), pp. 13–14.
[8] Gold (1993), p. 45.
[9] Ladd (1991), p. 480.
[10] Yinger and Ladd (1989).
[11] Advisory Commission on Intergovernmental Relations (1978).
[12] U.S. Conference of Mayors (1991a) and (1991b).
[13] Gold (1989).
[14] Hovey (1989) and Ladd and Yinger (1989).
[15] See Rusk (1993) for a provocative treatment of some of these issues.
[16] Oates (1972).
[17] Ladd and Yinger (1989), pp. 132–134, 300.
[18] O'Cléireacáin (1992).
[19] "Minnesota's Fiscal Disparities Program," Minnesota House of Representatives Research Department, 1991.
[20] Ladd and Yinger (1989), pp.304–306.
[21] Ladd and Yinger (1989), p. 307.
[22] Rivlin (1992).
[23] Economic Policy Council of the UNA-USA (1993).

# 8

## The Changing Fiscal
## Place of Big Cities
## in the Federal System

### PAUL E. PETERSON

The nation's cities were anticipating in the spring of 1993 new help from the federal government. During his campaign for the presidency, Bill Clinton secured strong mayoral backing in primary contests, and he carried the nation's cities by a decisive margin that significantly contributed to his overall victory. His economic stimulus package presented to the nation in February of 1993 called for an additional $3.75 billion for transportation, an additional $2.5 billion for community development, $850 million to comply with federal clean water standards, $300 million for immunization of children,

PAUL E. PETERSON is Henry Lee Shattuck Professor of Government and director of the Center for American Political Studies at Harvard University. He was a Guggenheim Fellow in 1977–78, and received the Woodrow Wilson Foundation Award from the American Political Science Association for the best book published in 1981 in politics, government, or international relations. In 1984 he was elected to the National Academy of Education. Dr. Peterson is the author or editor of numerous books and articles, most recently *The Urban Underclass,* edited with Christopher Jencks. Rick Hess, Don Lee, and Jerome Maddox assisted with the research for this chapter. Allison Kommer and Kristin Skala provided staff assistance.

and $1 billion for summer employment. The federal government seemed poised to reverse the cutbacks in federal aid that had begun during the last two years of the Carter administration and were accelerated during the Reagan-Bush years.

Yet big cities are well advised to keep their expectations modest. Although a limited expansion of the federal role is to be expected, the largess will probably be distributed widely among all states and localities. It is unlikely that federal programs will either expand rapidly or concentrate resources on the most needy communities. New federal assistance might very well do little more than offset the cuts that hard-pressed states are increasingly likely to impose. The fiscal problems of large central cities are deeply entrenched in the American federal system.

Much of the difficulty lies in the rigid legal boundaries that limit the territorial size of central cities even while metropolitan areas continue to expand. During the nineteenth century most central cities extended their political jurisdictions as their populations grew. Outlying areas agreed to be incorporated into the central city in order to get access to city-built sewers, roads, and streetcar lines. But as the twentieth century progressed, peripheral communities resisted, through state legislatures and local elections, takeover attempts by the central cities they surrounded. Rust Belt cities became locked into fixed political boundaries that usually encompassed less than half their metropolitan-wide population. Although cities of the rapidly growing South and West were less constricted, by the 1990s even many of these Sun Belt cities were less frequently annexing outlying areas.[1]

Without the ability to expand their territorial reach, big cities no longer shared equally in the growth of the U.S. population. Although the raw numbers of people living in large central cities (of more than 300,000 in population, the definition of big city that I shall use throughout this chapter) increased from 34 million to 42 million people between 1957 and 1990, the percentage of the U.S. population living in these cities declined from 19.8 percent to 16.8 percent.

Even bigger changes are detectable if regional distinctions are drawn. As can be seen in Table 1, the number of people living in Rust Belt cities fell from 25 to 20 million; their share of the U.S. population plummeted from 14.5 to 8 percent. Approximately 20 percent of this decline was due to the fact that four Rust Belt city populations fell below 300,000, thereby falling out of our definition of what constitutes a big city. The remaining 80 percent of the population decline occurred in the seventeen Rust Belt cities that continued to have populations in excess of 300,000 in 1990. The story of the cities of the Sun Belt is noticeably different. The number of residents living in these cities grew from 8.5 million to 23 million (Table 1). Much of this increase was due to annexation and to the fact that the number of cities with populations in excess of 300,000 increased from fifteen to thirty-four.

Big cities were also becoming increasingly differentiated from the suburban hinterland surrounding them. Central city residents, instead of being financially better off, became less well off than the average American. Median family income in big cities was 15.2 percent higher than the national median in 1950, but 7.8 percent lower in 1990. The percentage of big-city populations of non-European origin was 3 percentage points above the national average in 1950; by 1990 it was 22 percentage points above. Politically, central cities became heavily Democratic in their voting propensities, while suburban areas tended to be more Republican.

**Table 1. Proportion of U.S. Population Living in Big Cities, Selected Years**

| Proportion of U.S. Population | Year | | | |
|---|---|---|---|---|
|  | 1957 | 1972 | 1982 | 1990 |
| **All Big Cities** | | | | |
| Proportion | 19.8% | 19.0% | 16.8% | 16.8% |
| Annual % Change | — | − .2% | − 1.2% | 0.0% |
| Number of Cities | 36 | 48 | 48 | 51 |
| **Rust Belt Cities** | | | | |
| Proportion | 14.5% | 11.4% | 8.6% | 8.0% |
| Annual % Change | — | − 1.6% | − 2.7% | − 0.9% |
| Number of Cities | 21 | 20 | 18 | 17 |
| **Sun Belt Cities** | | | | |
| Proportion | 5.0% | 8.1% | 8.6% | 9.2% |
| Annual % Change | — | 3.2% | 0.6% | 0.8% |
| Number of Cities | 15 | 28 | 30 | 34 |

*Sources:* 1957: U.S. Bureau of the Census, *Compendium of City Government Finances in 1957.* (Washington, D.C.: U.S. G.P.O., 1958, pp. III–V. 1972: U.S. Bureau of the Census, *City Government Finances in 1971–72* (Washington, D.C.: U.S. G.P.O., 1974), Table 7 (Finances of Individual Cities Having 300,000 population or more, in Detail: 1971–72). 1982: U.S. Bureau of the Census, *City Government Finances in 1981–82* (Washington, D.C.: U.S. G.P.O., 1983), Table 7 (Finances of Individual Cities Having 300,000 population or more, in Detail: 1981–82). 1990: U.S. Bureau of the Census, *City Government Finances in 1989–90* (Washington, D.C.: U.S. G.P.O., 1991), Table 7 (Finances of Individual Cities Having 300,000 population or more, in Detail: 1989–90).

Once again, regional differences are striking. Median family income in the average Rust Belt city was 16.2 per cent *above* the national median in 1950 but 11.1 percent *below* the median in 1990. Changes were similar but less dramatic in the Sun Belt—from 12.4 percent above to 4.9 percent below the national median over this time period. The percentage of the population of European descent declined by 34.1 percent in the Rust Belt but only by 21.5 percent in the Sun Belt. Social change was occurring in all big cities, but the socially and economically most challenging transformations were occurring in the older, manufacturing based cities of the Northeast and Midwest.

Finally, central city governments differed from those in the outlying areas. Central cities established sizable bureaucracies with uniform policies for large, heterogeneous populations, while the surrounding suburbs consisted of many small governmental units. Each town, village, or special district was responsible for governing a small and usually quite homogeneous population. Though cities had the advantage of economies of scale that accrue to large jurisdictions, they also had the fiscal disadvantage of being vulnerable to wage demands and strike threats by their large municipal work forces.

## Changes in Big-City Revenues

These social and economic changes accelerated urban demand for public services. As a result, big cities made great efforts to increase their public sector revenues over the course of the three and one-half decades after 1957 (Table 2). But the patterns of change varied between the Rust Belt and the Sun Belt. As can be seen in Table 3, the revenues of Sun Belt cities increased from $752 to $1,739 per capita between 1957 and 1990. (All dollar figures in this chapter have been adjusted for changes in the cost of living over time and are reported in 1990 dollars.) The annual growth rate was fairly steady, hovering between 2 and 2.9 percent over the entire period. In the Rust Belt cities, revenue flow grew more steeply but less evenly. The overall per capita gain was from $818 to $2,942 over the course of the thirty-three years. But the rate of growth varied from an annual rate of 5.8 percent during the prosperous fifties and sixties, to 1.5 percent during the stagnant seventies, to 3.5 percent during the resurgent eighties.

An even more exact account of changing big-city finances can be ascertained by examining the share of the nation's gross national

**Table 2. Total Revenue Received by Big-City Governments ($1990)**

| Year | Revenue (Billions) | Annual Rate of Growth |
|---|---|---|
| 1957 | $27.2 | — |
| 1972 | 64.7 | 5.9% |
| 1982 | 71.2 | 1.0 |
| 1990 | 95.9 | 3.8 |

*Sources:* 1957: U. S. Bureau of the Census, *Compendium of City Government Finances in 1957.* (Washington, D.C.: U.S. G.P.O., 1958, Table 14. Also, see sources for Table 1.

**Table 3. Total Revenue Per Capita Received by Big-City Governments in Rust Belt and Sun Belt ($1990)**

| City Revenue | Year | | | |
|---|---|---|---|---|
| | 1957 | 1972 | 1982 | 1990 |
| **All Big Cities** | | | | |
| Revenue Per Capita | $800 | $1,616 | $1,826 | $2,229 |
| Annual % Change | — | 4.8% | 1.2% | 2.5% |
| **Rust Belt Cities** | | | | |
| Revenue Per Capita | $818 | $1,918 | $2,223 | $2,942 |
| Annual % Change | — | 5.8% | 1.5% | 3.5% |
| **Sun Belt Cities** | | | | |
| Revenue Per Capita | $752 | $1,161 | $1,426 | $1,739 |
| Annual % Change | — | 2.9% | 2.0% | 2.5% |

*Sources:* 1957: U.S. Bureau of the Census, *Compendium of City Government Finances in 1957* (Washington, D.C.: U.S. G.P.O.), Tables 14, 17. Also, see sources for Table 1.

product (GNP) that has been expended through big city halls. As can be seen in Table 4, the governments in big cities spent a slightly higher proportion of the nation's GNP in 1990 than they did in 1957. Here again, the differences between Rust Belt and Sun Belt are worth underlining. In the Rust Belt the percentage of GNP expended by big city halls remained essentially flat: it moved slightly upward from 1.04 to 1.06 percent. But this share of the nation's income remained constant even though the populations of these cities declined from 14.5 to 8 percent of the U.S. population. Rust Belt city government costs as a percentage of the national product remained level even while their population share was falling by 45 percent. These were the portents of an urban fiscal crisis. The share of the nation's GNP being spent by Sun Belt cities was much less— only 0.32 percent of GNP in 1957 and just 0.72 percent of GNP in

1990. Annual changes in city revenues over the entire period ran just moderately ahead of the annual increase in the Sun Belt city population.

In summary, one must distinguish between Rust Belt and Sun Belt cities in order to understand the contemporary fiscal problems of large central cities. In the older cities of the Rust Belt, changes in the composition of the central city population, coupled with an overall decline in the number of residents, were accompanied by increasing demands for city government services—demands that outpaced the nation's growth rate. The revenues of Sun Belt cities grew more in consonance with the overall growth of these cities and of the U.S. economy. Although per capita expenditures increased at a steady pace in the Sun Belt cities, the base from which this rate of increase began was particularly low. By 1990 Rust Belt cities, serving a population totaling 20 million people, were spending 1.06 percent of the nation's GNP. Sun Belt city governments, with a population of 23 million, were spending just 0.72 percent of the nation's GNP.

It is not possible to draw definite conclusions from these figures. It

**Table 4. Total Revenue as a Percent of GNP Received by Big-City Governments**

|  | Year | | | |
| --- | --- | --- | --- | --- |
| City Revenue | 1957 | 1972 | 1982 | 1990 |
| **All Big Cities** | | | | |
| Revenue/ GNP | 1.36% | 1.91% | 1.71% | 1.78% |
| Annual % Change | — | 2.0% | − 1.1% | 0.5% |
| Annual % Change in Population Share | — | − 0.2% | − 1.2% | 0.0 |
| **Rust Belt Cities** | | | | |
| Revenue/ GNP | 1.04% | 1.34% | 1.06% | 1.06% |
| Annual % Change | — | 1.5% | − 2.1% | 0.0% |
| Annual % Change in Population Share | — | − 1.4% | − 2.7% | − 0.9% |
| **Sun Belt Cities** | | | | |
| Revenue/ GNP | 0.32% | 0.57% | 0.67% | 0.72% |
| Annual % Change | — | 3.5% | 1.6% | 0.9% |
| Annual % Change in Population Share | — | 2.9% | 0.6% | 0.8% |

*Sources:* See sources for Tables 1, 2, and 3.

may be that in the Sun Belt, both states and special districts provide services that in the Rust Belt are the responsibility of municipal governments. But differences in responsibilities are unlikely to account fully for the markedly differentiated pattern of change in the two regions. The pattern of change in the Sun Belt seems to have been a fairly steady, quite predictable response to population growth. It seems not likely to culminate in fiscal crisis in the 1990s. On the other hand, the steep and erratic demands for more government revenues in the cities of the Rust Belt seem to be placing an ever increasing strain on their economies. This strain becomes more evident when one examines the changing structure of intergovernmental fiscal relations.

## Cooperative Federalism

Three decades ago the federal government invoked a theory of cooperative or "marble-cake" federalism to justify increasing attention to central city problems. As initially propounded by political scientist Morton Grodzins, cooperative federalism criticized the old, nineteenth century, dual sovereign theory of federalism as outmoded. The dual sovereign theory claimed that governments in the United States constituted a layer cake, each level separate from and independent of the other. Grodzins pointed out that, in practice, agencies from different levels of government typically worked together to solve problems, combining and intertwining their functions to such an extent that the intergovernmental system resembled a marble cake.

Grodzins's ideas about cooperative federalism were quickly absorbed into Lyndon Johnson's vision of a Great Society. All levels of government could work together, the president claimed, though the combination of governments appropriate to any given program would differ. Some federal grants went to states to assist in state run programs. Other federal funds were allocated directly to local governments. Still other federal grants were given to states to be distributed by each state to its local governments.

This new marble-cake federalism was well-dosed with yeast. Between 1962 and 1977, direct federal grants to all local governments increased tenfold—from $3.2 billion to $32.3 billion. The federal government also expanded its state grant program from $29.5 billion to $89.7 billion during this same time period.

Big cities were among those invited to the dessert table. Between

1957 and 1977 direct federal aid to big cities increased in real dollar terms from $.3 billion to $9.3 billion (Table 5). On a per capita basis, direct federal aid to cities climbed from $10 to $244 over this twenty-year period (Table 6).[2]

Remarkably, state aid to cities was also increasing during this period, though the growth was less spectacular than the growth in direct federal assistance to cities. As can be seen in Table 7, the jump

**Table 5. Federal Direct Grants to Big-City Governments in Rust Belt and Sun Belt (Billions of $1990)**

| Federal Aid | 1957 | 1972 | Year 1977 | 1982 | 1990 |
|---|---|---|---|---|---|
| **All Cities** | | | | | |
| Federal Aid | $.3 | $4.7 | $9.3 | $7.6 | $4.6 |
| Annual % Change | — | 19.0% | 14.4% | − 3.9% | − 6.3% |
| **Rust Belt Cities** | | | | | |
| Federal Aid | $.2 | $2.5 | $5.2 | $4.7 | $2.1 |
| Annual % Change | — | 19.3% | 16.2% | − 2.0% | − 9.5% |
| **Sun Belt Cities** | | | | | |
| Federal Aid | $.2 | $2.2 | $4.1 | $3.6 | $2.5 |
| Annual % Change | — | 18.4% | 13.1% | − 2.4% | − 4.5% |

*Sources:* See sources for Tables 1, 2, and 3.

**Table 6. Federal Direct Grants Per Capita to Big-City Governments in Rust Belt and Sun Belt ($1990)**

| Federal Aid | 1957 | 1972 | Year 1977 | 1982 | 1990 |
|---|---|---|---|---|---|
| **All Big Cities** | | | | | |
| Aid Per Capita | $10 | $118 | $244 | $195 | $109 |
| Annual % Change | — | 17.8% | 13.6% | − 4.3% | − 7.0% |
| **Rust Belt Cities** | | | | | |
| Aid Per Capita | $7 | $104 | $245 | $205 | $107 |
| Annual % Change | — | 19.7% | 18.7% | − 3.5% | − 7.8% |
| **Sun Belt Cities** | | | | | |
| Aid Per Capita | $20 | $133 | $238 | $184 | $110 |
| Annual % Change | — | 13.4% | 12.3% | − 5.0% | − 6.2% |

*Sources:* See sources for Tables 1, 2, and 3.

in state aid to cities between 1957 and 1977 was from $3.8 to $16.8 billion. On a per capita basis, this amounted to an increase from $112 to $442 per city resident.

These new federal and state resources were giving big cities the capacity to respond to a host of urban problems. Federal monies were directed toward ending poverty, financing welfare reform, educating disadvantaged children, subsidizing low-income housing, encouraging mass transit, and providing general fiscal support for city governments. Although space constraints preclude detailed attention to all of these programs, a brief review of the largest and politically most salient will reveal how widely the concept of cooperative federalism was being applied.

## War on Poverty

If any one initiative symbolizes the urban policy of Johnson's cooperative federalism, it was the modestly funded but politically explosive War on Poverty. Announced in the aftermath of the Kennedy assassination and on the eve of Johnson's triumphant 1964

**Table 7. State Total and Per Capita Direct Grants to Big-City Governments in Rust Belt and Sun Belt with a Population of 300,000 or more ($1990)**

| | | | Year | | |
|---|---|---|---|---|---|
| State Aid | 1957 | 1972 | 1977 | 1982 | 1990 |
| **All Big Cities** | | | | | |
| Total (Billions) | $3.8 | $16.0 | $16.8 | $14.0 | $17.8 |
| Aid Per Capita | $112 | $400 | $442 | $358 | $430 |
| Annual Per Capita % Change | — | 8.8% | 2.0% | −4.1% | 2.3% |
| **Rust Belt Cities** | | | | | |
| Total (Billions) | $3.2 | $14.3 | $15.1 | $12.0 | $15.2 |
| Aid Per Capita | $125 | $605 | $707 | $602 | $773 |
| Annual Per Capita % Change | — | 11.0% | 3.1% | −3.1% | 3.1% |
| **Sun Belt Cities** | | | | | |
| Total (Billions) | $.5 | $1.6 | $1.7 | $2.3 | $3.0 |
| Aid Per Capita | $64 | $99 | $101 | $116 | $131 |
| Annual Per Capita % Change | — | 2.9% | 0.4% | 2.8% | 1.5% |

*Sources:* See sources for Tables 1, 2, and 3.

presidential campaign, the Economic Opportunity Act of 1964, the statutory basis for the War on Poverty, directed the bulk of its fiscal resources to cities.

Several accomplishments remain evident two decades later. The popular Head Start program for preschoolers anticipated and paved the way for the child care and nursery school programs that subsequently diffused throughout the country. Job Corps, a residential education and training program, though expensive, paid off in better wages and employment prospects. The legal services program changed the standing of poor people in the courts by challenging the constitutionality of a wide variety of local police and administrative practices. And by providing political, administrative, and employment opportunities to emerging African-American, Latino, and other minority activists, the poverty program facilitated the incorporation of minority leaders into the fabric of urban political life. From the poverty warriors of the sixties and seventies emerged many minority mayors, state legislators, and members of Congress elected in the eighties and nineties.

Despite these achievements, the War on Poverty is better known for its warring factions than for its substantive results. Its modest size—an average of $4.9 billion annually over its nine-year existence—belied its pretension to be a warlike enterprise. Its efforts to coordinate local social services failed dismally. Most of its job search, worker readiness, summer job, and other short-term worker training programs had few long-term economic benefits.

The main objection to the War on Poverty was its emphasis on political action. In many cities, it antagonized local agencies and elected officials by encouraging protests, demonstrations, legal action, and minority electoral mobilization. To some Washington policy analysts, an emphasis on political action made sense. Involving the impoverished in the system could forestall political alienation and, perhaps, even reverse the social apathy that seemed endemic to inner city life. From a narrow partisan standpoint, energized African-American and Latino communities, newly enfranchised by civil rights legislation, could give Democrats a massive, energized bloc of supporters. But if these policy and partisan objectives made sense to some in Washington, local officials wondered why federal monies should fund their political opposition. Not surprisingly, the program was blamed for the wave of civil violence that swept through American cities in the two years immediately after its adoption. Some argued that it broke up the biracial Democratic coalition that had made a War on Poverty possible. Except where minority leaders had come to power, few local tears were shed in 1974 when Nixon, who had campaigned against the poverty war, persuaded Congress to transfer its popular components to other agencies and shut down the remainder.

## Welfare Reform

As part of the Social Security Act of 1935, Congress authorized federal grants to states to pay one-third of the cost of a program of income maintenance for needy mothers with dependent children. In 1939 Congress increased the federal share to 50 percent, and in 1959 it further increased its share of the payment to states whose per capita income was below the national average. The federal role nonetheless remained secondary to that of state and local governments. Benefit levels and most eligibility requirements were determined by state legislatures.

With the coming of cooperative federalism, income maintenance programs changed markedly. In 1962 the name of the program was changed to Aid to Families with Dependent Children (AFDC) when states were allowed—but not required—to aid two-parent families of low income. The passage of Medicaid in 1965 made AFDC families eligible for free medical services. Aides hired by the poverty program helped poor people obtain better access to AFDC assistance. Law suits brought by the War on Poverty's legal division challenged state administrative requirements. In response to one lawsuit, the U.S. Supreme Court, in *Shapiro v. Thompson* (1969), ruled that states could no longer deny AFDC benefits to families until they had been residents of the state for twelve months. With all these changes, the numbers of people receiving AFDC more than doubled between 1960 and 1970—from 3.1 million to 7.4 million.

Congress continued to make important changes in income maintenance policy after 1970 in response to Nixon's proposed Family Assistance Plan. While not passing the plan's most controversial features, Congress funded a national minimum benefit standard for the blind, deaf, aged, and disabled in 1972, expanded the food stamp program to all parts of the country (adding, in the average state, as much as $270 to the monthly budget of the most needy families), and approved in 1974 an earned income tax credit, which eliminated federal taxes and supplemented the income of the working poor.

## Education

Before cooperative federalism, Congress had authorized only three small education programs—impact aid, vocational education, and a combination of mathematics, science, and library programs. Although cities received some of the monies distributed through the three programs, no urban policy was implicit in any of them. A larger federal role had been inhibited by conservative opposition to federal control of education, southern opposition to desegregation, and public school opposition to sharing federal funds with nonpublic, sectarian schools.

To overcome these sources of opposition, Johnson proposed that federal aid to education be designed to help fight the war against poverty. Proposed in these terms, Johnson was able to obtain compromises on which public and nonpublic school officials could agree, and the large Democratic majority in Congress quickly passed the legislation. The resulting compensatory education programs had a strong urban emphasis: 37 percent of the pupils participating in compensatory education programs in 1985 lived in central cities (as compared to 25 percent of all pupils). Congress also appropriated in subsequent years monies for special education for the handicapped, bilingual education, and aid to assist in school desegregation. In 1978 Congress acknowledged the increased federal role in education by transforming the Office of Education into a cabinet-level department.

The compensatory education program, though controversial, continued into the 1990s. The propensity of the compensatory program to pull students out of regular classrooms and teach them in special remedial settings has been criticized for stigmatizing educationally disadvantaged children. But the program has been praised for symbolizing the country's commitment to equal educational opportunity and given some of the credit for the gains in educational achievement made by minority groups.

## Housing and Urban Development

Despite the fact that the Department of Housing and Urban Development was given cabinet-level status in 1965, two of its major programs, public housing and urban renewal, would soon be in disrepute. Public housing was symbolized by ugly, dirty, crime-infested, segregated, high-rise apartment buildings, while urban renewal became synonymous with African-American removal. To correct these failings, housing policy under the new cooperative federalism undertook two new initiatives.

The first, the 1966 Demonstration Cities and Metropolitan Development Act, called for a comprehensive, coordinated, carefully planned attack on a wide variety of physical and social problems within designated inner city neighborhoods. Known as the Model Cities Program, it came as close to a specifically urban policy as Congress had ever passed. But the program became bogged down in bureaucratic and intergovernmental infighting and, in the end, mainly demonstrated that the intergovernmental system could not easily plan comprehensive solutions to urban problems.

The second strategy relied more on the private market to provide low-income housing units. It encouraged developers to build low- and moderate-income housing by subsidizing the interest rates on its construction. The number of units constructed between 1968 and 1972 was more than 1.6 million, a figure larger than the total number of federally subsidized public housing previously erected. Then in 1970, 42,000 additional low-income families were assisted under a new rent subsidy program that paid for the portion of the cost of renting an approved housing unit in excess of 25 percent of the low-income family's income. Congress then greatly expanded rent subsidies with the passage of Section Eight of the Housing and Community Development Act of 1974, increasing the numbers served so that they were reaching an estimated 300,000 new families a year by the late 1970s.

### Transportation

Congress enacted in 1956 the Interstate Highway Act that created a highway trust fund into which went revenues from a sales tax on gasoline. From this fund the federal government paid for 90 percent of the cost of the construction and maintenance of the comprehensive system of limited-access highways that revolutionized American transportation. But even while the program was contributing to the growth of the U.S. economy, it was helping to intensify automobile traffic congestion within central cities. As commuters utilized the new interstate highways to get to work, usage of buses, trains, and trolleys declined. By 1960 only 26 percent of central city workers were using public transportation systems.

When central city officials asked for help in shoring up mass transit systems, Congress responded in 1961 by funding demonstration projects and offering to help cities better plan their mass transportation. In subsequent years, the scope of federal involvement increased. Congress authorized aid for mass transit construction in 1964; two years later, it established a Department of Transportation; in 1973 it antagonized the highway lobby by diverting to mass transit funds that had accumulated in the highway trust account; and in 1974 it, for the first time, appropriated funds for transit operations. But despite these efforts to support mass transit, Americans became increasingly dependent upon the automobile; by 1980 the percentage of central city workers commuting by public transport had declined to 14.3 percent.

## Block Grants and Fiscal Relief

The shape of cooperative federalism was modified somewhat with the election of two Republican administrations after 1968. Local officials had been complaining that federal bureaucrats were burdening local governments with unnecessary regulations. In his campaign for the presidency, Nixon made these demands his own. Instead of a system of *categorical grants,* which regulated the way in which state and local governments used federal dollars, he proposed *block grants* that distributed federal monies for locally defined purposes.

Congress responded by enacting three major block grant programs. The first, the General Revenue Sharing Act of 1972 (GRS), corresponded most closely to the Nixon administration's conception of an ideal federal system. Monies were distributed according to a strict formula that gave virtually no discretion to Washington bureaucrats. Local governments needed to submit no more than the most minimal application in order to receive the funds for which they were eligible, and monies were distributed with only minimal restrictions on their use. The program was expected to marry the federal government's ability to raise large amounts of funds equitably with the ability of local government officials to expend monies sensibly and efficiently. Although in some ways general revenue sharing was the very antithesis of an urban policy—the program had no substantive or territorial focus at all—many city governments were grateful for the financial relief it offered.

The second block grant program was the community development block grant (CDBG), established by Congress in 1974. It consolidated model cities, urban renewal, and five other categorical programs into a single grant that was to be used to provide decent housing, suitable environments, and economic opportunities for community residents, particularly residents of low and moderate income. The CDBG legislation represented a compromise between the Nixon administration and the Democratic Congress. On the one side, the Republican administration succeeded in achieving a substantial amount of deregulation: the number of pages contained in the relevant regulations was reduced from 2,600 to 120, and the average application was 50 instead of 1,400 pages in length. On the other side, the Democratic Congress was able to establish the Section Eight subsidy program to make both new and existing rental housing affordable for low- and moderate-income people.

Since CDBG distributed its funds widely to communities of all sizes and fiscal capacities, in 1977, Congress, at the prompting of the Carter administration, created an additional categorical grant program known as the urban development action grants (UDAGs). A modest substitute for urban renewal funds, UDAG assisted the economic and commercial development of cities with especially disadvantaged populations, until the program was terminated in 1985.

The third block grant program, the Comprehensive Employment Training Act of 1974 (CETA), replaced seventeen worker training programs established by the War on Poverty and related programs with a block grant that gave local governments considerable flexibility in designing training for jobless community residents. Congressional Democrats supported the legislation because it authorized funds for public sector employment in any community where the unemployment rate exceeded 6 percent. When Carter became president, the public sector employment component of CETA expanded rapidly, so that by 1978 it accounted for 58 percent of CETA funding. But the discretion that CETA gave to local governments came under criticism when it was discovered that many CETA workers were not particularly disadvantaged, and others were hired to perform traditional municipal functions.

While block grants were the Nixon and Ford administrations' most innovative urban policies, the 1975 New York City fiscal crisis had greater long-term impact: it prompted the most direct federal financial relief ever given to a big city and helped induce the backlash against big cities that would cause Congress's urban programs to contract. New York's steadily growing civic expenditure on an unusually broad range of public services, including hospitals, welfare, and a tuition-free university, combined with a tax base shrinking under the pressure of exceptionally high tax rates, produced a series of budget deficits first evident in the late 1960s. Several years later, when financial markets lost faith in the city's ability to repay its debts, New York City lurched toward bankruptcy. The Ford administration initially rejected New York's request for aid, provoking the notorious *New York Daily News* headline: "Ford to City: 'Drop Dead.' " Congress nonetheless authorized $2.3 billion in loan guarantees for New York on the condition that the city impose on itself a more disciplined budgeting system. Ford then lost the state of New York in his failed attempt at reelection in 1976, but New York became a symbol of urban profligacy that, along with a new conservatism and burgeoning federal deficits, would help undermine pro-urban forces in Congress.

### Rust Belt versus Sun Belt

The cities of the Rust Belt did well at garnering state and federal assistance during the era of cooperative federalism. These cities saw their per capita direct grants in aid increase from $7 to $245 between 1957 and 1977 (Table 6). State aid to Rust Belt cities also increased rapidly—from $3.2 billion in 1957 to $15.1 billion in 1977 (Table 7). As a result of all of these increments in outside assistance, the percentage of the local budget financed out of revenue sources internal to Rust Belt cities fell from 83 percent in 1957 to 58 percent twenty years later (Table 8).

The Sun Belt cities did not quite keep pace with their Rust Belt cousins during the golden years of marble-cake federalism. It is true that the total amount of direct federal assistance they received jumped from $.2 billion to $2.2 billion between 1957 and 1972, a gain only marginally short of the one enjoyed by Rust Belt cities. But when one calculates changes in per capita terms, the growth in aid to Sun Belt cities is less spectacular. Although per capita aid increased from $20 to $238 between 1957 and 1977, Sun Belt cities, which in 1957 had been receiving $13 more per capita in direct aid than Rust Belt cities, were by 1977 receiving $7 less.

The differences between the two regions are more striking when the role of the states is taken into consideration. In 1957 state aid per capita to Sun Belt cities was just half the amount going to Rust Belt cities. From this very low base, the rate of growth over the next

**Table 8. Sources of General Revenue of Big-City Governments in Rust Belt and Sun Belt**

| Revenue Sources | 1957 | 1972 | Year 1977 | 1982 | 1990 |
|---|---|---|---|---|---|
| **All Big Cities** | | | | | |
| Municipal | 83% | 67% | 63% | 69% | 75% |
| Federal | 1 | 7 | 13 | 10 | 5 |
| State | 14 | 24 | 23 | 19 | 19 |
| Other Local | 1 | 1 | 1 | 1 | 1 |
| Total | 100% | 100% | 100% | 100% | 100% |
| **Rust Belt Cities** | | | | | |
| Municipal | 83% | 62% | 58% | 63% | 69% |
| Federal | 1 | 5 | 10 | 9 | 4 |
| State | 15 | 32 | 31 | 27 | 26 |
| Other Local | 1 | 1 | 1 | 1 | 1 |
| Total | 100% | 100% | 100% | 100% | 100% |
| **Sun Belt Cities** | | | | | |
| Municipal | 89% | 78% | 73% | 78% | 84% |
| Federal | 3 | 11 | 18 | 13 | 6 |
| State | 8 | 8 | 7 | 8 | 8 |
| Other Local | 1 | 2 | 1 | 1 | 2 |
| Total | 100% | 100% | 100% | 100% | 100% |

*Sources:* See sources for Tables 1, 2, and 3.

fifteen years was only 2.9 percent per annum, well behind the rate of increase in the Rust Belt cities. After that, state aid increased hardly at all. By 1977 Sun Belt cities were receiving only $101 in state aid per capita—as compared to $707 going to Rust Belt cities.

One must be cautious in making these regional comparisons. It may well be that Sun Belt states assumed responsibility for public services that were being provided at the local level in the Rust Belt. Even so, it is quite remarkable that Sun Belt cities enjoyed only a pale reflection of the steep increases in state aid going to cities of the Rust Belt. In 1977 Sun Belt cities were covering 73 percent of the costs of city government from their own resources, but Rust Belt cities were digging into their own pockets for only 58 percent of the cost. When the day of state and federal fiscal retrenchment would arrive, the big cities of the Rust Belt would prove to be considerably more exposed than their Sun Belt counterparts.

## Urban Retrenchment

Few realized in 1977 that the dramatic expansion in federal aid to cities would soon be reversed by an almost equally rapid contraction. Yet the marble-cake was beginning to crumble under the impact of both intellectual and political change. The intellectual charge against cooperative federalism came from those who studied the implementation of federal programs. They pointed out that when small-scale, experimental, minimally funded programs are justified with grandiose rhetorical flourishes, program outcomes necessarily disappoint constituents. When many different governmental agencies must agree before action can be taken, delays and confusion are almost inevitable. If success is to occur, it will become evident only years, maybe decades, later, long after political support has begun to wane. And when liberal congressional subcommittees, responding to narrowly focused interest groups, sponsor innovative programs, local officials may find them politically threatening.

These difficulties bedeviled categorical grants more than block grant programs. Indeed, they provided the justification for the Nixon and Ford administrations' advocacy of block grants and general revenue sharing. But these less restrictive block grants generated their own critique. Why, it was asked, should the federal taxpayer give unrestricted money to local governments? Would not local officials be more accountable to their own citizens and taxpayers if they were not so dependent on federal assistance?

These intellectual challenges to marble-cake federalism were reinforced by conservative political trends. Even prior to Reagan, urban political muscle was growing flabby. Between 1960 and 1980, the percentage of the population living in big cities had fallen from 21 to 17 percent of the U.S. population. Though urban voters had helped put Jimmy Carter over the top in the general election, he had received only uneven assistance from big city mayors in his pursuit of the Democratic nomination. As budget deficits grew, Carter's urban and welfare policy initiatives encountered increasing resistance in Congress, and the president himself lost enthusiasm for new intergovernmental programs. His Republican successors, Ronald Reagan and George Bush, much less dependent on urban voters, urged deep cuts in social programs. By 1990 Congress's urban policies would be only modestly larger than they had been during the Eisenhower years.

Direct federal assistance to all local governments fell from $32.3 billion in 1977 to $18.4 billion in 1990. Cuts in benefits to big cities were even steeper than the overall cuts to local governments. Federal direct aid to the big cities fell from $9.3 billion in 1977 to $4.5 billion in 1990 (Table 5).

During this same thirteen-year period, federal aid to states rose from $89.7 to $118.4 billion. But states did not pass on much of this increase to local governments. For every dollar states were receiving from the federal government, states in 1990 were passing on to big cities only $0.15, down from $0.21 in 1972.

Two pieces of legislation provided the framework for the urban retrenchment: the 1981 Economic Recovery Tax Act (ERTA) and the Omnibus Budget Reconciliation Act. By cutting taxes more sharply than at any time in the nation's history, ERTA ushered in a decade or more of deficit politics that tightly constrained domestic spending programs and largely foreclosed the possibility of major urban initiatives. The 1981 budget act cut expenditures for most intergovernmental programs. Between 1980 and 1990, mass transit was cut from $5 billion to $3.7 billion. Compensatory education was reduced from $5.3 billion to $4.4 billion. Desegregation assistance was eliminated altogether. By 1990 eligibility for welfare benefits had been tightened, public sector employment abolished, urban development action grants eliminated, and only 52,000 new families were receiving rent subsidies. Only the highway program was still being funded at 1980 levels.

Congress was even less enthusiastic about block grants during the Reagan years. General revenue sharing was eliminated in 1985, and CDBG was cut from $6.1 billion in 1980 to $2.8 billion in 1990. Democrats on Capitol Hill acquiesced in the Reagan administration's proposed cuts in revenue sharing and many block grants, because they wanted to save monies for entitlement programs and the categorical grants over which they had greater control. Also, it was easier to cut block grants when local government coffers were swelling with additional revenues generated by the economic growth of the mid-1980s.

### Cuts in Aid to Rust Belt and Sun Belt Cities

Just as the expansion of the federal role had a disproportionate effect on Rust Belt cities, so did its contraction. Direct aid to Rust

Belt cities declined from $5.2 billion in 1977 to $2.1 billion in 1990
(Table 5). Some of this decline was a function of the population
decline in the cities of the Rust Belt. Yet even when adjustments for
the changing population are taken into account, the federal dollars
were rapidly disappearing. On a per capita basis, federal aid fell
from $245 in 1977 to just $107 thirteen years later (Table 6).

The cuts in federal direct aid were not offset by any increases from
state governments. Instead, state per capita assistance to Rust Belt
cities was only marginally higher in 1990 than it had been in 1977
(Table 7).

With the steep cuts in federal assistance, with state assistance only
barely stabilized, and with continuously rising costs, Rust Belt cities
by 1990 had to depend on their own tax resources for 69 percent of
their general revenues, as compared to 58 percent in 1977 (Table 8).

The changes in the Sun Belt during this period of fiscal retrenchment paralleled those in the Rust Belt. Federal direct aid to Sun Belt
cities slipped from $4.1 billion in 1977 to $2.5 billion in 1990. The rate
of decline over the course of the fifteen-year period closely paralleled
the rate of decline in the Rust Belt. Meanwhile, state aid per capita
climbed modestly from $101 to $131. Overall, Sun Belt cities by 1990
had to finance 84 percent of their revenue needs out of their own
fiscal resources, as compared to 73 percent in 1977 (Table 8).

## Federal Politics and the
## Fiscal Future of Big Cities

Much has been written about the competition among regions,
states, and communities for federal resources. It is often claimed that
the Democratic party, with its roots in cities of the Rust Belt, skews
the distribution of federal funds to the big cities of the Northeast and
Midwest. Conversely, it is claimed that Republicans distribute federal dollars to the suburbs and small towns of the South and West in
order to solidify their hold on these parts of the country. It is further
contended that the flow of federal dollars is significantly affected by
the decennial changes in the system of representation in the House
of Representatives. As regions and types of communities gain in
population, they gain power on Capitol Hill. As a result, they gain
better access to federal dollars.

There are reasons to doubt these claims. First, power in Washington was divided between the two political parties for twenty-four of
the thirty-six years between 1956 and 1992. Even when the Demo-

cratic party controlled both the executive and legislative branches, a conservative coalition of Republicans and southern Democrats exercised considerable influence on Capitol Hill. Legislative compromise, not naked, unconstrained pursuit of narrow partisan objectives, has generally constrained presidential initiatives and congressional responses.

Even more important than divided government is the system of representation required by the Constitution. Members of the House represent areas of the country in proportion to their population. Regardless of its population, each state is represented by two members in the Senate. Presidents represent the country as a whole. Federal grants must be authorized by one set of congressional committees. Monies for the authorized programs must be appropriated by another set of committees. All legislation must navigate a tortuous passage that requires votes in committees, passage on the floors of both Houses, renegotiation in a conference committee that includes representatives from both chambers, repassage on the chamber floors, and, finally, a presidential signature or two-thirds vote by each legislative chamber over the president's veto. Proponents of legislative initiatives have long known that any proposal that is to survive this labyrinth must be constructed in such a way as to weld together a broad, diverse set of interests. Legislative proponents would be taking a great risk if they left any major region or type of community seriously short-handed. Not every program must benefit every district equally, but, taken together, the sum total of federal aid to localities needs to be reasonably well balanced. Politically, it is preferable to find ways of building stable coalitions through logrolling that will distribute federal aid more or less evenly to almost all parts of the country.[3]

Congressional scholars have characterized the propensity of Congress to distribute benefits widely as following the universalism rule. According to this rule, when distributing monies, Congress develops formulas that benefit nearly the entire universe of states and congressional districts. If nearly everyone is likely to benefit, then nearly everyone has a reason for voting for the measure.

The universalism rule is not so powerful that all regional distinctions are eliminated. There is some evidence in our data that the Rust Belt does better when Democrats are in power and the Sun Belt does better when Republicans are in power. For example, the Rust Belt seems to have been helped disproportionately by the initial construction of cooperative federalism between 1957 and 1972, a time when Democrats controlled the Congress for all fifteen years and the presidency for eight of them. Over this period federal per capita aid to Rust Belt cities increased at an annual rate of 19 percent, while per capita aid to the Sun Belt cities rose at an 18.4 percent annual rate. Yet this gain in the Rust Belt simply reduced the original bias of federal aid formulas in favor of the Sun Belt. As of 1972 Sun Belt cities were still receiving $29 more in federal aid per capita than Rust Belt cities.

Ironically, it was while Richard Nixon and Gerald Ford held the presidency that Rust Belt cities finally reached a level playing field with the cities of the Sun Belt. Despite the talk of Richard Nixon's southern strategy, aid to the Rust Belt continued to increase more rapidly than aid to the Sun Belt. By 1977 the Rust Belt cities were receiving virtually the same amount of direct federal aid per capita as their counterparts in the Sun Belt.

Divided government probably explains these Rust Belt gains during a Republican presidency. In order to win congressional support for his revenue-sharing and block grant programs, President Nixon was forced to accept a distribution formula that favored a part of the country that was peripheral to his strategy for an emerging Republican majority. This pattern continued under Nixon's successor, Gerald Ford, who not only presided over the largest increment in federal aid to American cities passed by a Democratic Congress but acquiesced in a continuing shift in federal aid to the Rust Belt. In retrospect, President Ford hardly seems to have deserved the "Drop Dead" headline accorded him by the *New York Daily News*.

The cuts imposed on federal grants after 1977 were more partisan in nature. During the Carter years (1977 to 1982), Rust Belt cities suffered cuts in per capita aid that averaged 2 percent per annum, while Sun Belt cities suffered cuts that averaged 2.4 percent. In other words, the federal budget cutbacks were bad for all big cities, but were especially harsh for the Republican Sun Belt. Quite opposite effects occurred during the Reagan-Bush years. Between 1982 and 1990, Rust Belt cities were clobbered by cuts that averaged 9.5 percent per annum, while Sun Belt cities endured cuts of only 4.5 percent per annum. In the Reagan-Bush era, all cities suffered deeper cuts in federal aid than ever before, but it was the cities of the Rust Belt that had the biggest bite taken from their budget.

However, even these signs of partisanship in the federal grant-making mechanism should not be exaggerated. With all the partisan maneuvering that certainly took place, Sun Belt cities in 1990 were still receiving only $3 more in federal aid per capita than Rust Belt cities.

Not only have big cities in both regions been treated more or less equally over time, but big cities in general have fared about as well as smaller municipalities in the federal system. During the construction of cooperative federalism between 1957 and 1977, federal aid to all local governments increased at roughly the same rate at which federal aid to big cities increased. Since cities were losing a 2 percentage point share of the national population during this time, cities did well to gain as much in direct aid as other parts of the country. There seems to be some—but no more than some—truth to the conventional wisdom that John Kennedy and Lyndon Johnson paid their debt to Chicago Mayor Richard Daley and other big city politicians by giving them special favors.

Later, when cuts in direct federal aid to localities were promulgated, all local governments suffered the consequences. Between 1977 and 1990 direct federal aid to local governments declined by 43 percent. Cities were hit somewhat more severely. Direct federal aid to big cities fell by 51 percent. Thus there is some—but only some— truth to the conventional belief that Carter, Reagan, and Bush turned their backs on big cities in particular.

More important than the petty politics of partisan shading of funds to one part of the country or another are the tides in ideological opinion about the proper role to be played by the federal government in addressing the country's social problems. The enormous increments in federal dollars that came to the cities during the 1960s and early 1970s were rooted in a belief in cooperative federalism. Public officials were committed to the principle that all governments, working together, could ameliorate the country's social ills. In more recent years expectations that governments could solve social problems were sharply dampened. As a result, federal aid to states and localities was cut back to levels not much higher—as a percentage of GNP—than those prevailing when Dwight Eisenhower held the presidency. Big cities had to turn increasingly to their own resources not because of shifts in regional balances of power, but because of shifting ideological opinion about the appropriate role of government.

The fiscal future of big cities in the 1990s seems to be extremely dependent on the way in which the political climate evolves in this decade. If big cities are to be left to their own resources, the fiscal crises evident in some cities in the early 1990s may spread rapidly throughout the Rust Belt. But if state and federal governments are rethinking cooperative federalism and deciding that intergovernmental grants, for all their faults, are a necessary part of modern governance, then larger programs of intergovernmental assistance may again help cities avoid an impending fiscal crisis that otherwise seems especially likely in the Rust Belt. Cities do not need more or better representation in Congress in order to have their special interests taken specifically into account. What they need is a national political and policy commitment that sees urban needs as an intimate part of the country's broader social agenda.

## Notes

[1] The definition of the Rust Belt used in this chapter includes the cities and states of the Northeast, Midwest, and border state regions, together with Washington, D.C. Cities of the Sun Belt are defined as those cities located in the states of the Old Confederacy and west of the Mississippi River.

[2] Since our data are taken, for the most part, from the five-year U.S. census of governments, we report in the tables the fiscal situation for every fifth year beginning in 1957. The reader will notice that these dates do not always coincide exactly with the watershed political events that are discussed in the text.

[3] Markusen, Saxenian, and Weiss (1981), pp. 5–35.

# MAKING CHANGES: COMMUNITY INITIATIVES AND NEW POLICIES FOR CITIES AND THE NATION

# 9

## Emerging Approaches to Community Development

### PAUL C. BROPHY

The destinies of cities are dependent upon the successful inter-connections among the players critical to the growth and revi-talization of both downtowns and neighborhoods. The factors that shape our cities and the communities within them are a complex mix of governmental, civic, private for-profit and not-for-profit, commu-nity, and market forces. This chapter deals with four important di-mensions emerging in cities to rejuvenate communities:

- Some city governments have become increasingly entrepreneurial in their approaches to physical and economic improvement, play-

PAUL C. BROPHY is vice chair of The Enterprise Foundation, a charita-ble organization building a national system of housing for very poor peo-ple. From 1977–86, Mr. Brophy held positions in the city of Pittsburgh government, first as director of the city's Housing Department and then as executive director of the Urban Redevelopment Authority. Mr. Brophy has taught at the School of Urban and Public Affairs, Carnegie Mellon University, and the Graduate School of Public and International Affairs, University of Pittsburgh. He is co-author of *Housing and Local Government* and *Neighborhood Revitalization: Theory and Practice,* as well as author of numerous articles in professional journals.

ing the role of policy developer and dealmaker in leading city progress.

- More communities are tackling their revitalization agendas through partnerships between the public sector and the private sector, and these partnership approaches are extending beyond long-standing shared agencies, such as downtown renewal, into neighborhood improvement.
- A major new force—community based development organizations—has emerged in cities across the country, and they are working successfully to carry out neighborhood improvement.
- Comprehensive approaches to community development are underway in various localities in an effort to move beyond traditional physical revitalization approaches to improve the overall quality of life in neighborhoods—the physical, social, and economic.

These are critical changes in the ways cities are conducting their business, and they carry great potential for sustained success. But these promising approaches must be viewed in the dramatically changed world that cities have been facing over the past thirty years. In fact, in discussing changes in cities, a careful definition of "central cities" and "suburbs" is needed because cities and suburbs have changed in ways that challenge old stereotypes.

As Joel Garreau has reported in *Edge City,* today large numbers of Americans live, shop, and work in suburban employment, retail, and residential centers he calls "edge cities." These are areas that have developed their own identities and are their own destinations, like Tysons Corner, near Washington, D.C.; Las Colinas between Dallas and Fort Worth, Texas; and King of Prussia, Pennsylvania, outside Philadelphia. Garreau reports that there are more than 200 of these full-fledged "edge cities" and they have grown rapidly over the past thirty years. A great deal of suburban office space is now located in these places, and most of these facilities were developed in the 1970s and 1980s.[1]

"Edge cities" are not a surprising phenomenon, given the increased accessibility of much suburban land through the interstate highway system, the shift in jobs from manufacturing to information and services, and the willingness of many suburbs to encourage population growth and employment. The effect of suburban growth on central cities has been dramatic. Some cities, those David Rusk calls "elastic cities," have responded by annexing these growth areas.[2] Many other "inelastic cities"—those unable to stretch their boundaries—are suffering the financial challenge of serving as the core to a region while encountering an ever-dwindling tax base.

These older central cities have suffered deeply over the past twenty years. A few key indicators tell the story:

- *Central cities have lost population.*
  In 1950 almost 70 percent of metropolitan populations lived in central cities; in 1990, 60 percent of the population lived in suburbs, not central cities.
- *Poverty levels are higher in central cities, and poverty is increasingly segregated even within central cities.*
  The number of African-Americans living in concentrated areas of poverty increased 36 percent from 1980 to 1990, from 4.3 million to 5.9 million. The number of census tracts classified as ghettos grew 54 percent in the decade.
- *Children living in poverty increased 22 percent during the 1980s, mostly in central cities.*
  In 1989 the poverty rate for children under six was 30 percent in central cities, 16 percent for suburban areas.
- *Adjusting for inflation, federal aid to cities was cut 60 percent from 1980 to 1992.*
  This put these cities in a position where their dwindling tax base must serve to pick up costs once covered by the federal government.

This is the troubled context for most central cities. These changes threaten the health and vitality of cities. They have led to the important realization by city leaders that central cities must compete for survival and health.

## City Governments as Entrepreneurs

The best city governments in America are learning to be entrepreneurs in a wide range of their municipal functions.[3] This movement to entrepreneurship is evident in community development activities. Cities had a long way to go in learning how to conduct the business of physical and economic redevelopment. For many years the federal government discouraged local creativity and entrepreneurship.

The oldest federal housing program—public housing—has been administered as a top-down federal program, with the federal government setting detailed design constraints, funding levels, and approval processes. The local public authorities created as part of the program have had little room to connect to the broader community and to invent new approaches to local housing problems.

The widely used federally funded urban renewal program was a step in the right direction. Local redevelopment authorities submitted specific plans to the federal government for the acquisition, redesign, and redevelopment of blighted areas. Once approved, these authorities implemented the plan, involving the private real estate development industry as redevelopers with the local authorities handling the design review, land disposition, and relocation functions. Localities successfully operationized business relationships with private real estate developers.

In the 1970s federal programs shifted considerably, giving local governments more room to be creative. The community development block grant program of 1974 (CDBG) passed money to cities to benefit low- and moderate-income families, eliminate slums and blight, or meet urgent needs. This program represented a major shift of the policy process and program decision making to the local level. As a result, some cities become very entrepreneurial in their approach to urban development.

Faneuil Hall Marketplace in Boston is a good example of this kind of local government entrepreneurship. Heralded as a critical development in improving Boston's downtown, it is a mixed-use project developed by the Rouse Company and opened in the summers of 1976–78. The project consists of 215,000 square feet of retail and 170,000 square feet of office space near Boston's waterfront. The $30 million renovation was augmented by $12 million of public investment.

But to say that the Rouse Company was the developer is too simple. Both the Rouse Company and the Boston Redevelopment Authority (BRA) developed the Faneuil Hall Marketplace together as entrepreneurial partners. The BRA acted as the development partner that negotiated the purchase of two privately owned buildings that flanked the publicly owned Quincy Market. It relocated 400 businesses, installed new utilities, restored the facades, and improved streets. BRA then selected the Rouse Company as developer and manager of the market buildings, leasing the buildings for $1 per year for ninety-nine years. The city of Boston agreed to set property taxes as a percent of gross rental income. In exchange for its financing incentives, city government became a limited development partner getting a percentage of the center's net cash flow.

Faneuil Hall Marketplace is one of a genre of transactions that have occurred throughout American cities in which a public body has become a key partner in the execution of the urban project. Many of these projects obtained financial support from the urban development action grant program (UDAG), a federal program that emphasized entrepreneurial public-private ventures.

From 1977 to 1985 the federal UDAG program encouraged city governments to take on a more entrepreneurial role than earlier federal efforts. The UDAG program awarded grants to local governments for feasible, ready-to-go projects intended to create jobs and stimulate local economic development. Unlike urban renewal, local governments had to obtain binding financial commitments from developers, investors, and other project partners before the federal government would provide its support. There was no formula or maximum limit for the award of funds, so large projects, previously limited by numerous local demands on the annual community development block grant funds, became possible with UDAG. Priority for funding was given to projects with the highest private-to-public investment ratios. Cities were encouraged to make funds available to private development projects as loans instead of grants and to structure deals so that the local government would receive a return on its investment. Local governments were encouraged to become sophisticated real estate partners focused on "making deals happen."

The program produced results. By March 1990 the Department of Housing and Urban Development (HUD) had used $4.6 billion in UDAG funds to leverage $31.8 billion in private investment in 2,984 urban projects in 1,209 communities. These projects generated 592,-000 new jobs and created 113,000 new or substantially rehabbed housing units. Unfortunately, the UDAG program's funding was ended in 1988.

Of enduring importance, the program taught cities how to be entrepreneurs in housing and commercial real estate developments. This entrepreneurial approach was needed during the 1980s, when deep federal cutbacks in aid to cities required great inventiveness and political strength to keep improvement programs going and to find new sources of funds to partially substitute for declining of federal assistance.

The depth of these cutbacks was immense. For example, the Reagan administration cut federal funds for new housing from over $30 billion in 1981 to $8 billion in 1987. By 1986 city governments were raising about 72 percent of their total revenues from their own sources, compared to 63 percent in 1980. In 1979 Baltimore received federal assistance for 2,100 housing units. In 1989 the number was 400. Other cities suffered similar declines.

To cope with the loss of federal aid, many cities have developed creative approaches to tapping local sources of funds and dedicating them to housing and neighborhood development activities. One approach that cities have taken is to find special sources of revenues to place in housing trust funds—funds specifically earmarked for housing development in cities. Creative approaches for capital include:

- *Program income* such as loan repayments from the community development block grant program and the urban development action grant program.
- *Linkage fees* that, in strong market settings, require developers of commercial real estate to pay fees to help finance affordable housing needed because of the increased jobs produced by the new commercial developments.
- *Cable TV franchise proceeds.* San Antonio, Texas, took $10 million from its cable TV franchise fee and created the San Antonio Housing Trust Fund, an active funder of housing development in San Antonio.
- *Real estate transfer fees and documentation stamps* produced almost $90 million in Dade County, Florida, to finance the development of 2,850 new or rehabilitated homes from 1984 to 1992.
- *Escheat funds* (unclaimed property, bank accounts, and so on) are used in Ohio and Arizona for both housing finance guarantees and seed money loans to nonprofit, public, and limited dividend developers for the construction and rehabilitation of low-income housing.

Other entrepreneurial efforts by local governments involve leveraging private investment in affordable housing without direct subsidies. For example, jurisdictions have deposited cash and short-term public investments in financial institutions that agree to make mortgages available for targeted income groups or for multifamily and economic development projects in neighborhoods undergoing revitalization. These "linked deposit" programs are in place in eighteen states and twelve cities.

With more than $700 billion in assets, public pension fund investment in a wide range of commercial, housing, small business, and economic development projects is gaining credibility and momentum with state and local governments. Public pension investments are overcoming risk constraints through the use of intermediaries or through public or private credit enhancements. Some twenty-one states have made economically targeted investments, and this resource shows promise for much greater activity.

This creativity and entrepreneurship at the local level are far from uniform, however. Many cities have actually lost capacity to be effective as the result of the federal cutbacks of the 1980s, municipal budget reductions, and the growing poverty in their neighborhoods. Staffs had to be cut. A growing reregulation of the federal programs stymied creativity leading to local government efforts that are poorly administered in some cities. More energy goes into conforming to confusing regulations than to implementing aggressive efforts to improve community conditions.

In the most troublesome cases, scarce funds in an environment of greater needs have caused solid policy making about *what* the local community development agenda should be to deteriorate into the politics of *who* will control the funds and who will benefit politically. Such cities are clearly worse off than they were twenty years ago. Their problems are deeper, they have fewer resources, and their overall ability to be effective has declined. In these cities, much capacity-building work is needed to set in motion improved decision making, better trained staff, streamlined and more efficient program delivery, and improved organizational patterns—all leading to local governments that can emulate their peers, the cities that have succeeded in their efforts to implement a bold community development agenda despite federal cutbacks.

## Public-Private Partnerships

One of the enduring successful approaches that city leadership has used since World War II in tackling key city problems has been a sustained working relationship between local government and the business community.

It has become a standard practice for mayors and county executives to reach out to the business community for support for large-scale city projects such as downtown improvements, convention centers, and stadiums, just as the business community has looked to elected officials for support for their agendas. Where this working relationship has thrived, so have critical urban development efforts.

In Portland, Pittsburgh, Baltimore, Cleveland, and many other cities, the successful revitalization of downtowns has been the result of a long-standing relationship between government and business interests, represented by a professionally run business group. In Portland, it is Portland Progress Associates; in Pittsburgh, the Allegheny Conference on Community Development; in Baltimore, the Greater Baltimore Committee; and in Cleveland, Cleveland Tomorrow. These organizations have been the vehicle for the business community to express its voice and vision—and to apply its talent and resources—as partners with local governments to implement difficult, challenging projects and improvements that serve a region or a city. Examples of this success abound: Pittsburgh's Golden Triangle, Baltimore's Charles Center and Inner Harbor, and Cleveland's downtown revitalization are well-known illustrations of the benefits of effective working partnerships between local governments and local business communities.

The partnership lessons that have been learned from successful downtown and regional ventures are now being applied to neighborhood improvement efforts as well—and with very promising results.

- In 1983 in Pittsburgh, a group of bankers, corporate leaders, local foundations, civic leaders, local government and neighborhood leaders—with assistance from the Ford Foundation—joined to create the Pittsburgh Partnership for Neighborhood Development. The partnership's aim is to stimulate neighborhood recovery through housing and economic development projects, and through the strengthening of the capacity of neighborhood groups. The private sector partners are called on to lend funds, and to invest equity in projects. City government provides subsidy dollars to make housing and economic development projects feasible, and the foundations provide coordinated financial support to neighborhood groups.

  More importantly, the partnership acts as an ally and advocate for neighborhood reinvestment. By 1990 the partnership's sponsors numbered two dozen foundations, banks, and corporations, and the partnership was providing sustained project and operating funding to ten neighborhood development groups.

- In Atlanta, the Chamber of Commerce and the city government—with financial assistance from the Ford Foundation and technical help from The Enterprise Foundation—created the Atlanta Neighborhood Development Partnership (ANDP). ANDP's creation was a major breakthrough for Atlanta. Even though the city had a proud record of accomplishment on its downtown improvements, Atlanta did not have a structured way of tackling its neighborhood agenda. With solid corporate leadership and an energetic and creative executive director, ANDP has been able to raise $10.5 million of private capital for neighborhood investment, and is providing help to ten neighborhood based groups who are working on their grassroots improvement efforts.

ANDP's mission includes the development of housing for its own ownership, as well as assistance to other nonprofit housing and commercial developers. While still a young organization—it was launched in 1991—ANDP is likely to be a permanent fixture in Atlanta's civic machinery, acting as a key stimulant in combining the private interests and resources on its board with those in city government.

• In Boston, the Metropolitan Boston Housing Partnership is a full-service regional nonprofit corporation that develops and preserves affordable housing, administers a rental assistance program throughout the greater Boston area, and sponsors initiatives that encourage resident participation and control in housing, neighborhoods, social services, and economic opportunities. The partnership's board includes the CEOs of the areas largest financial institutions, neighborhood leaders, government officials, and prominent academics. Working together, this group has been able to solve problems that no one of the parties in the partnership could solve alone.

These partnerships are particularly valuable ways of involving lending institutions in neighborhood improvement efforts. Spurred by the federal Community Reinvestment Act that requires affirmative efforts to lend in underserved areas, lending institutions have found partnerships to be an effective way to exercise their community lending responsibilities.

Each of these partnerships is different in make-up and specific program thrust, but they all share the critical common feature that they build commitment and capacity to improve neighborhoods as a broad agreed-on urban mission. Partnerships like these exist in about fifty cities, according to the National Association of Housing Partnerships, a support organization formed to help local partnerships.

This extension of the partnership mode of conducting local civic businesses into neighborhoods, while positive, still has much growth before it. Although it is second nature for a mayor or county executive to work with the private sector on downtown-type issues, the commonality of interest in working on a neighborhood agenda is often not as obvious. Ongoing help is needed to solidify these new partnerships so that they can become a permanent vehicle for improving neighborhoods and thereby strengthen cities.

## The Community Based Development Movement

The spirit of entrepreneurship has grown not only in local governments. In cities throughout the country a similar phenomenon has occurred in neighborhoods. Alarmed by the growing deterioration of their communities, groups throughout the country have decided to take direct action, not only as advocates for improvement, but as the actual purveyors of the needed change.

Development by neighborhood based groups—called community development corporations (CDCs), community based development organizations (CBDOs), or community housing development organizations (CHDOs)—has become a major force in the 1990s for creating housing and neighborhood-scale commercial projects. The National Congress for Community Economic Development (NCCED), the trade association for these neighborhood based developers, reported that in 1991 there were 2,000 groups nationally—in virtually every city, and that they had produced over 320,000 units of housing and had created or retained almost 90,000 permanent jobs through neighborhood economic development activities.

These groups have a number of common characteristics. They are small-scale entrepreneurial developers; they produce housing and commercial projects in scale with the neighborhoods in which they are working; they are led by dedicated, able volunteers and professional staff; they are creative and unconventional in the approaches they take; and they are concerned with more than the physical improvement of their neighborhoods.

In addition to NCCED, three major national nonprofits provide assistance to these groups in helping them grow as a force for improving neighborhoods.

• The Local Initiatives Support Corporation (LISC), created by the Ford Foundation in 1979, has provided working capital and corporate equity to 875 community development corporations nationwide who have produced over 44,000 housing units. LISC has become a leading social investment banker, raising more than $800 million in donations and investments to help nonprofits succeed at their housing and economic development efforts. LISC has active programs in thirty cities.

- The Enterprise Foundation, launched in 1983 by Jim and Patty Rouse, has helped over 300 nonprofits in 100 cities in its first ten years. Enterprise has played a major role in strengthening nonprofit housing development groups, building local housing partnerships, helping local groups link needed services into the housing produced, and demonstrating creative approaches to low-income community development. Through 1992 Enterprise had raised $670 million in private capital for over 25,000 housing units produced by the groups with whom it is working.

- The Neighborhood Reinvestment Corporation was created by an act of Congress in 1978 to aid community groups in stimulating reinvestment in housing in city neighborhoods. Its role has been to stimulate neighborhood partnerships aimed at revitalizing deteriorating neighborhoods. These partnerships, operating in nearly 250 neighborhoods across the country, aim to improve the quality of life in low- and moderate-income neighborhoods through a range of housing rehabilitation and construction activities, economic development and commercial centralization, and related neighborhood improvement efforts.

Each of these organizations is working to institutionalize the neighborhood based development movement by providing organizing help, technical assistance, capital, and the transfer of learning from one group and city to another. The results—in new private investment and housing units produced—was clearly apparent by the start of the 1990s. Far more capacity exists at the neighborhood level to effect change than ever before. These neighborhood based groups have become a positive force in cities, able to be a partner with city governments, lenders, and others to produce needed, sustained change.

But there is also much fragility with many of these community groups, and much more help is needed to grow the strength of this urban asset. First, many of the groups—like most small, start-up businesses—are in need of assistance. They require basic skills training and funding to pay core staff, regular sources of working capital, and an ability to stabilize budgets over a multiyear time frame. Some important progress has been made in this regard as part of the federal HOME program. Passed by Congress in 1990, this program provides what is essentially an affordable housing block grant to state and local governments. Fifteen percent of the HOME funds (currently $2 billion a year) are set aside for nonprofit community based housing developers, and 5 percent of a city's funds can be used to support the operating costs of these groups.

Second, the relationship of community development groups with local governments must be solidified. Some city administrations—Dallas, New York City, Pittsburgh, for example—make it a policy to build the capacity of neighborhood based developers. Many local officials see the value of strong community development groups who can improve neighborhoods as important partners in a revitalization effort. Other local officials, however, view the notion of building and supporting neighborhood groups as a threat, since strong community based groups also constitute a demand system on city hall that can often exert considerable political pressure. Neighborhood groups succeed best where the environment includes a friendly city hall. In fact, in the best of circumstances, the entrepreneurial spirit in local government combines with that of community based groups, helping both players accomplish their mutual goal of urban revitalization.

Third, these community based groups must continue to find ways to work effectively with other players who can be helpful: as joint-venture partners with solid and experienced for-profit developers; as valued customers of lending institutions; as partners with social service agencies, able to provide services needed by the residents of the housing developed; and as political allies with others fighting for broad urban improvements.

Without question, the community based development corporations are on their way to becoming institutionalized in cities. They are likely to grow in importance and permanence on the urban scene.

## The Movement toward Holistic Approaches

There is a growing realization that community development efforts cannot be successful if they are limited to the physical improvement of cities and communities. This country has suffered through the pain of seeing well-designed urban development and housing projects fail because of socioeconomic conditions.

America's toughest neighborhoods are not slums just because they are physically deteriorated. They are undesirable places to live because their schools don't educate children well; they are unsafe; they lack job opportunities; health care is poor; and they are infested with illegal drugs. In short, they don't function as good places to live for the women, men, and children living there. The result of this deepening understanding of the multidimensional nature of the problems of these deeply distressed areas of America's cities has been a movement toward holistic approaches to community development.

The idea of comprehensive neighborhood approaches is not a new one. The Model Cities Program begun by the federal government in the 1960s had as its goal the demonstration of successful comprehensive approaches to neighborhood improvement. Designed to be a limited experiment in a few cities, by the time the program was approved by Congress, it had been expanded to 150 cities. Since program budgets were far below what was needed for effective results, the program had little or no permanent positive change in its cities—and it was generally viewed as a misfire.

One unfortunate outcome of the disappointing performance of the Model Cities Program was that it created a "nothing can be done" mood about deeply distressed neighborhoods that persisted through the 1980s. However, led in part by national philanthropies, a number of promising comprehensive approaches are underway. A report by Arlene Eisen in 1992 documented eleven "comprehensive neighborhood based community improvement approaches."[4] Eisen reports that these largely new efforts are based on three principles. They are:

- Comprehensive—they are based on the belief in a system approach that reflects the understanding that people, families, and neighborhoods are interdependent parts of a whole.
- Neighborhood based.
- Empowering of the community in both process and outcomes. "In the process of empowerment, neighborhood residents assume leadership to make decisions regarding all phases of program planning, implementation and evaluation. The outcome of empowerment is increased access to and control over resources—including organizational resources—by neighborhood residents."[5]

Key among the comprehensive efforts underway in various city neighborhoods are the Enterprise Foundation–city of Baltimore effort known as Community Building in Partnership, and former President Carter's Atlanta Project.

## The Enterprise Foundation's
## Neighborhood Transformation Program

In 1989 The Enterprise Foundation identified as one of its top goals the need to demonstrate that the transformation of America's most troubled neighborhoods is possible. Enterprise's work with neighborhood based housing developers around the country had shown very positive results in the production of housing and the improvement of the lives of the low-income families occupying the housing. But nowhere had the work led to the turning around of a complete neighborhood, because a far more comprehensive, multifaceted, radical approach was needed to literally transform a neighborhood.

Enterprise concluded that it "must demonstrate that these conditions can be transformed, that poor people in America can live decent lives in decent neighborhoods and that it will cost less for our people to live in healthy neighborhoods than in sick and painful ones."[6]

With strong support from Mayor Kurt Schmoke in Baltimore, the first neighborhood selected for the Neighborhood Transformation Program was the Sandtown-Winchester section of that city. In 1990 residents of the Sandtown-Winchester community, the city of Baltimore, and Enterprise launched the transformation effort known as "Community Building in Partnership," with the vision of redirecting all public and private support systems, including housing, education, health care, family support, public safety, and employment to benefit and empower community residents. An emphasis on changing fundamental systems and on family focused programs and services is basic to the transformation vision.

The neighborhood selected is one of Baltimore's most troubled: a population of 10,000; a 1990 median family income of $10,500; 45 percent of its households receiving public assistance; 44 percent unemployment or underemployment; 90 percent of births to unwed mothers; one of the top five high-crime neighborhoods in Baltimore; a school dropout rate of 20 percent per year; 600 vacant structures; and only 20 percent home ownership.

A strong partnership between the mayor, local residents, and The Enterprise Foundation, with financial support from foundations and corporations, has enabled community residents to organize and develop their own vision of how their neighborhood should be transformed.[7] The program's planning approach has involved neighborhood residents in setting goals and designing programs for all aspects of neighborhood and housing revitalization and the transformation of community services and systems.

Essential to the neighborhood transformation concept is that all of the dysfunctioning systems and destructive conditions must be dealt with at the same time in order to gain the reinforcing strength of change in all elements of life in these deeply distressed neighborhoods. The approach calls for radical results in improved delivery of community services. The Baltimore program has five basic goals:

- All children will be ready to succeed in school.
- All young adults will be prepared to enter the work force.
- All families will be able to support and care for themselves.
- All residents will live in a safe, nurturing environment and enjoy a significantly improved quality of life.
- The community will be mobilized and empowered to sustain an improved quality of life.

Detailed efforts are underway in physical and economic developments, education, human services, and community building to change the systems serving the neighborhood radically enough to reach the five stated goals.

The Sandtown-Winchester demonstration is a bold effort to prove that a radical transformation of a poverty neighborhood can be accomplished, with the result that the public cost of supporting the neighborhood in the future is less rather than more.

## The Atlanta Project

Dramatic in its scale and intent, the Atlanta Project led by former President Jimmy Carter is a community-wide effort aimed at increasing cooperation among levels of government, private industry, community leaders, and academic and other community institutions to address the social problems associated with poverty in urban areas. It is predicated on the idea that solutions require the pooling of individual efforts and resources, and envisions the use of massive numbers of volunteers. The Atlanta Project's aim is to reduce poverty, hopelessness, and despair in these neighborhoods, as well as the problems connected with poverty: school age pregnancy and dropout rates, juvenile delinquency, crime and violence, homelessness, drug abuse, and unemployment.

Organized into twenty cluster neighborhoods in Atlanta's Fulton, DeKalb, and Clayton counties, the Atlanta Project has successfully connected people and leaders within each neighborhood with corporations and volunteers from outside the neighborhoods to work toward its goals. The essential philosophy and goal of the project is to encourage the twenty target communities to identify their problems, devise their own solutions, and provide the resources for the community residents to empower themselves. Its grassroots efforts use cluster coordinators working in each area to organize steering committees of residents to be responsible for the program at the neighborhood level. A secretariat, with leaders in community development, economic development, education, health, housing, and criminal justice, provides leadership and initiatives in each of their areas. Atlanta based corporations have volunteered to partner with each of the project's clusters.

The energy level is high, and the potential is enormous for this effort to develop new creative approaches to overcoming problems of poverty. The Atlanta Project is working to bridge the social and class segregation that exists increasingly in older cities.

These comprehensive low-income neighborhood recovery efforts have similar goals, but use different techniques, organizational patterns, and points of emphasis. They share the common conviction that the approach taken must genuinely be rooted in the neighborhood, and that new ways of approaching persistent problems must be invented. They also challenge the long-standing categorical approach to service delivery, requiring bottom-to-top redeployment of resources so service delivery can be more effective for low-income people.

## Implications for Public Policy

The changes in central cities and the four key dimensions of changes in community development described briefly in this chapter have important public policy implications for reinventing the federal government's role in supporting community development efforts.

- Over the past decade, HUD has virtually limited its shrinking budget to housing assistance. The "urban development" in Housing and Urban Development has all but vanished. The federal government needs to become a friendly partner to local community development efforts. Playing such a partnership role requires a radical shift in the federal government's posture toward local community development efforts—one that puts more emphasis on enabling and fostering local creativity and entrepreneurship than on regulating every detail of expenditure.

• The comprehensive approaches to neighborhood improvement now underway call on the federal government to respond in innovative new ways—with vastly improved interagency cooperation and a willingness to support the proposition that programs that connect and work more effectively at the neighborhood level are needed for effective change to occur.

• Strengthening older central cities in the context of the widespread suburbanization of jobs and tax bases challenges the federal government to promote incentives to foster regional approaches that correct the imbalance in city and suburban fiscal arrangements, allowing central cities to become more capable of self-renewal. Cities need help in revitalizing the quality of the public services they can provide so as to attract and hold middle-income households and businesses.

• Local governments and community based groups need help to attract and hold the talent required to be successful with their community development agenda. A human resources development initiative, supported by the federal government, is needed to draw additional skilled people into the community development field.

• The federal government should use all of the incentives and programs possible to steer private capital into community development efforts. Capital is needed to rebuild inner city areas into stronger residential and commercial markets. These approaches can be uses of the tax code—such as the successful low-income housing tax credit and enterprise zones; new institutions like community development banks; and the continuation of the Community Reinvestment Act, requiring lending institutions to lend in low-income areas.

The entry of the federal government into the local community development agenda as an effective partner will greatly enhance the potential for successful and thriving programs and communities.

# Notes

[1] Garreau (1991), p. 5.

[2] Rusk (1993).

[3] See Duckworth, Simmons, and McNulty (1986) for a broad view of entrepreneurial approaches taken by cities outside of community development.

[4] Eisen (1992) reports on comprehensive efforts in sixteen locations sponsored by eleven foundations or collaborations.

[5] Eisen (1992), p. 1.

[6] Rouse (1992), p. 345.

[7] Part of the work of organizing the neighborhood residents is being undertaken by Baltimoreans United in Leadership Development (BUILD), a local affiliate of the Industrial Areas Foundation, as discussed in chapter 13.

# 10

## Quality of Life and Amenities as Urban Investment

### ROBERT H. MCNULTY

U rban revitalization is not a new business, and our complex urban ills necessarily require a complex solution. However, strategies that consume less capital, but that (1) foster pride; (2) enhance the sense of community; and (3) encourage economic development can play an important part in larger revitalization programs. Successful completion of the revitalization process is predicated on the skillful use of what are most often limited financial resources. One such low-cost strategy is cultural and amenity planning, whereby resources like museums, libraries, and other cultural institu-

ROBERT H. MCNULTY is founder and president of Partners for Livable Places, a nonprofit Washington, D.C. based coalition of 1,000 organizations concerned with economic health and quality of life. He formerly directed Columbia University's Historic Preservation Program in the Graduate School of Architecture, Planning and Preservation, and was assistant director of the Art and Architecture Program at the National Endowment for the Arts. He is the author of several articles and co-author of three books: *Economics of Amenity*, *Return of the Livable City*, and *Entrepreneurial American City*. Mr. McNulty would like to acknowledge the assistance of Daniel S. McCahan in the preparation of this chapter.

232 ROBERT H. MCNULTY

tions; parks and recreation programs; quality design standards; and arboretums and aquariums are used to promote the basic economic development that is essential to our cities. Such a strategy also seeks to instill a sense of place and a common purpose—two critical elements that are often missing in the most depressed areas.

## American and European Cities
## Can Learn from Each Other

Today it is generally acknowledged that U.S. inner cities are facing difficulties, left behind by a citizenry that for a variety of reasons prefers to live outside the core. But it is also a popular misconception that European cities are far more loved and much better cared for than their U.S. counterparts. Recent studies have uncovered a growing urban affliction in Western countries, even in wealthy, socially responsive countries like Germany and the Netherlands. While these afflictions—urban decay, underemployment, restless minority populations—are not nearly so pronounced in Europe as they are in the United States, they certainly foreshadow similar futures for urban areas on both sides of the Atlantic.

Experts and lay people alike tend to entertain a somewhat idealized notion of the European city, one that calls to mind human scale and pedestrian centered, almost medieval urban cores. However, modern development and technology have relegated areas that fit this description to a mostly symbolic role within the larger urban area. Today, European cities resemble their American counterparts in many ways, from their crowded superhighways to their decaying urban centers. Few would argue that European cities are in a state comparable to those in the United States, but recent studies suggest that they too have their problems, and they sound strikingly like those that U.S. cities have been burdened with.

### The State of the Cities Report

In 1992 a team of journalists and urban experts interviewed residents of three European cities—Rotterdam, Frankfurt, and Glasgow—and three North American cities—Atlanta, Chicago, and Toronto. Their findings, published as the "European–North American State of the Cities Report," sponsored by the German Marshall Fund of the United States, indicate that cities on both sides of the Atlantic face similar problems. To quote the report, "Even the most prosperous of the six cities . . . hide deep economic, social, and sometimes racial divisions which damage their ability to compete." For example:

- Frankfurt has drug and crime related problems cited by business-people as jeopardizing the city's role as a major financial center. Immigrants and refugees are being blamed for many of the city's problems.
- From 1965 to 1980 Rotterdam's population dropped from 731,000 to 579,000. At the same time suburbanization increased. Unemployment in the city, where minorities are concentrated, is around 17 percent.
- Glasgow, struggling to convert from manufacturing to a service economy, lost 27 percent of its population between 1971 and 1987.

Even with all the cultural, demographic, historical, and political differences among the cities, the report still cited four distinct similarities shared by all the cities in the report:

1. Dramatic declines in manufacturing.
2. Growth in white-collar jobs in the city center, usually filled by persons living in the suburbs.
3. Loss of population in city centers, coupled with rapid population growth in the suburbs.
4. Significant immigrant populations (except in Glasgow).

### Background from the Organization for Economic Cooperation and Development

In November of 1992, the Organization for Economic Cooperation and Development (OECD), an international group with representatives from all the Western European countries, the United States, Canada, Australia, and New Zealand, held its International Conference on the Economic, Social and Environmental Problems of Cities. The conference position paper cited economic growth, social development, the environment, finances, and geopolitical change as the most urgent challenges for *all* participating countries. Unlike the "State of the Cities" report, the members of the OECD did not go so far as to draw distinctions between regions, countries, and continents. Rather they sought to identify common issues and concerns that desperately need to be addressed. Comments from the conference position paper shed considerable light on urban conditions in these developed nations:

- Concentrations of the poor, and of ethnics and minorities who statistically are more likely to be poor, are characteristic of urban areas.
- There seems to be little connection between prosperous central business districts and the poorer surrounding neighborhoods.
- Children in poor families are the one group most at risk of living in poverty.

Again, these urban experts cite problems that are most drastically evident in the United States, but that underline the fact that European cities are beginning to suffer the same ills. If North American and European urban futures are converging, then certainly an opportunity exists to influence where on the spectrum of urban vitality that convergence occurs.

More importantly, Europeans and Americans have much to learn from each other. American local governments are becoming increasingly entrepreneurial, taking larger roles in promoting and marketing their cities. Frequently, Europeans look to the United States for assistance creating public-private partnerships that are able to accomplish what neither sector could do by itself. On the other hand, Americans look to Europe for lessons on improving the urban environment in such areas as use of public space, design management, architectural preservation, downtown development, and public animation. Cities on both sides of the Atlantic would be wise to consider amenities as part of any economic development strategy.

## Amenities: Resources to Revitalize Our Cities

It is important to remember that not all the news about our urban future is bad. Two things are happening that indicate more favorable economic development prospects for cities: (1) shifts in the structure and composition of the nation's economy are generating new opportunities for economic development in cities; and (2) urban leaders and urban institutions, both public and private, are organizing and acting in new and impressive ways to see that their cities' assets are employed as effectively as possible in overall development efforts. They are not letting the problems they face define the solutions, but are developing approaches to change the underlying structures of urban economies.

The issue, after all, is not whether cities will change, only whether the change will be for the better or worse. Realistic transition should be the objective. Each city contains within itself its own distinctive set of transition possibilities. These possibilities continue to be limited to some extent by natural forces, but the influence of these forces is much less decisive than in the past when a good deep harbor or a prime river location dictated a city's fate. Traditional geographic location factors exert a strong, direct influence on a decreasing proportion of private investment.

Many cities owe their problems to the increased mobility of capital, nationally and internationally, but that mobility offers opportunities as well. For an increasingly large share of the economy, a particular business does not have to be anywhere in particular. Among other things, this means that today, to a much greater extent than in the past, jobs can follow people rather than the reverse. In the most rapidly growing sectors, in fact, the critical factors are human intelligence and skill in the form of technical innovators and entrepreneurs. As a result, businesses are more likely to locate where these people want to live. Thus the changes in the nation's economy have made it much more important that cities link economic development and quality of life.

Cities that are not livable places are not likely to perform important economic functions in the future. Enhancing livability, therefore, should be a central objective in every city's economic transition strategy, and the elements of livability should be employed as economic development tools.

## The Role of Amenities in Urban Economic Development

Amenities can play the following roles in urban economic development:

- Certain amenity facilities or events, such as zoos, aquariums, performing arts centers, and festivals, can, in themselves, make important contributions to the local economy.
- Amenity industries, such as tourism, sports, and recreation, are growth sectors in the economy and are likely to have growth potential in most localities.
- Through the effective use of amenities, a city can capture a larger share of the disposable income of its residents, who will spend it at home instead of elsewhere, and generate more visitor spending to improve the local balance of payments.

- An amenity element, such as an attractive plaza, a well-designed retail complex, or public art, can improve the chances of success for a larger development project.
- Amenities help create and sustain a positive image for a city among residents and outsiders.
- Amenity projects can become the basis for cooperation between the public and private sectors in economic development efforts. They can energize the community, and successful projects can build the foundation for additional collaboration.

To start, consider amenities along with the other approaches and tools available for urban economic development. In every city there are opportunities for strengthening development programs through a more systematic inclusion of amenities. Developing this potential to fit local circumstances will probably require more than a business-as-usual approach; it will hinge on the development of a strategy more inclusive than those guiding most traditional development programs.

### The Key Elements of an Amenity Development Strategy

1. Identify and inventory amenity assets. Successful development must build on local strengths.
2. Build interest, consensus, and partnerships.
3. Plan projects and programs.
4. Organize funding and other resources.
5. Assign responsibility and implement the project or program.
6. Evaluate the impact.
7. Tell the story and maintain the momentum.

These suggested steps are not intended to be followed strictly, but can best serve as a guide to local planners. Any successful strategy must incorporate elements unique to a given city and must be a flexible, long-term venture.

### Animation: Breathing Life into the City

Cities work best when they are neither too organized nor too complex. Some seem to have the capacity to "spontaneously" generate and maintain a high level of varied activity, which development programs can take advantage of. In others, however, organized effort is needed to build vitality and the capacity to sustain that vitality. For individual developments, for specific areas of a city, or for a city as a whole, it is important to remember that what people are most interested in is people.

In his "festival marketplace" concept, developer James Rouse has expressed this perspective as it relates to successful city development projects; the term highlights the two necessary components: the setting and the activities. For Rouse, the test of success is crowds of people congregating for no better reason than being there. Rouse projects such as Boston's Faneuil Hall Marketplace, Baltimore's Harbor Place, and Norfolk's Waterside have passed that test.

Taking advantage of the potential of a physical setting to stimulate human activity is something that any city can do, but it will succeed only if the project fits. Festival marketplaces and downtown malls only work where conditions are right, and are not the solution for every city.

Animation pays off by increasing activity that strengthens the appearance and reality of security for individuals and businesses. Including well-designed open space as part of existing or new office developments creates more attractive environments for workers and managers, increases opportunities for daytime and evening activity, supports the long-term viability of those developments, and enhances the surrounding areas. In addition, frequent, varied, lively, and exciting activities attract outside visitors and strengthen civic pride among residents.

### Celebrating the City

Baltimore held its first city fair in the wake of the 1968 riots. The setting was the plaza area of the Charles Center, and its closely related purposes were to generate greater enthusiasm for the city and to get people to come downtown. The fair, with its neighborhood exhibits, arts and crafts displays, and other entertainment, attracted 180,000 people. Following its success with the fair, the city began creating public happenings—ethnic festivals, farmers markets, concerts, children's programs—in new spaces around the downtown area. In a 1984 interview, Sandra S. Hillman, the former director of promotion and tourism for the city of Baltimore, said:

We did it initially for one real reason—school spirit. What we wanted Baltimoreans to do was to begin to feel good about themselves, so that they could feel good about their city. . . . We did it in these brand new public spaces. The mayor wanted these spaces to become everybody's second neighborhood, the place where different kinds of people would come to share space, where they could become convinced that people could come downtown and go home happy.

Festivals in other cities, such as Pittsburgh's Three Rivers Festivals and the San Antonio Festival, are civic celebrations that strengthen interest and support in the community and serve as magnets for visitors and as pluses for the cities' reputations.

## Design Quality:
## Public and Private Profit

Urban policy prescriptions normally pay little attention to the design of the built environment. While it need not be provided in great detail, a design concept that establishes an image, theme, or strong idea for future development can guide and foster amenities, a sense of place, linkages, and activities that make a place function well as a center of economic and social life rather than as a sterile collection of buildings and facilities.

Some cities have taken significant steps to integrate a concern for high-quality design into their development strategies, design that includes everything from citywide development projects to attractive and functional directional signs. St. Paul's Lowertown redevelopment, a former warehouse district that today is a vibrant, mixed-use section of the downtown, is a good example. Lowertown planners preserved the historic architecture of the area during redevelopment, and were sensitive to street-level design elements that also contribute favorably to the sense of place.

## Cultural Resources

### What Are the Arts Worth?

Whenever people are asked to name what a city can contribute to their lives that cannot be found in suburban or rural locations, they are most likely to answer "culture." The visual arts, theater, music, dance, museums, and libraries are amenity assets concentrated in cities that make direct contributions to the economy and that, by enriching the lives of residents and attracting visitors, can exert a powerful influence on the community.

What are the arts worth to cities? To many, the answer is obvious. The arts, the institutions that foster them, and those who practice them make an invaluable contribution to the richness, excitement, and humaneness of a city and to society. Nevertheless, the issue of benefits and costs is legitimate for people in the public and private sectors who must make decisions about how to allocate scarce resources among many competing and worthy objectives. As a result, investing in the arts requires making decisions about the intrinsic value of the arts and about their role in helping to achieve other important objectives. Arts advocates repeatedly have demonstrated the conviction that the arts are major contributors to the economic vitality of cities—a conviction that is shared, at least to a degree, by academic analysts, business location specialists, and a growing number of people in government and business who are responsible for city development programs.

Urban advocates often assert that (1) cities are by their very nature uniquely equipped to generate and sustain artistic activity and that (2) this role is closely related to a city's continued economic vitality. The numbers back this up. An economic impact study of the Dallas Arts District estimated that arts and cultural organizations in the Dallas area generated $192 million in economic activity in 1990. St. Louis estimated that in 1987, nearly $290 million of direct spending was generated by museums and performing arts organizations in the metropolitan area. Studies completed in the late 1980s in Minneapolis estimate that educational and arts activities generate $360 million in economic activity per year.

The arts can fit into city development programs in various ways:

- The arts can contribute to an animation strategy for a specific development or city area.
- The arts can be incorporated explicitly into a strategy for attracting business.
- The arts are an attractive and productive focus for private investment in civic improvement efforts.
- The arts can improve a city's overall image, offering increased potential for tourism and for business investments.
- Entertainment and cultural facilities can be components of mixed-used projects, serve as anchors for larger development programs, or be used to structure area development and redevelopment.

## Cultural Resources in
## Downtown Development Projects

The developers of mixed-use projects are making the natural connection with the arts, and the arts community, faced with shrinking budgets, is looking for cooperative ventures. As a result, office buildings often double as art galleries. Retail marketplaces are transformed into performing arts stages, and plazas and museums host concerts. The arts not only decorate and enliven new projects, but also create environments that attract people willing to spend time and money.

Cultural facilities may serve as anchors for development of a larger area. In Portland, Maine, for example, the expansion of the Museum of Art with the new Charles Shipman Payson Building is not only a striking architectural achievement and a major cultural contribution to the city, but it also has exerted a strong, positive influence on the adjacent area and on the entire Portland central business district.

### Supporting the Arts

Cities can support and stimulate the arts in many ways—by providing direct funding and tax exemptions to artists and arts related projects, by enacting special zoning for projects, by providing display space for works of art, by licensing street vendors of original art, and by sponsoring arts and crafts fairs, to name a few. Many cities have linked painting and sculpture with development. Mixed-use development projects are making space available for public exhibitions, and public buildings are serving as settings for paintings, statues, and other visual art objects. Artists are being involved in the design of public facilities and, sometimes, in the enhancement of landscapes. In Pittsburgh and Oakland, urban sculpture parks were created. Some cities are notable for the display of major pieces of monumental and informal art, while others have incorporated into the daily life of their communities design features and visual art objects that emphasize the historical, social, cultural, and personal character of a particular place.

## The Meaning and Value of Image

All these elements contribute to a city's image, which is important for city improvement efforts in at least five separate but related ways. Image is a city's identity, its personality or character, which is made up of its strongest, most distinctive features. Without character or personality a city cannot be attractive, nor can it generate pride among its leaders and the citizenry. A clear image of a city's strongest, most distinctive, and most attractive features must guide development efforts in order to preserve and enhance the amenities that give a city its special appeal.

People are most likely to think of physical features when asked to characterize their city—a pleasant park, a striking view, an imposing building—but a city's identity includes as well the character and quality of its public and private leaders and institutions.

Image is also a vision of what the city should and could be. It is this vision that guides efforts to improve a city's quality of life and to strengthen its economy, and that stimulates interest, excitement, and enthusiasm. The importance of image as a guide to what a city can become was stressed by Edmund Bacon, one of the nation's urban design leaders, who wrote in 1984:

If American cities are to change into something worth having, there must be a clear image clearly conceived of what that city should be, and this image must be injected into and mature within the processes which actually dictate the form the city will take. If the image exists but does not make contact with the form-determining processes, the city will fail to achieve the humane character we seek for it.

Self-image, that is, the sum of the feelings that residents have about their city, is closely related to civic spirit. Low civic morale leads to a weak commitment to the city, pessimism, and little interest in working to improve the situation. Homeowners and businesses will doubt the wisdom of maintenance investments, and if the opportunity presents itself, they will move out rather than make an effort to change things.

The reputation a city has beyond its borders, whether it is accurate or inaccurate, is an image that influences decisions. A city's reputation as a place to live, work, and do business is always, to a degree, self-fulfilling. A city with no reputation or a negative reputation will lose out in competition for visitors, residents, and business involvement. In the 1940s, for example, Pittsburgh could hardly have been helped by Frank Lloyd Wright's response to the question of what should be done with Pittsburgh: "Abandon it." Fortunately, Pittsburgh has been on the upswing since then. It has successfully used amenities to spur revitalization. The city's transformation was reflected and reinforced when in 1984 the *Los Angeles Times* described Pittsburgh as the industrial city most likely to succeed in making an economic transition. A city with a strong, positive reputation gains an even greater advantage as the media carry the story and the feedback buoys the spirits of residents.

Finally, image is a promotion tool that can sell what a city has and, in the process, reinforce its strongest features. Most people know few cities firsthand, and they may have a poor understanding of the ones they do know. Promotion that is integrated with development programs can serve as a two-way street, increasing the development impact and expanding the base for additional action.

### Image and Action

The most important thing a city can do with amenity resources is to actively take advantage of them. No one can claim that amenity strategies are universally successful, or even appropriate. Even the best-conceived strategies cannot anticipate all eventualities, and resources sometimes prove insufficient to do what should be done. Some projects ultimately fail; some goals prove to be too ambitious or otherwise unrealistic. Nevertheless, without action the future of our cities will be much less promising. Clearly, amenities such as the performing arts, civic celebrations, innovative design, and public open space are important to development. They play a role in large-area, multistaged, mixed-use developments and in the neighborhood redevelopment programs in many cities.

## City Revitalization through Amenity Development: Three Strategies

Amenities generate economic benefits directly and also contribute to the overall climate for investment. For some cities they are key instruments for making the transition being forced on them by the changing national economy. The transition process requires the participation of government, business, and the nonprofit sector, and compels all three sectors to reconsider their responsibilities and to collaborate to achieve shared objectives. Success depends on imaginative and realistic strategies. For example, Pittsburgh has used amenities to help revitalize its decaying downtown and restructure the local economy for future growth. San Antonio has capitalized on its outstanding natural features and on the arts to promote tourism and economic development. Indianapolis set a goal to become an amateur sports and fitness center, and used its success in that area to expand the jobs base.

## Pittsburgh

Pittsburgh's current standing as one of America's most livable cities is based on the use of amenities and a strong public-private partnership to spur economic development and transition. Confronted with problems that have pushed lesser cities into deep distress, Pittsburgh has tapped its substantial civic resources to respond constructively to succeeding challenges. These resources, although not unique, would be coveted by any city wanting to undertake similar bold and sustained development. They include:

- Determined and powerful private business and foundation support.
- Consistently good political leadership by city officials who are able to work well with state and federal agencies and with local private sector leaders.
- A tradition of professionalism in government and business that has given top priority to civic purposes.
- The availability of significant federal financial assistance, beginning with federal grants for flood control in the 1940s.

*Civic Action.* Since late in the nineteenth century, the private sector has been cooperating with city officials to improve Pittsburgh. In 1943 Richard King Mellon and several other prominent members of the corporate community organized what became the Allegheny Conference on Community Development, a citizens group whose purpose was to stimulate and coordinate research and planning looking to a unified community plan for the region as a whole.

The Allegheny Conference is considered an initiator, broker, supporter, monitor, or facilitator that touches nearly every major development in the city. Its role is catalytic—to identify problems and to push for practical solutions. The conference has a reputation for consistently supporting action that serves the city's broad, long-term interests and for being able to develop a community consensus for strategies to serve those interests, and it has a proven ability to work closely with the public sector, which has been key as well.

In Pittsburgh today, a high quality of life is seen as a direct contributor to the community's economic growth. The implications of that view for the city's future may be seen in a report of the Quality of Life Task Force of the Allegheny Conference. The task force linked quality-of-life considerations to the area's economy under the following categories:

- *Service Industries*—Including entertainment, the arts, retail operations, hotel management, and tourism.
- *Attraction and Retention of Business*—Quality of life plays an important role in attracting new businesses and in strengthening bonds with existing companies.
- *Attraction and Retention of Skilled Employees*—The Pittsburgh area's negative national image is a particular problem in attracting and retaining businesses and technical, civic, and university talent.
- *Tax Base*—Quality of life can directly affect property values.
- *Averted Social Costs*—Lively streets and vital neighborhoods can contribute to reduced crime, vandalism, and juvenile delinquency.

***Downtown Investment: The Cultural District.*** The economic transformation that the city's public and private sector leaders are working to bring about depends on maintaining and improving the city's attractiveness as a hub for corporate headquarters and expanding investment in producer services. These leaders believe that second-rate development will not support a first-rate economy.

The Allegheny Conference sponsored a study to determine the most appropriate response to the problems and challenges of a major section of downtown Pittsburgh, the fourteen-square-block Penn Liberty corridor. The study recommended developing a performing arts district around 2,800 seat Heinz Hall. In 1984 the Allegheny Conference decided to form a separate nonprofit organization, the Pittsburgh Cultural Trust. The trust's mission is to support the development of the arts in the Pittsburgh area and participate in the economic rejuvenation of Pittsburgh by means of the Cultural District in downtown Pittsburgh. While the trust focuses its resources and management on the Cultural District, it also acts as a local arts agency for the city, servicing small and midsized arts organizations outside the district.

The trust is best known for its success in enlivening Pittsburgh's downtown through mixed-use development, such as the renovation of the Stanley Theater, a $42 million project now known as the Benedum Center for the Performing Arts and home to the Pittsburgh Opera, Ballet, Civic Light Opera, and Dance Council.

A third major cultural facility in the district opened in the fall of 1991. The Fulton Theater, a 1,370-seat house for drama and chamber music, was used by over twenty Pittsburgh organizations in its first full season. An adjacent movie theater, the 200-seat "Mini-Fulton," is leased by the trust to the Pittsburgh Filmmakers, an independent local group.

An economic impact report issued in 1989, the first comprehensive study of the arts as an aggregate industry in Pittsburgh, documented the following:

- Over $121 million was generated annually by 36 of the city's 175 nonprofit arts organizations in direct and indirect spending.
- A total of 2,617 jobs were generated through arts related spending.
- The 36 organizations themselves provided 1,265 full-time and part-time positions.
- Seventy-five percent of arts audiences, or 2.1 million people, came from outside the city, including 25 percent from outside the county.

Few industrial cities have capitalized on cultural amenities as catalysts for economic revitalization as well as Pittsburgh. Culture and the arts, highly visible components of the city's economic development strategy, deserve credit for helping Pittsburgh successfully make the difficult transition from industrial giant to postindustrial American city.

## San Antonio

Many American city dwellers desire the natural amenities that are San Antonians' birthright. Although semiarid, San Antonio's part of south Texas is the lovely, wooded hill country, where clear rivers feed clear lakes, and the average temperatures range only between a high of 86 degrees (F) in July and a low of 43 degrees (F) in January. One of the country's oldest cities, San Antonio is rich in history and architecture. It is also the center of finance, agribusiness, tourism, transportation, medical services, and wholesale and retail trade for the large and growing south Texas region. Aggressive efforts to attract high-technology and research centers were started by former mayor Henry Cisneros, who said, "In San Antonio we found that in biotechnology we were already close to national excellence, so we built part of our strategic vision for the future around that."

The arts, culture, and historic preservation are big factors in the city's high quality of life and have provided it with something very tangible: a tool for leveraging more high-tech firms into its economic orbit. High-tech firms often locate in cities with amenities that appeal to their generally well-educated employees along with good schools and good weather.

**Tourism.** The San Antonio River, a narrow channel that winds its way through the city's downtown, was not always regarded as one of the city's loveliest and most charming assets. During the 1920s and 1930s, frequent and disastrous flooding nearly caused city planners to convert the river into an underground storm sewer. However, with the help of dedicated preservationists, a 1939 Works Project Administration (WPA) project solved the flooding problem by creating a bypass channel. With the city's 250th birthday in 1968, San Antonio continued its commitment to the river by developing the celebrated San Antonio River Walk. A twenty-one-block tract of restaurants, shops, hotels, barges, subtropical greenery, and an outdoor theater, the River Walk has been described as a microcosm of the city itself.

The River Walk is also the centerpiece of San Antonio's tourism industry, which attracts approximately 10 million visitors annually and generated an overall economic impact of $1.6 billion in 1991. Over 32,500 persons are employed in the tourism industry making total annual wages of $459 million. In addition to the River Walk, the city is known for the Alamo and many other historic structures as well as the San Antonio Museum of Art, which is the result of an award-winning renovation of the former Lone Star Brewery.

**The Amenity of Art and Culture.** The arts and culture also are important in San Antonio. An economic impact study conservatively estimates that nonprofit cultural organizations had an overall economic impact of more than $596 million in the 1990–91 budget year, with over 1.5 million people attending nonprofit cultural events. Visitors from outside San Antonio and surrounding Bexar County account for $445 million of the overall economic impact.

The city provided $2.7 million in fiscal year 1992–93 in direct arts spending through the Department of Arts and Cultural Affairs, in addition to indirect support for such things as the Carver Cultural Center. Its support of the arts is one of the highest per capita in the nation. In addition, the city has inventoried the historically and architecturally significant buildings in the area to facilitate saving and reusing important structures. Mayor Cisneros was known for mediating disputes between preservationists and developers.

A fortunate mix of natural beauty, historic structures, a solid base for tourism, and a consensus building and visionary leadership has served San Antonio well. Today, the nation's tenth largest city is also known as one of its most livable. With its traditions and culture firmly rooted in its rich past and its development efforts looking towards the future, there is little doubt that San Antonio will continue to grow and thrive in the decades ahead.

## Indianapolis

Indianapolis is a striking example of a city whose leadership operates on entrepreneurial risk taking. Through careful planning and strategic use of public-private partnerships, Indianapolis's leaders set a new course for the city's future with amateur sports as the primary amenity investment. The city's overall success is largely attributed to:

- A series of active mayors, including Richard Lugar, William Hudnut III, and Stephen Goldsmith.
- "Unigov" legislation passed in 1970 that consolidated the city with surrounding Marion County and overnight made Indianapolis the twelfth largest city in the United States.
- The Greater Indianapolis Progress Committee (GIPC), a broad based, bipartisan, nonprofit advisory group whose activities and task forces help forge community consensus and are a catalyst for change.

Under Mayor Hudnut, the city set an economic development strategy designed to take advantage of Indianapolis's natural strengths. Because of the city's central location, proximity to agriculture, and transportation links, warehousing and distribution were obvious targets for development. The presence of Lilly Pharmaceutical and the Indiana Medical Center research facility served as the basis for further development in high technology and medical services. But it was amateur sports where Indianapolis has recently attained some striking success.

***The Sports and Fitness Industry.*** Indianapolis was able to link its economic development potential to an amenity enrichment program based on amateur sports and the fitness industry. The city set out to diversify its economy by giving the city a distinctive character as the amateur sports capital of the United States, building on existing institutions like the medical research facility and the local population's keen interest in amateur sports such as high school and college football and basketball.

By 1984 a combination of public and private investment of $180 million had built a 12,800 seat track and field facility; a first-rate natatorium and velodrome; state-of-the-art tennis, archery, and rowing facilities; and the 60,000 seat, $80 million Hoosier Dome. In 1987 the city hosted the Pan American Games, drawing over 6,000 athletes and generating an estimated economic impact of $175 million dollars. In 1991 the NCAA Men's Basketball Final Four drew 60,000 visitors to the city. The Hoosier Dome and other key investments also helped the city attract professional sports teams, most notably the National Football League's Indianapolis Colts.

***Civic Spirit and the Can-do Attitude.*** In addition to the direct economic impact and the international exposure garnered as a result of such events, there were other impacts as well. The citizens' civic pride and spirit gained a marked lift. Over 40,000 volunteered to help with the Pan American Games, and the city's reputation soared. Former Mayor Hudnut considers that sense of civic pride and a reputation for effectiveness as keys to later economic development achievements, including the successful attraction in 1991 of a United Airlines maintenance facility that will employ over 6,000 workers with an average annual wage and benefits package of over $45,000 per job.

Indianapolis's amenities do not end with sports, either. The City Market International, a collection of ethnically diverse shops and booths in the downtown, attracts nearly 2.5 million visitors yearly. White River State Park is a $200 million effort to reclaim 267 acres of downtown waterfront, and Monument Circle is the locus of the business district that saw massive reinvestment in the 1980s.

Called a "city on the rebound" in a feature article in the August 1987 *National Geographic,* Indianapolis has now rebounded and is moving forward. Today the city is positioning itself to be at the forefront of the air transportation and medical/fitness industries.

## Conclusion

Amenity strategies can be part of every city's development programs, but it is important to remember that they are not the answer in and of themselves. A city can recognize the importance of amenities and incorporate them into larger economic and human development strategies while acknowledging that they are but one facet of urban revitalization. However, it has been shown that cities that make efforts to link amenities and economic development have been successful in improving the quality of life and the economic opportunities for their residents.

For one thing, place does matter. The physical setting is vital for economic prosperity and for human comfort in our cities. Waterfronts like San Antonio's River Walk, parks and downtown open spaces, well-planned and well-designed real estate developments, festival marketplaces like those in Baltimore and Boston, and historic districts and historic preservation are all factors that contribute greatly to the prosperity of our cities.

Amenity investments like aquariums or downtown malls are perhaps no longer useful, but increasingly flagship *ideas* are replacing flagship *projects*. Communities that are able to take advantage of existing amenities like libraries and museums have been successful without making huge financial blunders.

In the end, a community's ability to establish an image that is the result of citizen involvement, political leadership, and creative projects is most essential. These cities are able to capitalize on the burgeoning tourism industry and better compete for jobs in an economy that puts increasing emphasis on quality of life.

Quality of life is a civic resource that cuts across race, class, inner city, and suburb and gets people working together. It is a civic factor that gives us some hope and a goal—to make our communities more livable places for our children.

# 11

# City Leadership in
# Human Capital Investment

## NATHAN GLAZER

A new national administration took office in 1993, one of whose defining characteristics is its commitment to human capital investment. It sees this as crucial for the restoration of vigor to the U.S. economy, the increase of good jobs for U.S. workers, and the effective competitiveness of the U.S. economy in a world in which international competition and the openness of all markets to penetration from abroad are a new and somewhat frightening reality. In the view of many today, investment in young people in school, in those who leave school prematurely, in those who even with high school diplomas flounder from one inadequate job to another, and in mature workers who lose jobs in an increasingly turbulent and volatile economy has become a key task for U.S. society. Human capital invest-

NATHAN GLAZER, professor of education and sociology at Harvard University, and co-editor of the quarterly *The Public Interest*, writes on American urban problems, ethnic and racial issues, and education. He is the author, among other books, of *Affirmative Discrimination: Ethnic Inequality and Public Policy, Ethnic Dilemmas, 1964–1982*, and *The Limits of Social Policy*, and the editor, with William Gorham, of *The Urban Predicament*.

ment—better education at all levels, better training for new jobs in businesses taking advantage of new technology, and new ideas of leaner organization—is seen as critical to global economic competitiveness.

The argument for new and strengthened initiatives in human capital investment has been made persuasively in books and reports that have received wide attention. Perhaps the defining text is the 1990 report, *America's Choice: High Skills or Low Wages,* by the Commission on the Skills of the American Workforce chaired by Ira Magaziner. Its argument is spelled out in detail in *Thinking for a Living* by Ray Marshall, cochair of the commission, and Marc Tucker. *The Work of Nations* by Robert Reich, now secretary of labor, *Head to Head* by Lester Thurow, and many other books and reports make the same case.

The central argument is that a U.S. economy that was dominant for twenty-five years after the end of World War II cannot maintain its preeminence without radical changes. The success of the U.S. economy was based on mass production, which the United States had pioneered, and in which jobs were reduced to simple tasks that unskilled or hardly skilled workers could fill. Powerful industrial trade unions guaranteed such workers high pay because the United States itself provided a huge market and foreign competition could not easily penetrate it. All this has changed. In addition to the buffeting of technological change and its demands, the United States now has more effective international competition. Manufacturing and other industries must become much more flexible, responding rapidly to the varied markets of an open and increasingly affluent world economy. Workers must become more flexible and resourceful. The jobs of unskilled or hardly skilled workers, which trade unions could protect in the former economy, and which provided high wages and benefits, are rapidly shrinking in number—as the troubles of General Motors, the former U.S. Steel, and many other pillars of American industry demonstrate.

Of course, one can present many other reasons why foreign competition has become such a powerful threat: higher savings rates in Japan and Germany, greater investment there in new capital, managements more attuned to the needs of production and less to those of the financial markets, and so on. Perhaps this argument places too great weight on human capital, on the presumed inferior capacities of U.S. workers. The argument is not foreclosed: U.S. workers are still the most productive in the world, overall, but it is true that their advantage over competitors such as Germany and Japan keeps on shrinking, they are no longer the most highly reimbursed workers in the world, and many comparisons, both of school children and young adults ready to enter the workforce, show they are far from the best educated.

If the case for human capital investment can be made persuasively for the nation, it can be made even more persuasively for the cities. If the country has lost manufacturing jobs, the cities have lost more. If its industry has been based on unskilled and scarcely skilled workers, that certainly defines one aspect of traditional city prosperity, built on the backs and with the hands of immigrants and migrants, generally with limited skills.

The cities have in general become poorer than their surrounding suburban belts, and the gap continues to widen. They have become areas of high concentrations of African-Americans and Latinos, as well as of new immigrants, and the combination of more poverty among their population and more immigrants of minority status with language difficulties inevitably means greater burdens on big-city educational systems. These school systems may have more resources than are found in rural areas and small towns, but generally have fewer resources than are available to suburban schools. State formulas to compensate cities, despite decades of litigation and many reforms, have not done much to redress the metropolitan imbalance.

The large-city school districts, organized in the Council for the Great City Schools, have recently issued baseline indicators as to where they stand in the effort to reach six key educational goals for the year 2000 set by the president and the state governors in 1990.[1] These large-city school systems enroll 13.1 percent of all public school children, but they enroll 37.1 percent of all African-American children, 31.8 percent of all Latino children, 36.1 percent of all children of limited English proficiency, and 24.5 percent of all children entitled to free or subsidized lunches. The aggregate enrollment of these large-city districts is 42.1 percent African-American, 26.5 percent Latino, 5.9 percent Asian-American, and 25 percent non-Latino white. There are 5.4 million students in the public schools of these city systems—54.8 percent of them are eligible for free or subsidized lunch. It comes as no surprise that on the whole they do worse academically than the U.S. norm, and the African-Americans or Latinos do worse among them. Thus only about one-third of the African-American and Latino students reach the national median in tests of reading, and less than 50 percent of the non-Latino white students score above the median.

One group of statistics in this compendium is particularly revealing. The number of graduates from these systems—high school graduates—is surprisingly small. Only half of the cohort of entering high school students can be expected to become graduates in four years. Thus, consider New York City. In 1991 it counted 955,514 students in its system, but graduated only 34,290. This is what happened to the cohort of 70,510 high school entrants of 1987:

After 4 years of high school, 17.2% had dropped out, 38.9% had graduated, 16.0% were discharged to other school systems, and 27.8% were still enrolled. Based on studies of previous cohorts, the dropout rate of individuals by age 21 is expected to be between 25.0% and 30.0%.[2]

New York City is not exceptional. Half of the cohort graduating in four years is typical for the large central cities. Nor is New York exceptional in what happens to them: 52 percent of the graduates are enrolled in four-year colleges, 19.8 percent are enrolled in two-year community colleges, 2.5 percent are enrolled in other postsecondary vocational programs, 2 percent are performing military service, 8 percent are employed full time, 15.8 percent are "undetermined."

Postgraduation enrollments in two-year and four-year colleges vary greatly, depending on the local system, but quite commonly well over half of the graduates are enrolled in postsecondary education: 65 percent in Chicago; 73 percent in Houston; 69 percent in Washington, D.C.; 67 percent in Dade County, Florida. Among the cities that fall well below this are Los Angeles (35 percent) and Boston (42 percent). In many respects, the system is working. When one considers the numbers who are not on track for employment or higher education, they do not seem overwhelming. Even for New York City, we cannot be speaking of more than 30,000 or 25,000 youths a year in need of some help. Given that New York City's public educational system spends $8 billion a year, and the local economy consists of 3 million jobs, one would think that the problem of high school dropout rates could be solved.[3]

There are other features of central cities that make the process of human capital improvement through social and public means more difficult, and more crucial. The percentage of families that are female-headed is greater; the number of young people connected through family and friends to stable workers who can help them get a job is fewer; and the initial jobs that help orient adolescents and non-college goers to the culture and requirements of the workplace are less accessible, as manufacturing and other business leave the inner city. This situation has been most dramatically described by William Julius Wilson in his 1987 book, *The Truly Disadvantaged.*

## The "Forgotten Half" Problem

A human capital approach for the cities means two things: education and job training. Urban education reform has received a good deal of attention in recent years. The report of the National Commission on Excellence in 1983, *A Nation at Risk,* appeared while many reform initiatives were stirring in the states, and had a significant impact in spurring yet further measures.

We will pay little attention in this chapter to those who go on to college, whether directly or through the route of community colleges. Whatever the failures of college education in the United States, college graduates do well enough. Indeed, a crucial initiating fact for the analysis of Robert Reich and the *America's Choice* report has been the fact that college graduates, and even college nongraduates, do so much better than high school graduates and high school dropouts.

One of the most surprising developments of the last fifteen years has indeed been the growing gap between the wages of high school dropouts and high school graduates, and college-goers and college graduates. Even as perceptive an analyst as Richard Freeman, in his 1976 book *The Overeducated American,* did not foresee this phenomenon—he felt that the United States was already educating to college standards more people than the jobs available for them. Many foresaw a future of college graduates driving taxicabs and selling shoes. Of course some of them do, but the United States is still very far from the "educated unemployment" of developing countries, or our own Great Depression.

The gap between the college educated and the high school dropout and high school graduate has widened. As *America's Choice* summarizes it: between 1979 and 1987, the earnings of men twenty-four to thirty-four who had less than four years of high school dropped 12 percent, income of high school graduates fell 9 percent, and earnings of those with two to three years of college declined 5 percent; while the income of college graduates increased 8 percent, and for those with more than four years of college, income rose 10 percent.[4] The story is clear that the college graduate does much better, whether prepared for specialized occupations or professions, or simply as a "symbolic analyst" (in Robert Reich's term from *The Work of Nations*), prepared to use words, understand concepts, write memoranda, and the like.

It is primarily for the "forgotten half"[5] that don't go on to college that the second major prong of human capital investment policy, the employment and training system, has been devised. We are not as much concerned with the others, the more than one-half of high school graduates who continue to prepare for work by going to community college or college. Whatever the strength of a liberal arts tradition in American colleges, it is clear that college education is a means of preparing for productive work. Many of the specific courses for which students enroll and the degrees for which they study are already directly work related—engineering, business, education. Those who are in fields not directly work related are very often preparing for further education that is directly work related— law, medicine, and other professions.

Work training for "the forgotten half" has been the focus of U.S. employment and training efforts for the past thirty years. A human capital approach must place as much weight on this vocational training system—whether remedial, or specialized to teach specific skills—as on education more narrowly understood, mainly the work of the public school systems. Of course the two are connected: the compulsory required education system, lasting for most a full twelve years, is the necessary base for further training for work, and its failures set the agenda for much of the employment and training system.

## Japan and Germany as Models?

When it comes to employment and training, the prevailing analysis of U.S. problems focuses on our successful international competitors, in particular Japan and Germany, and asks, can we do as well? In those countries we see remarkably coherent systems of training for work, systems that do not leave so many thousands out in the cold without skills and without jobs that will provide a decent income and basic benefits.

Japan and Germany fascinate us: we do not see aimless groups of youth populating the poorer parts of the city, without jobs, apparently without the education or motivation to get jobs, not only forming a threat to the effectiveness of the economy because their labor is not being well used, but also jeopardizing social peace. Indeed, this latter threat, so evident in American cities—the threat of crime— plays a large role in the flight of business and industry from the city.

Japan, Germany, Sweden, Denmark, and other countries seem to have much more effective and systematic approaches to preparing youth for productive work than the United States does. However, they do it in very different ways. In Japan, schools are strictly academic and have nothing to do with preparing young people for work directly. As Paul Osterman puts it:

After World War II, Japan faced a shortage of skilled labor. It had this in common with much of Europe. Yet whereas European nations developed extensive vocational training in the context of public education and created a large postschool training system, the Japanese solution involved very little provision of training, either in schools or job-training programs. In 1976, Japan spent .04% of its GDP on government-provided adult job-training programs, whereas Sweden, at the other extreme, spent .72% of its GDP and the United States .26%. The picture isn't very different with regard to vocational education in the schools. . . . Japanese public education has a very anti-vocational orientation. . . .[6]

In other words, the United States in 1976 already spent proportionately more than six times as much as Japan on work training, if only one-third as much as Sweden.

So why does Japan have such a highly qualified work force? One reason is that the quality of its public education is so good, and its students do so much better than U.S. students in those areas of education that are common enough to be tested and compared, such as mathematics and science. Even when taught in a purely academic context, the quality of thinking and the skills imparted by a strong education in these fields is critical to many kinds of work. Another important reason is that Japanese business and industry invest a great deal in training their workers, and look only for academic qualifications among those they select and train.

The Germans do it very differently. At school leaving, after ten years of education, those not going on to university take up an apprenticeship. Nearly 70 percent of all young Germans enroll in apprenticeships for two or three years, during which the apprentice gets paid training wages. In that period, he or she will attend a state school one day a week providing a related vocational-academic program. The apprentice will be trained in one of 380 occupations for which examinations exist. The examinations, passed after training, permit the apprentice to work at the trade for which he or she was trained. Apprentices very often graduate to work with the business or firm in which they have trained. German state and local governments spend $5.5 billion on vocational education, the federal government adds $4.5 billion, and the costs to business and industry are also very large. One estimate is that it costs $8,400 for each apprentice a year—far more than the United States spends in almost any work-training program. The German system is administered by the Federal Labor Agency, which employs 96,000 people. The program is huge: in 1992, 595,000 entered an apprenticeship program, and a total of 1.6 million are currently enrolled in apprenticeships, 6.5 percent of Germany's entire labor force.[7]

It is worth examining the German system because it seems to be more the kind of model the United States can follow than the Japanese system, which seems so different from anything in the United States. U.S. schools already emphasize preparation for work in our educational system through links with employers, and have developed these business and government connections substantially in the last ten years. The German model has had more influence than the Japanese on the ideas in the *America's Choice* report and on the proposal of the Clinton administration to expand apprenticeships.

But how do we get from here to there, can we get there, and should we get there? We do have real apprenticeship programs in the United States, but they enroll at best 200,000 or 300,000 young people, they are concentrated in the building trades, and they have a reputation for discriminating against African-Americans and other minorities.

Aside from America's very small apprenticeship programs, based, just as the far more extensive German system, on old guild traditions, we have also created in the United States during the past thirty years a very substantial but disorderly job training and retraining system. The 1960s poverty programs and varied successors created a huge network of providers of human capital improvement aimed at the poor and minorities. Most of these enterprises were maintained during the Nixon and Ford administrations. They saw a new burst of expansion in the Carter administration, with its substantial investments in employment and training programs. The work-training programs survived even the dry years of Republican administrations under the rubric of the Job Training Partnership Act.

These programs, many of them run by community organizations, provide assistance to those whose capacities for work are limited—antidropout programs; intensive residential job training; labor market preparation; temporary jobs for in-school and out-of-school youth; special intensive programs for welfare mothers, exoffenders, girls at risk of becoming pregnant or already mothers; and so on. Many programs have survived recent federal budget cutbacks and imaginatively found new sources of funds from private foundations and city and state governments, or have managed to connect in some way with whatever federal initiatives still exist. The results of all these efforts however have been somewhat thin.

Two major evaluations of the Carter administration's job-training programs came to similar and mostly critical conclusions.[8] American efforts at employment and training, despite the large sums of money that were invested, suffered from a number of consistent faults. One of the evaluations, of the projects of the Youth Employment and Demonstration Projects Act (YEDPA), points out that the legislation creating it combined too short a time schedule with too many different program elements and objectives. Quite typically, the aim in these programs was not only to provide training and employment, but to target dropouts, minorities, the hard-core unemployed, young women, or other special groups, and success was predicated on reaching these targeted groups. The legislation setting up the programs and their accompanying evaluations generally gave them too little time in which to show results before they had to make their case for further budgetary reauthorizations. There were also great changes from one administration to the next, and substantial changes from one fiscal year to the next. The various agencies created to carry out the programs had no assurance of continuity of funding, and lacked professionalized and experienced staff to carry out the program objectives.

The conclusion of the YEDPA evaluation is striking but typical. It describes a fundamental dilemma of the system of employment and training in the United States.

The employment and training system is trying to do what the education system should be doing. . . . Yet the employment and training system has not attained stability of funding, professionalization of staff, and delineation of authority, in short, institutionalization, of the sort that has given the educational system its accepted place in the mainstream of American life. As a result, in most communities, organizations involved in organization and training are considered marginal.

But the evaluators caution: "The educational system, on the other hand, should not be taken as an exact model for the institutionalization of the employment and training system, since it has not yet found an effective way to prepare a substantial part of the youth population for later employment."[9] Robert Taggart, looking at the entire employment and training enterprise in the Carter administration and before, came to conclusions consistent with the YEDPA evaluation. He was particularly unhappy with the fact that many of the job-training programs provided stipends regardless of any achievement, or without requiring steadiness in attendance. Some people enrolled more for the stipends than for the training, and the programs did not discipline them. Taggart's conclusions were, among others, that training programs should be more like school—(1) longer time frames; (2) programs should require more complex skills built on simpler, basic programs; (3) people should not be paid for attending; and (4) individuals should have to show clear evidence of progress. Short-term programs of the kind that were typical in the work-training world could not deal with many of the severe social problems.

Paul Osterman, in an informed and penetrating review of American programs for employment and training, also concludes that they achieve little and are hampered by organizational failings.

The changing federal legislation has so frequently shifted the respective roles of federal, state, and city governments that consistent governance has become difficult. However, it is at the point of program delivery that the true nature of the programs is apparent. Regardless of the particular federal legislation . . . the actual service deliverers have always been a collection of community action groups and social service agencies, national community-based organizations, and city agencies. The chief characteristic of many of these "program operators" has been their instability and lack of a consistent internal structure. In sharp contrast to the most analogous institution—the school system—these agencies come in and out of existence, there are no accepted certification or training requirements for staff, curriculum varies over space and time, and career lines for staff are virtually nonexistent. . . .

Equally indicative of its marginal character, and more damning of the possibility of success, is the tenuous relationship of the employment and training system to the private economy. . . . American business takes training seriously and expends considerable resources to accomplish it. . . . One might expect that firms would eagerly turn to a public system that was prepared to underwrite some of the costs. Yet this has not proved true . . .

(in a recent survey of firms concerning training programs) the Bureau of National Affairs found that only 9% had any involvement at all with the Job Training Partnership Act.[10]

The federally funded and locally and community managed employment and training system has become stigmatized as a form of welfare program. This was not necessarily so when the federal government first became involved, with the Manpower Development Training Act of 1962, which was predicated on the assumption that workers losing jobs because of technological and economic change could be assisted by retraining. But with the wave of programs of the War on Poverty, employment and training became identified with those who were hard to train and hard to employ. Current employment and training programs in the United States seem to suffer from the faults of other programs for the poor, such as public housing and welfare. They are not general entitlements for all workers, but are targeted to the most needy. Because they are targeted on the most difficult cases, it is hard to show success, and they are looked upon skeptically. Osterman gives the example of a test of one program, in which the government provided a subsidy to employers who hire a targeted group of work seekers drawn from the hard to employ. Similar applicants, with subsidies available, and without, were matched; employers preferred the applicants without subsidy.[11]

The United States is far from the German situation of public training in which no stigma is attached to those in the apprenticeship programs (after all, 70 percent of the workforce passes through them), or the Swedish situation, in which so much is spent on the retraining of workers throughout the occupational system. The United States has created a separate, poorly organized, complexly administered set of programs, based on variably competent community groups, with no great record of success. The Job Corps is regularly listed as the great success in this system.[12] When one looks at the measures by which it is considered successful—a few weeks more employment a year, a few hundred dollars more a year in earnings—it is enough to make one think, if this is considered success, how well do all the others do?

To all this must be added the inordinate complexity imposed on these systems at the state as well as the federal level. "The network of public training activities in this country has been created as a result of unrelated educational, social, and economic development goals rather than from any overall vision of human resource development," *America's Choice* tells us.

These various and often unintended origins of our adult training and employment "system" have created a bewildering array of services, programs and providers. . . . In Michigan, for example, $800 million in combined annual state and federal funds are scattered across 70 separate training and education funding programs, administered by nine different departments of state government, and offered by innumerable local providers. In New York, 19 different units of state government distribute $725 million in job training services through more than 85 different programs. At the local labor market level, where people seek training and employers seek workers, the picture is blurred. Lack of information on provision, price and quality continually frustrates the efforts of employers, agency officials, and customers. . . .[13]

## Promising Paths

If the evaluations of past training programs have been so critical, what can be different now? How can we improve on the course of the past, with a sympathetic administration, informed by a better understanding of our human capital problems and how they affect the nation and the cities than any before it?

Whether or not we can define new programs that are more effective than those of the 1960s, '70s, and '80s is still unclear, but certainly something new has been added in the 1990s, and that is the sense that these programs must not only lift up urban youth, they must also contribute to America's international competitiveness. Perhaps this additional task will concentrate the mind.

But whether or not it concentrates the mind, one must recognize regretfully it cannot concentrate the energy of our politically elected leaders and politically appointed officials to the extent that anything like the German system or even a great increase in order and systematic organization can be expected. These energetic and able people in the administration will have at most a few years in which to make an impact: they probably will not spend them in trying to make the current system more orderly, or in trying to create one big new system to replace it. Rather, more money will be put into old programs that look good or have sufficient political support, and into new ideas that look good. Americans are more fertile in thinking up new ideas than they are in creating new, stable institutions.

Many recent books and reports on employment training policy give us examples of success. To some extent these are replicable, and they are presented to us because they are replicable. Yet in each case, if one knows more, one sees distinctive features for each city, perhaps to be found in some others, perhaps not. Here there is an energetic and effective mayor, there a school superintendent, here an effective local community organization, there a coherent body of concerned businesspeople. Here one person or group takes the lead, there another. It is hard to see how it can be very different. We must build on what exists. What exists is diverse. It is impossible to summarize the various programs that try to bring greater work skills into the schools, or provide better work skills for those who leave school, with the help of local business, business organizations, community groups, foundations, mentors, volunteers, philanthropists, ethnic organizations, and so on. But we can describe some of these promising initiatives. I give two examples from Boston.

## The Boston Compact

The Boston Compact is a popular model for attempting to link the public educational system to higher skills and rewarding work through stronger connections to business. Begun in 1982 through the efforts of a very energetic school superintendent and a particularly coherent and enlightened business leadership, it promised business assistance to the schools and jobs for their graduates, in exchange for promises of increased school performance and reduced numbers of dropouts. This was the crude bargain.

*The Forgotten Half* gives a full account of the early years, and the varied supporting enterprises that tried to make a compact between top school leadership and top business leadership effective where it counts—at the school level, the classroom level, and the individual business level. Undoubtedly the compact was assisted by the "Massachusetts miracle" of rapid economic growth in the 1980s—as it was harmed by the very rapid collapse of the Massachusetts miracle, with the crisis in the computer industry, the decline in defense contracts, and the severe economic recession in the early 1990s.

The Boston Compact produced results: more students went on to higher postsecondary education. Of 2,700 graduates in 1987, 36 percent went on to full-time postsecondary education, 20 percent were working and studying part-time in postsecondary education, 1,000 got jobs at an average wage of $6.18, and 3,000 students were put in summer jobs in 669 companies at an average wage of $5.39.[14] However, the dropouts—almost as numerous as the graduates—were not affected much, and the graduates did not show great improvement in skills. The number of dropouts did not fall, which was a sticking point with the business side of the compact, and the achievement scores and general reputation of the Boston schools did not rise.

A detailed study of the Boston Compact's business-school connection offers this evaluation by a teacher and career counselor:

The combination of putting kids in a work situation with counseling and school-work had a great effect. It has increased attendance. . . . For students, the Compact shows the longitudinal picture, that there is a connection between school and work. Seeing this in real life does more to put pressure on the kids than anything teachers can say. It has made discipline problems less.

But as this study goes on to say, "Simply clocking hours in school will not overcome many youngsters' very real academic deficiencies." One active participant is quoted: "The biggest problem is still in the area of basic skills. If there's any weakness in the compact, it's . . . in its ability to tackle this problem." Another: "The greatest storm cloud is around the basic skills that kids enter ninth grade with and the relative inability of the high schools so far to change that."[15]

The compact persists, but it has not transformed the Boston schools, or much raised the capacity of the forgotten half on whom Boston's economy is in large part dependent.

## Project Protech

Another program from Boston gets us a little closer to the admired German model. Project Protech takes high school seniors who spend part of the school day learning a marketable skill, for which they get paid. An excellent description of the program focuses on two high school female seniors who are learning to be hospital technicians, in which they turn tissue samples into medical slides. Their high school studies seem unconnected to their hospital training, and they are described as bored by their physics class. (One wonders whether a related biology class would be more useful.) The Private Industry Council, the same business group responsible for the Boston Compact, runs Protech. It has a $970,000 federal grant, and serves 120 students, who enroll for a two-year program. Last year 115 students applied for seventy positions, which suggests there is not an overwhelming demand from the city's high school students. The program does have positive effects on the students—it "has raised their confidence and drive"—but neither of the two students on whom this article focuses "is sure she wants to be a histology technician.

Both are applying to four-year colleges, something they did not plan to do before entering the program. . . ."

The vice president for human resources at the esteemed Boston hospital at which the students work says the hospital entered the program because of altruism and self-interest. "We've got a lot of jobs to fill and we need highly technical people." The hospital now goes as far as Ireland to recruit them. It has taken on ten students at $6 an hour, but beyond that there is "an enormous commitment of time and resources." The students' salaries cost the hospital $74,000 in 1992, supervision another $20,000.[16]

The story illustrates some possible difficulties in introducing something like the German system. Job training is expensive. Will the business or firms or nonprofit organizations that pay for it get the benefit of the training in which they have invested, if, as is so possible, the trainees decide to take their new skills down the road, or to another city or region, or to go on to postsecondary education? The United States is a highly mobile and open country, with strong traditions of moving on, and many opportunities for second, third, and even further chances. That limits the enthusiasm of the employer for high-cost investment in workers who may not stay. But would we want it otherwise? We read in the accounts from Germany of similar problems there, as the postsecondary system expands and becomes more attractive to those who formerly could not have made it into the university system.

We could give examples of truly high-technology training, by companies with no government funding, to bring workers to the high level of skill that is common in Japan and Germany and essential for the United States—after all, U.S. industry is still very far from down the tubes and spends a great deal on training, basic and advanced, without government assistance. But many of the accounts that describe efforts to upgrade the American labor force concentrate on the enormous waste and cost of trying to instill, in the workplace, the minimal skills of reading and writing and mathematics that should be the task of the public schools.

So what is the defining vision for a city program in employment and training, in the new, more benign political environment in which national programs will be launched? There will undoubtedly be a national service program proposed by President Clinton, its dimensions and character undefined, perhaps something like the Peace Corps and its domestic equivalents, and more closely linked to the need to provide funds for college education. There will also be a

Clinton administration initiative for expanded federal apprentice-ship programs, trying to reach beyond the building trades.

For the cities, the aim must simply be more of the same, done better. It is not possible to build, in a country with our federal and political and social traditions, an all-embracing system such as the one that exists in Germany or Sweden. What we can do is encourage and press for the kind of activities at which we are best—new and varied ideas, introduced by voluntary organizations, foundations, community groups, funded from various sources, public and private. The advice from past experience that seems best is to spend less time on reorganization—bursts of reorganization leave matters very much as they were before—and more time seeking out and support-ing new ideas and energetic and committed program organizers, and perhaps most important, recognizing in all this the need for more of everything—more time, more money, more experienced staff. This is the advice of those who studied the programs of the Carter years, and it still makes sense. Literacy programs take more time and effort than we once thought, and changing behavior to adapt to the needs of the workplace also takes more time and money. For youth with weak education and weak motivation, learning new skills takes a long time. Job-training programs, if possible, should build on each other, as Taggart suggested, in effect becoming schools beyond school. Successful training programs require, for those with the most difficulty, steady support, even after, or particu-larly after, graduates get their first job.

It would be tempting to depend on a rising economy to solve all these problems: a rising economy and a labor shortage would induce employers to seek out and train the less qualified, and would moti-vate those who have not connected with a job because of a poor economy to do more to connect with work. But the experience of Boston and eastern Massachusetts in the few years of very low unem-ployment and easy availability of jobs in the latter half of the 1980s shows that the need for training still persists. The good times in Massachusetts did little to make inroads on the problem of unquali-fied and unmotivated youth.

It would be tempting to depend on the family, that great educa-tional agency that once provided the work habits and motivation necessary for effective participation in the labor force, but many families today cannot adequately handle this responsibility. In inner city schools, where one-parent families have already become the norm, we are now becoming familiar after the crack epidemic with

the "no-parent" family. Of course the United States must strengthen
both its economy and its families. But the basic remedial work-training system will still be essential. Half the high school graduates are
ready and able to go on to college, and much of the "forgotten half"
has the support of the family and work traditions and does not need
the remedial system in order to succeed at full-time employment.
The remedial system is still necessary for those worst off, and if work
training is somewhat stigmatized as a result, I do not see how we can
get out of that situation.

## What the Schools Can Do

It is true that if the schools did better, the demands on the work-
training system, at least that part of it devoted to basic skills that
should be learned in school, would be less. Ten years of reform effort
have done something to improve urban schools and suggest avenues
of greater promise in the future, but we are in very initial stages of
improvement.

The reform efforts of the ten years after the report *A Nation at Risk*
focused on state-level initiatives, and some national initiatives. At the
state level, many states have instituted measures to improve the
qualifications of teachers. These should continue. In the early stages
of this effort, the higher percentage of failing minority teachers and
prospective teachers raised a reasonable alarm that a minimum standard for qualifying teachers could mean fewer minority teachers, at
a time when the numbers of students from minority groups was
rising. This fear has been somewhat assuaged: enforcement of higher
standards has in some cases led to higher initial failure rates among
minority teachers, but the standards also induced more effort, and
performance has improved over time.

Many states have imposed higher requirements for high school
graduation and for entry into public colleges. Similar experiences
and similar fears as described above for higher standards for teachers
have surfaced, but the higher standards have in time induced more
effort. Again, we must continue along this track.

There are currently elaborate national foundation funded and
federally funded efforts to improve the quality of teachers through
new and more sophisticated methods of evaluation, as well as efforts
to create national curricula and national tests to assess student
achievement. One is impressed by how many such enterprises, federal and state, are launched, and wonders whether we could not save

money, reduce confusion, and increase impact by combining some of these varied efforts into one big push. But uniformity, as I have suggested above, is not the American way. According to many school experts, California has a good new mathematics and social studies curriculum. Why shouldn't other states adopt California's curriculum? They don't. Perhaps doing everything in many different ways, many times over, is worthwhile—it involves great numbers of people, and it may respond to some regional and state distinctiveness.

What advice can one give to cities on their school systems, which are, after all, the first line of defense in the creation of a motivated, qualified, and highly skilled labor force? Here once again U.S. cities must build on what they do best. School systems should be open to the involvement and participation of employers and business organizations, foundations, and voluntary groups. The examples given above such as the Boston Compact or Project Protech show some of the kinds of business and employer involvement that exist and I believe have value. They are to be found in all major cities, and their encouragement must be one of the chief sources of improvement. It seems America must face in two directions simultaneously, the creation of uniform national and state curricula and methods of assessment at the national and state level, combined with the greatest variety in achieving them at the school level. When one goes into the schools to examine how initiatives are working, one is impressed at their infinite variety, whether they involve the enterprise of teachers and principals, business-school partnerships, or the eruption of a good idea. They cannot be programed in advance.

Innovations are launched, often through the initiative of a single individual, that suddenly take off, expand, and have value. Consider the growth and impact of Eugene Lang's "I have a Dream" Foundation, which encourages wealthy individuals or groups of individuals to adopt and support the academic progress of a single class of inner city students. Or the rapid expansion of Wendy Kopp's "Teach for America," which recruits college graduates to spend a year or two in inner city schools. Neither involved any governmental initiative at the federal, state, or local level, or any government funds. Such examples are numerous.

The key element is for such variety to be encouraged, so that school principals and teachers keep on trying new ways of achieving high results, and business and voluntary organizations are stimulated to provide support and cooperation. This new orientation to variety also means the reduction of the role and size of central city school bureaucracies, which make it hard for diversity and creativity to flourish. In the late 1960s, another age of urban ferment, the New York City school system was partially decentralized, as community school systems were organized. Other school systems also underwent modest decentralization. In the last few years, decentralization and the shift of power to local schools has gone further, often under the name "school based management," sometimes on the basis of a thoroughgoing reorganization as in Chicago. The movement expands with the kinds of education reforms we label "choice." Unfortunately "choice" means so many things that its essential promise has been somewhat obscured. "Choice" is occasionally defended on the ground that if we can extend some public monies to the hard-pressed Catholic schools we will be saving some good schools, or on the ground that those who pay taxes for public schools but send their children to private schools should get some relief, or on the ground that the poor and hard-pressed should have the same kind of opportunity to attend private schools as the well-to-do. But the essential argument wrapped up in choice, possibly the wrong term because of the ideological baggage it carries, is that we want to free teachers and principals to employ their talents in creating good schools, and parents and children to be able to choose such schools, and to encourage communities of schooling with a common commitment from teachers, parents, and children to come into being.

Unleashing talent and creating community are the strongest arguments for choice. Where this kind of choice has come into effect, as in District 4 in East Harlem,[17] it has had remarkably good effects with a low-income, minority population. In East Harlem, choice is entirely within the public school system—to call it "choice" unfortunately means that it may be attacked by those who fear that choice will extend to private schools and weaken the public system. Those with such fears include teachers unions, advocates of stronger efforts at desegregation, and defenders of the idea of a common civic education. But the attacks on the kind of choice that is developing within the public system are misguided. There is no necessary threat to teachers, even if some of their rights under union contracts may not be exercised as freely. There is no threat to desegregation in systems that are already overwhelmingly minority. And there is no threat to the financing of city systems, which may receive more support if there is a greater degree of choice *within* that system and greater degree of freedom for the individual school.

What is crucial is that the current choice movement enables the creation of educational communities in which common commitment to some distinctive form of education and the achievement of a common high standard supersedes bickering over values education, multiculturalism, rules of discipline, how to teach about sex, AIDS, condoms, and so on. The breakup of large-city schools and the reduction of the powers of the large-city school bureaucracies permit the creation of small schools, and almost all education experts now believe that in the central city context, small is better. In Philadelphia with its charter schools, in Chicago, in New York, and in other cities, we now see a movement toward smaller big-city schools and faith in their success. The issue is not size as such: it is that smaller size promotes those values of community that are essential for good education. The argument for small, varied, flexible city schools has much in common with the argument that explains why mass production, turning out a standardized product efficiently, must bend under new influences toward more flexibility, flattened bureaucracies, and more responsibility for workers and managers at the point of production.

If there is a general school plan that will succeed in the cities, it is to encourage this burgeoning diversity, rather than to impose a new conformity. The old conformity failed for the cities as they became poorer and more diverse, and the frequency of social problems afflicting their students grew. Perhaps it once succeeded. I believe it did, just as mass production did, in an age when a common culture, working class or middle class, prevailed in our cities, when more families were intact and stable, and when the authority of the school and its principals and teachers was commonly accepted by parents. That has in large degree changed, and some of the reform initiatives described above, toward choice, smallness, community in school, are a necessary response.

The general plan can only be to encourage this diversity throughout the system. Such a plan is proposed in a book by Stephen F. Wilson based on a thorough study of the Boston school system.[18] It takes into account the reality that this school system, despite the intense involvement and concern of the business community, the cooperation of local foundations, and the attentions of the most qualified, is in trouble. It cannot find stable leadership; it cannot show substantial improvement. Wilson introduces new terminology—the "entrepreneurial" school—which encompasses what we have been learning from experiments in choice and small schools in

New York, Chicago, Philadelphia, and many other places.

In speaking of what the schools can do to enhance the human capital stock of the people of our cities, we have been concentrating thus far on the forgotten half, those who do not go on to college. One area of general success in employment training has been the growth of community colleges for those who do go on to postsecondary education. Between the colleges and the high schools stand the community colleges, America's unique contribution to educational systems. These already enroll half of those high school graduates going on to postsecondary education. They have seen remarkable growth over the past thirty years, and have seen their major initial function of providing two years of college education more cheaply than the four-year institutions and permitting transfer to such institutions radically reduced, while their functions as forms of occupational and vocational training have expanded enormously.

In 1965 only 13 percent of the students in community colleges were in vocational programs; in 1984, 66 percent. In 1983 no less than 69 percent of community colleges had specific contracts with some business or industry to provide training to a group of employees or potential employees. Such a pattern may appear somewhat compromising for the college or university, but it is a function that connects community colleges directly to the world of work. This connection is precisely what most of the students want, and what most of the employers want.

Consider, for example, a 1970s description of New York City Community College (NYCCC) of the City University of New York, located in Brooklyn, with a student body of 15,000:

About 80 percent of the students have chosen one or more of the occupational offerings, which are offered both day and evening: industry demands have an important impact on NYCCC's offerings. Located as it is near the center of the advertising industry, for example, the college has developed programs responding to the continuing demands for people trained in commercial art, graphic arts, and advertising technology. Of the students participating in cooperative education programs in engineering technologies, data processing, and accounting, better than 80 percent were offered permanent jobs in 1973 (a difficult placement year generally) by the companies with whom they had been gaining experience.[19]

Descriptions of community colleges in Pasadena, California; Charlotte, North Carolina; Cook County, Illinois; Eugene, Oregon; and other places show how widespread this successful pattern has grown.

The American educational system and the American employment and training system, even as they operate today in our large cities, offer hope for improvement. We are becoming increasingly aware of the enormous challenges posed by a racially and ethnically diverse society; by large numbers of non-English speaking immigrants concentrated in the cities; by the enormous fluidity of American society with its higher rates of mobility, family breakup, and crime; by the difficulties of our social programs, particularly in the area of health policy, which place great strains on families and additional burdens on the tasks schools and employment-training systems must undertake.

With all these challenges, America still manages to produce the workers for what is a highly productive society, though we can certainly do better. We cannot reproduce the admirable systems of other countries, though we must learn from them. What this country can do is build on our people's strengths—the variety and range and ingenuity of our voluntary and community initiatives and organizations, the willingness of business to contribute to social ends, the fertility of ideas and programs that surface in a society that is not finished or completed, and the energy of our political leaders ever willing to try something new. There are areas in our human capital programs where institutional change is necessary and is occurring, as in the efforts to create national curricula and national systems of educational standards and testing. There are areas in which we see little progress toward a basic institutional change, but in which such change would be desirable, as in the equalization of educational expenditures within states and between states. The major thrust of this discussion as to what cities can do is to continue experimenting with decentralized initiatives to encourage diversity and variety of programs, each one moving ahead a few students or workers to greater effectiveness.

## Notes

[1] The six goals are: all children will start school ready to learn; the high school graduation rate will increase to at least 90 percent; students will leave grades 4, 8, and 12 having demonstrated competency in challenging subject matter including English, mathematics, science, history, and geography; U.S. students will be first in the world in mathematics and science achievement; every adult will be literate and exercise the rights and responsibilities of citizenship; every school will be free of drugs and violence and will offer a disciplined environment conducive to learning.

[2] Council of the Great City Schools (1992).

[3] Council of the Great City Schools (1992).

[4] Commission on Skills of the American Workforce (1990).

[5] "The forgotten half" is the term devised for this group by the W.T. Grant Commission on Work, Family and Citizenship. See its 1988 report, *The Forgotten Half: Pathways to Success for America's Youth and Young Families.*

[6] Osterman (1988), p. 110.

[7] See Stephen Kinzer, "German's Apprentice System Seen as Key to Long Boom," *New York Times,* February 6, 1993, and Wilfried Prewo, "The Sorcery of Apprenticeship," *Wall Street Journal,* February 12, 1993.

[8] Taggart (1981) and Betsey et al. (1985).

[9] Betsey et al. (1985), p. 33.

[10] Osterman (1988), pp. 98–99.

[11] Osterman (1988), p. 105.

[12] See, for example, Taggart (1981), p. 28, and *The Forgotten Half* (1988), p. 121.

[13] Commission on the Skills of the American Workforce (1990), pp. 53–54.

[14] *The Forgotten Half* (1988), pp. 184–186.

[15] Farrar and Cipollone (1988), pp. 113–115.

[16] Jason De Parle, "Teaching High School Students How to Work," *New York Times,* November 26, 1992.

[17] Fliegel (1993).

[18] Wilson (1992).

[19] Marland (1974), pp. 224–227.

# 12

## Guaranteeing Liberty and Justice for All

### DENNIS W. ARCHER
### AND K. SCOTT HAMILTON

A substantial body of scholarship in recent years has testified to a growing danger that the American court system is overloaded to the point of collapse. Despite the fact that the great majority of criminal cases do not come to trial, "assembly line justice" has become the rule in most courts. A situation has developed in which lower courts race through their case loads on a batch or assembly line basis so that the whole process becomes a farce. Other courts, especially big city trial courts, fall behind in their calendars. The net effect of this overloaded system, as the American Friends Service Committee has concluded, is to make "justice" a hopelessly unattainable ideal: Enormous backlogs of cases in urban areas, generally coupled with administrative inefficiency and often with judicial or prosecutorial incompetence, create pressures in which defendants and society come out the losers.[1]

Although written almost two decades ago, these words unfortunately capture the current state of the American justice system

---

DENNIS W. ARCHER is a partner in the Detroit office of the law firm Dickinson, Wright, Moon, Van Dusen & Freeman. He served as an associate justice of the Michigan Supreme Court from 1985 to 1990, at which time he resigned from the Supreme Court and returned to private practice. In addition to serving as the president of the State Bar of Michigan, the in general, and the problems confronting the urban justice system in particular. Overloaded dockets, overworked judges, and unfunded and understaffed courts place upon the justice system enormous pressures that threaten its ability to fulfill its fundamental mission of guaranteeing justice to the injured individual, to the accused, and to society.

If the American justice system was on the brink of collapse in the 1970s, it is not difficult to envision what effects two decades' worth of steadily increasing pressures and just as steadily declining resources have had on it. In a 1992 report, the American Bar Association's (ABA) Special Committee on Funding the Justice System cautioned that "the combination of increased demand and shrinking resources now threatens the quality and availability of justice in our nation."[2]

The American justice system is in a state of crisis, and that crisis is felt most acutely in the nation's cities, where budgetary constraints, huge caseloads and backlogs, inadequate staffing, and the overwhelming demands of both civil and criminal case filings have crippled the justice system's ability to function.

An estimated two-thirds of all Americans now live in metropolitan areas. As the United States becomes more urbanized, the particular problems confronting the administration of justice in metropolitan America are to a large extent a measure of the condition of the justice system throughout the nation. As Herbert Jacob aptly stated:

Rarely do people think of justice as a municipal problem. They seek justice wherever they live, whether it be in a big city, in a small town, or out in the country. But most Americans now live in cities, and city life substantially

---

National Bar Association, and the Wolverine Bar Association, Justice Archer serves on and chairs several committees of the American Bar Association. He is a frequent lecturer and author of numerous articles and publications. In 1984, Justice Archer was named one of the 100 Most Influential Black Americans by *Ebony Magazine*. In 1985 and 1991, he was named one of the 100 Most Powerful Attorneys in the United States by *The National Bar Journal*. While a Supreme Court justice, he was named the Most Respected Judge in Michigan by the *Michigan Lawyers Weekly*.

K. SCOTT HAMILTON is an associate in the Detroit office of the law firm Dickinson, Wright, Moon, Van Dusen & Freeman. While in law school, he was editor-in-chief of *The Wayne Law Review*, after which he was law clerk to Judge Cornelia G. Kennedy of the United States Court of Appeals for the Sixth Circuit.

complicates the pursuit of justice. Moreover, the quest for justice illustrates many of the problems that characterize urban life, city politics, and municipal government.[3]

The condition of the nation's justice system is thus very much intertwined with the condition of the justice system in U.S. cities.

This chapter focuses on the condition of the justice system in the urban United States, and the causes of the most critical problems facing the administration of justice. The chapter briefly describes the justice system's place within the U.S. political framework and examines the traditional faith that people have had in the justice system as a mechanism for initiating social and political change when other mechanisms and institutions have failed. The chapter next examines the particular problems that confront urban courts, such as the chronic lack of resources, excessive backlog, the burden of ever-increasing criminal and civil case filings, discrimination within the justice system, and the tremendous expense of legal services that has effectively denied the poor access to the justice system. The chapter suggests particular policy changes that have the potential to resolve some of the most urgent needs of the justice system.

## The Institutional Role of the Justice System

In addition to the rather obvious functions of guaranteeing law and order, protecting the rights of the accused, and providing a mechanism by which individuals and corporations can obtain redress for injuries or other wrongs, the justice system serves a unique policy-making role as well. While commonly viewed as merely one component of a tripartite system of government, the judicial branch is of perhaps greater importance to the individual, society, and democracy than either the legislative or executive branches of government, for it is the judiciary that confines and restrains the excesses and abuses of the other two, even though the others are majoritarian institutions. Owing to its unique position in the American political structure, courts have stood guard over such rights as the right to obtain an abortion in the face of popularly enacted state and local laws prohibiting abortions, the right of African-Americans to use the same facilities and services as whites in the face of popularly enacted state and local laws requiring "separate but equal" facilities, and the right of individuals to use contraceptives in the face of popularly enacted state and local laws forbidding their use. It is one of the great ironies of democracy that an antimajoritarian judiciary is essential to the continued vitality of a system of government under which the majority rules by election.

The policy-making role of the justice system carries particular importance for individuals and minorities that cannot command popular support for their goals, agendas, and interests. Excluded from the legislative and policy-making process and frustrated by failure within the political arena, they often turn to the courts, where access does not depend upon electoral success at the polls. For example, although minorities could not achieve racial integration and desegregation through the political process in which they had little, if any representation, success could be achieved by resort to the judicial system. Thus long before the nationwide civil rights movement and resulting civil rights legislation of the late 1960s, minorities began racial integration and desegregation in the mid-1950s by asserting their cause in court. Similarly, decisions dealing with abortion rights, affirmative action, the right to government entitlements, prayer in public schools, and a host of other issues have shaped the social, religious, and political culture in cases where majoritarian institutions have failed.

Possessing the power neither of the purse nor of the sword like the other branches of government, the strength of the justice system depends solely upon the strength of the respect that people have for it. Justice Sandra Day O'Connor noted in *Planned Parenthood of Southeastern Pennsylvania* v. *Casey:*

the [Judiciary] cannot buy support for its decisions by spending and, except to a minor degree, it cannot independently coerce obedience to its decrees. The [Judiciary's] power lies, rather, in its legitimacy, a product of substance and perception that shows itself in the people's acceptance of the Judiciary as fit to determine what the Nation's law means and to declare what it demands.

It is therefore crucial that the justice system maintain the confidence of the public.

Individual decisions—even those causing explosive, violent, and deep-seated opposition from large groups of people—have not significantly diminished long-term faith in the justice system. From *Dred Scott* in 1857—which declared that African-Americans were not citizens, and which was a significant cause of the Civil War—to acquittal of police officers in the videotaped beating of Rodney King—

which resulted in the Los Angeles riots of 1992—particular decisions of the justice system have triggered extreme, violent, and widespread opposition, but they have not resulted in extreme, violent, or widespread distrust of the system. Despite the divisiveness of these and countless other controversial decisions involving racial desegregation, abortion, and other fundamental social issues, and despite the sometimes extreme criticism of those who disagree with particular decisions, the American judiciary has retained the faith of those over whom it adjudicates, and hence its own legitimacy.

Notwithstanding the traditional faith that people have in the justice system, that faith is not immutable. Indeed, long-term developments in the urban justice system have caused people to become increasingly disillusioned and frustrated by the institutional inadequacies of the system. Lack of funding and resources, tremendous criminal and civil case backlogs, and the inability of many urban courts to give adequate attention to the matters that come before them have made courts in many urban areas inaccessible and unresponsive to the needs of those they serve. The profound effects of the resulting widespread dissatisfaction that this situation causes can be neither underestimated nor overstated. The American Bar Association warned in its 1992 report:

The denial of access to justice produces disillusionment with, and disrespect for, a system designed to protect and defend fundamental rights and liberties. If this erosion continues without interruption, the ability to defend basic human rights will be decreased and the very underpinnings of our democracy weakened.

It is to the most pressing problems and causes of those problems that threaten respect for the urban justice system that this chapter next turns.

## Scope and Causes of the Problems Confronting the Urban Justice System

The problems confronting the American urban justice system are legion, reflecting the same kinds of social, economic, racial, and political problems that afflict the cities in which the nation's courts sit. While a thorough summary of all problems in the justice system is beyond the scope of this chapter, the chapter does consider three of the most critical problems facing urban courts—inadequate resources, discrimination within the urban justice system, and judicial delay.

## Inadequate Financial Resources

Acute and chronic inadequacies of resources, both in funding and in personnel, are a great impediment to the urban justice system's ability to accomplish even the most fundamental of its goals. Inadequate funding strikes both the state judicial system and the federal courts. At the federal level, Congress spends only approximately three-tenths of 1 percent of the budget on the federal court system. The nation's weak financial commitment to the federal judiciary can be placed in perspective by noting that the country spends almost as much money on one Stealth bomber as it spends on the *entire* federal judicial system, or that the whole federal judiciary could be funded for fifteen years for the cost of one space station. Moreover, only 3 percent of the federal government's spending goes to support all courts, both state and federal. At the appellate level alone, it has been suggested that the nation's commitment of resources should be doubled to guarantee proper functioning of the federal courts.[4]

The lack of resources in the state justice system is much more pronounced than in the federal courts, both in terms of the degree of the insufficiency, and the impact that the lack of resources has on individuals who become involved in the judicial process. In an investigative report covering forty-eight states and the District of Columbia, the American Bar Association found that in 54 percent of all cities, expenses exceeded revenues. More than half of the states were forced to cut their judicial budgets because of revenue shortfalls. Vermont stopped all civil jury trials for the last five months of 1990 because funds ran out. New York also temporarily closed its courthouse after a $51 million cut in the judicial budget. In eight states, no civil jury trials could be held during all or part of 1991 simply because there were no funds. By no means exhaustive, these examples highlight the severe impact that inadequate funding has on the administration of justice. The long-term scope of the financial crisis in state courts was noted by the American Judicature Society:

These are not problems simply caused by our recent recession and by current budget restrictions on our state and local governments. Rather, it is a chronic long-term situation that has simply become more noticeable recently because of the dramatic reduction in state budgets around the country.[5]

The lack of funding for state courts also has adverse consequences for local economies as well. For example, as a result of New York's defunding of county courts, the Long Island economy will lose an estimated $225 million annually. Similar repercussions can be anticipated in other local economies as the lack of funding for urban courts forces more courthouses to close.

Inadequate funding also impedes the ability to guarantee indigent defendants adequate representation. For example, in New Orleans inadequate funding of the public defender's office meant that one attorney had to handle 300 active criminal cases simultaneously. A judge ultimately declared that the insufficient financial support for public defenders, and the inability of counsel to give adequate attention to each case, made the system unconstitutional.

This funding crisis affects a significant portion of criminal defendants. Nationwide, almost 90 percent of all felony defendants cannot afford their own attorney. In addition to the lack of representation for indigent criminal defendants, studies show that only 20 percent of the legal needs of the poor are met each year. The legal profession has attempted to deal with such problems by encouraging pro bono public service, and some jurisdictions have considered establishing mandatory pro bono service. In addition to state funded public defender's offices, some jurisdictions have turned to "defense contracts" with private lawyers, law firms, and bar groups to fill the need of providing indigents with appointed counsel. Although only 6 percent of all counties used such a system in 1982, defense contracting is gaining use because it is less costly than funding full-time public defender's offices.

## Discrimination within the Urban Justice System

In many urban areas, minority membership of the bench and the bar is well below minorities' representation in the general population. The lack of minority representation in the justice system is particularly disturbing because it is the very institution charged with guaranteeing justice for all citizens. The American Bar Association stated in a report entitled "Achieving Justice In A Diverse America: Report of the American Bar Association Task Force on Minorities and the Justice System":

A court system should reflect the racial and ethnic composition of the community it serves. Yet, in many communities minorities are underrepresented in the judiciary. . . . When court facilities serving minorities are run-down and the courts' dockets are too heavy to provide fair consideration of each case, the promise of "equal justice" cannot be kept.

The same report quantified the degree of minority underrepresentation in both state and federal courts:

African Americans, Hispanic Americans and Asian Pacific Americans are represented on the federal bench by less than half the number of federal judges that their prevalence in the total U.S. population would warrant. State bias studies noted similar underrepresentation of minorities on their respective state judiciaries. A justice system which is not a racial and ethnic cross-section of the community it serves fosters the perception of racial and ethnic discrimination. . . .

The disproportionately high number of minorities within the court system, together with the disproportionately low number of minority attorneys, alienates minorities from the judicial process and fosters a belief that the justice system serves only majority interests. The Florida Supreme Court's Racial and Ethnic Bias Study Commission cautioned that "the underrepresentation of minorities as attorneys and judges serves to perpetuate a system which is, through institutional policies or individual practices, unfair and insensitive" to minorities. Such a perception of exclusion and a belief that the justice system cannot or will not dispense evenhanded justice for minorities erodes the public respect that is essential to the system.

## Judicial Overload, Backlog, and Delay

One of the most urgent problems in the urban justice system is the tremendous backlog currently clogging access to the courts. In 1972 Jeremy Main warned that because of judicial backlog:

the machinery of American justice is collapsing. Unless it is repaired quickly and thoroughly, the rule of law itself may disappear. . . . Professor Maurice Rosenberg . . . who contributed in 1965 to a book called *The Courts, the Public, and the Law Explosion,* says today, "My views have changed since 1965 to the extent that what we called a law explosion then looks like a pop by comparison with what we have now.[6]

Twenty years later, the American justice system is truly on the precipice of collapse. The volume of new civil and criminal cases filed annually in the federal court system has more than tripled in the last thirty years, from 80,000 in 1960 to 280,000 in 1990. The increase in litigation in the state system is even more significant. In a report entitled "State Court Caseload Statistics: Amended Report 1990," the National Center for State Courts found that the number of new civil and criminal case filings in state courts for 1990 was 31 million, more than 100 times greater than federal filings. In total, 100 million new cases were filed in state courts in 1990. Of those, 18.4 million were civil suits, 13 million were criminal, 1.5 million were juvenile, 67.5 million involved traffic or other kinds of ordinance violations, and 238,000 were appellate cases.

The report also showed that the increase in state civil and criminal case filings between 1984 and 1990 outstripped population growth by a factor of six. While the national population grew by 5 percent between those years, the civil caseload in the nation's state courts swelled by 30 percent, and the criminal caseload increased by 33 percent. In addition, the number of juvenile case filings went up by 28 percent, and the number of felony cases increased by over 50 percent. The demands placed upon the judicial system have been continually increasing, with no corresponding increase of resources to meet those demands. To the contrary, as discussed previously in this chapter, many urban courts have experienced a reduction in funding at a time when it is most needed.

Urban areas are especially affected by the judicial backlog caused by the ever-increasing demands placed on the justice system. As one observer noted, "Although the national judicial system is overloaded across the country, gridlock is particularly acute in metropolitan jurisdictions. . . ."[7] Multiple forces converge in urban areas to magnify the intensity of the problems of the urban justice system. Areas suffering most from lack of local resources also tend to have higher crime rates. High crime areas strain local judicial resources with higher criminal case filings. In some instances, high criminal caseloads have caused courts to ignore their civil dockets so they can deal with mounting criminal cases. For example, in Maine all state civil courts were closed for two months so that judges could deal with criminal cases. Civil courts in Minneapolis were shut down for three months in 1989 to deal with the backlog of felony cases. In New Jersey, seventeen judges had to be transferred from civil to criminal duty in order to deal with significant increases in the state's criminal docket.

Delay and backlog, while pervasive, are not uniform throughout the nation's cities. A three-year study by the National Center for State Courts covering eighteen urban jurisdictions concluded that "some urban trial courts handle their caseloads very expeditiously." However, others had significant backlog and delay. The "fastest" courts in the study completed half their civil cases within one year, while the slowest took over two years. In some urban jurisdictions, the state of the justice system is shocking. For instance, in Newark, New Jersey, it can take up to four years to get a civil trial date, while in Philadelphia it can take as long as five years.

Judicial delay and backlog are perhaps the most devastating problems in the justice system, since the most significant consequence of delay is its long-term impact on people's attitudes about the justice system. Court backlog and delay are possibly the single greatest source of public distrust and lack of faith in the justice system. A study by the National Center for State Courts entitled "Justice Delayed: The Pace of Litigation in Urban Trial Courts" reported a "remarkable lack of confidence in state and local courts . . ." as a result of judicial delay. Only 23 percent of those polled expressed a high degree of confidence in the urban justice system, and over one-third indicated little or no confidence. For an institution whose authority and ability to function are founded upon the respect of those whom it serves, the loss of public confidence and support for the justice system is debilitating.

Beyond the loss of public confidence in the justice system, there are several tangible effects from backlog and delay. First, backlog prevents the justice system from effectively protecting the public from crime, one of the justice system's primary missions. With a high backlog of criminal cases, prosecutors are often forced to plea bargain with defendants. As a result, individuals guilty of serious offenses may enter a guilty plea to a lesser offense and receive a shorter jail term, returning them to society sooner. Large backlogs also mean that trial dates, at least in state courts, can be delayed for many months while criminal defendants are free on bail. Empirical research indicates that one crime is committed for every 1,000 days of defendants' aggregate release time on bail, and one felony is committed for every 2,000 days of aggregate release time.[8] Thus the degree of delay in processing criminal cases is directly related to the growth of criminal activity.

Criminal trial delays caused by backlog also significantly reduce the likelihood of conviction once a case is tried because witnesses relocate or die and, even if they are available when the case is finally tried, memories inevitably fade. Delay, therefore, works to the distinct benefit of criminal defendants and to the distinct disadvantage of prosecutors and society.

A second effect is that backlog undermines the rights of the accused. While in theory criminal defendants are given a broad panoply of rights, the delay caused by judicial backlog often makes it impossible to assert them. Forced to dispense only "assembly line" justice, urban courts frequently give too little attention to the rights of those coming before the court. Similarly, defendants are encouraged to bargain away their rights by the court, the prosecutor, and, in some cases, their own counsel in an effort to keep the system moving.

Backlog and delay in the urban justice system also cause and reinforce racial tensions. Those who suffer most from the effects of backlog tend to be the poor, which includes many minorities. Thus "court delays may actually contribute to racial and social tensions: the people most disadvantaged by court backlogs are the indigent; many indigent persons are also members of racial, ethnic, or social minorities; thus, the courts are charged with perpetuating discriminatory treatment."[9]

Another effect of delay is that as courts become increasingly unable to handle steadily rising criminal caseloads in urban areas, citizens may resort to self-help and vigilantism. Professor Victor Williams of the John Jay College of Criminal Justice observed that:

Vigilantism increases as the courts are unable to handle the caseload of criminal cases adequately and prosecutors decide against bringing individuals to justice. Vigilantism challenges the very rule of law that is the basis of any civilized society. There is a nationwide, understandable, yet awfully disturbing trend toward citizen self-protection.[10]

## Causes of Backlog and Its Remedy

Many variables contribute to delay and backlog, only the most significant of which are considered here. For purposes of this analysis, they are divided into "external variables" (those existing outside the control of courts) and "internal variables" (those occurring within the court's administration).

The main external variables—inadequate resources and case overload—are often cited as the primary cause of judicial delay. In fact, "that delay is caused by an imbalance between available resources and mounting caseload is accepted by many commentators as almost an article of faith in both civil and criminal courts."[11] However, this simple assertion provides little insight for policy makers to reduce backlog and delay. It is necessary to first understand why there has been such a tremendous increase in caseloads.

At the federal level, a combination of uncoordinated policies and statutes has greatly contributed to judicial backlog and delay in recent years. The unintended synergism between three federal statutes in particular—the Sentencing Reform Act of 1984, the Anti-Drug Abuse Act of 1986, and the Speedy Trial Act of 1988—has both increased the volume of cases going into the justice system and simultaneously restricted the justice system's ability to process them efficiently. The Sentencing Reform Act of 1984 set mandatory minimums for a variety of crimes, the Anti-Drug Abuse Act of 1986 set mandatory sentencing minimums for drug offenders, and the Speedy Trial Act of 1988 required that criminal defendants must be tried within seventy days of indictment. In addition, the federal government increased the Department of Justice's drug enforcement resources by 137 percent from 1988 to 1991 and expanded the number of assistant U.S. attorneys who try drug cases by 62 percent.

These statutes and policies guarantee a tremendous increase in criminal drug cases. Even before their enactment, between 1980 and 1986 the number of drug cases filed annually in federal courts increased from 3,200 to over 7,800 and represented 40 percent of the total increase in criminal filings for that period. In 1989 the annual number of new drug cases grew to 12,000. Narcotics prosecutions account for almost half of all federal criminal trials, and those cases increase by 20 to 25 percent each year. State and local courts have also been delayed by drug cases. Felony drug cases in state, county, and municipal courts increased 46 percent between 1986 and 1988. In some urban jurisdictions, drug cases account for two-thirds of the criminal caseload. Because of their complexity, the growth of drug cases has been cited by many as a significant cause of congestion and delay.

Along with this increase in volume, the Speedy Trial Act and the Sentencing Reform Act both guarantee that criminal trials will take longer and that they will increase the delay in processing civil cases. The mandatory sentences of the Sentencing Reform Act "[have] stopped the plea bargaining process because no one is going to plea bargain where there is a mandatory minimum sentence facing them."[12] With mandatory sentencing, defendants are more likely to want trials because of the determinacy of the sentencing. Thus not only are more criminal defendants brought into the justice system, but they are much more likely to demand full trials given the entire statutory scheme.

Under the Speedy Trial Act, the government's case can be dismissed if the defendant is not tried within seventy days. Thus courts are forced to direct attention and resources to their criminal docket, while civil cases are ignored. The dedication of resources to drug enforcement and crime, the establishment of a determinate sentencing strategy, and legislation to expedite criminal trials each serve their own legitimate purposes. However, in concert they have the unintended effect of contributing to delay and backlog in the justice system, especially in urban areas that have the most severe drug problems. A 1991 study of the federal court for the Eastern District of New York concluded that "unless there is a commitment to increasing the resources of the court to meet these new demands, the criminal docket may well come close to overwhelming the civil justice system." The ABA reported that "the need to move the increased number of criminal cases through the justice system under the speedy trial requirements and limited—or even shrinking—resources has choked off access to the civil justice system." It noted that the "meager resources primarily committed to the civil justice system" are being drained away to deal with the burgeoning criminal caseload.

Another significant external cause of increased litigation is that individuals are afforded so many rights. For example, the rights of criminal defendants that were extended during the Warren era (e.g., Miranda rights, indigents' right to state sponsored counsel, and other procedural rights) caused each criminal prosecution to become inherently more complex and time consuming. With each individual's assertion of the full range of new rights, the criminal justice system had to dedicate more and more time, effort, and resources to each criminal prosecution. On the civil side as well, individual rights provided by legislation breed litigation to enforce them. According to Judge Carolyn Dineen King, the "primary reason [for the increase in the judiciary's caseload] is legislation which began in earnest in the 1960's . . . creating rights and entitlements and providing the mechanism to enforce or obtain them."[13] A 1990 study by the RAND Corporation and the Institute for Civil Justice entitled *Statistical Overview of Civil Litigation in the Federal Courts* found that in the period from 1971 to 1986, "civil rights actions grew fastest, falling just short of a fourfold increase." Lawsuits filed under other statutes comprised the largest portion of civil filings at the end of that period—61,676 cases out of a total civil caseload of 161,724.

Finally, social attitudes about lawsuits and the transformation of civil litigation into big business, together with acceptance by courts of diverse theories of liability and the high contingency fee awards available in litigation, have all contributed to increased civil suits. Walter Olson described, more or less accurately, the general evolution—both in the legal profession and in society—that caused the dramatic increase of civil suits in his book *The Litigation Explosion: What Happened When America Unleashed the Lawsuit*. For example, the rise of contingency fee based tort litigation and mass marketing of legal services has created a legal environment in which people are encouraged—and are enabled—to sue virtually anyone for anything.

Regardless of the cause, it is clear that the United States is the most litigious society in the world, possessing one lawyer for every 335 citizens. Japan, by contrast, has one for every 9,000 people. Since 1973 the number of attorneys in the United States doubled. Individuals, business, and the government spend an estimated $80 billion annually on direct litigation costs, and an estimated $300 billion indirectly. As a result of litigation, 49 percent of U.S. manufacturers have taken products out of the market, 25 percent have discontinued product research, and 15 percent have laid off employees because of product liability suits. Although some of these results stem from legitimate claims, and help remove dangerous products from the market, the general prolitigation attitude means that many marginal or frivolous suits are also filed, doing severe damage to the nation's economy as well as overburdening the justice system.

The National Center for State Courts concluded its three-year study of delay in the justice system by noting that there "is no simple model of a successful trial court delay reduction or prevention program. Successful courts have used a variety of techniques and have adapted the details of their program to local conditions." Moreover, resolving the problem of backlog and delay need not require a significant commitment of money and resources.

It would be very difficult to control the many external variables that overburden courts and cause delay. However, several policy reforms can be made within the justice system to reduce the delay and backlog that are caused by internal variables. Some of the most critical internal variables contributing to delay—and possible reforms to deal with them—are outlined below.

## Limiting Discovery

More than 92 percent of all civil lawsuits do not result in trial. It follows that efforts to streamline pretrial procedures offer the best solution to delay.

"Discovery" is the pretrial process by which each party in a civil case finds out facts from the other side by written interrogatories, depositions of witnesses, or demands to produce documents. In 1989 a Brookings Institution task force reported in *Justice for All: Reducing Costs and Delay in Civil Litigation* that "the most important cause of high litigation costs or delays is abuse by attorneys of the discovery process, which leads to 'overdiscovery' of cases rather than to attempts to focus on controlling issues." The Brookings Institution estimated that 60 percent of all litigation costs arise out of discovery. Others suggest that discovery abuse is 80 percent of the problem of cost and delay.

Under the current Federal Rules of Civil Procedure, and most state rules, it is not uncommon for a party to demand production of hundreds or thousands of documents in an average commercial lawsuit, or to take depositions of ten or fifteen witnesses. Moreover, when a party resists discovery by the opposing side, the normal reaction is to bring the matter before the court. One response to discovery abuse, and one that has been urged in federal courts, is to require the parties to disclose certain "core" information at the beginning of a lawsuit (e.g., names of witnesses, the location of key documents, etc.), and then greatly limit the number and scope of interrogatories and depositions that may be taken.

Discovery reform should also require the parties to first attempt to resolve discovery disputes without intervention of the court and then, if such intervention is necessary, require the loser to pay the winner's cost. Restructuring the discovery process in this way would foster cooperation between the parties and significantly reduce the amount of court involvement, since the threat of having to pay the opponent's costs provides a powerful incentive to withhold information in discovery only when it is justified, and it provides a disincentive for initiating judicial involvement in marginal cases.

## Reforming Case Management

Empirical research done on pilot programs over the past decade suggests several reforms that could effectively increase judicial efficiency and reduce backlog and delay. The following policy changes involve institutional reforms that have proven to reduce delay and backlog, and that involve only a minimal increase of judicial resources.

The use of "individual case calendering," rather than "master case calendering," can significantly increase judicial efficiency. The former system involves assigning one judge to a case at the time it is filed, while the latter system requires many different judges to handle different stages of the case (e.g., motions, conferences, trials, etc.). Research has found that civil courts with individual calendar systems dispose of cases approximately 200 days faster than master calendar systems.

"Differential case management" is another method of expediting case disposition. This entails assigning each case to a "track" or schedule based on the complexity of the case when it is filed. Rather than one uniform schedule for all cases, simple cases would be "fast tracked" with a discovery schedule of, for example, 50 to 100 days, standard cases a period of 100 to 200 days, and complex cases six to eighteen months. The Brookings Institution found that such a three-tier tracking system worked well in New Jersey, and recommended its adoption by other courts. Moreover, it reported that the vast majority of attorneys and judges support such a tracking system.

Early and rigid establishment of dates and deadlines has also proven to reduce litigation delay. In "Attacking Problems of Delay in Urban Trial Courts: A Progress Report," the National Center for State Courts found that the "point at which a court begins to become involved in monitoring the progress of litigation and in scheduling future events is important. The faster courts take cognizance of cases at the commencement of a lawsuit, and have mechanisms to enable periodic monitoring and early setting of schedules for future events."

Setting trial dates and disallowing continuances except for good cause is another important element of reducing delay. The Brookings Institution research indicates that "fixing early and firm dates for the completion of trial preparation and for the trial itself is probably the single most effective device thus far developed for encouraging prompt and well-focused case development." The Institute for Civil Justice similarly reported in *Court Efforts to Reduce Pretrial Delay* that "setting and monitoring firm trial dates is a critical factor in establishing court control over the caseload. Firm trial dates supposedly force case preparation and provide an incentive for attorneys to settle."

### Structural Reforms to Reduce the Burden on the Justice System

In addition to the internal policies that courts should adopt to more effectively use available resources, several other policy reforms can reduce the overload of urban courts. "Alternative dispute resolution" (ADR) is a mechanism by which cases are resolved by a nonjudicial process. ADR programs have been developed for both civil and criminal cases, and each is briefly described below. It should be noted at the outset, however, that ADR is not likely to significantly reduce delay by itself. The National Center for State Courts reported in *Implementing Delay Reduction and Delay Prevention Programs in Urban Trial Courts: Preliminary Findings From Current Research* that "these programs—by themselves—are not panaceas for resolving the problems of backlog and delay." However, the report found that such "programs can be useful components of an overall delay reduction or prevention effort, provided other elements of case management are present."

Arbitration involves a nonjudicial proceeding whereby an arbitrator or panel of arbitrators makes an award after considering the evidence of each party, usually with a limited right of appeal. Although this is normally a procedure to which parties contractually agree to submit, court-annexed arbitration has been used successfully to reduce court backlog in some jurisdictions. For example, in Allegheny County, Pennsylvania, court-annexed arbitration substantially reduced court backlog and delay. In just one year, the program disposed of 8,079 cases, each case taking about 100 days, while the civil court disposed of 5,758 cases with an average disposition time of 15.2 months. The final report to the chief judge entitled *Concerning the Causes of Unnecessary Delay and Expense in Civil Litigation in the Eastern District of New York* found that the "programs of [court-annexed] mandatory arbitration serve to expedite litigation."

Mediation is a procedure by which a mediator or panel of mediators considers each party's case, usually without testimony or evidence, and renders an evaluation as to the value of the claim. The parties can either accept the evaluation, which ends the case, or reject the evaluation and proceed to trial. Although there are no definitive research findings on the link between mediation programs and delay reduction, the fall 1985 *State Court Journal* estimated that "more than 90 percent of the people who use mediation reach agreement; in the absence of mediation, many of these disputes would have to be resolved in traditional court proceedings." The final report to the chief judge of the Eastern District of New York noted that the success rates of mediation "are usually in the range of 80 percent."

The "summary jury trial" is primarily a settlement device whereby both parties present a summary of their arguments and evidence (without calling witnesses) to a jury. Such a "trial" normally lasts only one half day. The judge or presiding officer then instructs the jury, which renders a nonbinding verdict that the parties can accept or reject. Although this ADR method involves judicial time and resources, it is much less of an investment than a full trial. Research shows that in instances where cases proceed to full trial, the actual jury verdicts are quite similar to the summary jury trial verdicts. Some studies have found that the parties, informed by the advisory jury's reaction to their case, are better able to negotiate a settlement, thus avoiding the need for an actual trial.

While these ADR mechanisms are designed for civil lawsuits, ADR has some limited application to criminal proceedings as well. "Criminal case diversion" programs, developed in the late 1960s and early 1970s, involve referring defendants charged with certain kinds of offenses to a diversion program that offers a variety of counseling, education, and vocational services designed to remediate the offender. The prosecutor must agree to such referral. The charges are dropped upon successful completion of the program. Experience with these programs has proven them relatively successful. For example, a pilot diversion program in Minneapolis served 404 felony cases and 46 misdemeanor offenders. The rearrest rate was only 7 percent.

Although criminal diversion by itself has not been shown to reduce delay, research indicates that diversion programs can be combined effectively with other aspects of a court's overall case management program to directly address problems of delay. For example, in Hudson County, New Jersey, diversion was a key part of an overall delay reduction program that resulted in dramatic reduction of case processing time over a four-year period.

The Brookings Institution, in its report *Justice for All: Reducing Costs and Delay in Civil Litigation,* recommended that because the evidence on ADR is far from definitive and because the most appropriate ADR device varies among cases, "it would be a mistake to freeze into the procedural rules one or more particular techniques." Instead, courts should implement so-called multidoor courthouses under which incoming cases are first screened to determine what kind of ADR is most appropriate.

## Reforming Fees and Punitive Damages

The general degree of litigiousness in this country cannot be controlled easily. A radical proposal designed to reduce litigation is adoption of the so-called English rule of fee shifting, under which the losing party of a lawsuit pays the winner's attorney fees. The United States is one of the few modern judicial systems that does not use the English rule. Under the current American rule, each party generally pays its own litigation costs whether it wins or loses. Plaintiffs, whose attorneys often work on a contingency fee basis, have no disincentive in bringing marginal or even frivolous claims if there is any chance that they may recover. An inordinate number of frivolous lawsuits are thus filed that take attention and resources away from legitimate claims. Proponents of the English rule argue that the fear of having to pay defendants' attorney fees provides a clear incentive for plaintiffs to bring only meritorious claims. Similarly, it provides an incentive for defendants to settle early or avoid altogether full litigation of meritorious claims brought by plaintiffs. Opponents argue that fee shifting will deprive legitimate parties access to court, since many do not have the financial means to pay two sets of legal fees if they lose. As a result, fee shifting may "chill" enforcement of meritorious claims if the party is anything less than certain of success.

Such a radical restructuring of the legal system should not be implemented immediately. Rather, fee shifting should be integrated incrementally to study its effects and determine whether its widespread application would tend to deprive litigants access to the justice system, as its detractors suggest.

## Reforming Expert Testimony

An increasing number of lawsuits are filed using the testimony of "experts" who are willing to testify in support of even the most ridiculous theories, whether it is cancer caused by automobile accidents, chemically induced AIDS, or a psychic's alleged loss of ESP resulting from a CAT scan. In "Agenda for Civil Justice Reform in America," the Bush administration's Council on Competitiveness observed that the uncontrolled use of expert witnesses has led to larger trials, more expensive litigation, and a reduction in the quality of expert testimony in many cases.

Restricting expert testimony to only widely accepted theories in the expert's field would greatly reduce the amount of "junk science" brought into the courtroom. Requiring plaintiffs and defendants to base their positions on accepted rather than fanciful scientific theories would also reduce the number of frivolous suits.

The reforms outlined in this chapter are not novel, and many have been the subject of long-term study. To the extent that immediate commitment of financial resources to the urban justice system is not practical or possible, it is critical that reforms be enacted to make the most efficient use of those resources that are available.

## Conclusion

The sober warning of the American Bar Association underscores both the scope and the immediacy of the current crisis in the U.S. justice system:

Today, the American justice system is under siege and its very existence is threatened as never before. . . . The justice system in 1992, and the very notion of justice in the United States, is threatened by a lack of adequate resources to operate the very system which has protected and extended our rights for more than two centuries.

Resolving the crisis confronting the urban justice system first requires addressing the crisis facing the nation's cities in general. Only then can the urban justice system fulfill its traditional role of guaranteeing liberty and justice for all.

# Notes

[1] Willard (1976).
[2] "Funding the Justice System: A Call to Action," a report by the American Bar Association, August 1992, p. i.
[3] Jacob (1973), pp. 1–2.
[4] Reinhardt (1993), p. 53.
[5] Chervick (1992), p. 83.
[6] Main (1972), p. 63.
[7] Williams (1992), p. 16.
[8] Church and Lee (1978), pp. 15–16.
[9] Willard (1976), p. 57.
[10] Williams (1992), p. 16.
[11] Church and Lee (1978), p. 19.
[12] Proceedings of the Fifty-Second Judicial Conference of the District of Columbia Circuit, June 5–7, 1991, p. 591.
[13] King (1991), p. 956.

# 13

# Reweaving the Fabric:
# The Iron Rule and the
# IAF Strategy for
# Power and Politics

## ERNESTO CORTÉS, JR.

## Introduction

The Industrial Areas Foundation (IAF) is the center of a national network of broad based, multiethnic, interfaith organizations in primarily poor and moderate-income communities. Created over fifty years ago by Saul Alinsky and currently directed by Ed Chambers, it now provides the leadership training for over thirty organizations representing nearly 1,000 institutions and over 1 million fami-

ERNESTO CORTÉS, JR. is the Southwest regional director of the Industrial Areas Foundation (IAF), founded by the late Saul Alinsky in 1940. Cortés has played a key role over the past twenty years in developing the IAF's successful approach to institution based community organizing. A native of San Antonio, Cortés returned to the city in 1974 and established the organization known as COPS (Communities Organized for Public Service), which has become a model for organizing efforts around the country. He went on to establish similar organizations in Los Angeles, Houston, and other cities in the Southwest. Cortés has received widespread recognition for his many accomplishments, including recognition as a MacArthur Foundation Fellow in 1984. His work has been highlighted in numerous publications on social change and in Bill Moyers's PBS series *A World of Ideas*.

lies. The central role of the IAF organizations is to build the competence and confidence of ordinary citizens and taxpayers so that they can reorganize the relationships of power and politics in their communities, in order to reshape the physical and cultural face of their neighborhoods. The IAF works with organizations in the New York City area, Texas, California, Arizona, Maryland, Tennessee, and the United Kingdom, and is assisting the development of about a dozen more in other regions.

## Challenges of the 1990s

There is a consensus that the quality of life in our cities has seriously deteriorated over the last twenty years. This thesis runs through a number of popular works, including Robert Reich's *The Work of Nations,* John Kenneth Galbraith's *Culture of Contentment,* William Julius Wilson's *The Truly Disadvantaged,* and William Schneider's *Atlantic Monthly* article on the growing suburbanization of American political life. Clearly what has occurred is Reich's "secession of the successful," that is, the distancing of the wealthy and fortunate from the fate and communities of the less fortunate. As a result, there has been a deterioration in the quality of life of our cities that has profoundly affected the economic, social, and political health of this nation.

There are, in fact, a number of serious crises affecting our society: (1) the decline of our cities, particularly the exodus of meaningful employment and leadership opportunities; (2) the crisis of our educational system; (3) the changing structure of our economy; (4) a pervasive cynicism and withdrawal from public life; and (5) an attenuated moral, cultural, and civic infrastructure. Unfortunately, to the extent that these issues are addressed at all, well-meaning people tend to develop solutions that deal with crises in isolation from one another, thereby limiting understanding of the mutually reinforcing and cumulative impact. This conceptual failing contributes to our political incompetence and lack of political imagination.

There has been widespread agreement heretofore that our politics and our political leaders have been unable to address these problems in any effective, relevant fashion. As a result, most of our adult population believes that politics is largely irrelevant to them. Our public discourse has become impoverished amidst a growing disillusionment and stasis inhibiting our ability to act collectively to acknowledge and confront urban decay.

At first glance, the decline in political institutions and public discourse may seem to have little place in a discussion on poverty. Yet clearly, one of the most significant causes of poverty in the United States is the inability of working people to absorb the costs of change in the economic and political institutions of the United States.[1] There are always costs to change in a dynamic economy, and invariably those who are the least articulate, least connected, and least well organized bear an inordinate share of the burden of these costs.

Reagan economics, excessive financial deregulation, the acquisition of enormous corporate debt, and the burden of financing that debt have disproportionately affected the poor and working people in the United States. The globalization of economic competition has left U.S. firms facing intense competition from lower-cost producers in other countries. These lower production costs are frequently due to lower wages paid by Third World employers. Additional competition is due to more efficient, higher-quality production methods by producers in industrialized nations like Germany and Japan that may actually pay higher wages than U.S. firms. U.S. companies are under intense pressure to cut costs, which usually means cutting jobs.

As documented in Frank Levy's *Dollars and Dreams,*[2] real income in the United States has been declining since 1973, affecting most seriously the incomes of the less well educated. Whereas one job used to be sufficient to keep a family above the poverty line, a similar standard of living now requires two or more such jobs. Families that used to survive on the income of just one adult worker now have to have at least two, and possibly three or four—the third or fourth often being children. This development has driven more and more families below the poverty line, leaving even those above poverty without the time or the energy for their children, their families, or their communities.

The potential impact of the North American Free Trade Agreement (NAFTA) is another case in point. Even though in the long run NAFTA will probably be beneficial to people who live in the United States and Mexico, in the short term there will be tremendous costs on both sides—costs that will once again be borne primarily by the least powerful and least articulate. For example, the immigration that is expected to result from NAFTA, particularly as Mexico phases out corn farming subsidies, will affect most severely the urban poor in the United States and the rural poor in Mexico. The influx of immigrants willing to work long hours for low wages has already depressed wage levels and increased competition for relatively unskilled, low-wage jobs in the Los Angeles area. As Jack Miles articulated in his disconcerting *Atlantic Monthly* article, the African-American underclass in Los Angeles has been largely squeezed out of the unskilled labor market by Latino immigrants, who in turn are forced to compete with even more recently arrived immigrants. By the end of the 1980s, 40 percent of all Los Angeles residents were first-generation immigrants.[3] Aside from the economic tension this situation has created, the lack of shared values or common history has made the Los Angeles community increasingly vulnerable to fragmentation. The resulting polarization makes it very difficult to identify shared interests.

Despite the obvious political nature of issues such as the costs of change in a dynamic economy and the divisiveness of competition for a limited pool of resources, political and social renewal is rarely discussed as a means of alleviating poverty. Instead, society focuses on the results of the crises rather than the causes, results such as hunger, homelessness, unemployment, violence, and so forth. Although attention to the immediate needs of the poor is an important facet of the resolution of these crises, such a short-term solution will have only limited success without corresponding long-term changes in social and political institutions.

## Importance of Political Renewal

The premise of the IAF is that the most important strategy for the alleviation of poverty is one that is imbedded in the re-creation of cultural and civic institutions that identify and mentor people capable of exerting the leadership to organize constituencies for the development of stronger, more active and cohesive communities. Such an approach recognizes that the problem of poverty is more than the lack of sufficient income. It is a crushing burden on the soul. Yet because such pressure is so deforming to the human spirit, the impoverished often view themselves as incapable of participating in the life of the civic culture and political community. This makes creating broad based institutions extraordinarily difficult. Yet there can be no transformation of the human spirit without development of practical wisdom and meaningful action through the practice of collaborative politics.

Politics, properly understood, is about collective action initiated by people who have engaged in public discourse. Politics is about relationships enabling people to disagree, argue, interrupt one another, clarify, confront, and negotiate, and through this process of debate and conversation to forge a compromise and a consensus that enables them to act. Practical wisdom is equivalent to good judgment and what the Greeks called *praxis,* the action that is aimed, calculated, and reflected upon. People must be given the opportunity to develop practical wisdom, to develop the kind of judgment that includes understanding and responsibility. In politics, it is not enough to be right, that is, it is not enough to have a position that is logically worked out; one also has to be reasonable, that is, one has to be willing to make concessions and exercise judgment in forging a deal. Elections understood in this sense are not to discover what people want, but to ratify decisions and actions the political community has reached through argumentative deliberations.

Aristotle said that we are political beings: there is a part of us that emerges only to the extent that we participate in public life. Sheldon Wolin, in *Presence of the Past,* describes as our birthright our political identity, which involves our capacity to collaboratively initiate action with other human beings.[4] This kind of action enables us to open schools, change the nature of schools, create job-training programs, or initiate flood control programs, and by so doing re-create and reorganize the way in which people, networks of relationships, and institutions operate.

Politics is where our moral dimensions emerge. We are social beings. We are defined by relationships to other people. These include family and kin. These also include the less familiar people with whom we engage in the day-to-day business of living our lives in a complicated society. When people do not have the opportunity to connect to meaningful power and participate in public life effectively, they learn to act irresponsibly—a complaint that is frequently voiced about the residents of our inner cities.

Focusing on the least important elements of political action—voting, elections, and turnout, trivializes our citizens by disconnecting them from the real debate and real power of public life. We fail to recognize that voter participation is the wrong measure of the health of our politics. Voter turnout was high in Pinochet's Chile. Voter turnout was never a problem in the totalitarian countries. Becoming mere voters, clients, taxpayers, and plaintiffs, rather than citizens, renders people incompetent, making them passive viewers of an electronic display. If there is to be genuine participatory politics in this country, there must be opportunities for ordinary people to initiate action about matters that are important to their interests.

## Power

Understanding politics requires understanding the nature of power. Frequently people shy away from the discussion of power. "Power tends to corrupt," said Lord Acton, and few people want to appear power-hungry and corrupted. What we must realize is that powerlessness also corrupts—perhaps more pervasively than power itself.

It is important to recognize that there are two kinds of power. Unilateral power tends to be coercive and domineering. The use of unilateral power is that in which one party of authority treats the other party as an object to be instructed and directed. Relational power is more complicated. It involves a personal relationship, subject to subject, developing the relational self. The IAF teaches people to develop the kind of power that is imbedded in relationships, involving not only the capacity to act, but the reciprocal capacity to allow oneself to be acted upon. In this context, relational power involves becoming calculatingly vulnerable—understanding that a meaningful exchange involves getting into other people's subject and allowing them to get into yours—in a word, empathy.

There is no power without relationships: two or more people come together, express and argue their concerns, develop a plan and the intention to exercise that plan, and take some sort of action. The challenge is how to teach them to get enough power to do the things they think are important. This can happen through two routes, organized people or organized money—obviously the poor have more of the former than the latter. Two or even ten people by themselves may not be able to do much, but if they begin to build coalitions with other people and learn the rules of politics, including relational power and reciprocity, then they begin to learn the process through which they can take advantage of the opportunities presented by economic, social, and political change.

The IAF believes in the importance of expanding the sphere of public participation. In every community throughout the nation there are literally thousands of people with the potential to participate successfully in public life. Such participation is the crux of the IAF's strategy for resolving the crises of poverty. It is not that we view other strategies as inappropriate policy, but rather that they should be connected to broad based institutions working to develop this human potential.

## The Iron Rule

The human potential of ordinary people emerges when they engage diverse human beings in the serious business of the *polis*, particularly the issues of family, property, and education—which have been the central work of the IAF for the last fifty years. IAF organizations have witnessed thousands of ordinary people developing extraordinary capacities to lead their communities into action and interpret those actions into the possibility of development and change—both for themselves and for their communities. The daily work of the IAF's organizers is searching for, identifying, challenging, testing, and developing potential leaders within our organizations. Each of the IAF's victories is the fruit of the personal growth of thousands of leaders—housewives, clergy, bus drivers, secretaries, nurses, teachers—who have learned from the IAF how to participate and negotiate with the business and political leaders and bureaucrats we normally think of as our society's decision makers. The IAF lives by the Iron Rule: "Never do for others what they can do for themselves." The IAF has won its victories not by speaking for ordinary people but by teaching them how to speak, to act, and to engage in politics for themselves.

This is the centerpiece of the IAF's organizing and educational philosophy. It is the practical consequence of Alfred North Whitehead's warning about the danger of teaching inert ideas—ideas that are merely received without being utilized, tested, or thrown into fresh combinations. Inert ideas make people the passive receptacles of disconnected information. The Iron Rule recognizes that the most valuable and important aspect of intellectual development is self-development, which is critical to the accountable utilization of power. The Iron Rule recognizes the preciousness of self-discovery. As John Stuart Mill said, "If a person possesses any tolerable amount of common sense and experience, his own mode of laying out his existence is the best, not because it is the best in itself, but because it is his own mode."[5]

The Iron Rule is a process that stimulates curiosity, inquiry, judgment, and mastery of new areas of understanding through action and reflection. It recognizes as John Stuart Mill did that people can only learn confidence through competent participation. We learn by doing.

The Iron Rule goes beyond the rejection of paternalism; it is centered in a vision of autonomous yet interdependent persons who respect each other and appreciate the values of reciprocal account-ability. In the IAF vision, healthy relationships in public life are developed through the back and forth of conversation, in contrast to the unilateral communication that our modern world directs at people in much of daily life. Just as conversation demands listening as well as speaking, public relationships demand reciprocity. They are a process that demands an openness, a willingness to suspend judg-ment, to argue and yet be willing to adjust one's own views. Public relationships demand an openness to others. One enters into public relationships not with self-righteousness, but with a commitment to the dignity and respect of others. As in a conversation, the exchange of a relationship does not have a foreclosed beginning and ending. It represents rather a moment in a relationship—a relationship that builds long-term trust through collaborative action.

## Role of Broad Based Organizations

The development of such public relationships will be possible only to the extent that there is an institution, a broad based organization, that teaches ordinary people how to engage others in conversations and arguments, to reflect upon their actions, and enable them to make informed political judgments. These must be mentoring insti-tutions that cultivate curiosity, imagination, and a vision of what is possible for citizens and their families. Simply designing isolated programs and making them available to a community will not ex-pand the capability, vision, and political acumen of the community's residents. The development of judgment is critical. In the modern political campaign, electioneering and voting have become our most common "political" encounters. This places an inordinate amount of importance on the measuring of opinions and preferences, which reinforces the learned helplessness that comes from being discon-nected and isolated. Such a focus reinforces dependency, rendering citizens incompetent as mere voters, customers, and clients. Too often our citizens have become professional plaintiffs who are unwill-ing to responsibly engage their fellow citizens and neighbors on any serious collaborative initiation, instead selecting a course of either costly litigation or exit strategies.

People in the United States have been left with litigation and exit as the most common mechanisms for the expression of dissatisfac-tion. As Albert Hirschman outlines in *Exit, Voice and Loyalty,* the ideology of exit is very powerful in America.[6] The nation was settled because of it, expanded westward because of it, and views upward social mobility as one of the most valuable expressions of it. "Love it or leave it" is a uniquely American expression, one that is embraced more and more frequently as citizens retreat into the walled security and complacency of the suburbs and enclaves. The theory behind the ideology of exit is that such an expression of dissatisfaction will force "management" to correct the problems that are driving people away. However, because the exit mechanism destroys social capital and weakens the mediating institutions of the community, it becomes in the self-interest of the "managers" for the vocal "troublemakers" also to exit, allowing the further disintegration of community to occur unimpeded. "Managers" are left with the most inarticulate, vulnerable, and compliant members of the community—those least likely to agitate for change.

The alternative to the exit mechanism is that of voice—designed to bring about change through internal agitation. This is the paradigm that the IAF is trying to teach, that people are citizens and neighbors who have to learn the art of making judgments and taking action. Institutions must be created to allow citizens to develop their alternative of voice, to learn to exercise their political nature, and to reclaim their political birthright. The importance of discourse and debate in the deliberative process exemplifies the need to make judgments in relationship with other people. Anyone can be rendered incompetent by not having access to interpretation or context, or by not having a frame of reference or access to other people's reactions and interpretations.

Because the art of making judgments is an interpretive process, one of the most important aspects of a broad based organization is that it be action oriented. What we mean by "action" is not just displacement of energy, not just reaction to a crisis, but rather *praxis*. In *praxis* the most important part of the action is the reflection and evaluation afterward. Our organizations plan "actions"—public dramas, where masses of ordinary people collaboratively and collectively move on a particular issue with a particular focus—which sometimes produce a reaction that is unanticipated. This reaction then produces the grist for the real teaching of politics and interpretation—how to appreciate the negotiations, the challenge, the argument, and the political conversation.

An IAF broad based organization is like a "mini-university." Our organizations have multiple agendas, traditions, independent dues based financing structures, and include a wide variety of individuals. Universities and broad based organizations are two types of institutions in which persons can engage in constrained conflict, opening the conflicts of our traditions to the inquiry and reflection of our citizens. Acknowledging and welcoming these tensions allows for the tempering of conflict to a manageable level. Repressing these conflicts can lead to war. Like a good university, a broad based organization does not just teach people about skills. It does not treat inquiry as a technique. It also teaches people about perspective. In the words of William Galston, there are two kinds of education: there is a philosophic education, which is about inquiry and the rules thereof, and there is also a civic education, which is about character formation, enabling persons to effectively conduct their lives and provide support for building and sustaining their community.[7] Civic education requires institutions, because character depends upon culture, values, and perspective. We do not learn those as isolated individuals. We learn those only in relationships with others, and in the context of our history and traditions. Institutions, be they familial, religious, cultural, or political, provide the framework within which civic education, character development, and leadership development must be nurtured. The IAF believes that both types of education are important, and indeed within a democratic society, each augments and supplements the other.

The organizations of the IAF are primarily federations of congregations; they are connected to institutions of faith and agitated by their traditions of faith. In this context the term "faith" does not mean particular religious beliefs, but rather a more general affirmation that life has meaning. Congregations are the conveyors of tradition, which connects people and holds them accountable to both their past and their future. They force us to recognize that we are encumbered beings who have a responsibility to deal regularly with the business of transformation, thereby engendering hope. These institutions, churches, synagogues, mosques, and temples, are built on networks of family and neighbors. Tragically, they are virtually the only institutions in society that are fundamentally concerned with the nature and well-being of families and communities. In addition, religious institutions have a commitment, albeit somewhat attenuated, to the vitality of the city. They are accountable to the vision of the prophet Jeremiah, who stated clearly, "Seek ye therefore the shalom [welfare] of the city. For there you shall find your own shalom."

Through these institutions we learn to accept the tension between what we are—our nature and our limits—and what we can be. We have to be able to embrace the dialectic of that tension and not yield either to cynicism or romantic sentimentality. We learn that there are always intended and unintended consequences to actions, and that to practice politics, citizens must be prepared to deal with both. Most importantly, and this is perhaps the crux of the tension, we must accept that the best often gets in the way of the good, and that there will never be total justice. This is a precept that is difficult to deal with unless one is situated in a political context. Political beings understand the limits and boundaries of power and action, and do not try to make inordinate claims on life. That is why there has to be in the teaching, the mentoring, and the evaluating the constant attempt to grapple with the human condition: what is the self, what is the relationship of the self to its situation and context, and how do we begin to understand the potential for the development of personhood. Our politics have to be connected to that search for meaning, for authenticity, and for identity.

Religious faith, history, and tradition are important because they embody the records of the struggles of those who have gone before—their struggles both to understand and to act. Others have made efforts, sometimes succeeding and sometimes not. In this context, one learns not to take one's self too seriously, and to recognize that there are limits to what one can accomplish in a lifetime or in a generation. Traditions, to the extent that they are meaningful and useful, enable us to deal with the realities of ambiguity, irony, and tragedy. They convey to us, through symbols, those dimensions of the human experience.

The root of the word "religion," *re-ligare,* means to bind together that which is disconnected. There is always an effort to connect. The best of religious traditions try to be inclusive. They respect diversity. To the extent that they are good traditions, they convey a plurality of symbols that incorporate the experiences of diverse peoples. The whole concept of the mixed multitudes in Sinai and Pentecost is central to the Judeo-Christian tradition; there is a constant incorporation of different traditions in the reweaving of the social and political fabric.

## Social Capital

The IAF is concerned with the social capital embodied in relationships among adults in a democratic public life. Broadly defined, "social capital" is a term identifying the value of a community's relationships. In contrast to human capital, which is locked up in the skills of an individual, social capital is a measure of how much collaborative time and energy people have for each other: how much time parents have for their children, how much attention neighbors will give to each other's families, what kind of relationships people in congregations have with each other, the relationships in organizations like PTAs and scout troops, and the quality of many other potential webs of relationships in a community. The social capital of a democratic public life comprises relationships among adults who are equal in essential aspects and yet unequal in their virtues. The IAF is concerned with the relationships of people who aspire to learn and to grow—to acquire the virtues of leadership and satisfactions of becoming, in the phrase of Thomas Jefferson, "participators in the affairs of government."

Social capital is not a familiar term in the current debate, but it is as crucial to the resolution of crises and the alleviation of poverty as are the other forms of capital we already understand. In order for community development (both economic and social) to be successful, there have to be investments in human capital, physical capital, and social capital so that financial capital or entrepreneurial activity can be productive. The 1980s were absorbed by concern with financial capital, and now the United States is paying the price for that narrow focus. Differing types of capital must be mixed with each other to be productive. The items of "physical capital" such as machinery alone are not enough, but require workers with the "human capital" of skills to operate them. Teams of workers need not only tools and skills, but the trusting relationships of "social capital" to work together. They all need "financial capital" to facilitate the exchanges and investments central to economic life. Men and women of vision must be able to coordinate these different kinds of capital.

To think of our relationships as "capital" suggests a different way of thinking about other people. To create capital we must invest labor, energy, and effort in the here-and-now to create something for later use. We must expend energy now in creating a tool, or learning a skill, or saving money, or building a relationship in order to put it to use in the future. Investment requires the ability and discipline to defer gratification, to invest energy not only in the needs or pleasures of the present, but also in the potential demands of the future.

Capital also requires maintenance and renewal. Workers find that their tools wear out with use and rust with disuse. Knowledge and skills must be updated and refined. Similarly, the partners in a venture must renew the means of trusting one another. Neighbors in a community or members of a family must maintain their relationships to renew the social capital they represent.

University of Chicago sociologist James Coleman has examined a particular example of the importance of social capital in the context of education.[8] He identifies the social capital of a school as "attention from responsible adults" that students receive in the various institutions of their daily lives—their schools, families, churches, and neighborhoods.

Coleman studied public, Catholic, and non-Catholic private schools in Chicago, and found that Catholic schools had been more successful at educating students than either public or non-Catholic private schools. Even when he took into account the advantages and disadvantages of varying family backgrounds and incomes (i.e., different levels of "human" and "financial" capital), students at Catholic schools had slightly higher achievement rates on math and verbal skills and *dramatically* lower dropout rates. In fact, the dropout rates were *one-quarter* the level of public schools and *one-third* the level of other private schools.

Coleman argues that the strong, informal adult-student relationships of the Catholic school and community were responsible for the significantly lower dropout rates. Even when children had relatively diminished attention from adults at home—as in the case of single-parent families—the Catholic schools were able to keep them in school. He suggests that adults in the Catholic community were attentive to the children's growth and willing to intervene early when they saw trouble. They provided role models and mentored children. By their example and their actions, they taught children how to relate collaboratively with others. They were available to ask for help or guidance.

The concept of social capital places credence as much in the quality of relationships among people as simply their number or availability. Social capital implies a richness and robustness of relationships among people, that the members of a community are willing and eager to invest in one another. Our broad based organizations are trying to build, expand, and agitate the social capital that is imbedded in the networks of human relationships.

## The Development of Leadership

IAF leaders begin their development in one-on-one conversations with a skilled organizer. Individual meetings are not interviews. Rather than a communication of information, convictions, or instruction, they represent an exchange of views, judgments, and commitments. The organizers see themselves as teachers, mentors, and agitators who cultivate leadership. Their job is to teach people how to form relationships with other leaders and develop a network, a collective of relationships able to build the power to enable them to act. They begin with small, winnable issues—fixing a streetlight, putting up a stop sign. Then they move into larger concerns—making a school a safe and civil place for children to learn. Then they move to still larger issues—setting an agenda for a municipal capital improvement budget; strategizing with corporate leaders and members of the city council on economic growth policies; developing new initiatives in job training, health care, and public education. When ordinary people become engaged and begin to play large, public roles, they develop confidence in their own competence.

IAF leaders are women like Virginia Ramirez of San Antonio's Communities Organized for Public Service (COPS), who was afraid to speak out because she felt she wasn't educated. But she was angry at the injustice done to her neighborhood—at watching a neighbor die because she did not have heat in the winter. COPS taught Mrs. Ramirez to tap that anger and forge it into a tool for the renewal of hope in herself and her community. She learned to speak publicly, to lead actions, to take risks with herself, and to guide others. The IAF process taught her to develop relationships within which she could challenge the indifference and apathy of corporate and government officials. She learned how to negotiate with the holders of power: how to compromise, how to confront when necessary, and how to rebuild collaboration. She gained the confidence to negotiate with the City Council and mayor. She went back to school at age forty-four, earned her general equivalency diploma, and entered college.

Virginia Ramirez is now president of her parish council. She is also a cochair of COPS and represents her community at the negotiating table with the head of the Chamber of Commerce, the mayor, and the bankers of San Antonio. She leads a team of community leaders and clergy engaged in transforming the public hospital system to truly serve the inner city. She guides and mentors young leaders, some of whom are the sons and daughters of founders of COPS from twenty years ago.

Mrs. Ramirez, as a result of being part of COPS, has learned how to exercise power—relational power. She has learned not only how to act, but how to be acted upon. She has learned how to collaborate. She has learned how to develop a political institution inside the COPS organization. She has learned how to leverage that institution in a relationship with the city government and the corporate community. As a result, San Antonio has one of the most creative community development block grant (CDBG) programs in the country. In addition, a new, innovative housing strategy has been created, including a $10 million Housing Trust Fund. COPS has used public dollars to leverage many more private dollars for construction and purchase of single-family homes. As a result, the organization has literally physically and spiritually revitalized neighborhoods so their residents have the opportunity to generate stability and growth.

Virginia Ramirez and her personal and political growth are extraordinary but not unique. The IAF has developed more than twenty institutions that have transformed the lives of thousands of persons like her, who felt a deep anger at the injustices done to their lives but believed they had no ability nor right to speak out to make their communities more just and more fully human. The IAF organizations have been schools for the development of politics and community.

## What Politics Has Brought

One of the twelve Texas IAF organizations is Allied Communities of Tarrant (ACT) in Fort Worth, composed of 14,000 families from twenty-two congregations of diverse faiths and ethnic backgrounds. ACT is a very broad based institution, involving African-American, Anglo, and Hispanic leaders from both protestant and Catholic congregations. Formed in 1982, ACT has organized its families in a number of efforts to direct public investment to the inner city. Among other accomplishments, it guaranteed the passage of a bond referendum to finance $57 million of new streets, sewers, and other improvements in 1985.

In 1986 ACT leaders began to work closely with the principal of Morningside Middle School, a predominantly African-American school that had all but ceased to function as anything other than a holding place for children and adults. Its students ranked dead last on measures of performance among the district's twenty middle schools. Half of the children were failing at least one subject. Half failed the state's writing skills test. The police were called to the school two to three times a day. The school's parent-teacher organization had one or two persons attending meetings.

In collaboration with the principal, ACT leaders developed a plan to rebuild the relationships among the parents, teachers, and students of the school to revitalize the school. The principal took the lead in building a leadership team within the school's staff. ACT built leadership among the parents through a two-pronged strategy.

First, ACT congregations near the school organized periodic "Recognition Days" in which the congregation as a whole would applaud children for progress at school. Each congregation took care to recognize every child for some form of progress, no matter how small. These ceremonies generally formed part of the worship service. Often the homilies were directed toward recognizing and supporting families in their efforts. Nearly twenty local congregations held "Recognition Days" for the children of the school.

Second, ACT leaders organized a series of individual meetings in which they met or attempted to meet with the parents or guardians of every child, regardless of whether or not they belonged to an ACT congregation or to any congregation at all. The building of relationships in individual meetings is slow, hard work, but there is no shortcut or substitute. It is the means by which people begin to recognize and understand their own interests. It is how they articulate their vision of themselves and their hopes for their families. It is how they build reciprocal relationships with others.

Over 600 meetings were conducted in a period of a year and a half. While leaders learned about parents' concerns, the more important result was that they began to build relationships to draw them into involvement with the school. Parents attended training sessions on how to support their children's study habits. They began to meet more often with their children's teachers individually.

The most visible sign of change was the school's transformation into a successful institution. The children's performance on standardized tests rose from twentieth of the district's twenty middle schools to third. The percentage of students passing the state writing skills test increased from 50 to 89 percent. The percentage of children failing at least one subject decreased from 50 to 6 percent. Police calls fell off to virtually none. Now it is not unusual for 200 or more to attend parent assemblies at the school to learn about drug awareness, study habits, or other education related themes. Parents also staff an after-school enrichment program that ACT and the principal of the school jointly conceived and implemented. Leaders in other churches and schools have begun to duplicate this effort in another middle school and three feeder elementary schools.

Beyond making the school a more successful institution, parents became successful in ACT, a mediating institution, and developed the capacity to negotiate with other institutions to pursue their interests and the interests of their children. In the second middle school, parents identified the need for substantial physical renovation of the building. They drew up a $1.8 million plan and negotiated it with the school board. The board approved the plan and doubled the capital spending originally allocated to the school.

Such accomplishments are only the outward signs of the organization's real achievement—the development of mediating institutions that shape and support their families in both their private and public lives. Whereas before, the children had been failing, the new relationships built among parents strengthened their family lives and enabled them to succeed in school. One ACT leader has commented that the project calls parents to be parents, changing the culture within families. Through their experiences in ACT, parents learned how to organize and how to act. They no longer merely celebrate their values and their hopes as fantasies in the privacy of home or pew, but have acquired the power to make them a real part of the public life of Fort Worth.

Communities Organized for Public Service in San Antonio is the oldest and most established of the IAF organizations. For twenty years, one of COPS' focal points has been pioneering a strategy to rebuild the infrastructure of its inner city community. With its sister organization, the Metro Alliance, COPS has brought over $750 million of sewers, streets, sidewalks, parks, libraries, clinics, streetlights, and other infrastructure to the poor west, east, and south sides of the inner city. The IAF organizations in San Antonio have helped working families build over 1,000 units of new housing, rehabilitate 2,600 existing units, and purchase 1,300 more. Beyond these new homes and infrastructure, however, the most important accomplishment of the IAF organizations is the leadership development of people like Virginia Ramirez.

In the early years of the San Antonio housing efforts, professional organizers worked intensively to identify and mentor individuals who would form a core of leadership, equipping them to reshape city policy. This core group, and the thousands of others whom they led and collaborated with, organized hundreds of house meetings, neighborhood actions, and research visits, which built both the COPS housing agenda and the power to move it forward.

COPS' first major housing initiative came to be known as the "Select Housing Target Areas" program. Unlike many other cities, in which substandard housing was razed or refurbished without regard to the original low-income residents, COPS was able to develop a strategy in which community improvements did not dislocate residents. Their aim was not to redevelop real estate, but to rejuvenate communities. Formulated in cooperation with city officials and the San Antonio Development Agency (SADA), the program has built over 900 new homes and rehabilitated 2,600 more since its inception in 1974. Ninety-five percent of homeowners have chosen to rebuild their homes in the redeveloped neighborhoods, rather than seek housing in the suburbs.

COPS leaders, when encountering obstacles or gaps in the community redevelopment strategy, have been able to initiate new programs to complement existing ones. One gap identified from the experience of the Target Areas program was the need to help young families purchase their own homes. Working families in San Antonio, like others in the United States, have seen their wages and incomes fall in real terms over the last decade, while the price of housing has risen. In the words of one COPS leader, they saw young families "losing the American dream of owning their own home." Many were able to afford monthly payments, but were unable to raise the lump sum of down payment, closing costs, and prepaid insurance and taxes.

To address this barrier, COPS and Metro Alliance leaders worked with SADA to create the Homeownership Incentive Program (HIP) to help young families finance the lump-sum payments. HIP enables moderate-income families who qualify for FHA insured loans to receive a thirty-year, zero-interest second mortgage to use as a down payment. Since 1988 the city has made loans to leverage private mortgage funds to over 1,300 families. These families have an average annual income of $17,500, and 18 percent are headed by single mothers.

The central component of the San Antonio IAF organizations' work to redevelop the city's neighborhoods has been the annual community development block grant program, $4 million of which remains the principal funding for the Target Areas and the HIP effort. Designed to replace numerous federal categorical programs with a single, flexible grant to cities, the CDBG program since 1974 has been a steady, though small and diminishing, source of funds for the redevelopment of inner cities across the country. COPS and the Metro Alliance have ensured that the funds are used carefully and effectively, maximizing expenditures for durable capital improvements and minimizing the demands on CDBG for ongoing operating expenditures of city and private agencies. In fact, San Antonio's program has been recognized nationwide as a model CDBG project.

COPS leaders drive the annual CDBG process, in which residents of eligible neighborhoods meet in their homes, schools, and churches to draw up their lists of potential projects, the costs of which are always three or four times their neighborhood's CDBG allocation. People begin their bargaining, trimming some projects and delaying others in exchange for mutual support. They proceed from house meetings concerned with one street or drainage issue, to neighborhood meetings proposing a package of projects, to meetings in each City Council district to shape a proposal with the council member, and then, in collaboration with the City Council member, community leaders finalize the selection of the year's project. COPS leaders have incorporated into the organization's collective culture the expertise to plan projects and the skills of negotiating and facilitating the bargaining among neighborhoods.

The principal constraint on COPS' efforts has been the lack of resources. San Antonio had received roughly $40 million a year in federal aid in the early 1970s in various categorical urban programs. Now that amount has fallen to $14 million through the CDBG program.

COPS and Metro Alliance leaders have sought new sources of funds to complement the limited resources from CDBG. In 1988 leaders from the two organizations developed a plan for the creation of a City Housing Trust Fund. They researched the operation of local trust funds across the country, designed their own proposal, and negotiated with the City Council to establish it. The City Council was more willing to create the fund than to actually fund it, but a windfall of $22 million from the sale of San Antonio's cable television franchise gave the IAF organizations an opportunity. IAF leaders negotiated with the council and representatives advocating other capital spending priorities to set aside $10 million of the $22 million sale to endow the City Housing Trust Fund, ensuring an annual stream of $500,000 to $1 million in new funding for housing.

San Antonio's City Housing Trust Fund provides an important source of flexible financing to fill gaps left by other sources too restricted or too highly taxed to be accessible to low-income families. So far the City Housing Trust Fund has financed the planning of several housing projects for the elderly and one affordable single-family development—the Brighton Park subdivision.

The Brighton Park story is one that begins not with a government housing program, but with the frustrations of neighbors with a trashy vacant lot. House meetings were convened to discuss possible uses for the lot. Each house meeting, where ten or fifteen neighbors would gather for an hour or so of conversation, reported back to the leadership with the same issue: housing for young families. Neighbors became excited when they imagined the prospect of new, modern, single-family homes as good as the ones in the new subdivisions outside San Antonio's Outer Loop.

The story proceeds through the development of a core of dedicated and competent neighborhood leaders who for five years worked doggedly to secure the participation of the city government, commercial banks, the San Antonio Development Agency, the City Housing Trust Fund, and private builders. In essence, the COPS leaders became developers. The story concludes with young families moving into a new neighborhood of sixteen custom designed homes—the first new subdivision in the south side of San Antonio in over twenty years.

Time and again, COPS and the Metro Alliance have initiated new ideas for the creative use of local, federal, and state public dollars to help working families rebuild their neighborhoods, both physically and socially. They formulate their goals and strategies from the experiences and dreams of working families. These IAF organizations have institutionalized a culture of politics in which citizens have both the real power to act on their hopes for their communities, as well as the responsibility to put forward not just complaints but constructive plans. They have created a culture of reasoned debate, accountability, negotiations, respect, and compromise within which the powers of a city can collaborate to guide its destiny.

Other situations in which disenfranchised citizens have developed the power to initiate action to improve their communities include the following.

**The Nehemiah Homes Project in Brooklyn and Bronx, New York.** East Brooklyn Congregations has built over 3,000 new single-family homes for working families, renewing completely devastated neighborhoods. This was possible because the broad based church organization, under the auspices of the Industrial Areas Foundation, leveraged land and tax abatements from the city of New York and no-interest construction financing from religious institutions. In addition, each home carries an interest-free second mortgage loan from the city government of $15,000 as a lien repayable whenever the house is sold. A similar Nehemiah program was established in Baltimore by BUILD, also an IAF organization.

**Job Training in San Antonio.** COPS and the Metro Alliance, the business community, the city of San Antonio, the local Private Industry Council (PIC), the governor of Texas, and several other state and local agencies have collaborated to create a $7 million, high-skill job-training effort. Employers have committed several hundred high-skill positions—primarily in health care. The governor committed $2.3 million in state funds for development. The city government committed $2 million for income maintenance. The PIC committed $2.6 million for job training. COPS and Metro committed the sweat equity of neighborhood leaders to holding job trainees accountable to the community for a commitment to long-term training.

**Commonwealth in Baltimore.** The corporate community in Baltimore contributed $20 million in scholarship funds, to be matched by funds from local universities, for high school graduates achieving good grades and attendance. The BUILD organization helps to raise additional resources from government sources, and mobilizes the participation of families and local schools. COPS and the Metro Alliance created a similar program called the San Antonio Education Partnership.

**Colonias in South Texas.** The state of Texas has pledged $250 million in grants and low-interest loans (which is helping to leverage federal and local funds) to build water and sewer systems in the 400-plus unincorporated rural communities along the Texas-Mexico border. *Colonia* is a Spanish word for neighborhood, and along the border in Texas it is a word for communities of people who were deceived by unscrupulous land developers—hard-working people who were promised complete utility services but were left with open sewage ditches, unpaved streets, no running water, and an unfathomable number of public health problems. Valley Interfaith, the Border Organization, and the El Paso Interreligious Sponsoring Organization (EPISO), with support from the entire network of Texas IAF organizations, initiated and promoted the legislation in collaboration with the elected leadership of the state government, the Texas Water Development Board, and local providers.

***Moral Minimum Wage.*** In 1987, after nine months of hard dialogue and negotiation with Southern California IAF, the California Industrial Welfare Commission raised the state's minimum wage to $4.25 an hour, then the highest in the nation. This case is one in which the work of the Southern California IAF made a positive difference in the real income of families, and contrary to the prophecies of the opposition, subsequent studies have demonstrated no adverse effect on levels of employment.

***Community Policing in Hudson County, New Jersey.*** The Interfaith Community Organization (ICO) in Jersey City and Hoboken has for three years worked with police departments to create a new culture of "community policing"—an approach to public safety that involves the commitment of a city's resources to the day-to-day work of building ongoing relationships between police and neighborhood residents. Although the struggle ran the gamut from replacing the police chief to developing a true public consensus on community policing as a priority, ICO's work has led to a firm commitment of resources and personnel for eight neighborhoods in Hudson County.

***Texas Alliance Schools.*** The Texas Education Agency has pledged additional resources to thirty-two schools that are collaborating with local community organizations to seriously reorganize neighborhood schools. Modeled on the experience of Fort Worth's Morningside Middle School, in which leaders of Allied Communities of Tarrant rewove the fabric of community linking families, teachers, administrators, and community leaders, the Alliance Schools project works to build a constituency and commitment among stakeholders in education to make dramatic improvements in the performances of the schools and develop an effective constituency for education reform.

## The Role of the Government

Reinvigorating urban life requires a new vision of civil society appropriate to the challenges of this age. The IAF believes, with Arthur Okun, that the two primary institutions of modern times, the market and the state, have their places in social life, but must be kept in their places.[9] Without strong countervailing institutions, the imperialism of the market will dominate and penetrate all relationships, in both public and private spheres, as it did in the 1980s. The healthy functioning of an enterprise-market system depends on balanced relationships among society's major institutions—family, community, and church—and market mechanisms. These institutions teach the values of social intercourse, reciprocity, trust, exchange, and accountability, which are requisite for the effective functioning of the market system.

Americans have already seen contemporary politics—both electioneering and governing—reduced to marketing strategies. Politics no longer mediates the market but is part and parcel of it. The advertising executives and media consultants now shape campaigns centered not around debates of public philosophy or the governance of what Daniel Bell called the "public household," but around negative thirty-second television ads. Even worse, the media advisors now attempt to govern, fashioning the rationale of war and peace by opinion polls. The result is an incoherent, inarticulate, and trivial political leadership, and a growing, cancerous cynicism and alienation in the community. The failure to center public life around genuine discourse is poisoning the reservoirs of good will in social relationships. Trust is unraveling not just in the political sphere, but in other public spheres—between doctors and patients, pastors and parishioners, teachers and students.

The tools of a market mechanism—money and prices—are effective signals for what is to be produced, how much, and for whom. The market is also an effective mechanism for the creation of wealth, the coordination of economic activity, and the buffering of citizens from the state. Yet the market has fundamental limits. It accepts grossly unequal distributions of income and power, which distort the very workings of the market process. The market cannot deal with external factors, nor can it calculate intergenerational costs. Market mechanisms often seem oblivious to the many examples of market failures that lead to air and water pollution, environmental degradation, and social imbalance—what John Kenneth Galbraith called private affluence in the midst of public squalor.

Government provision of consumer goods, services, transfer payments, or tax credits will provide some relief from the conditions of poverty. To the extent that they allow some people more choices, such policies are useful. Yet these consumables, however benignly bestowed, will not provide a long-term solution to the culture of poverty and despair that exists in communities today. The alleviation of poverty requires not just an increase in income, but the development of the capacity to act—to make choices. This means that any strategy to alleviate poverty must also address the question of inequities of power. The role of those who have power in shaping political and economic decisions is critically important. If poor people are to have any real dignity, they must play a meaningful role in making these decisions. Market oriented strategies are not sufficient. There must also be strategies for developing political entrepreneurship.

Just as the government cannot create entrepreneurial economic activity, neither can it create political entrepreneurship. The government cannot "empower" people, because power is not something that can be bestowed. Government can facilitate, encourage, recognize, and reward grassroots organizing, but it cannot create it. Government cannot create local initiatives, but it can understand the importance of these initiatives having an institutional base rooted in people's imagination, curiosity, values, and search for meaning.

The IAF has developed an innovative proposal that is rooted in our organizational community base. We propose that the federal government structure a matching grant strategy to leverage the commitments of states, local municipalities, and communities. The strategy would be based on the concept of an augmented community development block grant program and a more flexible Job Training Partnership Act. Communities would receive a certain minimum entitlement based on need, as in the current program. The federal government could then increase the amount of the grant to the extent that a results oriented strategy had been developed that would reward the achievement of certain outcomes. These outcomes could include some combination of the following: increases in meaningful employment, reduction of a percentage of poverty, increased access to health care, improvements in infrastructure and security, facilitation of first-time housing purchases, and so forth. Essentially, the federal government would provide matching grants for local investments of money, resources, and "sweat equity." Ideally these efforts should be developed as part of a larger strategy for state and local governments, corporations, and private sector institutions to make available resources to match the social capital of authentic indigenous local community based organizations.

Theoretically, the granting of additional monies to cities in which such strategic organizing is taking place should generate interest in other locales, thus facilitating the replication and dissemination of a new institution-building process. At the same time this strategy recognizes the necessity for macroeconomic initiatives to ensure a growing economy and full employment. In addition, it also recognizes potential labor demand and supply problems. Thus there is the need to develop job-training initiatives strategically, with consideration for the future as well as the current situation in which the local economic structure is embedded.

## Conclusion

The task of rebuilding our civic and political institutions is an urgent one. People in modern industrial societies, particularly those living in the cities, are atomized and disconnected from each other. Particularly in the suburbs, far too much of the American search for "fulfillment" is centered on the individual, making his or her relationships utilitarian and narcissistic in nature. This fragmentation leaves people increasingly less capable of forming a common purpose and carrying it out. Vaclav Havel pointed out in his address to the World Economic Forum in February 1992 that global civilization is in danger of destroying itself through inattention to any number of massive threats—the population explosion, the greenhouse effect, AIDS, and so on.

The large paradox at the moment is that [the hu]man—a great collector of information—is well aware of all this, yet is absolutely incapable of dealing with the danger. Traditional science, with its usual coolness, can describe the different ways we might destroy ourselves, but it cannot offer us truly effective and practicable instructions on how to avert them. . . . What is needed is something different, something larger. . . . The way forward is not in the mere construction of universal systemic solutions, to be applied to reality from the outside; it is also in seeking to get to the heart of reality through personal experiences. Such an approach promotes an atmosphere of tolerant solidarity and unity in diversity based on mutual respect, genuine pluralism and parallelism. In a word, human uniqueness, human action, and the human spirit must be rehabilitated.[10]

As Havel indicates, this rehabilitation can only be done through a different kind of politics, that is, a politics that creates authentic democratic political institutions that teach, mentor, and build a constituency of leaders and a network of stakeholders to initiate and support appropriate public policies that can rebuild our cities and reinforce the development of viable communities and mediating institutions.

The work of the IAF is in fact designed to create a different kind of politics. Developing a strategy that deals with the structural inequalities built into our dynamic economy requires an organized constituency with the power and imagination to initiate and support policies for change. If we are to create such a constituency and restore health and integrity to our political process, mitigating the distorting role and influence of organized concentrations of wealth, then we must be vigilant in the development of real democratic institutions. The work of the IAF is to create organized constituencies that are effective in teaching real politics.

## Notes

[1] Mishel and Frankel (1991).
[2] Levy (1990).
[3] Miles (1992), pp. 41–68.
[4] Wolin (1989).
[5] Thompson (1976).
[6] Hirschman (1990).
[7] Galston (1989), pp. 89–101.
[8] Coleman (1989).
[9] Okun (1975), p. 119.
[10] Havel (1992), pp. 8–14.

# Bibliography

Advisory Commission on Intergovernmental Relations. 1978. *State Mandating of Local Expenditures*. Washington, D.C.: ACIR.

———. 1992a. *Federal Statutory Preemption of State and Local Authority: History, Inventory, and Issues*. Washington, D.C.: ACIR.

———. 1992b. *Significant Features of Fiscal Federalism. Volume #1: Budget Processes and Tax Systems*. Washington, D.C.: ACIR.

Aschauer, David. 1989. "Public Investment and Productivity Growth in the Group of Seven." *Economic Perspectives: A Review from the Federal Reserve Bank of Chicago,* Vol. 13, September-October 1989.

Betsey, Charles L. et al. 1985. *Youth Employment and Training Programs: The YEDPA Years*. Washington, D.C.: National Academy Press.

Bluestone, Barry, Mary Stevenson, and Chris Tilly. 1991. "The Deterioration in Labor Market Prospects for Young Men with Limited Schooling: Assessing the Impact of 'Demand Side' Factors." Paper presented at the Eastern Economic Association Meeting, Pittsburgh, March 14–15.

Bureau of the Census. 1968–1992. *Current Population Survey, March (Annual Demographic File)*. Washington, D.C.: Government Printing Office.

———. 1969. *1967 Census of Manufactures—Geographic Area Series*. Washington, D.C.: Government Printing Office.

———. 1982. "Characteristics of the Population Below Poverty Level:

1980." *Current Population Reports.* P-60, No. 131. Washington, D.C.: Government Printing Office.

———. 1991. *1987 Census of Manufactures—Geographic Area Series.* Washington, D.C.: Government Printing Office.

———. 1992. "Poverty in the United States: 1991." *Current Population Reports.* P-60, No. 181. Washington, D.C.: Government Printing Office.

Burtless, Gary. ed. 1990. *A Future of Lousy Jobs? The Changing Structure of U.S. Wages.* Washington, D.C.: The Brookings Institution.

Cannan, Edwin. 1896. *The History of Local Rates in England: Five Lectures.* London: Longmans, Green.

Castells, Manuel. 1989. *The Informational City.* New York: Basil Blackwell.

Chervick, R. 1992. "Funding State and Local Courts: Increasing Demands and Decreasing Resources." *Judicature, Journal of the American Judicature Society,* Vol. 76.

Chubb, John, and Terry Moe. 1990. *Politics, Markets, and America's Schools.* Washington, D.C.: The Brookings Institution.

Church, T., and J. Lee. 1978. *Pretrial Delay: A Review and Bibliography.* Williamsburg, VA: National Center for State Courts.

Coleman, James. 1989. "Schools and Communities." *Chicago Studies,* November 1989.

Commission on the Skills of the American Workforce. 1990. *America's Choice: High Skills or Low Wages!* Rochester, NY: National Center on Education and the Economy.

Council of the Great City Schools. 1992. *National Urban Education Goals, Baseline Indicators, 1990–91.* September 1992.

Department of Housing and Urban Development. 1974. *The Costs of Sprawl.* Washington, D.C.: Government Printing Office.

Dertouzos, Michael, Richard K. Lester, and Robert Solow. 1989. *Made in America: Regaining the Competitive Edge.* Cambridge: Massachusetts Institute of Technology Press.

Doeringer, Peter et al. 1991. *Turbulence in the American Workplace.* New York: Oxford.

Douglas, G. Bruce. 1990. "Suburban Trip Generation and Some Notions about Changing Traffic Patterns." *Travel Characteristics at Large Scale Suburban Activity Centers,* Transportation Research Circular #323. Washington, D.C.: Transportation Research Board.

Downs, Anthony. 1992. *Stuck in Traffic.* Washington, D.C.: The Brookings Institution.

Duckworth, Robert, John Simmons, and Robert McNulty. 1986. *The Entrepreneurial American City.* Washington, D.C.: Partners for Livable Places.

Duncan, Otis D., Ray Cuzzort, and Beverly Duncan. 1961. *Statistical Geography.* Glencoe, IL: The Free Press.

Economic Policy Council of the UNA-USA. 1993. *The Social Consequences of a North American Free Trade Agreement.* New York: UNA-USA.

Eisen, Arlene. 1992. *A Report on Foundations' Support for Comprehensive Neighbor-hood-Based Community-Empowerment Initiatives.* New York: The New York Community Trust.

Farrar, Eleanor, and Anthony Cipollone. 1988. "After the Signing: The Boston Compact, 1982–1985." In Levine and Trachtman 1988.

Fliegel, Sy, with James MacGuire. 1993. *Miracle in East Harlem.* New York: New York Times Books.

*The Forgotten Half: Pathways to Success for America's Youth and Young Families.* 1988. The William T. Grant Foundation Commission on Work, Family and Citizenship.

Freeman, Richard. 1976. *The Overeducated American.* New York: Academic Press.

Galston, William. 1989. "Civic Education in the Liberal State." In Rosen-blum 1989.

Garreau, Joel. 1991. *Edge City: Life on the New Frontier.* New York: Double-day.

Gold, Steven D. 1989. *Reforming State & Local Government Relations: A Practical Guide.* Denver: National Conference of State Legislatures.

———. 1993. "Changes in State and Local Tax Systems over the Past 20 Years." *State Tax Notes,* January 4, 1993.

Goldberg, Arthur. 1990. "Americans and their Cities." City University of New York, Office of Urban Affairs (mimeo), November 1990.

Havel, Vaclav. 1992. "Politics and the World Itself." *Kettering Review,* Sum-mer 1992.

Hirschman, Albert. 1990. *Exit, Voice and Loyalty.* Cambridge: Harvard Uni-versity Press.

Hovey, Harold A. 1989. "Analytical Approaches to State-Local Rela-tions." In Liner 1989.

Hughes, Mark Alan. 1989. "Mispeaking Truth to Power: A Geographic Perspective on the 'Underclass' Falacy." *Economic Geography,* Vol. 65.

*International Conference on the Economic, Social, and Environmental Problems of Cities Issues Paper.* 1992. Paris: Organization for Economic Cooperation and Development.

Jacob, Herbert. 1973. *Urban Justice: Law and Order in American Cities.* Engle-wood Cliffs, NJ: Prentice-Hall.

Jargowsky, Paul A., and Mary Jo Bane. 1991. "Neighborhood Poverty: Basic Questions." In Lynn and McGeary 1991.

Kahn, Alfred. 1991. Comments at Conference on the Future of Telecom-munications Regulation, sponsored by Columbia Institute for Tele-communications and Information, Columbia University, Fall 1991.

Jencks, Christopher. 1988. "Deadly Neighborhoods." *The New Republic,* June 13, 1988.

Jencks, Christopher, and Paul Peterson, eds. 1991. *The Urban Underclass.* Washington, D.C.: The Brookings Institution.

Kasarda, John D. 1985. "Urban Change and Minority Opportunities." In Peterson 1985.

———. 1989. "Urban Industrial Transformation and the Underclass." *Annals of the American Academy of Political Science,* Vol. 501.

———. 1990. "Structural Factors Affecting the Location and Timing of Urban Underclass Growth." *Urban Geography,* Vol. 11.

Kasarda, John D. et al. 1992. *Urban Underclass Database: An Overview and Machine-Readable File Documentation.* Chapel Hill, NC: Kenan Institute of Private Enterprise.

Kearns, David, and Dennis Doyle. 1988. *Winning the Brain Race.* San Francisco: ICS Press.

King, Carolyn Dineen. 1991. "A Matter of Conscience." *Houston Law Review,* Vol. 28.

Ladd, Helen F. 1991. "The State Aid Decision: Changes in State Aid to Local Governments, 1982–87." *National Tax Journal,* December 1991.

Ladd, Helen F., and John Yinger. 1989. *America's Ailing Cities.* Baltimore: Johns Hopkins University Press.

Ledebur, Larry C., and William R. Barnes. 1993. *"All in it Together": Cities, Suburbs and Local Economic Regions.* Washington, D.C.: National League of Cities.

Levine, Marsha, and Roberta Trachtman. eds. 1988. *American Business and the Public Schools: Case Studies of Corporate Involvement in Public Education.* New York: Teachers College Press.

Levy, Frank. 1990. *Dollars and Dreams: The Changing American Income Distribution.* New York: Basic Books.

Lineberry, W.P. ed. 1972. *Justice in America: Law, Order, and the Courts.* New York: H.W. Wilson.

Liner, E. Blaine. ed. 1989. *A Decade of Devolution: Perspectives on State-Local Relations.* Washington, D.C.: Urban Institute.

Lynn, Lawrence E. Jr., and Michael G.H. McGeary. eds. 1991. *Inner-City Poverty in the United States.* Washington, D.C.: National Academy Press.

Main, Jeremy. 1972. "Justice on the Verge of Collapse." In Lineberry 1972.

Markusen, Ann R., Annalee Saxenian, and Marc A. Weiss. 1981. "Who Benefits from Intergovernmental Transfers?" *Publius,* Winter 1981.

Marland, Sidney. 1974. *Career Education: A Proposal for Reform.* New York: McGraw-Hill.

Marshall, Ray, and Marc Tucker. 1992. *Education and the Wealth of Nations.* New York: Basic Books.

Massey, Douglas, and Mitchell Eggers. 1990. "The Ecology of Inequality: Minorities and the Concentration of Poverty, 1970–1980." *American Journal of Sociology,* Vol. 95.

Meisenheimer, Joseph R. II. 1992. "How Do Immigrants Fare in the U.S. Labor Market." *Monthly Labor Review,* December 1992.

Miles, Jack. 1992. "Blacks vs. Browns." *Atlantic Monthly,* October 1992.

Mincy, Ronald B., Isabel Sawhill, and Douglas Wolf. 1990. "The Underclass: Definition and Measurement." *Science,* Vol. 248.

Mishel, Lawrence, and David Frankel. 1991. *The State of Working America.* Armonk, N.Y.: M.E. Sharpe.

Moss, Philip, and Chris Tilly. 1991. *Why Black Men Are Doing Worse in the Labor Market: A Review of Supply-Side and Demand-Side Explanation.* New York: Social Science Research Council.

Munnell, Alicia. 1990. "Why Has Productivity Growth Declined?" *New England Economic Review,* January/February 1990.

*1992 European-North American State of the Cities Report.* 1992. Washington, D.C.: German Marshall Fund of the United States.

Oates, Wallace E. 1972. *Fiscal Federalism.* New York: Harcourt Brace Jovanovich.

O'Cléireacáin, Carol. 1991. "The Costs of the New Federalism: From Revenue Sharing to Deficit Sharing." *Dissent,* Spring 1991.

———. 1992. "A Case Study in Fiscal Federalism: New York City and New York State." *Fordham Urban Law Journal,* Vol. 19.

Okun, Arthur. 1975. *Equality and Efficiency.* Washington, D.C.: The Brookings Institution.

Osterman, Paul. 1980. *Getting Started: The Youth Labor Market.* Cambridge: Massachusetts Institute of Technology Press.

———. 1988. *Employment Futures: Reorganization, Dislocation, and Public Policy.* New York: Oxford.

Pagano, Michael A. 1991. *City Fiscal Conditions in 1991.* Washington, D.C.: National League of Cities, July 1991.

Peirce, Neal R. (with Curtis W. Johnson and John Stuart Hall). 1993. *Citistates: How Urban America Can Prosper in a Competitive World.* Arlington, Va.: Seven Locks Press.

Penne, L. 1985. *Urban Amenities: Linking Livability and Economic Development.* Washington, D.C.: National Council for Urban Economic Development.

Persky, Joseph, Elliott Sclar, and Wim Wiewel. 1991. *Does America Need Cities?* Washington, D.C.: Economic Policy Institute.

Reich, Robert. 1991. *The Work of Nations.* New York: Knopf.

Reinhardt, S. 1993. "Too Few Judges, Too Many Cases." *American Bar Association Journal,* Vol. 79.

Reischauer, Robert D. 1987. *The Geographic Concentration of Poverty: What Do We Know?* Washington, D.C.: The Brookings Institution.

Ricketts, Erol, and Isabel Sawhill. 1988. "Defining and Measuring the Underclass." *Journal of Policy Analysis and Management,* Vol. 7.

Rivlin, Alice M. 1992. *Reviving the American Dream: The Economy, the States and the Federal Government.* Washington, D.C.: The Brookings Institution.

Rosenblum, Nancy. ed. 1989. *Liberalism and the Moral Life.* Cambridge: Harvard University Press.

Rouse, James. 1992. "Rational Visions Generate Energy." *Vital Speeches,* Vol. 86.

Rusk, David. 1993. *Cities Without Suburbs.* Washington, D.C.: Woodrow Wilson Center Press.

Sassen, Saskia. 1991. *The Global City: New York, London, Tokyo.* Princeton: Princeton University Press.

Taggart, Robert. 1981. *A Fisherman's Guide: An Assessment of Training and Remediation Strategies.* Kalamazoo, MI: W.E. Upjohn Institute for Employment Research.

Tax Foundation. 1992. *Facts and Figures on Government Finance.* Washington, D.C.: Tax Foundation.

Thompson, Dennis F. 1976. *John Stuart Mill and Representative Government.* Princeton: Princeton University Press.

Thurow, Lester. 1992. *Head to Head.* New York: William Morrow & Company.

*Trends and Forecasts of Highway Passenger Travel.* 1987. The Future National Highway Program, 1991 and Beyond, Working Paper 2, FHWA, U.S. Department of Transportation, December 1987.

U.S. Conference of Mayors. 1991a. *City Fiscal Conditions 1980–1990.* Washington, D.C.: U.S. Conference of Mayors.

———. 1991b. *Impact of the National Recession on America's Cities.* Washington, D.C.: U.S. Conference of Mayors.

Weiss, Marc A. 1987. *The Rise of the Community Builders.* New York: Columbia University Press.

Willard, C. 1976. *Criminal Justice on Trial: A Basic Overview of the American System of Criminal Justice.* Skokie, IL: National Textbook Co.

Williams, Victor. 1992. "Help Wanted—Federal Judges: Judicial Gridlock: Solving an Immediate Problem and Averting a Future Crisis." *Loyola University Chicago Law Journal,* Vol. 24.

Wilson, Stephen F. 1992. *Reinventing the Schools: A Radical Plan for Boston.* Boston: Pioneer Institute.

Wilson, William Julius. 1987. *The Truly Disadvantaged: The Inner City, the Underclass, and Public Policy.* Chicago: University of Chicago Press.

Wolin, Sheldon S. 1989. *The Presence of the Past: Essays on the State and the Constitution.* Baltimore: Johns Hopkins University Press.

Woolhandler, Stephanie, and David U. Himmelstein. 1986. "Cost without Benefit: Administrative Waste in U.S. Health Care." *New England Journal of Medicine,* Vol. 314.

———. 1991. "The Deteriorating Administrative Efficiency of the U.S. Health Care System." *New England Journal of Medicine,* Vol. 324.

Yinger, John, and Helen F. Ladd. 1989. "The Determinants of State Assistance to Central Cities." *National Tax Journal,* December 1989.

# Final Report
## of the
## Eighty-second American Assembly

At the close of their discussions, the participants in the Eighty-second American Assembly, on *Interwoven Destinies: Cities and the Nation*, at Arden House, Harriman, New York, April 15–18, 1993, reviewed as a group the following statement. This statement represents general agreement; however, no one was asked to sign it. Furthermore, it should be understood that not everyone agreed with all of it.

### Values and Vision

America and its cities are at a crossroads.

If they choose to make their separate ways into the future, decline and decay almost surely lie ahead for both. But if they stride together as partners into the twenty-first century, the nation and its great urban areas will compete and brilliantly succeed in the new global economy.

The past and present are studded with dramatic and conflicting facts and figures:

- Productivity and real income in the United States have barely grown in the past two decades—yet during the same period we have created millions of new jobs.

- One of every two African-American children is born into poverty—yet countless immigrants still consider this country the land of opportunity.
- The infant mortality rate in our inner cities is at Third World levels—yet our medical technology is the envy of the First World.

The problems and promise of America and its cities are tightly interwoven. For our country to remain competitive, we must strengthen our metropolitan areas and central cities where 80 percent of Americans live and work. We must also fully use all our human and physical capital. There is no shortage of such resources—the challenge is to develop them through more effective education and management.

To create prosperity and give everyone a chance to share the American dream, our country must reaffirm and deliver on six basic principles:

First is the promise of economic opportunity, which has made America a beacon to the world. This promise can only be fulfilled if good jobs at good wages are available for all who want to work.

Second is the concept of individual responsibility—part of the social contract that assumes we will help ourselves and each other achieve a better life. Our government, in turn, is called upon to encourage and support these efforts.

Third, there is the idea of community. This encompasses a national diversity strengthened by shared values and common bonds. The communitarian ideal, with its spirit of neighborly self-help, lies at the very heart of the American character.

Fourth, a commitment to quality education is equally central to our national heritage. Traditionally, education in America has been a liberating force, promoting economic and social mobility and providing the civic glue that binds us together.

A fifth belief is equality for all people. Our country was founded on this "self-evident" truth. Yet today, racism—the most profound cancer in our body politic—is preventing millions of Americans from being judged on the basis of "the content of their character rather than the color of their skin." Racial divisions and discrimination deprive many citizens of equality of opportunity; a just society will never be built until these barriers are removed.

Sixth, we highly value the freedom to enjoy the blessings of "life, liberty, and the pursuit of happiness." Sadly, countless numbers of our fellow citizens today are denied a bright future by violent crime and an atmosphere of hopelessness and fear.

Our cities and our nation must confront these problems and solve them. Racism must give way to equal opportunity. Freedom from fear must replace violence and lawlessness. We must revitalize community, improve education, and establish an environment that encourages personal responsibility. Accomplishing these tasks will help assure our country's continuing competitiveness in the global economy and will speed the realization of America's promise to itself.

## Regional Solutions

If America is to thrive, metropolitan regions must thrive, and if they are to thrive, both our core cities and suburbs must thrive.

America should resist the urge to blame its core cities for the growing social disorder of many low-income inner city neighborhoods that suffer from crime, drugs, homelessness, poverty, and despair.

Core cities are the victims of a number of external forces:

- the shift of higher-income groups to the suburbs;
- the migration of many manufacturing and service jobs to outlying areas;
- federal and state policies regarding highways, mortgage lending, taxation, gasoline pricing, and education funding systems that favor suburban areas; and
- concentration of immigrants within and outside America's borders.

America and its government officials would serve themselves better by thinking and acting in terms of comprehensive geographic areas rather than competing individual localities.

Direct aid should be established between the federal government and core cities within metropolitan areas based upon resource needs created by national economic and social forces beyond local control.

The federal government should also "level the playing field" within metropolitan areas by the use of incentives or sanctions that foster a fairer distribution by the states of metropolitan-wide tax collections. Such a redistribution could:

- help unite cities and suburbs as interdependent thriving metropolitan areas;
- increase core-city funding of public safety programs;
- promote racially and economically integrated private and public housing throughout the metropolitan area that is both affordable to the poor and uplifting to families moving to independence;

- improve funding and programs in core-city schools, which must grapple with the most difficult student populations;
- redress the imbalance between highway and mass transit funding to make mobility of people, not vehicles, the goal;
- promote region-wide economic development and planning;
- revitalize neighborhoods and downtowns; and
- equalize tax incentives for investment in industry, commerce, and housing among cities, suburbs, and non-metropolitan areas.

Economic activity in metropolitan regions clearly links core cities to their suburbs. Government and political institutions do not reflect the economy and cannot, therefore, provide effective leadership or coordination.

Contrary to legislation in the last few years charting new directions for transportation, energy, and clean air, federal funding continues dramatically to favor highways over transit. It thus encourages rather than deters less efficient, less cost-effective settlement patterns while abdicating responsibility for city infrastructure and the mobility needs of the poor. This trend further isolates the poor in the ghettos—inaccessible to jobs in the suburbs—and deters use of the more efficient multiple occupancy vehicles throughout the metropolitan area. Ironically, such policies are contributing also to the rapidly worsening gridlock on our suburban highways and declining rates of speed on such highways as well.

## The New Economic Environment

The advanced industrialized countries are transforming themselves into information and service economies, causing a dramatic impact on the nature, size, and life cycles of economic organizations.

Fueled by continuing improvements in computer and telecommunications technologies, we are moving from a world of long-standing, large hierarchical organizations to small adaptive enterprises; from General Motors and IBM to community development corporations and Silicon Valley start-ups. In this transformation, America's economic vitality will be improved by the ability of cities to play a leadership role in ensuring our global economic competitiveness.

Cities have a substantial portion of the resources needed for entrepreneurial growth:

- a large and diverse work force;
- a rich and extensive network of financial, educational, cultural, business, and scientific institutions; and

- diversity and density of public and private infrastructure and human capital that are the necessary ingredients to experiment and innovation.
  At the same time, cities face irreversible challenges:
- financial and human capital has become much more mobile, subjecting America's cities, like the nation itself, to greater economic competition; and
- our new economy requires higher levels of education and expertise. As large corporate and governmental organizations downsize, the American workforce faces a greater risk of unemployment and requires substantial and expensive retraining and job placement.

To ensure that cities lead the way through this economic transformation, we must:

- redesign taxes, regulations, and governmental decision making to create incentives for new organizations and their workers;
- ensure collaborative efforts among educational institutions, businesses, government, nonprofit organizations, and community groups, to create economic opportunities and new innovations;
- use public assistance to provide incentives to workers and employers to move individuals from welfare to work;
- promote equal access to a superior education and training for all Americans;
- encourage the concentration of public and private investments in inner city zones; and
- reduce the barriers to the flow of investment capital into small start-up organizations and into urban areas.

The future productivity of our urban workforce will profoundly influence the productivity of our national workforce; and it is this productivity that will contribute to the rate of our economic growth in the twenty-first century. In an information economy, the cost of excluding any of our citizens from the growing job sectors will not only harm our national spirit, but diminish our material prosperity as well.

## Redesigning Government

Government at all levels can become monopolistic, fragmented, and rule-driven. When that occurs, the people served are viewed as passive recipients. Redesigned properly, government can provide coherent services to prideful citizens.

The first principle for redesign is for government to avoid doing for others what they can do for themselves. The second principle is to provide choices to the people served. Thus, government must commit to the goals of public service but it should also be flexible in its methods.

An entrepreneurial government would:

1. jointly venture with private for-profit corporations;

2. subcontract with private nonprofit groups;

3. invite competition permitting citizens choice of systems that serve them best.

Applying the first principle, such a government might let people serve themselves within communities, then repay communities the cost savings. For example, if neighbors can help seniors to prolong self-sufficiency and avoid nursing homes, the results may not only be more humane, but more cost-effective.

Government should offer rewards to merge activities where fragmentation or duplication can be reduced. Cases abound in which health services, job training, and housing assistance are provided as a package. What is needed is public policy that rewards such work.

A redesigned local government will improve service delivery and operate more cost-effectively. It will strip away redundant regulations and encrusted practices that burden enterprises, profit and nonprofit, large and small. By engaging citizens in shaping their own governance, greater personal responsibility and a deepened sense of community will be sure to follow.

Just as we can redesign local government, we should also address the tangled responsibilities and resource allocations within the federal and state governments. The roles of each level of government must be redefined. Funding needs and sources of revenue are not well matched, particularly within metropolitan areas.

The federal government should be responsible for assuring and financing basic levels of health care and income support. In addition, it should absorb the costs of national policies, such as those relating to immigration, which now place disproportionate burdens on some local governments. State governments should continue to increase their role in equalizing educational opportunity, with the federal government playing an enhanced role in financing educational support for children from disadvantaged households and with special needs.

State and local governments should take primary responsibility for transportation and other infrastructure, whose benefits are primarily local. For infrastructure that is crucial to the national economy and environment, such as major airports, highways, ports, rail, and mass transit, the federal government should continue to play the major role. Programs that are mandated by the federal or state governments should be financed by those governments. This rearrangement of responsibility will require significant increases in federal taxation, but such increases should be offset, at least partially, by reductions in state and local taxes.

Fragmentation of local governments within metropolitan areas is a major problem. State and local governments should be encouraged to establish metropolitan tax-sharing arrangements, jurisdictional reforms, and state equalization funding.

This redefinition of roles should be only the beginning of a national examination of how governance can be organized to match the changed economy. The restructuring of governmental roles should be part of a major reexamination of federal priorities that includes conversion of both the level and distribution of defense spending to better meet the needs of the domestic and metropolitan economies.

## Human Capital: The Crucial Investment

One theme that must find expression in any urban policy initiative is investment in the skills, talents, and potential of our people. While it is not possible to anticipate or chart every future economic turn, it is possible to prepare our human assets so we can adapt and make adjustments as global and national economic trends become clear.

Such preparation will require sustained and expanded commitment to education and training at the national level. The redirection of priorities toward investment in human capital would be a powerful first step.

States and cities must also stress the enhancement of their human resources. There is a long tradition of city planning for land use, water resources, transportation systems, parks, and library systems. But few cities have explicit plans for integrating education, training, and the means to finance them. The elements of a broad-based human capital plan would include early childhood education, quality public schools, work related technical education, excellent community colleges, comprehensive higher education, literacy education, worker retraining, and life-long learning.

Restructuring our public schools to meet the needs of all of our citizens is an imperative. The federal government has established national goals. We need now to create high educational standards of excellence and develop tools of assessment to ensure we meet our goals.

Although goals and standards need a national perspective, we must recognize that they can only be achieved by students, teachers, and parents working collaboratively on the local level.

Communities that want such strategies to open doors for their citizens to the jobs of the new economy will have to collaborate with existing businesses as well as with economic development planners. To assure that such strategies penetrate the barriers of poverty, racial inequities, and central city isolation, cities and states must design pathways of access and outreach and a sustainable system of financing.

The federal government should encourage this kind of human capital development at the local level by comprehensive planning and by integrating the efforts of federal departments.

The safest insurance policy for uncertain economic times is to prepare a citizenry whose people are educated enough and confident enough to be masters of their destinies both as individuals and as members of a community.

## A Place to Live

Essential elements of urban revitalization and community stability are quality affordable housing and strong neighborhoods for all citizens. Decent housing is a fundamental necessity for people to succeed in life. Construction and rehabilitation of housing generate jobs and economic development for communities, and the improvement of the housing stock is a vital sign of neighborhood prosperity, individual mobility, and social well-being.

While America has a high national home ownership rate and a great deal of good housing in cities and suburbs, there are also important problems that must be addressed. Millions of people pay too much for housing, in many cases from 50 to 70 per cent of their incomes. Millions also live in substandard dwellings. More than half a million people are homeless every night, yet abandoned housing blights a large percentage of central city neighborhoods. Many people, especially minorities, face daily discrimination in being denied access to housing.

Many families are unable to afford the down payment to buy a first home, and home ownership rates have declined substantially among young adults. Racial minorities are denied mortgage credit at an unacceptable rate. At the same time, much of the national housing credit and tax policies favor housing for higher-income people, plus second homes and the suburbanization of residences in a way that does not fully account for the environmental or transportation costs.

To build more affordable housing, expand the range of housing choices for all citizens, particularly minorities, make existing housing more affordable for low- and moderate-income people, strengthen urban neighborhoods, and reduce homelessness, additional financing is needed from a variety of public and private sources. Secondary mortgage market institutions such as Fannie Mae and Freddie Mac should play a larger role in supplying funds for affordable housing, and private lending institutions can provide additional financing with the encouragement of credit enhancement. Federal mortgage insurance programs must now be redesigned with public and private partners to make certain that capital is available to rebuild areas where there is real but manageable risk in real estate lending. The Community Reinvestment Act should be used as a tool to expand private capital for affordable housing and community development and to reverse discrimination in lending practices.

The talent and resources of the private sector can be encouraged to participate in the redevelopment of our cities and the production of affordable housing. New partnerships can be forged to address a community's housing needs and the need to revitalize neighborhoods. These partnerships involve pension funds, nonprofit community organizations, for-profit housing developers, state and local housing finance agencies, and private investors through incentives such as the Low-Income Housing Tax Credit.

Real estate tax policies should be revised. Alternative sources of revenue rather than property taxes can be used to pay for programs and services that are not property-specific. To help increase housing affordability, it is important to encourage private investment and development through real estate tax incentives.

What is needed is greater stability and long-term commitment to maintaining permanent housing affordability. Also necessary is a substantial expansion of resources for supportive housing to assist homeless people and people with special needs such as the frail elderly, and the physically and mentally disabled. A fresh effort to revitalize older deteriorated neighborhoods is needed—one that goes beyond physical renewal to include social, economic, and community-building dimensions. Specific efforts are recommended to improve the physical, economic, and social fabric of our nation's public housing stock. Fair housing laws and regulations should be vigorously enforced to eliminate discrimination and promote equal housing opportunity. Finally, greater initiatives are required for mixed-income housing and neighborhoods, and increased assistance to help poor people and minorities live throughout metropolitan areas and create healthy economic and social integration.

## Creating Quality Places

Our communities are "billboards" of aspiration and values. If we allow our urban areas to deteriorate with trash-littered streets, unkempt parks, and worsening environmental air and water quality, if our cultural institutions are isolated from community needs, if our public housing states by design and maintenance that no one valuable lives here, if our downtowns are empty and dangerous after dark, then we have said a great deal about how we as citizens view our future.

Amenities of civic life are not a "frill"—they are an essential resource for urban development. This precious resource can be nurtured by promoting cultural facilities, enhancing urban design through public planning and private development standards, creating programs and incentives to establish lively and safe gathering places, using tax credits and other incentives to preserve historic structures and districts, building community parks and green spaces, managing the location and level of automobile and truck use, and maintaining environmental quality.

Amenities can become an urban economic development strategy by attracting business, promoting tourism and convention trade, and creating a positive change.

Cultural programs can become a bridge of good will and provide the first key steps for cooperation between diverse people to use urban culture to create coalitions for broader civic goals. Cultural institutions, including churches and educational facilities, can also rededicate themselves to serving those most at risk in our communities, such as youth and families in need of support.

Subsidized housing can reflect the best practices of adaptive reuse of historic buildings. Scattered-site, low-income housing can be designed to complement existing neighborhoods and encourage community conservation.

We should build and rebuild livable communities for all citizens and create places to be respected and enjoyed.

## A Just Society

Access to an effective urban justice system is essential to the social and economic well-being of cities. Particularly in urban areas, too many Americans believe the civil justice system is not available to them even as a means for resolving disputes. Adequate funding of legal services for the poor at federal and local levels is essential to give all citizens access to our democratic system.

The fear of crime corrodes our national spirit. In many communities, our justice system is overwhelmed and in crisis. It is time for innovative thinking and bold action to forge a new consensus in reversing the scourge of drugs, violence, gangs, and crime.

Our leaders must direct intellectual and financial assets toward understanding and confronting the underlying causes of crime. We must run the justice system with greater flexibility and responsiveness to what works.

Expenditures for parts of the criminal justice system cannot be made in isolation, but must be made with a comprehensive understanding of how they will affect the whole system.

From prevention to policing to correction, the importance of community responsibility belongs at the center of discussions of crime policy. The demand for drugs and guns flowing unremittingly across our borders must be halted by families, schools, and neighborhoods. Fifty thousand deaths by guns per year is convincing proof that indiscriminate sales of handguns and ammunition must cease.

Local coalitions of resident organizations, business, education, and government can generate concerted action from within each community to stop crime. Clearly, within this context, the community policing concept has special value and should be supported. In this concept, police officers are assigned to walk a neighborhood beat and work actively as partners and organizers with local residents to prevent criminal activity and engage in community improvement.

The alarming rise in crimes by and against children requires early intervention with a variety of services. Appropriate punishments for juvenile offenders must be balanced with the commitment to teaching young people to be peaceful citizens. At the local level, we should modernize and adequately fund our juvenile courts; at the federal level, provide stable funding and enlist the most qualified professionals.

The major crime threat to our communities comes from the drug crisis, and too little innovative thinking is being applied to the problem. Although money for law enforcement is critical, we must devote adequate funds to education, prevention, and treatment, and perhaps more importantly, we must speak out on the importance of early intervention and prevention.

Until recently, victims of crime were ignored within the system. State and federal laws have attempted to remedy this neglect. Hate crimes have emerged as a new concern, and it is impossible to ignore the public perception of bias in the justice system.

There is substantial evidence that the justice system, intentionally or unintentionally, treats minorities inequitably, and that past efforts to respond to such findings have been relatively ineffective. We must build confidence in the criminal justice system and work to ensure that the system treats all individuals with fairness and equity.

Programs must be fostered to ease community-police tension in minority communities, such as hiring minority officers and cross-cultural training for officers.

Underrepresentation of minorities on the bench and among court personnel, poor court facilities, and heavy caseloads should also be addressed to assure that our justice system has credibility and is used by all Americans to redress their grievances. Ultimately, we must commit adequate resources to our justice system and make reforms to assure that our justice system protects its citizens from crime and provides timely resolution of disputes. On the criminal side, more crime prevention and more effective alternatives to incarceration are new ways of thinking with promise. On the civil side, alternative dispute resolution systems and similar nonjudicial methods must be instituted to resolve conflicts more quickly and cheaply.

## Healthy Citizens, Healthy Cities

Access to decent, affordable health care is a right that should be available to all Americans, and the federal government has a responsibility to guarantee this right.

For too many of our citizens, rising health care costs are taking a bigger piece of the paycheck, for both coverage and treatment. For others, in rural and urban areas alike, health care is simply unavailable; there is no money or insurance, or there are no doctors or medical facilities. It is not uncommon in our cities today for primary health care to be obtained in the emergency room of the local hospital.

It is axiomatic that a thriving, working city rests on the good health of its citizens. Community clinics and physicians practicing in the neighborhood will bring medical attention to the people.

Beyond such issues of availability, there is a growing list of medical ills that should be addressed. Infant mortality rates in our major cities are a national disgrace. Local government can reverse these trends by providing access to prenatal and infant care.

Immunization for all at the appropriate age will ensure a better chance for our children. Educating parents on proper nutrition is critical to the healthy development of our young people and their ability to learn, to grow, and to work.

The growing number of homeless people speaks to the need for community and mental health care in our cities. Mental illness, in fact, is a growing problem for the many children being raised in dysfunctional conditions today.

Domestic violence is a growing problem as well, and must be addressed as a matter of national policy. The growth in the number of people infected with HIV reinforces the need for education, research, and treatment.

Paying for health care remains the thorniest issue. Some 25 percent of health care expenditures go for administrative costs. More efficient, cost-effective solutions must be found, such as alternatives to institutional care and insurance reforms.

Efforts to reform the nation's health care system are now under way in the federal government. We believe the reformed system should include basic coverage for all Americans and consumer choice.

## Promoting Racial Justice

The most malignant strain in American history has been the inability of our country to come to terms with the issue of race. Discrimination has diminished hope and opportunity for many racial and ethnic groups, and has been especially pernicious and persistent with respect to African-Americans. For more than 300 years, the ravages of racial prejudice have destroyed families and lives and our sense of national community. Our Constitution identified human beings in slavery as three-fifths of a person. We fought our bloodiest war over slavery. We have denied individuals such basic rights as the right to vote, to use public facilities, to work and to live where they choose, and to equitably-funded education.

Despite a non-violent civil rights movement in the 1950s and 1960s that stirred the conscience of the nation, despite landmark voting rights and equal access laws, and despite instances of inspiring personal progress, too many Americans today live with daily reminders that the color of their skin is the shaping reality of life. We all pay a tremendous price for this flaw in the American ideal.

- We waste human talent and potential that could contribute immeasurably to solving urgent national problems.
- We expend resources to fix social and economic problems that would be greatly diminished if we extended fairness of opportunity.
- We have created such vast separation in American institutions— our schools, our places of work, even our churches—that we are becoming separate societies and violating our most precious ideals.
- We create the conditions of social unrest when we fail to address pent-up anger and frustration.
- We damage ourselves and our children when we allow artificial divisions and misconceptions to deny the richness of diversity and respectful human contact.

The price we pay for failure to come to terms with race is too high, but we *can* do something about it. Public policies can be reshaped and implemented to eradicate racial discrimination and inequality. Among these policies are:

- Access to equal employment opportunity through the creation of voluntary affirmative measures and the enforcement of all equal employment legislation.
- Access to fair housing opportunity through the affirmative application of principles, laws, and regulations that guarantee the rights to full residential mobility and housing choice without discrimination.
- Access to equal educational opportunity through availability of

advanced curricula, quality facilities, and well-trained faculty for all students.
- Access to health care through availability of quality medical services and neighborhood-based health care facilities.
- Access to equal justice through availability of legal services, pretrial diversion programs, and community mediation clinics.

We will never fulfill our hopes for a society that enshrines the ideals of "liberty, equality, and fraternity," unless each of us assumes personal responsibility for embracing diversity and developing common environments where people of different races can relate to each other as persons with dignity and respect. As we seek out and create these windows of opportunity in our housing and neighborhoods, our schools and athletics, our professional and civic associations, and the institutions that carry the cultural heritage of our communities, we will take small steps forward for each of us that will some day add up to a giant step for our country.

## The New Civics

To fulfill our dreams for new cities in a renewed nation, the ethics of a new civics will have to replace the current decline in civic virtue. Our society has legitimated selfishness, violence, rebelliousness, and greed; the new civics can reconnect people with each other in partnership for their gain and our common good. This is a task not for legislation but for moral and civic guidance by our political, cultural, and community leaders. They must voice their support for the values that undergird any community.

How? By:

- celebrating diversity and encouraging an inclusive approach to decision making that transcends the barriers of race, gender, economic station, and political party that so often divide us;
- encouraging corporations and institutions to make it possible for their employees to participate in civic life;
- supporting a National Service Corps, including those who are not attending college as well as the college-bound, to assist in restoring sections of our cities;
- promoting responsible public awareness, enlightened public dialogue, and creative public activity; and challenging the media to join in their effort;
- cultivating involvement in those traditional activities that promote

civic virtue, such as churches, block associations, service clubs, and the like;
- enlisting the self-help efforts of urban residents to strengthen their neighborhoods;
- helping our schools to educate children for citizenship in a democracy;
- introducing immigrants to our culture and helping them understand the basic American compact;
- providing assistance and support for the political organization of those in our society who are voiceless and powerless; and
- persuading families, neighborhoods, media, churches, schools, not-for-profit agencies, labor unions, businesses, and other social and civic institutions to join together to develop better communities in which to live and work and raise a family.

We will work for new civic leadership to emerge in the public, private, not-for-profit, and volunteer sectors. It will recognize that we can change behavior without a government grant. Its aim will be to rebuild the infrastructure of the spirit that has been so seriously eroded today. If self-control is given higher value than self-indulgence, if enthusiasm replaces weariness, if optimism overcomes cynicism, then a new civics will appear that emphasizes "we" rather than "I" and couples affirmation of rights with assumption of responsibility. It will encourage individuals to fulfill themselves through perseverance, honesty, and hard work; discipline, self-sacrifice, and respect; compassion, tolerance, and love.

Practicing the new civics will move our cities from old ways that did not work, and lead to the realization of our dreams for economic freedom, social cohesion, political reform, and personal fulfillment.

# Participants

DENNIS W. ARCHER
Former Justice, Michigan
    Supreme Court
Dickinson, Wright, Moon, Van
    Dusen & Freeman
Detroit, MI

ROSANNE K. BACON
Executive Committee
National Education
    Association
Washington, DC

AL BILIK
President
Public Employee Department
AFL-CIO
Washington, DC

JORGE BOLANOS
President
Mivia Corporation
Miami, FL

\*\*DONALD J. BORUT
Executive Director
National League of Cities
Washington, DC

JOYCE BOVE
Vice President
The New York Community
Trust
New York, NY

PAUL BROPHY
President
Enterprise Foundation
Columbia, MD

V. JEAN BUTLER
President
Louisiana Housing Finance
    Agency
Baton Rouge, LA

DAVID F. CHAPPELL
City Councilman
Chappell & Handy, P.C.
Fort Worth, TX

‡HENRY G. CISNEROS
Secretary
U.S. Department of Housing &
    Urban Development
Washington, DC

MICHAEL CLARK
Executive Director
Citizens Committee for New
    York City, Inc.
New York, NY

DELMAS VERNON COLE
Housing Development
    Coordinator
Office of the Bronx Borough
    President
Bronx, NY

†ERNESTO CORTÉS
Director
Texas Industrial Areas
    Foundation
Austin, TX

STEPHEN COYLE
Chief Executive Officer
Housing Investment Trust
AFL-CIO
Washington, DC

THOMAS M. DE
    MARTINO
Vice President
Brooklyn Union Gas Company
Brooklyn, NY

*OSBORN ELLIOTT
Chairman
Citizens Committee for New
    York City, Inc.
New York, NY

ROBERT C. EMBRY, JR.
President
The Abell Foundation, Inc.
Baltimore, MD

**C. AUSTIN FITTS
President
The Hamilton Securities
    Group, Inc.
Washington, DC

MARTY FLEETWOOD
Founder & Executive Director
HomeBase/The Center for
    Common Concerns
San Francisco, CA

HENRY FLORES
Executive Director
Texas Department of Housing
    & Community Affairs
Austin, TX

JERRY FRANKLIN
President & CEO
Connecticut Public
    Broadcasting, Inc.
Hartford, CT

ELLEN V. FUTTER
President
Barnard College
New York, NY

LOUIS GAMBACCINI
General Manager
Southeast Pennsylvania
    Transportation Authority
Philadelphia, PA

HERBERT J. GANS
Robert S. Lynd Professor of
    Sociology
Columbia University
New York, NY

†DAVID R. GERGEN
Editor-at-Large
*U.S. News & World Report*
Washington, DC

†ELI GINZBERG
Professor
Director
The Eisenhower Center for the
    Conservation of Human
    Resources
Columbia University
New York, NY

NATHAN GLAZER
Professor of Education &
    Sociology
Graduate School of Education
Harvard University
Cambridge, MA

RICHARD G. GROSE
Executive Director
Missouri Housing
    Development Commission
Kansas City, MO

K. SCOTT HAMILTON
Dickinson, Wright, Moon, Van
    Dusen & Freeman
Detroit, MI

*†KAREN V. HILL
Executive Director
The City of Yonkers Fair
    Housing Implementation
    Office
Yonkers, NY

WALTER HOOK
Institute for Transportation
    and Development Policy
Brooklyn, NY

†WILLIAM H. HUDNUT, III
Senior Fellow
Hudson Institute
Former Mayor of Indianapolis
Indianapolis, IN

R. WILLIAM IDE, III
Long, Alderidge & Norman
Atlanta, GA

KENNETH TERRY
JACKSON
Barzun Professor in History &
Social Science History
Columbia University
New York, NY

†INGRID SAUNDERS
JONES
Vice President
Corporate External Affairs
The Coca-Cola Company
Atlanta, GA

HELEN F. LADD
Terry Sanford Institute of
Public Policy
Duke University
Durham, NC

**†VINCENT LANE
Chairman
Chicago Housing Authority
Chicago, IL

**†GEORGE LATIMER
Professor
School of Law
Hamline University
Former Mayor of St. Paul
St. Paul, MN

KENT LAWRENCE
Director & President
M. R. Bauer Foundation
Chicago, IL

JAMES L. LOGUE III
Executive Director
Michigan State Housing
Development Authority
Lansing, MI

HERBERT MAGIDSON
Executive Vice President
New York State United
Teachers
Vice President
American Federation of
Teachers
Albany, NY

ROBERT H. MCNULTY
President
Partners for Livable
Places
Washington, DC

*KIRSTEN MOY
Vice President
Equitable Real Estate
New York, NY

RAYMOND D. NASHER
President's Committee on the
Arts & Humanities
Chairman, The Nasher
Company
Dallas, TX

JEAN NOLAN
Assistant Secretary for Public
Affairs
U.S. Department of Housing
and Urban Development
Washington, DC

†CAROL O'CLÉIREACÁIN
Commissioner
New York City Department of
Finance
New York, NY

ROBERT M. O'TOOLE
Senior Staff Vice President
Mortgage Bankers Association
  of America
Washington, DC

PAUL E. PETERSON
Henry Lee Shattuck Professor
  of Government
Director, Center for American
  Political Studies
Department of Government
Harvard University
Cambridge, MA

PETER B. PRESTLEY
Chair
Tort and Insurance Practice
  Section
American Bar Association
Hartford, CT

HUGH B. PRICE
Vice President
The Rockefeller Foundation
New York, NY

ALFRED RAMIREZ
President
2000 Regional Partnership
Los Angeles, CA

NICOLAS RETSINAS
Assistant Secretary-Designate
  for Housing
Federal Housing
  Commissioner
U.S. Department of Housing
  and Urban Development
Washington, DC

BETSY REVEAL
Director
Seattle Department of Finance
Seattle, WA

REBECCA R. RILEY
Vice President of Chicago
  Affairs
Director of Community
  Initiatives Program
John D. and Catherine T.
  MacArthur Foundation
Chicago, IL

BENSON F. ROBERTS
Director of Policy and
  Program Development
Local Initiatives Support Corp.
Washington, DC

HIPOLITO ROLDAN
President
Hispanic Housing
  Development Corporation
Chicago, IL

DAVID RUSK
Former Mayor, Albuquerque,
  NM
Washington, DC

PETER D. SALINS
Chairman
Department of Urban Affairs
  & Planning
Hunter College
New York, NY

ELLIOTT D. SCLAR
Professor of Urban Planning
School of Architecture,
  Planning and Preservation
Columbia University
New York, NY

CHARLES H. SHAW
Chairman
The Shaw Company
Chicago, IL

FRED SIEGEL
Editor, *City Journal*
Professor of History
The Cooper Union
New York, NY

OTTO A. SILHA
Chairman & President
City Innovation
Minneapolis, MN

LORIE A SLUTSKY
Chairman
Council on Foundations
New York, NY

JAMES J. SOLEM
Commissioner
Minnesota Housing Finance
  Agency
St. Paul, MN

JACK R. STOKVIS
President
Stokvis Associates, Inc.
Haworth, NJ

JANET W. THOMPSON
Vice President
Corporate Contributions
Citibank, N.A.
New York, NY

SOL TRUJILLO
President & CEO
US West Marketing Resource
  Group
Englewood, CO

JULIA VITULLO-MARTIN
New York, NY

FRITZ WAGNER
Professor & Dean
National Center for the
  Revitalization of Central
  Cities
College of Urban and Public
  Affairs
University of New Orleans
New Orleans, LA

MARC A. WEISS
Director
Real Estate Development
  Research Center
Associate Professor
School of Architecture,
  Planning and Preservation
Columbia University
New York, NY

JAMES C. WORTHY
Professor of Management
J. L. Kellogg Graduate School
  of Management
Visiting Scholar
Center for Urban Affairs &
  Policy Research
Northwestern University
Evanston, IL

KNEELAND C.
  YOUNGBLOOD, M.D.
Dallas, TX

** Discussion Leader
* Rapporteur
‡ Delivered Formal Address
† Panelist

## The American Assembly

The American Assembly was established by Dwight D. Eisenhower at Columbia University in 1950. It holds nonpartisan meetings and publishes authoritative books to illuminate issues of United States policy.

An affiliate of Columbia, the Assembly is a national, educational institution incorporated in the state of New York. The Assembly seeks to provide information, stimulate discussion, and evoke independent conclusions on matters of vital public interest.

## American Assembly Sessions

At least two national programs are initiated each year. Authorities are retained to write background papers presenting essential data and defining the main issues of each subject.

A group of men and women representing a broad range of experience, competence, and American leadership meet for several days to discuss the Assembly topic and consider alternatives for national policy.

All Assemblies follow the same procedure. The background papers are sent to participants in advance of the Assembly. The Assembly meets in small groups for four or five lengthy periods. All groups use the same agenda. At the close of these informal sessions participants adopt in plenary session a final report of findings and recommendations.

Regional, state, and local Assemblies are held following the national session at Arden House. Assemblies have also been held in England, Switzerland, Malaysia, Canada, the Caribbean, South America, Central America, the Philippines, and Japan. Over one hundred sixty institutions have cosponsored one or more Assemblies.

## Arden House

The home of The American Assembly and the scene of the national sessions is Arden House, which was given to Columbia University in 1950 by W. Averell Harriman. E. Roland Harriman joined his brother in contributing toward adaptation of the property for conference purposes. The buildings and surrounding land, known as the Harriman Campus of Columbia University, are fifty miles north of New York City.

# THE AMERICAN ASSEMBLY

*Columbia University*

# Index